THE *HIGH SCHOOL*

BIOLOGY TUTOR®

Staff of Research and Education Association
Dr. M. Fogiel, Chief Editor

Research and Education Association
61 Ethel Road West
Piscataway, New Jersey 08854

THE HIGH SCHOOL BIOLOGY TUTOR®

Printed in the United States of America

Library of Congress Catalog Card Number 97-75747

International Standard Book Number 0-87891-907-4

THE HIGH SCHOOL TUTOR is a registered trademark of Research & Education Association, Piscataway, New Jersey 08854

WHAT THIS BOOK IS FOR

For as long as biology has been taught in high schools, many students have found this subject difficult to understand and learn. Despite the publication of hundreds of textbooks in this field, each one intending to provide an improved approach to the subject over previous textbooks, students continue to be perplexed by biological principles. As a result, biology often becomes a course taken only to meet school or departmental curriculum requirements.

In a study of the problem, REA found the following basic reasons underlying the difficulties that students experience with biology as it is taught in schools:

(a) No systematic rules of analysis have been developed which students may follow in a step-by-step manner to solve the usual problems encountered. This results from the fact that the numerous different conditions and principles which may be involved in a biology problem, lead to many possible different methods of solution. To prescribe a set of rules to be followed for each of the possible variations, would involve an enormous number of rules and steps to be searched through by students, and this task would perhaps be more burdensome than solving the problem directly with some accompanying trial and error to find the correct solution route.

(b) Biology textbooks currently available will usually explain a given principle in a few pages written by a professional who has an insight of the subject matter that is not shared by high school students. The explanations are often written in an abstract manner which leaves the students confused as to the application of the principle. The explanations given are not sufficiently detailed and extensive to make students aware of the wide range of applications and different aspects of the principle being studied. The numerous possible variations of principles and their applications are usually not discussed, and it is left for the students to discover these for themselves while doing exercises. Accordingly, the average student is expected to rediscover that which has been long known and practiced, but not published or explained extensively.

(c) The examples usually following the explanation of a topic are too few and too simple to enable the student to obtain a thorough grasp of the principles involved. The explanations do not provide sufficient basis to enable students to solve problems that may be subsequently assigned for homework or given on examinations.

The examples are presented in abbreviated form which leaves out much material between steps, and requires that students derive the omitted material themselves. As a result, students find the examples difficult to understand—contrary to the purpose of the examples.

Examples are, furthermore, often worded in a confusing manner. They do not state the problem and then present the solution. Instead, they pass through a general discussion, never revealing what is being sought.

Examples, also, do not always include diagrams/illustrations, wherever appropriate, and students do not obtain the training to draw diagrams to simplify and organize their thinking.

(d) Students can learn the subject only by doing the exercises themselves and reviewing them in class, to obtain experience in applying the principles with their different ramifications.

In doing the exercises by themselves, students find that they are required to devote considerably more time to biology than to other subjects of comparable credits, because they are uncertain with regard to the selection and application of the principles involved.

(e) When reviewing the exercises in classrooms, instructors usually request students to take turns in writing solutions on the boards and explaining them to the class. Students often find it difficult to explain in a manner that holds the interest of the class, and enables the remaining students to follow the material written on the boards. The remaining students seated in the class are, furthermore, too occupied with copying the material from the boards, to listen to the oral explanations and concentrate on the methods of solution.

This book is intended to aid high school students taking biology in overcoming the difficulties described, by supplying detailed illustrations of the solution methods which are usually not apparent to students. The solution methods are illustrated by problems selected from those that are most often assigned for class work and given on examinations. The problems are arranged in order of complexity to enable students to learn and understand a particular topic by reviewing the problems in sequence. The problems are illustrated with detailed step-by-step explanations, to save the students the large amount of time that is often needed to fill in the gaps that are usually found between steps of illustrations in textbooks or review/outline books.

The staff of REA considers that biology is best learned by allowing students to view the methods of analysis and solution techniques themselves. This approach to learning the subject matter is similar to that practiced in various scientific laboratories, particularly in the medical fields.

In using this book, students may review and study the illustrated problems at their own pace; they are not limited to the time allowed for explaining problems on the board in class.

When students want to look up a particular type of problem and solution, they can readily locate it in the book by referring to the index, which has been extensively prepared. It is also possible to locate a particular type of problem by glancing at just the material within the boxed portions. To facilitate rapid scanning of the problems, each problem has a heavy border around it. Furthermore, each problem is identified with a number immediately above the problem at the right-hand margin.

To obtain maximum benefit from the book, students should familiarize themselves with the section, "How To Use This Book," located in the front pages.

To meet the objectives of this book, staff members of REA have selected problems usually encountered in assignments and examinations, and have solved each problem meticulously to illustrate the steps which are difficult for students to comprehend. Special gratitude is expressed to them for their efforts in this area, as well as to the numerous contributors who devoted their time to this book.

The difficult task of coordinating the efforts of all persons was carried out by Carl Fuchs. His conscientious work deserves much appreciation. He also trained and supervised art and production personnel in the preparation of the book for printing.

Finally, special thanks are due Helen Kaufmann for her unique talent to render those difficult border-line decisions and constructive suggestions related to the design and organization of the book.

Max Fogiel, Ph.D.
Program Director

HOW TO USE THIS BOOK

This book can be an invaluable aid to biology students as a supplement to their textbooks. The book is subdivided into 11 chapters, each dealing with a separate topic. The subject matter is developed beginning with an Overview of Biology, and extends through Life Processes and Biochemistry, Interrelationship of Living Organisms, The Cell, Mendelian Genetics, Heredity, Kingdom Protista and Kingdom Fungi, Plant Kingdom, Animal Kingdom-Invertibrates and Vertibrates, and finally an extensive chapter discussing Human Anatomy.

TO LEARN AND UNDERSTAND A TOPIC THOROUGHLY

1. Refer to your class text and read the section pertaining to the topic. You should become acquainted with the principles discussed there. These principles, however, may not be clear to you at that time.

2. Then locate the topic you are looking for by referring to the "Table of Contents" in the front of this book.

3. Turn to the page where the topic begins and review the problems under each topic, in the order given. For each topic, the problems are arranged in order of complexity, from the simplest to the most difficult. Some problems may appear similar to others, but each problem has been selected to illustrate a different point or solution method.

To learn and understand a topic thoroughly and retain its contents, it will be generally necessary for students to review the problems several times. Repeated review is essential in order to gain experience in recognizing the principles that should be applied and in selecting the best solution technique.

TO FIND A PARTICULAR PROBLEM

To locate one or more problems related to a particular subject matter, refer to the index. In using the index, be certain to note that the numbers given there refer to problem numbers, not to page numbers. This arrangement of the index is intended to facilitate finding a problem more rapidly, since two or more problems may appear on a page.

If a particular type of problem cannot be found readily, it is recommended that the student refer to the "Table of Contents" in the front pages, and then turn to the chapter which is applicable to the problem being sought. By scanning or glancing at the material that is boxed, it will generally be possible to find problems related to the one being sought, without consuming considerable time. After the problems have been located, the solutions can be reviewed and studied in detail. For this purpose of locating problems rapidly, students should acquaint themselves with the organization of the book as found in the "Table of Contents."

In preparing for an exam, it is useful to find the topics to be covered on the exam in the "Table of Contents," and then review the problems under those topics several times. This should equip the student with what might be needed for the exam.

Contents

CHAPTER 1

OVERVIEW OF BIOLOGY

The Scientific Method

● **PROBLEM 1-1**

What is the scientific method?

SOLUTION:

The scientific method is a set of procedures used for scientific investigation of a problem. The procedure includes: defining the problem; formulating a hypothesis; experimenting to test the hypothesis using a control group and an experimental group; observing and recording data; and drawing a conclusion.

● **PROBLEM 1-2**

Define the term "biology."

SOLUTION:

The term "biology" refers to the study of life. "Bios" is Greek for "life" and "logos" is Greek for "discourse." Biology is a comprehensive term for the science of living organisms and life processes which include structure, function, growth, origin, and behavior.

Distinguish between the terms "in situ," "in vitro," and "in vivo."

SOLUTION:

These terms are all used to refer to where a biochemical reaction or process takes place. "In situ" is Latin for "in place"; it refers to a reaction that occurs in its natural or original position. "In vitro" is Latin for "in glass"; it refers to a reaction that does not occur in the living organism, but instead occurs in a laboratory such as a test tube. "In vivo" is Latin for "in the living" and refers to a reaction that occurs in the living organism.

● **PROBLEM 1-4**

A biologist deals with things on a microscopic level. To describe cellular dimensions and the amount of materials present at the cellular level, units of an appropriately small size are needed. What are these units of measurements?

SOLUTION:

In biology, the units of length commonly employed include the micron (abbreviated by μ) and the Ångstrom (abbreviated by Å). A micron is equivalent to 10^{-3} millimeters (mm) or 10^{-10} meters. An Ångstrom is equivalent to $10^{-4} \mu$ or 10^{-7} mm or 10^{-6} meters.

Weights are expressed in milligrams (10^{-3} grams) micrograms (10^{-6} grams), and nanograms (10^{-9} grams). The unit of molecular weight employed is the dalton. A dalton is defined as the weight of a hydrogen atom. For example, one molecule of water (H_2O) weighs about 18 daltons. One dalton weighs 1.674×10^{-24} grams.

● **PROBLEM 1-5**

By photographic and optical means, an image can be enlarged almost indefinitely. However, most light microscopes offer magnifications of only 1000 to 1500 times the actual size, while electron microscopes offer magnifications of 100,000 times or more. Explain.

SOLUTION:

All microscopes are characterized by limits of resolution. Resolution refers to the clarity of the image. Objects lying close to one another can not be distinguished (resolved) as separate objects if the distance between them is less than one half the wavelength of the light being used. The average wavelength of visible light is 550 nanometers (or 5500 Å). Thus, for light microscopes, objects can be distinguished only if they lie farther apart than about 275 nanometers. Objects closer together than 275 nm are not resolved and appear to be one object. Increasing the size of the image, or the magnification, will not give meaningful information unless resolution is also increased. Increasing magnification without increasing resolution results in a larger image that is still blurred.

Electron microscopes offer resolution of details separated by .1 to .5 nanometers. Electrons, rather than light, are the radiation used in electron microscopes. Recall that electrons have a wave property in addition to a particle property and may be regarded as a radiation of extremely short wavelength. Since the wavelength of an electron in motion is so much shorter than the wavelength of light, resolution is more than a thousandfold better. Structures such as the plasma membrane, endoplasmic reticulum, ribosomes, microtubules and microfilaments were not visible until the advent of the electron microscope. These structures are all less than 275 nm in width. The plasma membrane has a thickness of 7.5 to 10 nm (or 75 to 100 Å). The ribosome is 15 to 25 nm in diameter (or 150 to 250 Å). Microtubules are 20 to 30 nm in diameter, and microfilaments range from 5 to 10 nm. Electron microscopy has also made possible the visualization of the nuclear envelope and the internal membranes of mitochondria and chloroplasts.

SHORT ANSWER QUESTIONS FOR REVIEW

Choose the correct answer.

1. The scientific method is a set of procedures used for scientific investigation of a problem. Which of the following is not part of the procedure? (a) formulating a hypothesis (b) drawing a conclusion (c) defining the problem (d) experimenting with errored data

2. Experimentation involves data collection. Length and weight are two dimensions that are frequently measured in the laboratory. Which of the following do not represent units of length or weight? (a) gram (b) ampere (c) dalton (d) micron (e) millimeter

3. Two objects separated by a distance of 3000 Å are viewed under a light microscope. The light source has a wavelength of 0.7μ. An observer looking through the eyepiece of the microscope would see (a) two distinct and separate objects. (b) a single object. (c) nothing, because the objects would cancel out.

Fill in the blanks.

4. Biology is a comprehensive term for the science of living organisms and life processes which include _____, _____, _____, _____, and _____.

5. Resolution refers to the _____ of the image.

6. The electron microscope uses _____ as the source of radiation.

Determine whether the following statements are true or false.

7. When testing the hypothesis, one always needs both a control group and an experimental group.

8. The resolution of an electron microscope is much better than a light microscope because of the greater magnification in the former.

9. A professor performed an experiment in vitro and deduced the mechanism for a certain biochemical reaction. He can conclude that this is the mechanism by which the reaction occurs within a cell.

ANSWER KEY

1. d   2. b   3. b

4. structure, function, growth, origin, behavior

5. clarity   6. electrons

7. True   8. False   9. False

CHAPTER 2

LIFE PROCESSES AND BIOCHEMISTRY

Properties of Chemical Reactions

● **PROBLEM 2-1**

Define the following terms: atom, isotope, ion. Could a single particle of matter be all three simultaneously?

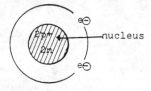

Figure 1. Atom of helium

SOLUTION:

An atom is the smallest particle of an element that can retain the chemical properties of that element. It is composed of a nucleus, which contains positively charged protons and neutral neutrons, around which negatively charged electrons revolve in orbits. For example, a helium atom contains 2 protons, 2 neutrons, and 2 electrons.

An ion is a positively or negatively charged atom or group of atoms. An ion which is negatively charged is called an anion, and a positively charged ion is called a cation.

Isotopes are alternate forms of the same chemical element. A chemical element is defined in terms of its atomic number, which is the number of protons in its nucleus. Isotopes of an element have the same number of protons as that element, but a different number of neutrons. Since atomic mass is determined by the number of protons plus neutrons, isotopes of the same element have varying atomic masses. For example, deuterium (^2H) is an isotope of hydrogen, and has one neutron and one proton in its nucleus. Hydrogen has only a proton and no neutrons in its nucleus.

A single particle can be an atom, an ion, and an isotope simultaneously. The simplest example is the hydrogen ion H^+. It is an atom which has lost one electron and thus developed a positive charge. Since it is charged, it is therefore an ion. A cation is a positively charged ion (i.e., H^+) and an anion is a negatively charged ion (i.e., Cl^-). If one compares its atomic number (1) with that of deuterium (1), it is seen that although they have different atomic masses, since their atomic numbers are the same, they must be isotopes of one another.

● PROBLEM 2-2

Describe the differences between an element and a compound.

SOLUTION:

All substances are composed of matter in that they have mass and occupy space. Elements and compounds constitute two general classes of matter. Elements are substances that consist of identical atoms (i.e., atoms with identical atomic numbers). This definition of an element includes all isotopes of that element. Hence O^{18} and O^{16} are both considered to be elemental oxygen. A compound is a substance that is composed of two or more different kinds of atoms (two or more different elements) combined in a definite weight ratio. This fixed composition of various elements, according to law of definite proportions, differentiates a compound from a mixture. Elements are the substituents of compounds. For example, water is a compound composed of the two elements hydrogen and oxygen in the ratio 2:1, respectively. This compound may be written as H_2O, which is the molecular formula of water. The subscript "2" that appears after the hydrogen (H) indicates that in every molecule of water there are two hydrogen atoms. There is no subscript after the oxygen (O) in the molecular formula of water, which indicates that there is only one oxygen atom per molecule of water. Hence water is a compound whose molecules are each made up of two hydrogen atoms and one oxygen atom.

What properties of water make it an essential component of living matter?

SOLUTION:

The chemistry of life on this planet is essentially the chemistry of water and carbon. Water is the most abundant molecule in the cell as well as on the earth. In fact, it makes up between 70 and 90 percent of the weight of most forms of life.

Life began in the sea and the properties of water shape the chemistry of all living organisms. Life developed as a liquid phase phenomenon because reactions in solution are much more rapid than reactions between solids, and complex and highly structural molecules can behave in solution in a way that they cannot behave in a gas. Water is an excellent solvent for living systems. It can stay in the liquid stage throughout a very wide range of temperature variation. Almost all chemicals present in living matter are soluble in it.

Water serves many functions in the living organism. It dissolves waste products of metabolism and assists in their removal from the cell and the organism. Water functions in heat regulation almost as an insulator would. It has a high heat capacity or specific heat in that it has a great capacity for absorbing heat with only minimal changes in its own temperature. This is because water molecules bond to one another by hydrogen bonds. Excess heat energy is dissipated by breaking these bonds, thus the living material is protected against sudden thermal changes. In addition, plants and animals utilize water loss to cool their bodies. When water changes from a liquid to a gas, it absorbs a great deal of heat. This enables the body to dissipate excess heat by the evaporation of water. In animals this process is sweating. Also, the good conductivity properties of water makes it possible for heat to be distributed evenly throughout the body tissues. Water serves as a lubricant, and is present in body fluids wherever one organ rubs against another, and in the joints where one bone moves on another. Water serves in the transport of nutrients and other materials within the organism. In plants, minerals dissolved in water are taken up by the roots and are transported up the stem to the leaves.

Water is also very efficient in dissolving ionic salts and other polar compounds because of the polar physical properties of water molecules. The proper concentration of these salts is necessary for life processes and it is important to keep them at extremely constant concentrations under normal conditions. These salts are important in maintaining osmotic relationships.

What are the three laws of thermodynamics? Discuss their biological significance.

SOLUTION:

The first law of thermodynamics states that energy can be converted from one form into another, but it cannot be created or destroyed. In other words, the energy of a closed system is constant. Thus, the first law is simply a statement of the law of conservation of energy.

The second law of thermodynamics states that the total entropy (a measure of the disorder or randomness of a system) of the universe is increasing. This is characterized by a decrease in the free energy, which is the energy available to do work. Thus, any spontaneous change that occurs (chemical, physical, or biological) will tend to increase the entropy of the universe.

The third law of thermodynamics refers to a completely ordered system, particularly, a perfect crystal. It states that a perfect crystal at absolute zero (0° Kelvin) would have perfect order, and therefore its entropy would be zero.

These three laws affect the biological as well as the chemical and physical world. Living cells do their work by using the energy stored in chemical bonds. The first law of thermodynamics states that every chemical bond in a given molecule contains an amount of energy equal to the amount that was necessary to link the atoms together. Thus, living cells are both transducers that turn other forms of energy into chemical bond energy and liberators that free this energy by utilizing the chemical bond energy to do work. Considering that a living organism is a storehouse of potential chemical energy due to the many millions of atoms bonded together in each cell, it might appear that the same energy could be passed continuously from organism to organism with no required extracellular energy source. However, deeper consideration shows this to be false. The second law of thermodynamics tells us that every energy transformation results in a reduction in the usable or free energy of the system. Consequently, there is a steady increase in the amount of energy that is unavailable to do work (or increase in entropy). In addition, energy is constantly being passed from living organisms to nonliving matter (e.g., when you write you expend energy to move the pencil, when it is cold out your body loses heat to warm the air, etc.). The system of living organisms thus cannot be a static energy system, and must be replenished by energy derived from the nonliving world.

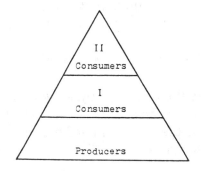

Figure 1. Food pyramid

The second law of thermodynamics is also helpful in explaining the loss of energy from the system at each successive trophic level in a food pyramid. In the following food pyramid, the energy at the producer level is greater than the energy at the consumer I level which is greater than the energy of the consumer II level. Every energy transformation between the members of the successive levels involves the loss of usable energy, and this loss serves to increase the entropy. Thus, this unavoidable loss causes the total amount of energy at each trophic level to be lower than at the preceding level.

Acids and Bases

● PROBLEM 2-5

Differentiate between acids, bases, and salts. Give examples of each.

SOLUTION:

There are essentially two widely used definitions of acids and bases: the Lowry-Brønsted definition and the Lewis definition. In the Lowry-Brønsted definition, an acid is a compound with the capacity to donate a proton, and a base is a compound with the capacity to accept a proton. In the Lewis definition, an acid has the ability to accept an electron pair and a base the ability to donate an electron pair.

Salts are a group of chemical substances which generally consist of positive and negative ions arranged to maximize attractive forces and minimize repulsive forces. Salts can be either inorganic or organic. For example, sodium chloride, NaCl, is an inorganic salt which is actually best represented with its charges Na^+Cl^-; sodium acetate, CH_3COONa or $CH_3COO^-Na^+$ is an organic salt.

Some common acids important to the biological system are acetic acid (CH_3COOH), carbonic acid (H_2CO_3), phosphoric acid (H_3PO_4), and water. Amino acids, the building blocks of protein, are compounds that contain an acidic group (–COOH). Some common bases are ammonia (NH_3), pyridine

(C_5H_5N), purine (C_4N_2), and water. The nitrogenous bases

important in the structure of DNA and RNA carry the purine or pyridine functional group. Water has the ability to act both as an acid [$H_2O - H^+ \rightarrow OH^-$] and as a base ($H_2O + H^+ \rightarrow H_3O^+$) depending on the conditions of the reaction, and is thus said to exhibit amphiprotic behavior.

Vinegar is classified as an acid. What does this tell you about the concentration of the hydrogen ions and the hydroxide ions?

SOLUTION:

Compounds can be classified as acidic or basic depending upon the relative concentrations of hydrogen and hydroxide ions formed in aqueous solution. In an aqueous solution, acidic compounds have an excess of hydrogen ions, and basic compounds have an excess of hydroxide ions. Since vinegar is considered to be an acid, it will have an excess of hydrogen ions with respect to hydroxide ions when in solution. Thus, it can be deduced that the pH of an aqueous solution of vinegar will be within the range of 0 to 7.

Acetic acid is the constituent that gives vinegar its acidic properties. Acetic acid has a pH of 2.37 at a one molar concentration.

What are acid-base reactions? In what way are they analogous to oxidation-reduction reactions?

SOLUTION:

An acid-base reaction involves proton transfer between two species: the proton donor and the proton acceptor. The proton donor is better known as a Brønsted acid and the proton acceptor as a Brønsted base. The general equation for an acid-base reaction can be written as:

Proton donor→ H^+ + proton acceptor.

For example, the following reaction occurs between acetic acid (CH_3COO) and water (H_2O):

$$CH_3COOH + H_2O \rightarrow CH_3COO^- + H_3O^+$$

Acetic acid is the Brønsted acid because it donates a proton to become the acetate anion, and water is the Brønsted base since it accepts a proton to form the hydronium ion. The acetate anion now has the capacity to accept a proton, and therefore is a Brønsted base by definition. The acetic acid and the acetate anion together constitute a conjugate acid-base pair. The generalized formula of these types of reactions would be:

Brønsted acid$_J$ + Brønsted base$_K$→ conjugate
Brønsted base$_J$ + conjugate Brønsted acid$_K$

where the compounds written with the subscript J are one conjugate acid-base pair and the compounds written with the subscript K are the other conjugate acid-base pair.

11

An oxidation-reduction reaction includes the transfer of electron(s), rather than proton(s), between two species. We can write the following general equation for oxidation-reduction (also known as redox) reactions, analogous to the one we wrote for acid-base reactions:

Electron donor → e⁻ + electron acceptor

The electron donor is the species that is undergoing oxidation (loss of electrons), and is also called the reducing agent (i.e., one that reduces another species). The electron acceptor is the species undergoing reduction (gain of electrons), and is also known as the oxidizing agent (i.e., one species that oxidizes another). The electron donor and acceptor together constitute a conjugate redox pair or couple. In some oxidation-reduction reactions, the transfer of one or more electrons is made via the transfer of hydrogen. Dehydrogenation is thus equivalent to oxidation. One example of a redox reaction is the one between NAD+ and NADH + H⁺:

$$NAD^+ \; + \; H_2 \; \underset{\text{oxidation}}{\overset{\text{reduction}}{\rightleftarrows}} \; NADH \; + \; H^+$$

● **PROBLEM 2-8**

What does the "pH" of a solution mean?

SOLUTION:

The pH (an abbreviation for "potential of hydrogen") of a solution is a measure of the hydrogen ion concentration. Specifically, pH is defined as the negative log of the hydrogen ion concentration. A pH scale is used to quantify the relative acid or base strength. It is based upon the dissociation reaction of water: $H_2O \rightarrow H^+ + OH^-$. A pH of 7 is considered to be neutral since there are equal concentrations of hydrogen and hydroxide ions. The pH scale ranges from 0 to 14. Acidic compounds have a pH range of 0 to 7 and basic compounds have a range of 7 to 14.

● **PROBLEM 2-9**

All organic matter is made up entirely or mostly of the basic elements carbon and hydrogen. In view of this, why is there such a diversity of organic compounds present?

SOLUTION:

The diversity of organic compounds is so vast that these organic compounds have been divided into families, such as alkanes, alkynes, and aromatic compounds, which have no counterparts among inorganic compounds. The tremendous variety of these compounds is made possible by the unique properties of carbon. To be able to understand how carbon can form such a huge number of compounds with a great variety of properties, the way in which the atoms in these molecules are bonded together must be looked at.

Carbon has a valence number (the number of bonds an atom of an element can form) of four. This means that each carbon atom always has four bonds which can be either bonded to four other atoms, as in methane; to three other atoms, as in formaldehyde; or to two other atoms as in hydrogen cyanide. In other words carbon is capable of forming single, double, and triple bonds:

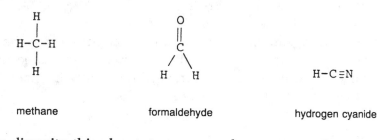

methane   formaldehyde   hydrogen cyanide

But the diversity this element possesses does not stop here. It is capable of bonding to other carbon atoms in an almost unique variety of chain and ring structures. This property is called catenation and accounts for the tremendous variety seen in the following compounds:

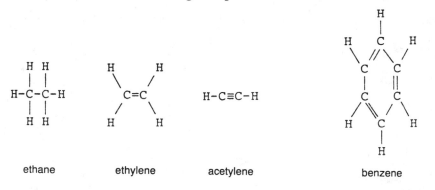

ethane   ethylene   acetylene   benzene

These examples show the use of a minimum number of carbon atoms. The diversity possible is apparent when one considers the fact that these different types of bonds can be joined together in infinite numbers. To exemplify this, look at the compound:

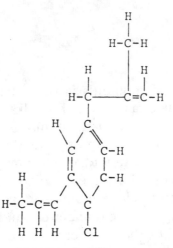

As it can be seen, a multitude of different variations could be made with the only constraining factor being that carbon must have four bonds. The freedom allowed carbon is apparent when contrasted with the halogens (iodine, chlorine, bromine, and fluorine) which are monovalent and thus can only form one bond, for example:

H-Cl   Br-Br
hydrochloric acid   bromine

Another feature of the compounds of carbon that contributes to their variety is the existence of isomers (compounds composed of the same number and kind of atoms, but with the atoms arranged differently in space). Look, for example, at the compound C_4H_{10}. This can exist as:

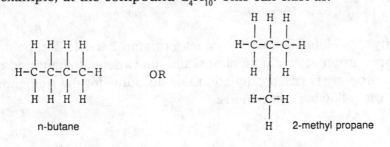

or look at C_5H_{10}. It can exist as:

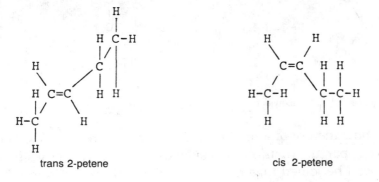

Although these compounds have the same chemical formulas they have different chemical, physical and biological properties due to their arrangement in space.

14

Distinguish between covalent and ionic bonds.

SOLUTION:

A covalent bond is a bond in which two atoms are held together by a shared pair of electrons. An ionic bond is a bond in which oppositely charged ions are held together by electrical attraction.

In general, the electronegativity difference between two elements influences the character of their bond (see Table 1).

IA	II A	III A	IV A	VA	VI A	VII A
H 2.1						
Li 1.0	Be 1.5	B 2.0	C 2.5	N 3.0	O 3.5	F 4.0
Na 0.9	Mg 1.2	Al 1.5	Si 1.8	P 2.1	S 2.5	Cl 3.0
K 0.8	Ca 1.0		Ge 1.8	As 2.0	Se 2.4	Br 2.8
Rb 0.8	Sr 1.0		Sn 1.8	Sb 1.9	Te 2.1	I 2.5
Cs 0.7	Ba 0.9		Pb 1.7	Bi 1.8		

Table 1. Electronegativities of main groups of elements

Electronegativity measures the relative ability of an atom to attract electrons in a covalent bond. Using Pauling's scale, where fluorine is arbitrarily given the value 4.0 units and other elements are assigned values relative to it, an electronegativity difference of 1.7 gives the bond 50 percent ionic character and 50 percent covalent character. Therefore, a bond between two atoms with an electronegativity difference of greater than 1.7 units is mostly ionic in character. If the difference is less than 1.7 the bond is predominately covalent.

What are hydrogen bonds? Describe fully the importance of hydrogen bonds in the biological world.

SOLUTION:

A hydrogen bond is a molecular force in which a hydrogen atom is shared between two atoms. Hydrogen bonds occur as a result of the uneven distribution of electrons in a polar bond, such as an O-H bond. Here, the bonding electrons are more attracted to the highly electronegative oxygen atom, resulting in a slight positive charge (δ^+) on the hydrogen and a slight negative charge (δ^-) on the oxygen. A hydrogen bond is formed when the relatively positive hydrogen is attracted to a relatively negative atom of some other polarized bond. For example:

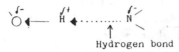

Hydrogen bond

Figure 1. Polar bond with electrons being attracted to the more electronegative element, oxygen.

The atom to which the hydrogen is more tightly linked or specifically the atom with which it forms the polar bond, is called the hydrogen donor, while the other atom is the hydrogen acceptor. In this sense, the hydrogen bond can be thought of as an intermediate type of acid-base reaction. Note, however, that the bond is an electrostatic one — no electrons are shared or exchanged, between the hydrogen and the negative dipole of the other molecule of the bond.

Hydrogen bonds are highly directional (note the arrows in the figure), and are strongest when all three atoms are colinear.

Bond energies of hydrogen bonds are in the range of about 3 to 7 kcal/mole. This is intermediate between the energy of a covalent bond and a van der Waals bond. However, only when the electronegative atoms are either F, O, or N, is the energy of the bond enough to make it important. Only these three atoms are electronegative enough for the necessary attraction to exist.

Hydrogen bonds are responsible for the structure of water and its special properties as a biological solvent. There is extensive hydrogen bonding between water molecules, forming what has been called the water matrix. This structure has profound effects on the freezing and boiling points of water, and its solubility properties. Any molecule capable of forming a hydrogen bond can do so with water, and thus a variety of molecules will dissociate and be soluble in water.

Hydrogen bonds are also most responsible for the maintenance of the shape of proteins. Since shape is crucial to their function (as both enzymes and structural components), this bonding is extremely important. For example, hydrogen bonds maintain the helical shape of keratin and collagen molecules and gives them their characteristic strength and flexibility.

It is hydrogen bonds which hold together the two helices of DNA. Bonding occurs between the base pairs. The intermediate bond strength of the hydrogen bond is ideal for the function of DNA — it is strong enough to give the molecule stability, yet weak enough to be broken with sufficient ease for replication and RNA synthesis.

Properties of Enzymes, Coenzymes, and Cofactors

● PROBLEM 2-12

Enzyme behavior may be described by the lock-and-key theory. Explain and describe this theory.

SOLUTION:

Millions of chemical reactions occurring in the body require catalysts to make them go to completion. Enzymes serve as these catalysts. Their behavior and/or function is described by the lock-and-key theory.

According to this theory, enzymes have definite three-dimensional structures. They are arranged so that the substrate (the substance upon which the enzyme acts) fits into the enzyme's structure. Only a specific kind of substrate can fit into a given enzyme. When the substrate and enzyme unite, i.e., form an aggregate, the substrate is exposed for a reaction to occur. In Figure 1, the three-dimensional shape of the enzyme is arranged to accommodate the substrate. The active site is that portion of the enzyme that catalyzes the reaction. In Figure 2, the substrate is held in position by the enzyme while the reaction occurs. In Figure 3, the product(s) of the reaction leaves the enzyme, thus, freeing the enzyme to catalyze another reaction.

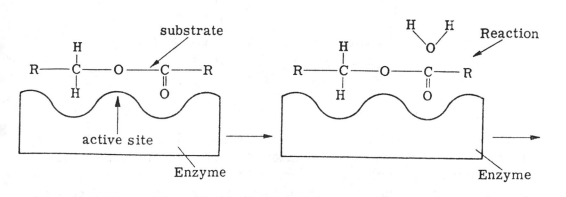

Figure 1   Figure 2

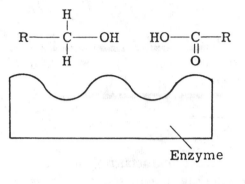

Figure 3

● **PROBLEM 2-13**

Meat possesses a large amount of connective tissue that can be ten-derized by the action of proteolytic enzymes. Can such enzymes harm the stomach lining when the food is eaten?

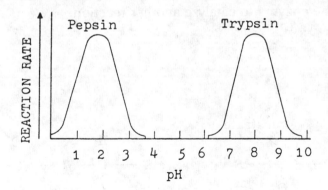

SOLUTION:

This question deals with proteolytic enzymes, which may be defined as protein degradation catalysts. Two factors that affect enzymic activity are pH, and temperature. Whether these enzymes damage the stomach or not will depend, to a great extent, on the conditions in the stomach. The accompa-nying figure shows how pH can alter enzyme activity of pepsin and trypsin. From the diagram, you see that these enzymes do not function well at ex-tremely low pH. Due to the presence of HCl in the stomach as a hydrolysis agent, the acidity of the stomach is high, which means an environment of low pH exists. It becomes doubtful that these proteolytic enzymes would have much activity at the low pH of the stomach. This means that little, if any, damage would be done to the stomach. Heating alters enzymic activity, also. It is likely that most of the enzyme would be inactivated by the cooking of the meat.

● PROBLEM 2-14

The rate of a certain biochemical reaction at body temperature in the absence of enzyme has been measured in the laboratory. The rate of the same reaction, when enzyme-catalyzed in the human body, is 10^6 times faster. Explain this phenomenon.

SOLUTION:

For any reaction to proceed, a certain amount of energy is needed. This energy is called the energy of activation. When a catalyst, such as an enzyme, is added to the system, the energy of activation is lowered. Because the energy requirement for the reaction is less, the reaction proceeds more quickly.

● PROBLEM 2-15

Catalase, the enzyme that assists the breakdown of hydrogen peroxide into oxygen and water, has a turnover number of 2×10^8. In one hour, what weight of hydrogen peroxide could be decomposed by one molecule of catalase?

SOLUTION:

Enzymes may be defined as catalysts. A substrate is the compound that the enzyme acts upon to form the product. One aspect of enzymatic reactions is the rate at which the enzyme-substrate complex is formed and shifted to product. One can express this rate as the turnover number. It is defined as the number of molecules of substrate converted to product by one molecule of enzyme in one minute at optimum conditions.

In this problem, you are given one molecule of enzyme, and excess substrate. The turnover rate is given as 2×10^8. You are asked for the weight of the substrate decomposed in one hour. To find the weight, you need the number of molecules decomposed. According to the definition of turnover number, 2×10^8 molecules decompose in one minute. Thus, in 1 hour, 60 minutes $\times 2 \times 10^8 = 1.2 \times 10^{10}$ molecules of hydrogen peroxide (H_2O_2) is decomposed.

To calculate the total weight of these molecules, one uses Avogadro's number. It states that there are 6.02×10^{23} molecules in one mole. Thus, 1.2×10^{10} molecules represents $1.2 \times 10^{10}/6.02 \times 10^{23} = 1.99 \times 10^{-14}$ moles of H_2O_2 decomposed. A mole is defined as weight in grams/molecular weight. The molecular weight of H_2O_2 = 34. Thus, weight of H_2O_2 decomposed = $(1.99 \times 10^{-14}$ moles$)(34$ g/mole$) = 6.766 \times 10^{-13}$ grams.

SHORT ANSWER QUESTIONS FOR REVIEW

Choose the correct answer.

1. All of the following are parts of an atom except: (a) neutrons. (b) protons. (c) isotopes. (d) electrons. (e) nucleus.

2. A positively or negatively charged atom or group of atoms is named a(n) (a) isotope. (b) element. (c) proton. (d) ion. (e) electron.

3. Water is the most abundant molecule on the earth and inside of the cell. Which of the following is not a property of water? (a) dissolves nonpolar substances such as lipids (b) dissolves waste products (c) functions in heat regulation (d) dissolves ionic salts and other polar substances

4. The helical structure of nucleic acids are maintained by (a) anhydride bonds. (b) phosphodiester bonds. (c) H bonds. (d) covalent bonds.

Fill in the blanks.

5. The _____ states that a perfect crystal at absolute zero would have zero entropy.

6. A Lewis acid has the ability to _____ an electron pair, and a Bronsted base has the ability to _____ a proton.

7. Oxidation can involve the removal of _____ or _____, as well as the addition of _____.

8. The theory that describes enzyme behavior as allowing a specific substrate to fit into a given enzyme is the _____.

9. A substance in the pH range of 0 to 7 is considered to be _____ because it has an excess of _____ ions.

10. The rate at which the enzyme-substrate complex is formed and converted to product is expressed as the _____.

Determine whether the following statements are true or false.

11. Ammonia (NH_3) is a compound because it is composed of more than one element, which occur in definite proportions.

12. When a liter of water at 100°C is combined with a liter of water at 0°C in a closed system, the resultant temperature is 50°C. In this process, entropy has increased and *usable* energy has decreased.

13. An oxidizing agent is one which reduces a substance, and is itself oxidized.

14. Trans-3-hexene and cis-3-hexene are organic isotopes of each other.

15. If the electronegativity difference between two atoms is zero, the bond is predominantly covalent.

16. Since an enzyme is a catalyst, a reaction would proceed more quickly in the presence of an enzyme because the enzyme raises the activation energy.

17. Trypsin and pepsin does very little damage to the stomach because they do not function well at low pH ranges.

ANSWER KEY

1. c

2. d

3. a

4. c

5. third law of thermodynamics

6. accept, accept

7. hydrogen, electrons, oxygen

8. lock-and-key theory

9. acidic, hydrogen

10. turnover number

11. True

12. True

13. False

14. False

15. True

16. False

17. True

CHAPTER 3

INTERRELATIONSHIP OF LIVING ORGANISMS

Taxonomy of Organisms

● **PROBLEM 3-1**

What is the basis of classification of living things used today and why is it better than some of the older methods?

SOLUTION:

The modern day basis of the classification of living things was developed by Linnaeus. Linnaeus based his system of classification upon similarities of structure and function between different organisms. Previously used, was a system based on the similarities of living habitats. Before Linnaeus, animals were categorized into three groups: those that lived in water, on the land, and in the air. We use structure and function today as a basis for grouping, since similar characteristics may indicate evolutionary relationships. For example, porpoises and alligators both live in the water, whereas cows and lizards both live on the land. Using Linnaeus's system of classification, porpoises are grouped with cows, and lizards with alligators. Porpoises and cows both give birth to live young, and maintain constant body temperature. Structurally, they both possess mammary glands, from which milk is obtained to feed their young. Alligators and lizards both have scales on their skins, and have similar respiratory and circulatory systems. Cows and porpoises are members of the class of mammals, even though their habitats are different. Alligators and lizards are members of the class of reptiles. This systematic method of biological classification based on evolutionary relationship is termed taxonomy. At present, both genetics and evolution are important in understanding taxonomy. Because of similarities in structure and function, both cows and porpoises are believed to have a common ancestor in the very distant past. A separate ancestor was probably shared by alligators and lizards.

● **PROBLEM 3-2**

> The following are all classification groups: family, genus, kingdom, order, phylum, species, and class. Rearrange these so that they are in the proper order of sequence from the smallest grouping to the largest. Explain the scientific naming of a species.

SOLUTION:

Closely related species are grouped together into genera (singular–genus), closely related genera are grouped into families, families are grouped into orders, orders into classes, classes into phyla (singular–phylum), and phyla into kingdoms. Classes and phyla are the major divisions of the animal and plant kingdoms.

In order to give the scientific name for a certain species, the genus name is given first, with its first letter capitalized; the species name, given second, is entirely in lower case. For example, the scientific name of the cat is *Felis domestica* and that of the dog is *Canis familiaris*. The cat and dog both belong to the class of mammals and the phylum of chordates.

An example of a complete taxonomic classification for a Manx cat is:

Kingdom - Animalia
Phylum - Chordata
Subphylum - Vertebrata
Class - Mammalia
Subclass - Eutheria
Order - Carnivora
Family - Felidae
Genus - Felis
Species - domestica
Variety - manx

As this example shows, important divisions may exist within a class or phylum, and the use of subclasses and subphyla is an aid to classification.

Note that the group "variety" allows us to refer exactly to the type of domesticated cats we are considering, not Siamese cats, not Persian cats, but Manx cats.

List some organisms which are difficult to assign to either the plant or animal kingdom. Does classifying these as members of a third kingdom, the Protista, solve the problems raised by attempts to divide the living world into "plants" and "animals"?

SOLUTION:

Many one-celled organisms are difficult to classify as either animals or plants. Some have characteristics of both animals and plants. Euglena are an example of this. Like plants, they contain chlorophyll and are capable of photosynthesis; like animals they are able to move about within the environment, ingesting and absorbing organic nutrients. Other organisms have characteristics strikingly different from either plants or animals. Bacteria, like plants, have a cell wall; however, unlike plants, their cell wall is not composed of cellulose. Certain bacteria are capable of photosynthesis, while other bacteria must obtain organic nourishment. Amongst the bacteria which do not rely on organic nourishment, some, like plants, obtain energy from sunlight, and some, unlike any other organism, obtain energy from the oxidation of inorganic compounds.

The formation of a third kingdom solves some of the problems which arise in attempting to classify these organisms. However, a problem still exists with the classification Protista since classification is based upon structural and functional similarities within groupings of organisms.

Many diverse organisms are included within the Protista which bear no closer relationship to each other than to plants or animals. For this reason a fourth and a fifth kingdom have also been proposed, the Monera and the Fungi. The Monera kingdom includes the bacteria and blue-green algae. These have cell walls different from plant cell walls, and lack nuclear membranes. Their ultrastructure differs from that of organisms in the other kingdoms. The members of the Fungi kingdom lack photosynthetic pigments but have cell walls and multiply in a manner more like plants or protists than animals.

The problems inherent in any classification system can never be fully resolved. In attempting to classify bacteria or Euglena, the problem is not in determining what the organism is, but in determining to what other organisms it bears the closest resemblance. As more is learned about the structure and function of different organisms, and about the relationships between different organisms through fossil records and biochemical analysis of their genetic compositions, more complete taxonomic systems can be established.

Principles of Ecology

How would you define ecology? Differentiate between autecology and synecology.

SOLUTION:

Ecology can be defined as the study of the interactions between groups of organisms and their environment. The term autecology refers to studies of individual organisms or populations, of single species and their interactions with the environment. Synecology refers to studies of various groups of organisms which are associated to form a functional unit of the environment.

Groups of organisms are characterized by three levels of organization — populations, communities, and ecosystems. A population is a group of organisms belonging to the same species which occupy a given area. A community is a unit composed of a group of populations living in a given area. The community and the physical environment considered together is an ecosystem. Each of these designations may be applied to a small local entity or to a large widespread one. Thus a small group of sycamore trees in a park may be regarded as a population, as could be the sycamore trees in the eastern United States. Similarly, a small pond and its inhabitants or the forest in which the pond is located may be treated as an ecosystem. From these examples, we see that the limit of an ecosystem depends on how we define our ecosystem. However each ecosystem must consist of at least some living organisms inhabiting a physical environment.

Various ecosystems are linked to one another by biological, chemical, and physical processes. The entire earth is itself a true ecosystem because no part is fully isolated from the rest. This global ecosystem is usually referred to as the biosphere.

● PROBLEM 3-5

Explain what is meant by an animal's ecological niche, and define competitive exclusion.

SOLUTION:

Ecologically, niche is defined as the functional role and position of an organism within its ecosystem. The term niche should not be confused with habitat, which is the physical area where the organism lives. The characteristics of the habitat help define the niche but do not specify it completely. Each local population of a particular species has a niche that is defined with many variables. Each has a temperature range along with other climatic factors. There are required nutrients and specific activities that also help characterize the niche.

The principal of competitive exclusion states that unless the niches of two species differ, they cannot coexist in the same habitat. Two species of organisms that occupy the same or similar ecologic niches in different geographical locations are termed ecological equivalents. The array of species present in a given type of community in different biogeographic regions may differ widely. However, similar ecosystems tend to develop wherever there are similar physical habitats. The equivalent functional niches are occupied by whatever biological groups happen to be present in the region. Thus, a savannah-type vegetation tends to develop wherever the climate permits the development of extensive grasslands, but the species of grass and the species of animals feeding on the grass may differ significantly in various parts of the world.

● PROBLEM 3-6

What factors determine the characteristics of particular organisms that exist in an ecosystem.

SOLUTION:

Temperature and precipitation are among the most crucial physical factors in determining what type of vegetation will exist in a certain area. It is often possible to predict the type of biome at a given locality from the characteristics of the climate. However, other physical factors are also important. The structure and chemistry of the soil can be equally vital. There are, for example, certain trace elements known to be essential for the full development of plants. These include boron, chlorine, cobalt, copper, iron, manganese, molybdenum, sodium, vanadium, and zinc. When one or more of these substances is not present in sufficient concentration, land which should carry a forest according to the temperature — precipitation features, will instead be covered with shrubby vegetation, or be grassland bearing a few scattered trees. Where grassland was indicated, there may exist sparse vegetation typical of a desert. Any single factor such as the amount of sunlight, temperature, humidity, or the concentration of trace elements is capable of determining the presence or absence of species and thus the characteristics of the entire biome. The Law of Minimum is a generalization that is sometimes used to explain this phenomenon. It states that the factor that is most deficient is the one that determines the presence and absence of species. It does not matter, for example, how favorable temperature and sunlight are in a given locality, or how rich the nutrients and trace elements of the soil are if the precipitation is very low, because the result will still be a desert. Only a consideration of all the climatic and soil characteristics of a region can reveal the reasons for the existence of certain plant formations. In turn, animals are indirectly influenced in their distributions by soil types because of their dependence upon plants as the source of high-energy organic nutrients.

Nutritional Requirements and Procurement

● PROBLEM 3-7

Why are autotrophic organisms necessary for the continuance of life on earth? Do all autotrophs require sunlight?

SOLUTION:

Autotrophic organisms have the capacity to generate all needed energy from inorganic sources. Heterotrophic organisms can only utilize the chemical energy present in organic compounds. There are two main types of autotrophs — photosynthetic organisms and chemosynthetic organisms. Photosynthetic autotrophs obtain energy from sunlight, and convert the radiant energy of sunlight to the chemical energy stored in the bonds of their organic compounds. Green plants obtain CO_2 from the atmosphere and minerals and water from the soil. Algae and photosynthetic bacteria absorb dissolved CO_2, water, and minerals through their cell membranes. Using energy from sunlight, the photosynthetic autotrophic organism converts CO_2, water, and minerals into all the constituents of the organism. Chemosynthetic organisms are much less common than photosynthetic organisms, and are always bacteria. Chemosynthetic bacteria do not require sunlight, and obtain energy by oxidizing certain substances. Two examples are the nitrifying bacteria which oxidize ammonia to nitrite (NO_2^-) or nitrate (NO_3^-) ultimately, and the sulfate bacteria, which oxidize sulfur to sulfates. The energy released from these chemical reactions is converted to a form of chemical energy utilized by the organism.

All the organisms which carry on respiration, that is, oxidize organic compounds to carbon dioxide and water, require oxygen. Respiration is the process by which heterotrophs obtain energy. Chemosynthetic bacteria also require oxygen in order to carry out oxidations of inorganic substances. The only source of oxygen on earth is the photosynthetic autotrophs. These organisms convert CO_2 and water to organic compounds, utilizing sunlight to provide energy, and generate O_2 in the process. If there were no green plants or photosynthetic marine organisms, the oxygen present in the atmosphere would quickly be used up by animals, bacteria, and fungi.

The autotrophs are also responsible for providing the heterotrophs with organic nourishment. Sunlight is the most important source of energy on the earth, and it is only the photosynthetic autotrophs which can utilize this energy, converting it to chemical energy in organic compounds. Heterotrophs utilize the organic compounds produced by the autotrophs. Heterotrophs which obtain organic nourishment from other heterotrophs are also ultimately dependent upon autotrophs for nourishment, because the animals which are the prey have either directly or indirectly (through another animal) utilized the organic material of plants or algae. Photosynthetic autotrophs provide the earth with an energy source for living organisms and with oxygen. If photosynthetic autotrophs were not present, all life on earth would eventually cease as the food and O_2 would become depleted.

● PROBLEM 3-8

Differentiate between the several types of heterotrophic nutrition and give an example of each.

SOLUTION:

The different types of heterotrophic nutrition are defined according to either the type of food source used or the methods employed by the organism in utilizing the food to obtain energy. Holozoic nutrition is the process employed by most animals. In this process, food that is ingested as a solid particle is digested and absorbed. Holozoic nutrition can be further classified as to the food source: herbivores, such as cows, obtain food from plants; carnivores, such as wolves, obtain nutrients from other animals; omnivores, like man, utilize both plants and animals for food.

Saprophytic nutrition is utilized by yeasts, fungi, and most bacteria. These organisms cannot ingest solid food; instead they must absorb organic material through the cell membrane. They live where there are decomposing bodies of animals or plants, or where masses of plant or animal by-products are found. A saprophyte obtains nutrients from nonliving organic matter. An example of a saprophyte is given by yeasts which produce ethanol. Utilizing grape sugar as their energy source, they ferment glucose to carbon dioxide and ethanol. These yeasts are used to produce wine.

In parasitic nutrition, organisms called parasites obtain nourishment from a living host organism. Most parasites absorb organic material and are unable to digest a solid particle. This is true also of saprophytes; however, saprophytes do not require a living host in order to supply them with nourishment. Parasites are found in many classes of the plant and animal kingdoms, and frequently are bacteria, fungi, or protozoa. All viruses are parasites, requiring the host not only for nutrition, but also for synthetic and reproductive machinery. Some parasites exist in the host causing little or no harm. Parasites causing damage to the host are well known to man, and are termed pathogenic. Examples of these are the tapeworm, which lives in the intestine and prevents the host from obtaining adequate nutrition from the food which is eaten, and the tubercle bacillus which causes tuberculosis. Certain organisms are saprophytic in their natural habitat, but are capable of living in a host organism and causing disease. *Clostridium tetani* is an example. In forests, these bacteria obtain nutrients from decaying plant and animal material. When the bacteria enter a wound in a human, the toxic substances they release cause the disease tetanus.

● PROBLEM 3-9

Why are parasites usually restricted to one or a very few host species?

SOLUTION:

Parasites usually have extremely specific requirements for growth. They may grow only within a narrow range of pH and temperature, a certain oxygen concentration, and may require a large number of different organic nutrients. The specific combination of optimal growing conditions which is required by a particular parasite can be found only in one host species, or in several closely related host species. Usually the parasite can live only in certain locations within the host. The tapeworm, for example, can live only in the intestine of a human and will not infect the kidneys or the bones. Saprophytes, on the other hand, will grow within a broad range of temperature, pH, and O_2 concentration, and they require very few organic nutrients. Yeasts, an example of a saprophyte, are able to grow at many different oxygen concentrations, oxidizing glucose to CO_2 and water if oxygen is present, and fermenting glucose to CO_2 and ethanol if oxygen is not present in sufficient amounts. Parasites, in general, are unable to switch from oxidative to fermentative metabolism, and must utilize either one or the other. In addition, yeasts can synthesize all their constituent proteins, nucleic acids, and other components if they are supplied with glucose. Parasitic bacteria lack the enzymes needed for this and must be supplied with amino acids, vitamins, and a mixture of sugars.

These complex growth requirements make it difficult to culture parasitic organisms in the laboratory. Many parasites can grow only if supplied with extracts from animal tissues. Some parasites, such as viruses and rickettsias, can grow only in the presence of living cells.

Energetics and Energy Flow

● PROBLEM 3-10

Sunlight is the ultimate energy source on earth. Energy from sunlight is not returned to its source but is transformed to other forms of energy which are closely tied together in an energy cycle. Describe the energy cycle.

SOLUTION:

The energy cycle starts with sunlight being utilized by green plants on earth. The kinetic energy of sunlight is transformed into potential energy stored in chemical bonds in green plants. The chemical bonds are synthesized by the process of photosynthesis. The potential energy is released in cell respiration and is used in various ways. Thus, fundamental to the energy cycle is the ability of energy to be transformed.

Inorganic (nonliving) matter in the ecosystem is closely tied to organic (living) matter in the energy cycle. For example, photosynthesis requires carbon dioxide from the air and water and minerals from the soil to occur besides sunlight. These are the nonliving components of photosynthesis. Chlorophyll in green plants captures the sunlight, and organic substances (i.e., glucose) are generated from inorganic ingredients via a series of enzymatic reactions in the plant cell.

Chlorophyll, enzymes, and other cellular components form the living part of photosynthesis.

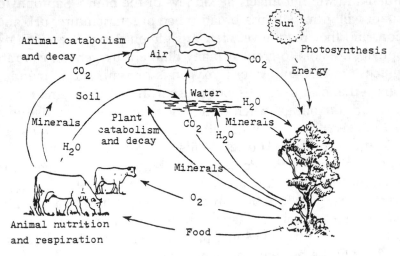

Figure 1. The energy cycle. This diagram shows the relationships between plants and animals and the nonliving materials of the earth. The energy of the sunlight is the only thing that is not returned to its source.

In the energy cycle pictured above, some of the food synthesized by green plants are broken down by the plants for energy, and consequently carbon dioxide and water are released. These again become available for green plants in capturing more energy of the sunlight. Some of the synthesized compounds are used in building the bodies of the plants and are hence stored as potential energy until the plants die. The bacteria and fungi of decay break down the bodies of the dead plants, using the liberated energy for their own metabolism. In these processes, carbon dioxide and water are released, and the minerals go back into the soil. These substances are thus recycled. Animals which feed on plants utilize a part of the energy from the food in cell respiration, with a release of carbon dioxide and water which are again recycled. Some of the minerals in the plant food are excreted by the animals and are thus available to be reused. Animals which feed on other animals utilize some energy from the food in building their own bodies. They break down some of their stored food to yield energy for daily activities such as locomotion. Food degradation is accompanied by release of carbon dioxide and water, which are returned to the ecosystem. When animals die, their bodies decay and all of the materials that were used in the construction are restored to a state which can be reused by the action of the bacteria and fungi of decay.

It must be remembered that at no point in the cycle is energy destroyed. The energy from sunlight is not destroyed but is transformed into heat, chemical, or mechanical energy.

● PROBLEM 3-11

In contrasting a food chain and a food web, which one do you think actually operates in a real community?

SOLUTION:

Food is the common word used to describe the various nutrients that all living heterotrophic organisms must ingest in order to obtain energy to sustain their life processes. Autotrophic photosynthetic organisms, such as the green plants, can manufacture their own food from simple inorganic molecules with the energy from sunlight. Life on earth ultimately depends on food energy which in turn is dependent on the sun.

The radiant energy from the sun that reaches the photosynthetic green plants is responsible for the transformation of basic raw materials such as water, carbon dioxide, nitrogenous compounds, and minerals into the development of the plants themselves. Plants store nutrients (starches and sugars) within them and in turn are eaten by heterotrophic organisms such as animals.

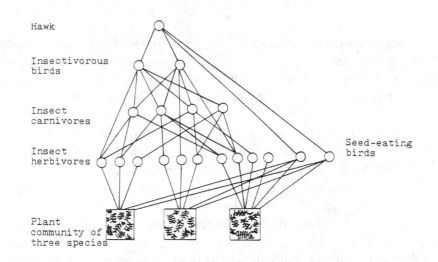

Figure 1. Hypothetical food web. It is assumed that there are three hundred species of plants, ten species of insect herbivores, two bird herbivores, two bird insectivores, and one hawk. In a real community, there would not only be many more species at each trophic level but also many animals that feed at more than one level, or that change level as they grow older. Some general conclusions emerge from even an oversimplified model like this however. There is an initial diversity introduced by the number of plants. This diversity is multiplied at the plant-eating level. At each subsequent level the diversity is reduced as the food chains converge.

A food chain is most commonly a sequence of organisms that are related to each other as prey and predators. One species is eaten by another, which is eaten in turn by a third, and so on. Each species forms a step or link in one or more food chains.

Every food chain begins with the autotrophic organisms (mainly green plants) that serve as the producers of the community. Any organism that does not produce its own food and must therefore depend on another for nutrients is a consumer. Every food chain ends with decomposers, the organisms of decay, which are usually bacteria and fungi that degrade complex organic materials to simple substances which are reusable by the producers. The links between the producers and the decomposers are variable because the producers may die and be acted upon directly by the decomposers, or the producers may be eaten by primary consumers, called the herbivores. The herbivores consume the green plants and in turn may be either acted upon directly by the decomposers or fed upon by the secondary consumers, the carnivores (animal eaters). Some food chains consist of tertiary consumers, or secondary carnivores, which eat the secondary consumers and sometimes also the primary consumers. In almost all ecosystems there are top carnivores: one or more large, specialized animal species that prey on organisms on the lower steps, but are not ordinarily consumed by predators themselves. The larger whales enjoy this status, as do lions, wolves, and man. The decomposers can feed on any dead organism in the food chain. In addition, there are parasite chains in which small organisms live on or within larger ones from where they obtain food.

The successive levels in the food chains of a community are referred to as trophic levels. Thus all the producers together constitute the first (or lowest) trophic level and the primary consumers (herbivores) constitute the second trophic level. The herbivore-eating carnivores constitute the third trophic level, and so on.

Energy-flow in an ecosystem is actually more complicated than the flow of nutrients that simplified food chains imply. In most real communities, there are many different possible food chains that are tied together by cross link-ages. Any one animal usually eats a variety of food and thus may be part of several food chains that intersect. Also, food chains starting from a common plant source may radiate outward as the plant food is eaten by different her-bivores, and as the latter are eaten by different carnivores, and so on. Thus, there is actually a complex food web formed as the food chains first radiate outward from the plants and then come together at the top carnivore level of the web (see Figure 1). For example, the grasshoppers of the grasslands of Canada eat grass and are eaten by robins. Robins eat many kinds of insects as well as grasshoppers. The great horned owl feeds upon the robin as well as other mammals such as the prairie vole. But the prairie vole is also eaten by the coyote. Hence, even though organisms in a community can be classi-fied into the various trophic levels according to the nature of their prey, it is more characteristic to assign organisms to a food web than to a food chain in a real community.

● **PROBLEM 3-12**

The biomass of each trophic level is usually much less than that of the preceding lower trophic level. Define the term biomass and explain the factors that determine the biomass of trophic levels in ecosystems.

Figure 1. Biomass and energy pyramids for two very different ecosystems. The form of energy pyramids is similar from one system to another, but form of biomass pyramids varies considerably.

SOLUTION:

Biomass is the total mass of the living material present in a certain category, whether it is a trophic level or an ecosystem. The distribution of biomass within some ecosystems can be represented by a pyramid, with the first trophic level (producers) at the base and the last consumer level at the apex. In general, the decrease of energy at each successive trophic level means that less of the biomass can be supported at each level.

If the animals of each trophic level were of the same size, they would have to be rarer and rarer toward the top of the pyramid where energy is in shortest supply. Since the animals at the top are usually larger, they are sharing an even smaller supply of energy. The animals high in food chains therefore, must be few, and the pyramid of biomass is a direct consequence of this. Thus the total mass of carnivores in a given community is almost always less than the total mass of herbivores. The size, growth rate, and longevity of the species at the various trophic levels of a community are important in determining whether or not the pyramidal model will hold for the biomass of the community. In fact, biomass pyramids of different communities vary greatly.

The variability of biomass pyramids exist because the plant producer organisms exhibit extreme variability in their ability to undergo photosynthesis. The small algae of some ocean communities can greatly outproduce most land plants on a per gram basis. This is also because of the high metabolic and reproductive rates of algae. Consequently, they are able to support a proportionately much larger biomass of herbivores. The production of ocean herbivores is still only about ten percent (due to ecological efficiency) that of algae. But the biomass of the herbivores is increased because the turnover rate (the rate at which they are consumed and replaced) of the algae is very high. Biomass normally tends to decrease with each successive trophic level, forming the shape of a pyramid. Some communities show an inverse pyramid biomass relationship, such as the case of open ocean algae primary producers.

● PROBLEM 3-13

What factors limit the number of trophic levels in a food chain?

SOLUTION:

As energy flows through the various food chains, it is being constantly channeled into three areas. Some of it goes into production, which is the creation of new tissues by growth and reproduction. Energy is used also for the manufacture of storage products in the form of fats and carbohydrates. Some of the energy is lost from the ecosystem by way of decomposing dead organic materials. The rest of the energy is lost permanently to the ecosystem through respiration. The loss of energy due to respiration is very high and only a small fraction of energy is transferred successfully from one trophic level to the next. Each trophic level depends on the preceding level for its energy source. The number of organisms supportable by any given trophic level depends on the efficiency of transforming the energy available in that level to useful energy of the subsequent level. Ecological efficiencies may vary widely from one kind of animal to another, even at the same trophic level. It has been shown that the average ecological efficiency of any one trophic level is about 10 percent.

The rate at which energy can be transformed by plants is controlled by the carbon dioxide concentration of the atmosphere, by the amount of photosynthetic surfaces available to light and by various limiting factors of the environment such as water and nutrients.

Animals have their energy supply already in the usable form of high-energy compounds. The efficiency of an animal trophic level is primarily a function of the food-getting and digesting process of that trophic level.

The actual energy flow into primary consumers or herbivores is a small fraction of the total energy converted by plants because a substantial part of what they eat cannot be digested and must be returned back to the environment. Moreover, much of the energy converted by vegetation is used by the vegetation itself for respiration.

Carnivores face similar but even more rigorous restrictions on their energy supplies, because their energy depends on how many of the herbivores they can manage to catch, eat, and digest. For secondary carnivores the restrictions are even more rigorous and increase through the successive trophic levels.

Since energy is so important to animals, and is in restricted supply, the number of animals that can be supported is determined by the efficiency with which they utilize energy. From this can be calculated the frequency of a species and the total number that a given area can support. The number of trophic levels or steps in a food chain is normally limited to perhaps four or five because of the great decrease (90 percent) in available energy at each level; i.e., only 10 percent of the energy is transferable to the next trophic level.

Species Interactions

> What is mutualism? Give three examples of this type of relationship.

SOLUTION:

Mutualism, (or symbiosis) like parasitism and commensalism, occurs widely through most of the principal plant and animal groups and includes an astonishing diversity of physiological and behavioral adaptations. In the mutualistic type of relationship, both species benefit from each other. Some of the most advanced and ecologically important examples occur among the plants. Nitrogen-fixing bacteria of the genus Rhizobium live in special nodules in the roots of legumes. In exchange for protection and shelter, the bacteria provide the legumes with substantial amounts of nitrates which aid in their growth.

Another example of plant mutualism is the lichens. They are actually "compound" organisms consisting of highly modified fungi that harbor blue-green and green algae among their hyphae (filaments). Together the two components form a compact and highly efficient unit. In general, the fungus absorbs water and nutrients and forms most of the supporting structure, while the algae provides nutrients for both components via photosynthesis.

In a different form of mutualism, many kinds of ants depend partly or wholly upon aphids and scale insects for their food supply. They milk aphids by stroking them with their forelegs and antennae. The aphids respond by excreting droplets of honeydew, which is simply partly digested plant sap. In return for this sugar-rich food, the ants protect their symbionts from parasitic wasps, predatory beetles, and other natural enemies.

In man, certain bacteria that synthesize vitamin K live mutualistically in the human intestine which provides them with nutrients and a favorable environment.

● PROBLEM 3-15

> In a commensalistic relationship between two species living symbiotically what are the consequences of their interactions?

SOLUTION:

Commensalism is a relationship between two species in which one species benefits while the other receives neither benefit nor harm. The advantage derived by the commensal species from its association with the host frequently involves shelter, support, transport, food, or a combination of these. For example, in tropical forests, numerous small plants called epiphytes usually grow on the branches of the larger trees or in the forks of their trunks. They use the host trees only as a base of attachment and do not obtain nourishment from them. A similar type of commensalism is the use of trees as nesting places by birds. Such relationships do not produce any apparent harm to the hosts.

Commensalism is widespread throughout the animal kingdom, and is especially common among the marine invertebrates. The host organisms are typically slow moving or sessile and live in shells or burrows, which can be readily shared by the smaller commensal species. One example is a certain species of fish that regularly lives in association with sea anemones, deriving protection and shelter from them and sometimes sharing some of their food. These fish swim freely among the tentacles of the anemones even though these tentacles quickly paralyze other species of fish that touch them. The anemones feed on fish, yet the particular species that live as commensals with them can actually enter the gastrovascular cavity of their host, emerging later with no ill effects. This implies a certain amount of physiological and behavioral adaptation between members making up a commensal relationship.

Still another example is a small tropical fish (Fierasfer) that lives in the rectum of a particular species of sea cucumber. The fish periodically emerges to feed and then returns by first poking its host's rectal opening with its snout and then quickly turning so that it is drawn tail first into the rectal chamber.

● PROBLEM 3-16

Why would it be disadvantageous for a host-specific parasite to kill its host?

SOLUTION:

In the course of their evolution, parasites usually develop special features of behavior and physiology that make them better adjusted to the particular characteristics of their host. This means that they often tend to become more and more specific for their host. Where an ancestral organism might have parasitized all species in a particular family, its various descendants may parasitize only one species of host at each stage in its development. This means that many parasites are capable of living only in one specific host species and that if they should cause the extinction of their host, then they themselves would also become extinct. A dynamic balance exists where the host usually survives without being seriously damaged and at the same time allowing the parasites to moderately prosper. Probably most long-established host-parasite relationships are balanced ones. The ideally adapted parasite is one that can flourish without reducing its host's ability to grow and reproduce. For every one of the parasitic species that cause serious disease in man and other organisms, there are many others that give their hosts little or no trouble. It is generally true that the deadliest of the parasites are the ones that are the most poorly adapted to the species affected. Relationships that result in serious disease in the host are usually relatively new ones, or ones in which a new and more virulent form of the parasite has recently arisen, or where the host showing the serious disease symptoms is not the primary host of the parasite. Many examples are known where man is only an occasional host for a particular parasite and suffers severe disease symptoms, although the wild animal that is the primary host shows few ill effects from its relationship with the same parasite.

Succession

● PROBLEM 3-17

What are the characteristics of ecological succession?

SOLUTION:

Succession is a fairly orderly process of changes of communities in a region. It involves replacement, in the course of time, of the dominant species within a given area by other species. Communities succeed each other in an orderly sequence in which each successive stage is thought to be dependent on the one which preceded it. Each community in the succession is called a seral stage.

The first stage of succession is usually the colonization of barren space such as a sandy beach or a rock, by simple pioneer species such as grasses. The pioneer species are able to grow and breed rapidly. They have adopted the strategy of finding and utilizing empty space. Then, gradually the pioneers are replaced by more complex and bulky species until finally the community is characterized by climax species which represent the final stage of succession. Climax communities are the most stable and will only appear if some outside agent such as new species or a geographic change displaces them. Most succession can be classified into either primary or secondary successions. Primary successions proceed by pioneering new uninhabited sites. Secondary successions occur on disturbed land where a climax community that existed before had been destroyed by such occurrences as fire, severe wind storms, flooding, and landslides.

Although succession in different places and at different times is not identical (the species involved are often completely different) some ecologists have nevertheless formulated generalizations that hold true for most cases where both autotrophs and heterotrophs are involved:

1) The species composition changes continuously during the succession, but the change is usually more rapid in the earlier stages than in the later ones. 2) The total number of species represented increases initially and then becomes fairly stabilized in the older stages. This is particularly true of the heterotrophs, whose variety is usually much greater in the later stages of the succession. 3) Both the total biomass in the ecosystem and the amount of nonliving organic matter increase during the succession until a more stable stage is reached. 4) The food webs become more complex, and the relations between species in them become better defined. 5) Although the amount of new organic matter synthesized by the producers remains approximately the same, except at the beginning of succession, the percentage utilized at the various trophic levels rises.

In summary, the trend of most successions is toward a more complex ecosystem in which less energy is wasted and hence a greater biomass can be supported.

● PROBLEM 3-18

Why does succession occur? Why can the first colonists not simply seize an area and hold it against subsequent intruders?

SOLUTION:

Succession occurs independently of the climate. Climate may be a major factor in determining what types of species will follow one another, but succession itself results from other changes. The most important of these are the modifications of the physical environment produced by the community itself. Most successional communities tend to alter the area in which they occur in such a way as to make it less favorable for themselves and more favorable for other communities.

In effect, each community in the succession sows the seeds of its own destruction.

Consider the alterations initiated by pioneer communities on land. Usually these communities will produce a layer of decay matter or litter on the surface of the soil. The accumulation affects the runoff of rainwater, the soil temperature, and the formation of humus (organic decomposition products). The humus, in turn contributes to the soil development and thus alters the availability of nutrients, the water, the pH and aeration of the soil, and the types of soil organisms that will be present. But the organisms that are characteristic of the pioneer communities that produced these changes may not prosper under the new conditions, and they may be replaced by invading competitors that do better in an area with the new type of soil. In another manner, plants sometimes foreclose future reproduction by the process of their own growth. In Australia, for example, the Eucalyptus trees of the open, sunny savannas provide shade in which young tress from the nearby rain forests can sprout and grow. When these intruders reach their full size, they cast too much shade for the Eucalyptus to reproduce themselves. The Eucalyptus finally die out as the rain forest takes over the land completely.

Not all successional stages prepare the way for their own decline and fall. In the eastern United States, mixed forests of pine and oak modify the soil in a way that makes it more favorable for the growth of their own seedlings than for those of their competitors. Succession in such cases occurs simply because slower growing trees rise to dominance at a later time and alteration of the environment therefore may have nothing to do with replacement.

An orderly sequence of communities in a succession usually occurs because as the species specialized for each stage persists and changes the environment, an excellent habitat for the next set of species is provided. In fact, ecologists recognize two broad classes of species involved in this ordered kind of succession. Opportunistic species are able to disperse widely, and they grow and breed rapidly. The opportunistic species include the pioneers and the species involved in the early succession stages. They have adopted the strategy of finding and utilizing empty space before other species preempt it. *Stable species*, on the other hand, specialize in competitive superiority. Forest trees of most kinds belong to this category. They grow and disperse more slowly, but in their encounters with opportunistic species, they are able to grow successfully at the expense of the other species and remain for longer periods of time. Forest trees commonly make up a large percentage of the land climax communities.

● PROBLEM 3-19

Describe the sequence of succession leading to a climax community from a bare rock surface.

SOLUTION:

Ecological successions are common in most regions, including those which develop on bare rocks. The first pioneer plants may be lichens (algae and fungi living symbiotically) which grow during the brief periods when the rock surface is wet and lies dormant during periods when the surface is dry. The lichens release acids and other substances that corrode the rock on which they grow. Dust particles and bits of dead lichen may collect in the tiny crevices formed and consequently pave the way for other pioneer communities. Mosses can gain anchorage in these crevices and grow in clumps. These clumps allow the formation of a thickening layer of soil composed of humus rotted from dead mosses, lichen parts, and also grains of sand and silt caught from the wind or from the runoff waters of a rainstorm. A few fern spores or seeds of grasses and annual herbs may land on the mat of soil and germinate. These may be followed by perennial herbs. As more and more such plants survive and grow, they catch and hold still more mineral and organic materials, and the new soil layer becomes thicker. Later, shrubs and even trees may start to grow in the soil that now covers what once was a bare rock surface. This type of succession is referred to as primary succession in that the region involved has never supported life forms before.

Secondary succession is best understood by considering what happens to a farm field when it is abandoned. In the very first year, the abandoned field is covered with annual weeds. By the second summer the soil is completely covered with short plants, and the perennial herbs have seized the available space. Grasses start to form a turf. In the next few years, the turf of herbs thickens, but also woody plants, such as brambles and thorny shrubs, become established. The shrubbery grows until the field is blocked by an almost impenetrable tangle of thorny plants. Trees grow up through them, changing the field in a decade or two into a rough wood forest. Other communities of trees replace these trees in the succession. The stages from ploughed fields to forests have been witnessed many times and the successions of vegetation before the climax community is reached are better known as seral stages.

Population Dynamics and Growth Patterns

● PROBLEM 3-20

Why does population growth follow a logistic (S-shaped) form until it reaches the carrying capacity of the environment?

SOLUTION:

Since nearly all mature individuals in a population can produce offspring, the rate at which an unrestricted population increases is a function of the generation time, which is the period required for an organism to reproduce. When a population initially grows, the size of the population will double every generation time. This kind of growth rate is referred to as exponential growth (Figure 1).

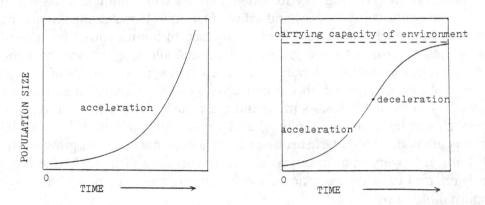

Figure 1. Exponential (unrestricted) growth   Figure 2. Logistic (restricted) growth

A population of animals has a potential through reproduction to increase at a given rate which is termed the intrinsic rate of increase. The intrinsic rate of increase is equal to the difference between the average birth rate and average death rate of a population. It varies enormously from species to species.

In a typical experiment, 40 individual paramecia were placed in a small tube of water and each day thereafter fresh food was added. Therefore, a constant but limited daily input of food to the system was provided. Under these conditions, the paramecia reproduced quickly at first, with their number increasing exponentially until there were about 4000 animals in the tube. Then the rate of growth leveled off, and the population remained at a steady state. The rate of replacement was finally about equal to the death rate, and the population became balanced. It seems likely that the balance reached by experimental populations is equivalent to the general balance existing in nature.

If animals breed prolifically when there is plenty of space and food, but cease to do so when crowded, then it is reasonable to suggest that cessation may be a result of increasing intraspecific (between the members of one species) competition for the resources of the habitat. Breeding may also become suppressed by some effect of the environment which inhibits the population more strongly as crowding increases. The growth of a population in a confined space with a limited input of energy is described by an "S"-shaped graph (see Figure 2). The number of individuals increases rapidly, but in time there is a leveling off of the rate of growth of the population so that the growth rate eventually becomes zero. This suppressing effect of competition gets stronger as the animals get more numerous, until it is strong enough to bring the rate of increase down to zero and an upper limit is reached where the environment in which they live cannot support any more of them.

The limiting size is called the carrying capacity of the environment. At this population size, the death rate equals the birth rate, and therefore the rate of increase in the number of individuals is zero. Temporary deviations from zero growth will probably occur causing the population to grow for a short time, or to decline, but the average value over long periods of time will be zero.

The actual value of the carrying capacity of the environment for a specific species is determined by the interaction of several factors, including the total energy flow in the ecosystem, the trophic level to which the species belongs, and the size and metabolic rate of the individuals. Eventually, energy from food will be a limiting factor for any population.

● **PROBLEM 3-21**

Suppose a fisherman was interested in trying to extract the maximum number of fish from a pond or lake. Why would it not be to his economic advantage to reduce the fish populations by excessive harvesting?

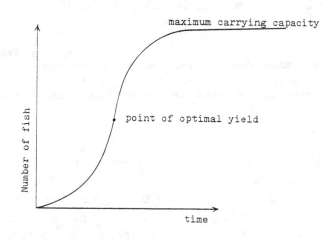

Figure 1. An S-shaped growth curve showing the point of optimal yield.

SOLUTION:

The ideal economic strategy for the fisherman to follow would be to catch only enough fish so as to keep the population at a level of optimal yield. If the population is allowed to reach the maximum that the environment can support, or if it is exploited to the point where the organisms become scarce, the yield will decline. This phenomenon exists because the greatest amount of increase in population size does not occur either when the population is very low or when the population has reached the carrying capacity of the environment. The point of greatest growth and hence the maximum replacement capacity of a population occurs at a point midway on the exponential part of an S-shaped growth curve, that is, halfway between the baseline and the maximum carrying capacity (see Figure 1).

This point corresponds to the point of steepest rise on the S-shaped curve. At this point, the greatest number of new individuals are added to the population in a given amount of time. This maximum rate of population growth is referred to as the optimal yield.

Fish populations, as well as other animal populations that man harvests, can be obtained with much less effort at a point of optimal yield than populations reduced by overfishing. Moreover, the greater the exploitation of populations, the more the population will come to consist of younger and smaller individuals, which are usually the least valuable commercially. The proportion of large fish caught is higher when the population is at a point of optimal yield. Consequently, as the fish populations are reduced, more expensive and sophisticated ships and trawling techniques are required to produce the same amount of yield.

Biotic Potential and Limiting Factors

● **PROBLEM 3-22**

Explain how density dependent controls of population occur.

SOLUTION:

An important characteristic of a population is its density, which is the number of individuals per unit area. A more useful term to ecologists is ecologic density, which is the number of individuals per *habitable* unit area. As the ecologic density of a given population begins to increase, there are regulatory factors that tend to oppose the growth. These regulating mechanisms operate to maintain a population at its optimal size within a given environment. This overall process of regulation is known as the density dependent effect.

Predation is an example of a density dependent regulator. As the density of a prey species rises, the hunting patterns of predators often change so as to increase predation on that particular population of prey. Consequently, the prey population decreases; the predators then are left with less of a food resource and their density subsequently declines. The effect of this is often a series of density fluctuations until an equilibrium is reached between the predator and prey populations. Thus, in a stable predator-prey system, the two populations are actually regulated by each other.

Emigration of individuals from the parent population is another form of density dependent control. As the population density increases, a larger number of animals tend to move outward in search of new sources of food. Emigration is a distinctive behavior pattern acting to disperse part of the overcrowded population.

Competition is also a density dependent control. As the population density increases, the competition for limited resources becomes more intense. Consequently, the deleterious results of unsuccessful competition such as starvation and injury become more and more effective in limiting the population size.

Physiological as well as behavioral mechanisms have evolved that help to regulate population growth. It has been observed that an increase in population density is accompanied by a marked depression in inflammatory response and antibody formation. This form of inhibited immune response allows for an increase in susceptibility to infection and parasitism. Observation of laboratory mice has shown that as population density increases, aggressive behavior increases, reproduction rate falls, sexual maturity is impaired, and the growth rate becomes suppressed. These effects are attributable to changes in the endocrine system. It appears that the endocrine system can help regulate and limit population size through control of both reproductive and aggressive behavior. Although these regulatory mechanisms have been demonstrated with laboratory mice, it is not clear to what extent they operate in other species.

● **PROBLEM 3-23**

In contrast to density dependent effects, there are also density independent effects which operate without reference to population size. Elaborate on the major density independent effects and their relationship to population size.

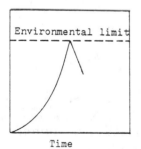

Time

Figure 1. A growth curve in which the environmental limiting factors did not become effective until late, and then produced a sudden sharp decline.

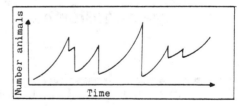

Figure 2. Growth curve under density independent effect.

SOLUTION:

There is no scientific principle which states that populations must be controlled as a function of density. Density effects will always be working in crowded populations, but it is also possible for actual control of population

45

size to be exercised before crowding occurs. Control agents that are not dependent on density can take the form of sudden events that are catastrophic to animal populations. Catastrophic events can solve the problem of overcrowding just as efficiently as a density dependent device.

Hurricanes and volcanic explosions can destroy entire populations but these events are too scattered and local to be used as examples for general population controls. More applicable are the common catastrophes which we know as changes in the weather. Nearly all places on the earth suffer seasonal changes from summer to winter, from warm to cold, and from wet to dry. Each of these cyclic changes represents hazards to the animals of each area. Thus, growing populations are frequently cut back, making their normal lives a race to reproduce so quickly that there shall be at least some survivors following the next catastrophe. Unless something happens to prevent the catastrophe from occurring, such a population may never grow large enough to suffer the effects of crowding.

Density independent factors may play an important role in limiting some organisms, particularly those with very short life cycles characterized by a growth curve in which the environmental limiting factors do not become effective until after many generations (see Figure 1). A sudden strong density independent limitation then brings growth to an end before density dependent factors can become operative.

The density independent effects are definite factors in moving population growth upward or downward, but they cannot hold the population size at a constant level. As a result, populations effected by density independent factors are under control but their numbers fluctuate within wide limits (see Figure 2) and can hardly be described as "in balance."

Biosphere and Biomes

● PROBLEM 3-24

Describe the various land biomes that are usually encountered by a traveler going from the equator to the arctic polar ice cap.

SOLUTION:

In the equatorial regions of several continents (Africa, Asia, and South America) are tropical rain forests with enormous trees. The interlocking canopy of leaves blocks out the sun and allows only dim light to penetrate. As a result, the ground is sparsely covered with small plants. The canopy also interrupts the direct fall of the plentiful rain, but water drips from it to the

46

forest floor much of the time, even when it is not raining. It also shields the lower levels from wind and hence greatly reduces the rate of evaporation. The lower levels of the forest are consequently very humid. Temperatures near the forest floor are nearly constant.

The pronounced differences in conditions at different levels within such a forest result in a striking degree of vertical stratification. Many species of animals and epiphytic plants (plants growing on large trees) occur only in the canopy, while others occur only in the middle strata, and still others occur only on the forest floor. Decomposition of fallen leaves and dead wood is so rapid that humus is even missing in spots on the floor. The diversity of life here is the greatest found anywhere on earth. In a single square mile of the richest tropical rain forests, hundreds of species of trees, hundreds more of birds, butterflies, reptiles and amphibians, and dozens of species of mammals make their habitat.

Huge areas in both the temperate and tropical regions of the world are covered by grassland biomes. These are typically areas with relatively low total annual rainfall or uneven seasonal occurrence of rainfall. This type of climate is unfavorable for forests but suitable for growth of grasses. Temperate and tropical grasslands are remarkably similar in appearance, although the particular species they contain may be very different. In both cases, there are usually vast numbers of large herbivores, which often include the ungulates (hoofed animals). Burrowing rodents or rodentlike animals are also often common.

North of the tropics, in the temperate regions of Europe and eastern North America, are deciduous forests. Small creepers and epiphytes such as lichens and mosses may be found, but they are not so conspicuous as in the rain forests. There is richer vegetation on the ground below, which is often covered by a carpet of herbs. Such a forest may be called temperate deciduous forest. In those parts of the temperate zone where rainfall is abundant and the summers are relatively long and warm, the climax communities are frequently dominated by broad-leaved trees, whose leaves change color in autumn then fall off in winter and grow back in the spring.

North of the deciduous forest of temperate North America and Eurasia is a wide zone dominated by coniferous (cone-bearing) forests sometimes referred to as the boreal forests. This is the taiga biome. Instead of being bushy-topped, the trees are mostly of the triangular Christmas-tree shape. The trees of the boreal forest are evergreens, cone-bearing, and needle-leaved consisting mostly of spruce, fir, and tamarack. They branch over most of their height and are relatively close-packed. The land is dotted by lakes, ponds, and bogs. The winters of the taiga are very cold and during the warm summers, the subsoil thaws and vegetation flourishes. Moose, black bears, wolves, lynx, wolverines, martens, squirrels, and many smaller rodents are important in the taiga communities. Birds are abundant in summer.

The territory of the boreal forest is hundreds of miles wide, but eventually it meets the completely treeless vegetation of the tundra. The tundra is the most continuous of the earth's biomes, forming a circular band around the North pole, interrupted only narrowly by the North Atlantic and the Bering Sea. The vegetation of the tundra resembles grassland but it is actually made up of a mixture of lichens, mosses, grasses, sedges and low growing willows, and other shrubs. There are numerous perennial herbs, which are able to withstand frequent freezing and which grow rapidly during the brief cool summers, often carpeting the tundra with brightly colored flowers. A permanent layer of frozen soil lies a few inches to a few feet beneath the surface. It prevents the roots of trees and other deep growing plants from becoming established, and it slows the drainage of surface water. As a result, the flat portions of the tundra are dotted with shallow lakes and bogs, and the soil between them is exceptionally wet. Reindeer, lemmings, caribou, arctic wolves, foxes, and hares are among the principal mammals, while polar bears are common on parts of the tundra near the coast. Vast numbers of birds, particularly shorebirds and waterfowl (ducks, geese, etc.), nest on the tundra in summer, but they are not permanent inhabitants and migrate south for the winter. Insects are incredibly abundant. In short, the tundra is far from being a barren lifeless land; but the number of different species is quite limited.

The succession of biomes between the equator and the Arctic is roughly mirrored in the Southern Hemisphere, although the absence of large landmasses makes the pattern less complete. There are also some other biomes that are more irregularly scattered about the world, but which have a distinctive form. These are the biomes of the desert regions and the sclerophylous bushlands.

The bushlands, common in the chaparral of California, maquis of the Mediterranean, and the mallee heath of Australia, are made up of different species of plants, but have much in common. They have gnarled and twisted, rough and thorny plants. The leaves tend to be dark and are hairy, leathery, or thickly cutinized. All grow in places with hot dry summers and relatively cool moist winters. A climatic pattern such as this is rare and is always accompanied with vegetation of this form. In places where rainfall is very low grasses cannot survive as the dominant vegetation and desert biomes occur. Deserts are subject to the most extreme temperature fluctuations of any biome. During the day they are exposed to intense sunlight, and the temperature of both air and soil may rise very high. But in the absence of the moderating influence of abundant vegetation, heat is rapidly lost at night, and a short while after sunset, searing heat has usually given way to bitter cold. Some deserts, such as parts of the Sahara, are nearly barren of vegetation, but more commonly there are scattered drought-resistant shrubs and succulent plants that can store much water in their tissues. Most desert animals are active primarily at night or during the brief periods in early morning and late afternoon when the heat is not so intense. Most of them show numerous remarkable physiological and behavioral adaptations for life in their hostile environment.

We have thus seen that one moving North or South on the earth's surface may pass through a series of different biomes. The major biome types have been mentioned with the exception of the comparatively unproductive biomes such as the polar ice caps. Ecologists often differ in their classifications of the major patches of the biosphere because the biomes are strictly defined by the elements put into them. The borders of the biomes shift as we add or subtract species. The point to remember is that the biomes seldom exist as sharply defined patches. They have broad borders, and the species that comprise them have weakly correlated geographical ranges.

● **PROBLEM 3-25**

Why isn't a biome map of the earth a true representation of the vegetation formations found on land?

SOLUTION:

The naturalist travelers of the eighteenth and nineteenth centuries saw strikingly different kinds of vegetations parceled out into formations. They drew maps showing the extent of each formation. However, drawing a map involves drawing boundaries. Where there are real, distinct boundaries on the ground this is an easy task. Such boundaries include those between sea and land, along deserts or beside mountain ranges. But often there are no real boundaries on the ground. In fact, most of the formation boundaries of the earth are not distinct. Real vegetation types usually grade one into another so that it is impossible to tell where one formation ends and another begins.

The apparent distinctness of the vegetation formations, when viewed from afar, is largely an optical illusion as the eye picks out bands where individual species are concentrated. A vegetation mapmaker could plot the position of a tree line well enough, if he had a few reports from places with distinct treelines which he could plot and link up. However, the gradual transitions, such as between the temperate woods and tropical rain forests would be much more difficult to plot. So map-makers draw boundaries using what seems to be the middle of the transitions. When the map is finished, the area is parceled out by blocks of formations of plants. A map like this shows the vegetation of the earth to be more neatly set into compartments than it really is.

Environmental Chains and Cycles

Animals at the top of a food pyramid may be larger in individual size than animals more immediate to the primary source of food, yet they represent a smaller total weight (biomass) in the aggregate. Explain.

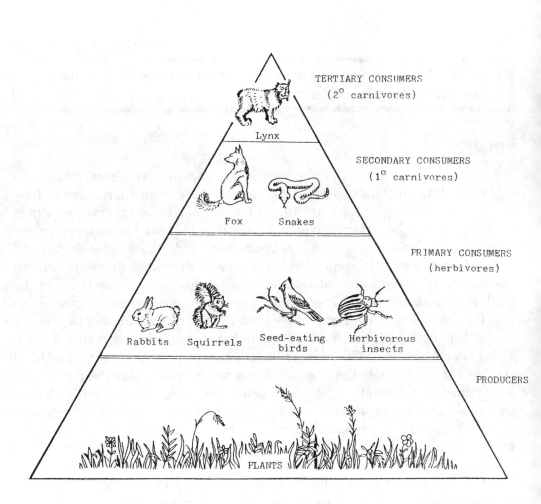

TERTIARY CONSUMERS
(2° carnivores)

Lynx

SECONDARY CONSUMERS
(1° carnivores)

Fox   Snakes

PRIMARY CONSUMERS
(herbivores)

Rabbits   Squirrels   Seed-eating   Herbivorous
                         birds   insects

PRODUCERS

PLANTS

Figure 1. A hypothetical food pyramid. The amount of energy found at each level can be represented as: energy at producer level > energy at primary consumer level > energy at secondary consumer level > energy at tertiary consumer level. The decrease in the amount of biomass (the mass of living organisms) going up the pyramid is also evident.

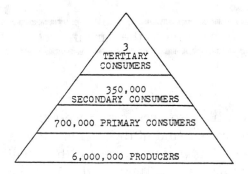

Figure 2. Pyramid of the biomass in a bluegrass field with respective approximate numbers.

SOLUTION:

The food pyramid is the term that describes the successive transfer of the radiant energy trapped by plants through a series of consumers. In its simplest form, plants are eaten by primary consumers (herbivores), which are in turn eaten by secondary consumers (carnivores). Ultimately, decomposers (bacteria and fungi) degrade unused plant and animal matter into components useful to themselves or the green plants. At each level there is a decrease in the amount of usable energy because in the process of each transfer, energy is lost as heat. There is more energy available to plants than there is available to herbivores, more energy available to herbivores than to carnivores, more energy available to primary carnivores (carnivores that eat only herbivores) than to secondary carnivores (carnivores that also eat other carnivores). With each step, the animal must oxidize the food it eats to obtain energy to synthesize its own cellular constituents and to perform other life functions. The energy that is liberated is not all converted to the animal's cellular constituents, rather a large proportion is lost as heat. The amount of available energy limits the number and mass of each organism which can utilize that energy to support life.

The total mass of the animals at the top of the food pyramid, the secondary carnivores, is less than the total mass of the animals closer to the plant source of food, the herbivores, because there is less energy available to the secondary carnivores. An individual secondary carnivore is usually very large. Large body size is useful to these animals, since it enables them to capture and kill their prey. However, the number of such carnivores is small. In considering the total mass of the secondary carnivores, both the individual body mass and the number of individuals must be taken into account (See Figures 1 and 2).

Discuss the role of bacteria in the carbon cycle and the nitrogen cycle.

SOLUTION:

Cycling of the earth's resources is a process by which life is able to continue on earth. The carbon and nitrogen atoms that are present on the earth today are the same atoms that were present three billion years ago, and have been used over and over again. They are the fundamental constituents of organic compounds, and are present in large quantities in all organisms. Carbon and nitrogen atoms that were present in a dinosaur might now be found in an oak tree since matter is not destroyed, and cannot be created. The same carbon and nitrogen atoms are constantly being recycled.

In the carbon cycle, atmospheric carbon dioxide is converted into organic material by plants. Animals and bacteria convert some of this organic matter into CO_2 by respiration, however, most of the carbon remains fixed as organic matter in the bodies of plants and animals. Bacteria play a crucial role in the carbon cycle. Bacteria, as well as fungi, convert the carbon atoms in the organic matter of decaying plants, animals, and other bacteria and fungi to CO_2, which returns to the atmosphere (see Figure 1).

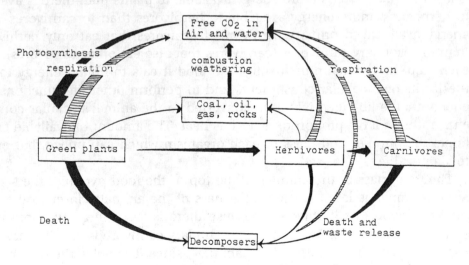

Figure 1. The carbon cycle.

Plants obtain nitrates from the soil, taking them up through their roots, and convert the nitrate into organic compounds, mainly proteins. Animals obtain nitrogen from plant proteins and amino acids and they excrete nitrogen-containing wastes. These nitrogenous wastes are excreted in one of the following forms, depending on the species — urea, uric acid, creatinine, and ammonia. Certain bacteria in the soil convert nitrogenous waste and the proteins of dead plants and animals into ammonia. Another type of bacteria present in the soil is able to convert ammonia to nitrate. These are termed nitrifying bacteria. They obtain energy from chemical oxidations. There are two types of nitrifying bacteria: nitrite bacteria, which convert ammonia into nitrite, and nitrate bacteria, which convert nitrite into nitrate. Nitrogen is thus returned to the cycle. Atmospheric nitrogen, N_2, cannot be utilized as a nitrogen source by either animals or plants. Only some blue-green algae and certain bacteria can convert N_2 to organic compounds. This process is termed nitrogen fixation. One genus of bacteria, Rhizobium, is able to utilize N_2 only when grown in association with leguminous plants, such as peas and beans. The bacteria grow inside tiny swellings of the plant's roots, called root nodules. Nitrogen is also returned to the atmosphere by certain bacteria. Denitrifying bacteria convert nitrites and nitrates to N_2, thus preventing animals and plants from obtaining biologically useful nitrogen. A summary of the nitrogen cycle is provided in Figure 2.

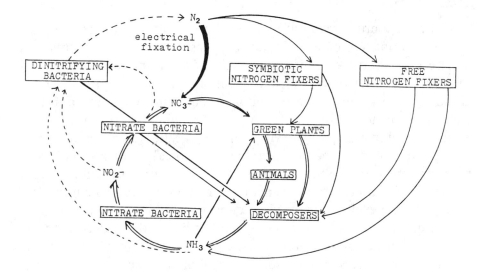

Figure 2. The nitrogen cycle.

In what way does the phosphorus cycle differ from the carbon and nitrogen cycles? In what way does the energy cycle differ from all other cycles?

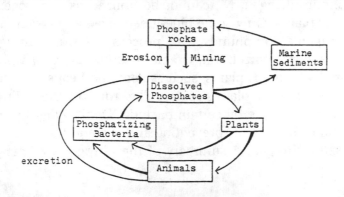

Figure 1. A simple version of the phosphorus cycle.

SOLUTION:

The phosphorus cycle differs from the carbon and nitrogen cycles in that it is not completely balanced, and relies less on living organisms to maintain it. The phosphorus cycle is an example of a sedimentary cycle in which the minerals cycle between land and sediments in the sea. Inorganic phosphate is found in rocks on the earth and is available to plants and animals as inorganic phosphate in their water supply. The phosphate is then converted to various organic phosphates, which are an additional source of phosphate for animals in the food they eat. In degrading dead plant and animal material, bacteria return phosphate to the soil. The phosphate is then leached out of the soil and carried into the sea. Sea birds and fish return some of this phosphorus to the cycle. Marine birds deposit phosphorus-containing wastes on the land. Until the advent of chemical fertilizers, these deposits were an important source of phosphorus for agricultural use. Animals which eat fish and marine invertebrates recover some phosphorus. Despite these recovery methods, more phosphate is lost to the sea bottom than is returned. Over time, however, phosphorus may be returned to the cycle by geologic upheavals which bring the sea bottom up to the earth's surface, creating mountains and new land masses.

The energy cycle differs from other cycles in that no cycling of useful energy occurs. The energy is converted into other forms of energy. However, in the process, energy is lost as heat, which is not biologically useful. The energy cycle, thus, is not actually a cycle. All energy is derived from sunlight. Plants convert solar energy to chemical energy. Only three percent of the sun's radiation energy is trapped by the photosynthetic process. The chemical energy that is stored in plants is utilized by animals or bacteria. Since the process is not completely efficient, not all of the energy stored within the plant can be converted into useful energy by the animal; about 40 percent of the energy is lost as heat. If the animal is eaten by another animal, a further reduction in the amount of useful energy occurs, as additional heat is generated and lost when the chemical energy of the first animal is converted to the cellular constituents of the second animal. Eventually all the energy trapped by green plants is converted to heat, and all the carbon of organic compounds is converted to CO_2 and fossil fuels.

Diversification of the Species

Suppose you were given a cage full of small, rat-like animals from the Rocky Mountain region and another cage full of similar animals from the Appalachian Mountains. How would you determine if the two groups were of the same or different species?

SOLUTION:

The species is the fundamental unit of biological classification. A species is defined as a group of organisms that is closely related structurally and functionally, which in a natural environment interbreeds and produces fertile offspring, but which seldom, if ever, breeds with organisms of another species. A species is reproductively isolated. The dog and the cat are examples of two different species. Dogs and cats cannot breed with one another.

Closely related species may interbreed, however, the offspring are rarely fertile. The horse and the donkey are examples of closely related species which can mate and produce viable offspring. This offspring is the mule, which is unable to reproduce. A mule can only result from the union of a horse and a donkey. The fact that mules are sterile helps to establish the fact that the horse and the donkey are of different species.

Species may be subdivided into subspecies, varieties, or races. The varieties are kept distinct either through geographic isolation, seasonal differences in reproductive patterns, or by the intervention of man. Dogs offer an example of controlled breeding. If unrestrained by man, the different varieties interbreed to produce mongrels. In certain cases, interbreeding between different subspecies is very difficult. The greatest problem in the case of dogs would be size; however, sexual attraction between different varieties exists and it can be proven that both varieties belong to the same species because they are structurally and functionally similar. Both the small and large varieties could breed with a medium sized variety, proving that the varieties are not reproductively isolated. If interbreeding between varieties is prevented by seasonal variation of reproductive patterns, careful regulation of laboratory conditions could enable two different subspecies to be ready for reproduction at the same time.

In the case of the rat-like animals, the two groups should be studied to see if they are similar structurally and functionally. If so, it must be determined whether the animals could breed with one another. If they could and if they produce fertile offspring, the two groups would be classified as members of the same species. If the offspring were all sterile, it would mean that the two groups of animals belonged to two different, closely related species. If the two groups seemed similar after studying their structural and functional characteristics, but did not breed with one another, an examination of their natural reproductive patterns might offer information as to why breeding did not occur under laboratory conditions. If conditions were altered and fertile offspring were produced, the two groups of animals could be members of the same species. If breeding did not occur under any conditions, or through an intermediate species, one would conclude that the two were members of different species.

● PROBLEM 3-30

Explain how a new species may arise after it has been separated from its ancestors for a considerable period of time.

SOLUTION:

Gene mutation and natural selection are two processes which enable a certain group of organisms to become a distinct species, different from its ancestral species. As a certain species distributes itself over a large geographical area, different subgroups become isolated in different environments. As genes mutate to give rise to different traits, certain traits are proven to be more valuable in certain environments and less valuable in others. The traits that enable the organism to be better adapted to its environment will tend to be conserved. This is because the organisms which express these traits will be more likely to survive and reproduce than organisms not so well adapted to their environment. Eventually, the genetic composition of an isolated group becomes so different from the genetic composition of the ancestral species, that breeding can no longer occur between the two groups of organisms. In addition, the isolated group will have different structural and functional characteristics. The new group has thus become a distinct species.

An example of this type of evolutionary divergence from a common ancestor is given by the camels and their relatives. Through study of fossil records, it has been determined that the ancestral species was similar to the South American llama. At some time in the distant past, some of these animals migrated across a land bridge to Africa. These animals, the immediate ancestors of the camels, evolved adaptive mechanisms that enabled them to survive in the desert environment. For example, the camel's hump can store food and water for a long time over great distances. This is an adaptive structure which llamas and their American relatives do not possess.

SHORT ANSWER QUESTIONS FOR REVIEW

Choose the correct answer.

1. The classification system used today is based upon (a) similarities of habitats between different organisms. (b) similarities of phenotypes between different organisms. (c) similarities of structures and functions between different organisms. (d) similarities of ecological niches between different organisms.

2. Which of the following classification groups are in the proper sequence from the largest grouping to the smallest? (a) phylum, class, order, family (b) kingdom, family, class, phylum (c) family, order, genus, species (d) kingdom, class, species, genus

3. The genus and species of a fruit fly is correctly written: (a) *Drosophila melanogaster.* (b) *Drosophila Melanogaster.* (c) *drosophila melanogaster.* (d) *drosophila Melanogaster.*

4. The greatest similarity in structure occurs between members belonging to the same (a) species. (b) genus. (c) family. (d) class.

5. The kingdom Monera includes: (a) only bacteria. (b) bacteria and blue-green algae. (c) blue-green algae and red algae. (d) all fungi.

6. Organisms which absorb organic material through the cell membrane because they cannot ingest solid food, and live where there are decomposing bodies of animals or plants are: (a) holozotes. (b) omnivores. (c) parasites. (d) saprophytes.

7. Nitrogenous wastes are excreted by different species of animals in all of the following forms, except: (a) creatinine. (b) uracil. (c) ammonia. (d) urea.

8. In order for plants to obtain the necessary nitrogen, the free nitrogen in the air must be converted to nitrates. This is done by (a) legumes. (b) bacteria of decay. (c) nitrogen fixing bacteria. (d) denitrifying bacteria.

9. Which of the following pairs represents ecological equivalents? (a) squirrel and rattlesnake (b) house cat and lion (c) sea gull and codfish (d) wild horse and zebra

10. The character of an ecosystem is determined by the environmental factor that is in shortest supply. This is (a) the law of minimum. (b) Borty's law. (c) the law of diminishing returns. (d) Dollo's law.

11. A sequence of species related to one another as predator and prey is a(n) (a) trophic level. (b) ecosystem. (c) food chain. (d) climax.

12. The "10 percent rule" (a) refers to the percentage of similar species that can coexist in one ecosystem. (b) refers to the average death total of all mammals before maturity. (c) is the percent of animals not affected by DDT. (d) refers to the level of energy production present in a given trophic level and used for production by the next higher level.

13. The relationship between fungi and the algae in lichens is known as (a) mutualism. (b) parasitism. (c) commensalism. (d) saprophytism.

14. Choose the statement that best describes the climax stage of an ecological succession. (a) It is usually populated only by plants. (b) It remains until there are severe changes in the environment. (c) It represents the initial phases of evolution. (d) It changes rapidly from season to season.

Fill in the blanks.

15. Some organisms are difficult to assign to either the plant or animal kingdom. Thus three more kingdoms have been proposed, the _____, _____, and _____.

16. The binomial system of classification which is being used today is based on the model developed by _____.

17. _____ organisms can produce energy by using inorganic sources.

18. _____ is the process in which plants can convert the light energy of sunlight to chemical energy.

19. Most animals employ _____ nutrition in ingesting their food as a solid particle and then digesting and absorbing it.

20. Atmospheric nitrogen cannot be utilized as a nitrogen source by plants or animals. It must first be converted to _____ and/or _____ in order for it to be usable.

21. _____ refers to studies of individual organisms, or populations of single species, and their interactions with the environment.

22. _____ refers to studies of various groups of organisms which are associated to form a functional unit of the environment.

23. Within a given area, a group of organisms belonging to the same species is called a _____.

24. A group of populations living in a given area is considered a _____.

25. The community and the physical environment considered together is a(n) _____.

26. Two species of organisms that occupy the same or similar ecological niches in different geographical locations are termed _____.

27. The steady replacement of one species by another as the environment changes due to the actions of organisms is known as _____.

28. The phenomenal human population growth has been a result of the striking drop in the early _____.

29. Six important terrestrial biomes are recognized. They are: _____, _____, _____, _____, _____, and _____.

Determine whether the following statements are true or false.

30. Taxonomy is the science of classification.

31. A group of related species is called a genus.

32. Green plants change inorganic materials into carbon dioxide.

33. A parasite can usually grow in many varied environments.

34. Rodent-like creatures were collected from three different locations and brought back to a laboratory where they could be studied. They mated and produced viable young. This proved they were all of the same species.

35. The reason that the amount of energy available to organisms is less as you proceed up a food pyramid is because energy is lost to the environment as heat.

36. Host-specific parasites establish short-term relationships with hosts.

37. Food chains seldom have more than five levels because the top carnivores are too sparse and contain too few calories to make predation worthwhile.

38. The increase in the world population today is partially due to an increased birth rate.

39. A population of frogs protected from all predation would increase indefinitely.

40. Biomes that resemble one another in physical appearance but differ in species composition belong to the same type biome.

41. A land biome is identified primarily by its dominant animals.

ANSWER KEY

1. c	2. a	3. a
4. a	5. b	6. d
7. b	8. c	9. d
10. a	11. c	12. d
13. a	14. b	15. Protista, Monera, Fungi
16. Linnaeus	17. Autotrophic	18. Photosynthesis
19. holozoic	20. nitrites, nitrates	21. Autecology

22. Synecology   23. population   24. community

25. ecosystem   26. ecological equivalents

27. ecological succession   28. death rate

29. desert, grassland, equatorial forests, deciduous forests, coniferous forests, tundra

30. True   31. True   32. False

33. False   34. False   35. True

36. False   37. True   38. False

39. False   40. True   41. False

CHAPTER 4

THE CELL

Cell Structure and Function

What is a cell?

SOLUTION:

A cell is the fundamental organizational unit of life. One of the most important generalizations of modern biology is the cell theory. There are two components of the cell theory. It states: (1) that all living things are composed of cells and (2) that all cells arise from other cells. Living things are chemical organizations of cells and capable of reproducing themselves.

There are many types of cells, and just as many classifications to go with them. There are plant cells, animal cells, eucaryotic cells, procaryotic cells, and many others. Also within each of these divisions, there are smaller subdivisions pertaining to the specific properties or functions of the cells. Cells exhibit considerable variation in properties based on different arrangements of components. Cells also vary in size, although most of them fall in the range of 5 to 20 mμ.

What are the chief components and structures of a eukaryotic cell?

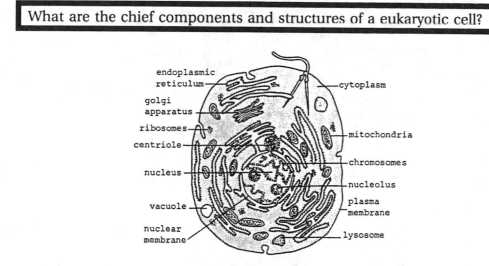

Figure 1. Typical animal cell

SOLUTION:

Membranes are a crucial component of both animal and plant cells. The plasma membrane surrounds the cell and serves to separate the internal living matter from the external environment. Plant cells have in addition a cell wall external to the plasma membrane. It is composed mainly of cellulose and is fairly rigid but permeable. Selectivity of materials entering the plant cells is not a function of the cell wall but of the plasma membrane. Membranes are also present inside the cell, dividing the cell into compartments distinctive in both form and function. All membranes are composed basically of lipids and proteins. For this reason the plasma membrane and the membranes inside the cell are termed unit membranes. Subcellular structures in the cytoplasm are known as organelles. When these are surrounded by membranes, they are termed membrane-bounded organelles. Each organelle performs some specific functions.

The nucleus is the controlling center of the cell. The nucleus is surrounded by two layers of unit membrane which form the nuclear envelope. Within the nucleus are found the chromosomes, the substances of inheritance. Chromosomes are composed chiefly of deoxyribonucleic acid (DNA) and protein. Genes located within the chromosomes direct cellular function and are capable of being replicated in nuclear division. The nucleolus is a specialized region in the nucleus involved in the synthesis of ribosomal RNA, the material making up the ribosomes.

Mitochondria and chloroplasts are membrane-bounded organelles involved in energy production in the cell. Since energy can neither be created nor

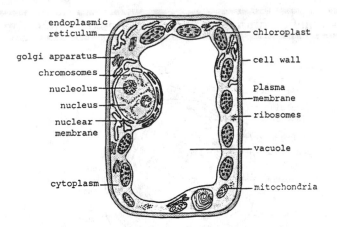

endoplasmic reticulum
golgi apparatus
chromosomes
nucleolus
nucleus
nuclear membrane
cytoplasm

chloroplast
cell wall
plasma membrane
ribosomes
vacuole
mitochondria

Figure 2. Typical plant cell

destroyed, these organelles actually convert one form of energy to another. Chloroplasts found in plant cells, convert solar energy to chemical energy contained in organic substances; the latter are oxidized in the mitochondria to yield energy useful to the cell in the form of ATP.

Cells which utilize food for energy must take food into the cell and degrade it. Lysosomes are membrane-bound organelles whose digestive enzymes break down organic substances to simpler forms, which can be used by the cell to yield energy for its life-sustaining process.

Most cells contain membrane-delimited bodies called vacuoles. Small vacuoles may be termed vesicles. These structures may contain the ingested materials taken from the cell exterior or materials to be released by the cell. Mature plant cells usually contain a single large fluid-filled vacuole. This vacuole aids the cell in maintaining an internal pressure and thus rigidity.

Organelles involved in the synthesis and transport of cellular components are the ribosomes, endoplasmic reticulum, and Golgi apparatus. Ribosomes are involved in protein synthesis. The endoplasmic reticulum is a system of membranes providing transport channels within the cell. It transports the synthesized protein to other parts of the cell. The Golgi apparatus is involved in the packaging of cellular products before they can be released by the cell to the outside.

Organelles involved in the maintenance of cellular shape and in movement are the microfilaments and microtubules, also known as the skeleton of the living cell. Microfilaments are involved in the connection of adjacent cells for intercellular communication. They also function in the transport of products within the cell. The microtubules are the basic substance in the cilia and flagella of motile cells. By the contracting action of microtubules, flagella and cilia beat and propel the cell. The microtubules have also been identified as the fundamental substance in the spindle apparatus during cell division. Both microfilaments and microtubules are protein structures.

What are the chief differences between plant and animal cells?

SOLUTION:

A study of both plant and animal cells reveals the fact that in their most basic features, they are alike. However, they differ in several important ways. First of all, plant cells, but not animal cells, are surrounded by a rigid cellulose wall. The cell wall is actually a secretion from the plant cell. It surrounds the plasma membrane, and is responsible for the maintenance of cell shape. Animal cells, without a cell wall, cannot maintain a rigid shape.

Most mature plant cells possess a single large central fluid sap, the vacuole. Vacuoles in animal cells are small and frequently numerous.

Another distinction between plant and animal cells is that many of the cells of green plants contain chloroplasts, which are not found in animal cells. The presence of chloroplasts in plant cells enable green plants to be autotrophs, organisms which synthesize their own food. As is generally known, plants are able to use sunlight, carbon dioxide, and water to generate organic substances. Animal cells, devoid of chloroplasts, cannot produce their own food. Animals, therefore, are heterotrophs, organisms that depend on other living things for nutrients.

Some final differences between plant and animal cells are in the process of cell division. In animal cells, undergoing division, the cell surface begins to constrict, as if a belt were being tightened around it, pinching the old cell into two new ones. In plant cells, where a stiff cell wall interferes with this sort of pinching, new cell membranes form between the two daughter cells. Then a new cell wall is deposited between the two new cell membranes. During cell division, as the mitotic spindle apparatus forms, animal cells have two pairs of centrioles attached to the spindles at opposite poles of the cell. Even though plant cells form a spindle apparatus, most higher plants do not contain centrioles.

Cell Wall

Describe the composition and structure of the plant cell wall.

SOLUTION:

Because plant cells must be able to withstand high osmotic pressure differences, they require rigid cell walls to prevent bursting. This rigidity is provided primarily by cellulose, the most abundant cell wall component in plants. Cellulose, a polysaccharide, is a long, linear, unbranched polymer of glucose molecules. In the cell wall cellulose molecules are organized in bundles of parallel chains to form fibrils. The fibrils are often arranged in criss-cross layers reinforced and held together by three other polymeric materials: pectin and hemicellulose (complex polysaccharides) and extensin (a complex glycoprotein). Lignin is an additional polymeric substance found in the wood of trees. Together these substances provide a matrix capable of withstanding enormous stress.

A layer known as the middle lamella lies between and is shared by adjacent cells. The lamella is composed primarily of pectin. By binding the cells together, it provides additional stiffness to the plant.

The cell wall is usually interrupted at various locations by plasmodesmata. These are tiny holes in the cell walls through which run protoplasmic connections between adjacent cells. This provides for intercellular exchange of such materials as water and dissolved substances. Being extremely small, the plasmodesmata do not prevent the cell wall from exerting pressure on a swollen cell.

● PROBLEM 4-5

Plant cells are able to withstand much wider fluctuation in the osmotic pressure of the surrounding medium than animal cells. Explain why.

SOLUTION:

A plant cell is able to withstand much greater fluctuations in the makeup of the surrounding fluids than can an animal cell. This can be best understood by examining the role played by the plants' cell wall, a structure absent in animal cells.

First, take the case in which the cell is placed in a hypotonic medium. This means that the surrounding fluid has a lower concentration of solute molecules and a higher concentration of solvent (water) than the cell. Thus, the cell has a higher osmotic pressure than the medium, which means that the net movement of water should be into the cell. This is exactly what happens in an animal cell (see Figure 1). An animal cell will take in water by osmosis causing it to swell. It will take in enough water so that the osmotic pressure of the cell is equal to the osmotic pressure of the medium, thus they will be isotonic to each other. However, if the original difference in pressure was great, the animal cell may have to take in more water than its membrane can allow. Then the animal cell would burst. This is called lysis. If the original cell was a red blood cell, this is hemolysis. A plant cell placed in a hypotonic medium would also have water enter into it, causing it to swell (see Figure 2). However, an upper limit as to how much water can enter is imposed by the cell wall. As the cell swells, its plasma membrane exerts pressure on the cell wall which is called turgor pressure. The wall exerts an equal and opposing pressure on the swollen membrane. When the pressure exerted by the cell wall is so great that further increase in cell size is not possible, water will cease to enter the cell. Thus, plant cells will only absorb a certain amount of water, even in an extremely dilute medium.

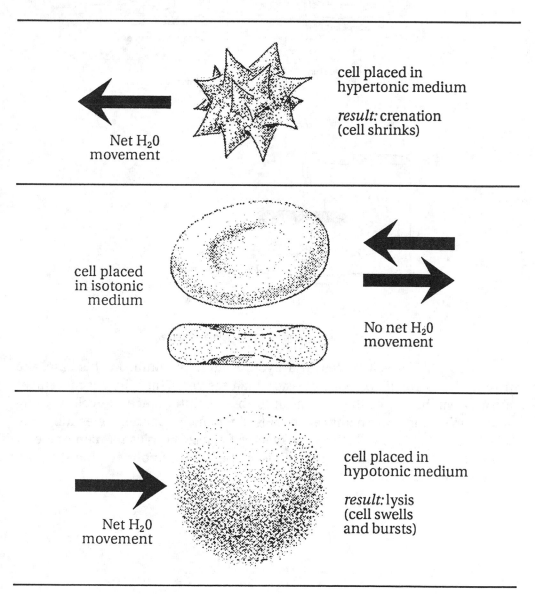

cell placed in
hypertonic medium

result: crenation
(cell shrinks)

Net H$_2$0
movement

cell placed
in isotonic
medium

No net H$_2$0
movement

cell placed in
hypotonic medium

result: lysis
(cell swells
and bursts)

Net H$_2$0
movement

Figure 1. A typical animal cell in varying environments.

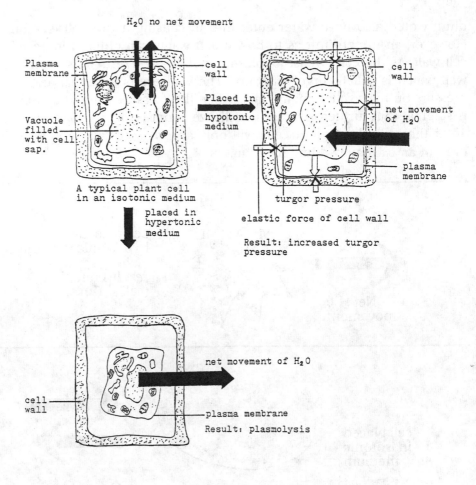

Figure 2. A typical plant cell in varying environments.

Now consider a cell placed in a hyperosmotic medium. In this case, the medium has a greater osmotic pressure than the cell. Thus, the net movement of water will be out of the cell and into the medium. Since the cell is losing water it will shrink. In an animal cell this phenomenon is called crenation (see Figure 1). In a plant cell, the shrinkage will cause the plasma membrane to pull away from the cell wall. The cell is said to be plasmolyzed, and the phenomenon is plasmolysis (see Figure 2).

Plasma Membrane and Movement of Materials Across Membranes

Describe the structure and functions of the plasma membrane.

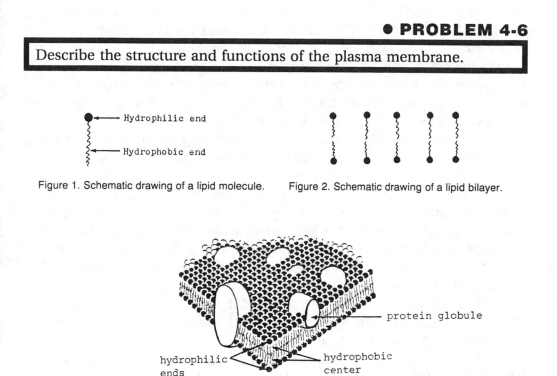

Figure 1. Schematic drawing of a lipid molecule.   Figure 2. Schematic drawing of a lipid bilayer.

Figure 3. Model of the unit membrane.

SOLUTION:

Each cell is surrounded by a selective membrane, a complex elastic covering that separates the cell protoplasm from the external environment. The structure of this covering, called the plasma membrane, has been under major investigation for many years. Studies of membrane permeability, electron microscopy, and biochemical analysis have enabled biologists to better understand the structure and composition of the plasma membrane. The plasma membrane contains about 40 percent lipid and 60 percent protein by weight, with considerable variation from cell type to cell type. The different types and amounts of lipids and proteins present determine to a great extent the characteristics of different membranes. As seen in electron micrographs, all membranes appear to have a similar fundamental structure. The plasma membrane is revealed by electron microscopy to resemble a railroad track in cross-section — two dark lines bordering a central lighter line. The membranes of cellular organelles also display this characteristic. The two dark lines were suggested to correspond to two layers of protein and the light middle layer to lipid. It was soon revealed that the lipid actually exists in two layers.

The lipid molecules of the plasma membrane are polar, with the two ends of each molecule having different electric properties. One end is hydrophobic ("fear of water"), which means it tends to be insoluble in water. The other end is hydrophilic ("love of water"), which means it has an affinity for water (see Figure 1). The lipid molecules arrange themselves in two layers in the plasma membrane so that the hydrophobic ends are near each other, and the hydrophilic ends face outside toward the water and are stabilized by water molecules (see Figure 2). In this bilayer, individual lipid molecules can move laterally, so that the bilayer is actually fluid and flexible.

Protein molecules of the plasma membrane may be arranged in various sites but embedded to different degrees in relationship to the bilayer. Some of them may be partially embedded in the lipid bilayer, some may be present only on the outer surfaces, and still others may span the entire lipid bilayer from one surface to the other (see Figure 3). The different arrangements of proteins are determined by the different structural, conformational, and electrical characteristics of various membrane proteins. Like the lipid bilayer, the protein molecules tend to orient themselves in the most stable way possible. The proteins are usually naturally folded into a globular form which enables them to move laterally within the plane of the membrane at different rates. Certain proteins can actually move across the membrane. Thus membrane proteins are not static but dynamic.

The functions of the plasma membrane are highly specific and directly related to its structure, which is in turn, dependent on the specific types and amounts of proteins and lipids present. The discriminating permeability of the membrane is its primary function. It allows certain substances to enter or leave the cell, and prevents other substances from crossing it. Whether or not a molecule can cross a membrane depends on its size after hydration, electric charge, shape, chemical properties, and its relative solubility in lipid as compared to that in water. This selective permeability of the plasma membrane gives the cell the ability to keep its interior environment both chemically and physically different from the exterior environment.

The plasma membrane is also found to be particularly important in cell adherence. Because of the specificity of protein molecules on the membrane surface, cells can recognize each other and bind together through some interaction of their surface proteins. Surface proteins are believed to provide communication and linkage between cells in division so that cells divide in an organized plane, rather than in random directions giving rise to an amorphous mass of cells as in cancer. Surface proteins of the plasma membrane are also proposed to recognize foreign substance due to their remarkable specificity; they can bind with the foreign substance and inactivate it. Membrane proteins are further suggested to interact with hormones, or convey hormonal messages to the nucleus so that a physiological change can be effected. The plasma membrane also is involved in the conduction of impulse in nerve cells. The axon of nerve cells transmits impulse by a temporary re-distribution of ions inside and outside the cell, with a subsequent change in the distribution charges on the two surfaces of the membrane.

Differentiate clearly between diffusion, dialysis, and osmosis.

SOLUTION:

Diffusion is the general term for the net movement of the particles of a substance from a region where the substance is at a high concentration to regions where the substance is at a low concentration. The particles are in constant random motion with their speed being directly related to their size and the temperature. When the movements of all the particles are considered jointly, there is a net movement away from the region of high concentration towards regions of low concentration. This results in the particles of a given substance distributing themselves with relatively uniform density or concentration within any available space. Diffusion tends to be faster in gases than in liquids, and much slower in solids.

The movement or diffusion of water or solvent molecules through a semipermeable membrane is called osmosis. The osmotic pressure of a solution is a measure of the tendency of the solvent to enter the solution by osmosis. The more concentrated a solution, the more water will tend to move into it, and the higher is its osmotic pressure.

The diffusion of a dissolved substance through a semipermeable membrane is termed dialysis. Dialysis is the movement of the solute, while osmosis is the movement of the solvent through a semipermeable membrane. Dialysis and osmosis are just two special forms of diffusion.

Diffusion is too slow a process to account for the observed rate of transport of materials in active cells. Explain why.

SOLUTION:

The cytoplasm of a living cell is a watery medium separated by the plasma membrane from the external environment. The cytoplasm resembles a loose gel which is somewhat denser than pure water. In order to move from one part of a cell to another, materials have to move through this relatively dense gel. Thus diffusion of materials through a cell is necessarily a much slower process than diffusion of materials through water. Diffusion is a relatively slow method of transport of materials also because the molecules in motion are constantly colliding with other molecules. This causes them to bounce off in other directions and to take a zig-zag path instead of a straight one. Therefore molecules have to travel a longer distance, which requires more time, in order to get to their destinations.

Diffusion is only a passive process: it does not require energy. Its rate depends on the viscosity (thickness) of the medium, the difference in concentrations of molecules in the two regions, the distance between the two regions, the surface area of the two regions if they are in contact, and the temperature. Often the transport of materials in living cells occurs at so rapid a rate that it is not possible to be accounted for by simple (passive) diffusion alone. Instead, some active processes involving expenditure of energy are believed to be responsible.

● PROBLEM 4-9

The concentration of sodium ions (Na^+) inside most cells is lower than the concentration outside the cells. Why can't this phenomenon be explained by simple diffusion across the membrane and what process is responsible for this concentration difference?

SOLUTION:

Since the cell membrane is somewhat permeable to sodium ions, simple diffusion would result in a net movement of sodium ions into the cell, until the concentrations on the two sides of the membrane became equal. Sodium actually does diffuse into the cell rather freely, but as fast as it does so, the cell actively pumps it out again, against the concentration difference.

The mechanism by which the cell pumps the sodium ions out is called active transport. Active transport requires the expenditure of energy for the work done by the cell in moving molecules against a concentration gradient. Active transport enables a cell to maintain a lower concentration of sodium inside the cell, and also enables a cell to accumulate certain nutrients inside the cell at concentrations much higher than the extracellular concentrations.

The exact mechanism of active transport is not known. It has been proposed that a carrier molecule is involved, which reacts chemically with the molecule that is to be actively transported. This forms a compound which is soluble in the lipid portion of the membrane and the carrier compound then moves through the membrane against the concentration gradient to the other side. The transported molecule is then released, and the carrier molecule diffuses back to the other side of the membrane where it picks up another molecule. This process requires energy, since work must be done in transporting the molecule against a diffusion gradient. The energy is supplied in the form of ATP.

The carrier molecules are thought to be integral proteins; proteins which span the plasma membrane. These proteins are specific for the molecules they transport.

● **PROBLEM 4-10**

Distinguish between the terms "endocytosis" and "exocytosis."

SOLUTION:

The transport of macromolecules through the plasma membrane is accomplished by the processes of endocytosis and exocytosis. In exocytosis an intracellular vesicle is transported to the plasma membrane where it fuses with the plasma membrane. The fusion process releases the contents of the vesicle to the extracellular space. Endocytosis is essentially the reverse of this process.

Endoplasmic Reticulum

● **PROBLEM 4-11**

Explain the importance and structure of the endoplasmic reticulum in the cell.

SOLUTION:

The endoplasmic reticulum is responsible for transporting certain molecules to specific areas within the cytoplasm. Lipids and proteins are mainly transported and distributed by this system. The endoplasmic reticulum is more than a passive channel for intracellular transport. It contains a variety of enzymes playing important roles in metabolic processes.

The structure of the endoplasmic reticulum is a complex of membranes that traverses the cytoplasm. The membranes form interconnecting channels that take the form of flattened sacs and tubes. When the endoplasmic reticulum has ribosomes attached to its surface, we refer to it as rough endoplasmic reticulum and when there are no ribosomes attached, it is called smooth endoplasmic reticulum. The rough endoplasmic reticulum functions in transport of cellular products; the role of the smooth endoplasmic reticulum is less well known, but is believed to be involved in lipid synthesis (thus the predominance of smooth end reticulum in hepatocytes of the liver).

In most cells, the endoplasmic reticulum is continuous and interconnected at some points with the nuclear membrane and sometimes, with the plasma membrane. This may indicate a pathway by which materials synthesized in the nucleus are transported to the cytoplasm. In cells actively engaged in protein synthesis and secretion (such as acinar cells of the pancreas), rough endoplasmic reticulum is abundant. By a well regulated and organized process, protein or polypeptide chains are synthesized on the ribosomes. These products are then transported by the endoplasmic reticulum to other sites of the cell where they are needed. If they are secretory products, they have to be packaged for release. They are carried by the endoplasmic reticulum to the Golgi apparatus, another organelle system. Some terminal portions of the endoplasmic reticulum containing protein molecules bud off from the membranes of the reticulum complex, and move to the Golgi apparatus in the form of membrane-bounded vesicles. In the Golgi apparatus, the protein molecules are concentrated, chemically modified, and packaged so that they can be released to the outside by exocytosis. This process is necessary because some proteins may be digestive enzymes which may degrade the cytoplasm and lyse the cell if direct contact is made.

● PROBLEM 4-12

In microscopy, small spherical bodies are often seen attached to the network of endoplasmic reticulum. What are these bodies? What function do they serve in the cell?

SOLUTION:

The small spherical bodies that we see studding the endoplasmic reticulum — more accurately, the rough endoplasmic reticulum — are the ribosomes. The rough endoplasmic reticulum owes its rough appearance to the presence of ribosomes. The smooth endoplasmic reticulum appears smooth because it lacks ribosomes. Ribosomes consist of two parts, a large subunit and a small subunit. Both the large and small subunits are made of proteins and ribonucleic acid (RNA). However, the two subunits differ both in the number and in the type of proteins and RNA they contain. The large subunit contains large and more varied RNA molecules than the small subunit. It also has more protein molecules than the smaller one. An interesting point to note is that when we put together all the chemical components of a ribosome, under favorable conditions, these parts will rearrange themselves and come together, without direction from pre-existing ribosomes, to form a functional assembly. This ability to self-assemble may provide us with a clue of the origin of living things.

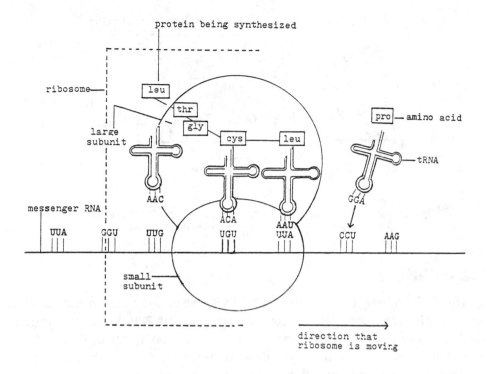

Figure 1. The role of the ribosome in protein synthesis.

Ribosomes are the sites of protein synthesis in the cell. Messenger RNA (mRNA), which carries genetic information from the nucleus, associates with the small ribosomal subunit first and then binds to the large subunit in a prelude to protein synthesis. This association of mRNA to ribosomes holds the components of the complex system of protein synthesis together in a specific manner for greater efficiency than if they are dispersed freely in the cytoplasm. The mRNA then pairs with complementary molecules of transfer RNA (tRNA), each carrying a specific amino acid. The linking up of tRNA molecules into a chain complementary to mRNA brings together amino acids which bind with each other to form a highly specific protein molecule. Thus ribosomes are the sites whose proteins are synthesized under genetic control.

The Golgi Complex

● PROBLEM 4-13

How is the Golgi apparatus related to the endoplasmic reticulum in function?

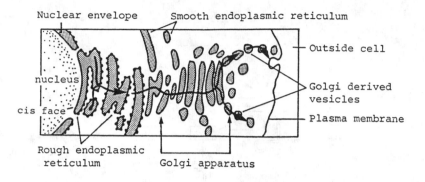

Figure 1. Schematic representation of the secretion of a protein in a typical animal cell.
The solid arrow represents the probable route of secreted proteins.

SOLUTION:

The Golgi apparatus is composed of several membrane-bounded, flattened sacs or cisternae arranged in parallel array about 300 Å apart. The sacs are disc-like and often slightly curved. Note the concavity on the trans face near the plasma membrane and the convexity of the cis face are thinner (more like reticulum membrane than like plasma membrane).

The function of the Golgi apparatus is best understood in cells involved in protein synthesis and secretion. The protein to be secreted is synthesized on the rough endoplasmic reticulum. Vesicles containing small quantities of the synthesized protein bud off from the endoplasmic reticulum. These vesicles carry the protein to the convex face of the Golgi complex. In the Golgi apparatus, the protein is concentrated by the removal of water. In addition, chemical modifications of the protein, such as glycosylation (addition of sugar) occur. The modified protein is released from the concave surface in the form of secretory granules. The secretory granules containing the protein are from the cytoplasm by a membrane that can fuse with the plasma membrane, its content (protein in this case) is expelled from the cell, a process known as excytosis.

Most of the cell organelles are found in a specific arrangement within the cell to complement their function. For example, the Golgi apparatus is usually found near the cell membrane and is associated with the endoplasmic reticulum. Since they are relatively close to each other, transport of materials between them is considerably efficient.

Nucleus and Nuclear Membrane

What are the functions of the nucleus? What is the evidence that indicates the role of the nucleus in cell metabolism and heredity?

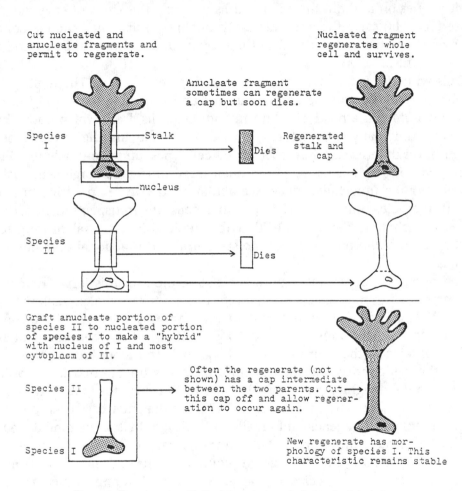

Cut nucleated and anucleate fragments and permit to regenerate.

Nucleated fragment regenerates whole cell and survives.

Anucleate fragment sometimes can regenerate a cap but soon dies.

Species I

Stalk

Regenerated stalk and cap

Dies

nucleus

Species II

Dies

Graft anucleate portion of species II to nucleated portion of species I to make a "hybrid" with nucleus of I and most cytoplasm of II.

Species II

Often the regenerate (not shown) has a cap intermediate between the two parents. Cut this cap off and allow regeneration to occur again.

Species I

New regenerate has morphology of species I. This characteristic remains stable

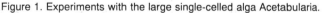

Figure 1. Experiments with the large single-celled alga Acetabularia.

SOLUTION:

If the cell is thought of as a miniature chemical plant designed to carry out all the processes of life, then the nucleus can be compared to a central computer that controls a network of sophisticated and highly complicated biochemical machinery. This is because the nucleus contains the chromosomes, which bear the genes, the ultimate regulator of life.

The genes comprise a library of programs stored in the nucleus, programs that specify the precise nature of each protein synthesized by the cell. The nucleus monitors changing conditions both inside the cell and in the external environment, and responds to input of information by either activating or inhibiting the appropriate genetic programs.

Control of protein synthesis is the key to controlling the activities and responses of the cell, since a tremendous array of important biological and biochemical processes are regulated by enzymatic proteins. By switching particular genes on and off, the cell controls not only the kinds of enzymes that it produces, but also the amounts. Both qualitative and quantitative control of enzyme synthesis are crucial to the proper functioning of the cell and the whole organism.

Cells without nuclei have a very limited range of function. The mammalian red blood cell does not contain a nucleus and is unable to reproduce; it is functional only for a relatively short period. Egg cells, from which nuclei have been experimentally removed, may divide for a while, but the products of division never differentiate into specialized cell types, and eventually die. Fragments without a nucleus, cut from such large unicellular organisms as the amoeba or the unicellular algae Acetabularia, survive temporarily; but ultimately they die, unless nuclei from other cells are transplanted into them. These experiments demonstrate that the nucleus is essential to long term continuation of life processes, and to structural and functional differentiation of cells.

The nucleus is of central importance also in the transmission of hereditary information. The nucleus carries the information for all the characteristics of the cell. This information is found in the chromosomes, which consist of protein and deoxyribonucleic acid (DNA). DNA is the hereditary material which contains all the information for the growth and reproduction of the cell. When the cell divides, the nuclear information is transmitted in an orderly fashion to the daughter cells by replication of the chromosomes and division of the nucleus. Thus, in this type of division, the daughter cells each possess a single complement of genetic information identical to that of the mother cell.

The hereditary importance of the nucleus can be demonstrated experimentally (see Figure 1). If a fragment containing the nucleus is cut from an Acetabularium of one species, characterized by a given appearance, the fragment will regenerate a whole cell of that species. This regenerative ability permits experiments of the type shown in the accompanying figure, in which nuclei of one species are grafted onto the cytoplasm of a different species. The observation from these experiments shows that the appearance of the regenerated cell eventually resembles that of the organism from which the nucleus is taken. Hence, we conclude that the nucleus, as a controlling center, produces information that controls the cytoplasm and participates in the regulation of cell growth and structure. Since the crucial information comes from the nucleus, the regenerated cell will resemble the organism from which the nucleus is taken.

Describe the structure and function of the nuclear membrane.

SOLUTION:

The nuclear membrane actually consists of two leaflets of membrane, one facing the nucleus and the other facing the cytoplasm. The structure of each of these two leaflets is fundamentally similar to the structure of the plasma membrane, with slight variations. However, the two leaflets differ from each other in their lipid and protein compositions. The nuclear membrane is observed under the electron microscope to be continuous at some points with the membranes of the endoplasmic reticulum.

Nuclear pores are the unique feature of the nuclear membrane. They are openings which occur at intervals along the nuclear membrane, and appear as roughly circular areas where the two membrane leaflets come together, fuse, and become perforated. Many thousands of pores may be scattered across a nuclear surface.

The nuclear pores provide a means for nuclear-cytoplasmic communication. Substances pass into and out of the nucleus via these openings. Evidence that the pores are the actual passageways for substances through the nuclear membrane comes from electron micrographs which show substances passing through them. The mechanisms by which molecules pass through the pores are not known. At present, we know that the pores are not simply holes in the membrane. This knowledge comes from the observation that in some cells, small molecules and ions pass through the nuclear membrane at rates much lower than expected if the pores were holes through which diffusion occurs freely.

Lysosomes

Why do cells contain lysosomes?

SOLUTION:

Lysosomes are membrane-bounded bodies in the cell. All lysosomes function in, directly or indirectly, intracellular digestion. The material to be digested may be of extracellular or intracellular origin. Lysosomes contain enzymes known collectively as acid hydrolases. These enzymes can quickly dissolve all of the major molecules that comprise the cell, and presumably would do so if they were not confined in structures surrounded by membranes.

One function of lysosomes is to accomplish the self-destruction of injured cells or cells that have outlived their usefulness. Lysosomes also destroy certain organelles that are no longer useful. Lysosomes are, in addition, involved in the digestion of materials taken into the cell in membranous vesicles. Lysosomes fuse with the membrane of the vesicle so that their hydrolytic enzymes are discharged into the vesicle and ultimately digest the material. Lysosomes play a part in the breakdown of normal cellular waste products, and in the turnover of cellular constituents.

Peroxisomes (or microbodies) are other membrane-bound vesicles containing oxidative enzymes. Peroxisomes play a role in the decomposition of some compounds.

Mitochondria and Chloroplasts

● **PROBLEM 4-17**

Why is the mitochondria referred to as the powerhouse of the cell?

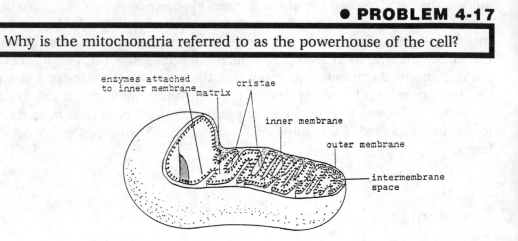

Figure 1. The internal structures of a mitochondrion through a cutaway view.

SOLUTION:

Mitochondria are membrane-bounded organelles concerned principally with the generation of energy to support the various forms of chemical and mechanical work carried out by the cell. Mitochondria are distributed throughout the cell, because all parts of it require energy. Mitochondria tend to be most numerous in regions of the cell that consume large amounts of energy and more abundant in cells that require a great deal of energy (for example, muscle and sperm cells).

Mitochondria are enclosed by two membranes. The outer one is a continuous delimiting membrane. The inner membrane is thrown into many folds that extend into the interior of the mitochondrion. These folds are called cristae. Enclosed by the inner membrane is the ground substance termed the matrix (see Figure 1). Many enzymes involved in the Krebs cycle are found in the matrix. Enzymes involved in the generation of ATP by the oxidation of $NADH_2$, or, the electron transport reactions, are tightly bound to the inner mitochondrial membrane. The enzymes for the specific pathways are arranged in sequential orders so that the products of one reaction do not have to travel far before they are likely to encounter the enzymes catalyzing the next reaction. This promotes a highly efficient energy production.

The reactions that occur in the mitochondria are all related in that they result in the production of ATP (adenosine triphosphate), which is the common currency of energy conversion in the cell. Some ATP is produced by reactions that occur in the cytoplasm, but about 95 percent of all ATP produced in the cell is in the mitochondria. For this reason the mitochondria are commonly referred to as the powerhouse of the cell.

● **PROBLEM 4-18**

What is the structure and function of the chloroplasts in green plants?

SOLUTION:

The chloroplasts have the ability to transform the energy of the sun into chemical energy stored in bonds that hold together the atom of such foods (fuel) as glucose. By the process of photosynthesis, carbon dioxide and water react to produce carbohydrates with the simultaneous release of oxygen. Photosynthesis, which occurs in the chloroplasts, is driven forward by energy obtained from the sun.

Photosynthesis involves two major sets of reactions, each consisting of many steps. One set depends on light and cannot occur in the dark; hence, this set is known as the light reaction.

It is responsible for the production of ATP from sunlight and the release of oxygen derived from water. This process is known as photophosphorylation. The other set, referred to as the dark reaction, is not dependent on light. In the dark reaction, carbon dioxide is reduced to carbohydrates using the energy of ATP from the light reactions.

Chlorophyll, the pigment contained in chloroplasts which gives plants their characteristic green color, is the molecule responsible for the initial trapping of light energy. Chlorophyll transforms light energy into chemical energy; then it passes this energy to a chain of other compounds involved in the light and dark reactions.

81

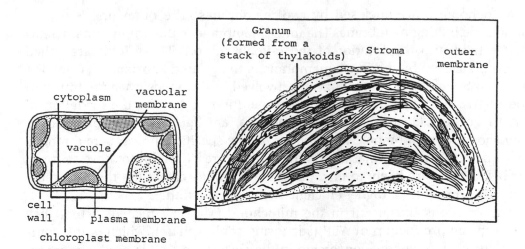

Figure 1. The internal structures of a choroplast.

Plastids are organelles which contain pigments and/or function in nutrient storage. Chloroplasts are but one example of a plastid; they give the green color to plants. Each chloroplast is bounded by two layers of membranes; the outer one is not connected with the other membranes of the cell. The inner membrane gives rise to the complex internal system of the chloroplast. Surrounding the internal membranes is a ground substance termed the stroma. The stroma contains the enzymes which carry out the dark reactions of photosynthesis. Granules containing starch are also found in the stroma. The internal membrane system of the chloroplast are usually in the form of flattened sacs called thylakoids (see Figure 1). A stack of thylakoids is called a granum (plural–grana). The lamellae contain the chlorophyll molecules and other pigments involved in photosynthesis. The layered structure of the granum is extremely crucial for the efficient transfer of energy from one pigment molecule to another without the dissipation of a great deal of energy in the process.

Cytoskeleton

● **PROBLEM 4-19**

Microtubules and microfilaments both appear to be involved in intracellular motion and in intracellular structural support. How do the two organelles differ in structure and function and how are they similar?

Microtubules are thin, hollow cylinders, approximately 200 to 300 angstroms in diameter. Microfilaments are not hollow, and are 50 to 80 angstroms in diameter. Both microtubules and microfilaments are composed of proteins. The protein of microtubules is generally termed tubulin. Tubule proteins can be made to assemble into microtubules in a test tube, if the proper reagents are present. Some of the narrower microfilaments have been shown to be composed of proteins similar to actin. Actin is a protein involved in muscle cell contraction. The composition of thicker microfilaments has not been completely determined.

Microtubules are often distributed in cells in an arrangement that suggests their role in maintaining cell shape (a "cytoskeletal" role). For example, microtubules are arranged longitudinally within the elongated processes of nerve cells (axons) and the cytoplasmic extensions (pseudopods) of certain protozoa. Microtubules are arranged in a circular band in the disc-shaped fish red blood cells. Microfilaments may also play a structural role. They are often associated with some specialized region of the plasma membrane, such as the absorptive plasma membrane of the intestinal cells, or the portions of the plasma membrane which serve to anchor adjacent cells together so that they can intercommunicate.

Microtubules are components of cilia and flagella, and participate in the rapid movements of these structures. Microtubules are involved in directional movement within the cell during cell division, and are involved in certain types of oriented rapid intracellular movement. Microfilaments seem to be involved in many different types of cytoplasmic movement. They are believed to play a role in amoeboid motion of cells, and in the rapid streaming of the cytoplasm of plant cells about a central vacuole. Close associations between microfilaments and membrane-bound organelles suggests that microfilaments assist in intracellular transport and exchange of materials.

Centrioles, Flagella, and Cilia

● **PROBLEM 4-20**

Describe the structure of a centriole. What hypothetical function does it serve?

SOLUTION:

Centrioles are small bodies located just outside the nucleus of most animal cells and some plant cells in a specialized region of cytoplasm that has been known to play a role in cell division. Centrioles usually occur as a pair in each cell oriented at right angles to each other. Each centriole of the pair is composed of nine groups of tubules arranged longitudinally in a ring to form a hollow cylinder. Each group is a triplet composed of three closely associated tubular elements called microtubules. (See Figures.) The space immediately surrounding a pair of centrioles is called the centrosome. The centrosome appears to be clear or empty in the light microscope.

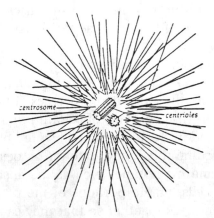

Figure 1. Diagram showing the relationship of the centrioles and centrosome.

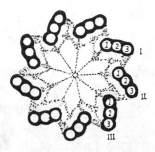

Figure 2. Diagram of centriole structure.

Centrioles do not occur in most higher plant cells, although they are found in some algae and fungi and in a few reproductive cells of higher plants. The centrioles seem to play some part in directing the orderly distribution of genetic material during cell division. At the beginning of cell division the centrioles replicate, and the two pairs of centrioles that result move to opposite poles of the dividing cell. Under the electron microscope each pair is seen to send out spindle fibers, structures involved in separating and moving chromosomes to the opposite ends of the cell. This observation leads to the hypothesis that centrioles are needed in the formation of the spindle fibers. However, the existence of cells without centrioles yet capable of spindle formation seems to refute this hypothesis.

● **PROBLEM 4-21**

Explain the structural and functional aspects of cilia and flagella.

SOLUTION:

Some cells of both plants and animals have one or more hair-like structures projecting from their surfaces. If there are only one or two of these append-

84

ages and they are relatively long in proportion to the size of the cell, they are called flagella. If there are many that are short, they are called cilia. Actually, the basic structure of flagella and cilia is the same. They resemble centrioles in having nine sets of microtubules arranged in a cylinder. But unlike centrioles, each set is a doublet rather than triplet of microtubules, and two central singlets are present in the center of the cylinder. At the base of the cylinders of cilia and flagella, within the main portion of the cell, is a basal body. The basal body is essential to the functioning of the cilia and flagella. From the basal body fibers project into the cytoplasm, possibly in order to anchor the basal body to the cell.

Both cilia and flagella usually function either in moving the cell, or in moving liquids or small particles across the surface of the cell. Flagella move with an undulating snake-like motion. Cilia beat in coordinated waves. Both move by the contraction of the tubular proteins contained within them.

PERPETUATION AND REPRODUCTION

Mitosis

● PROBLEM 4-22

Outline briefly the events occurring in each stage of mitosis. Illustrate your discussion with diagrams if necessary.

SOLUTION:

Mitosis refers to the process by which a cell divides to form two daughter cells, each with exactly the same number and kind of chromosomes as the parent cell. In a strict sense, mitosis refers to the division of nuclear material (karyokinesis). Cytokinesis is the term used to refer to the division of the cytoplasm. Although each cell division is a continuous process, in order for it to be studied, it can be artificially divided up into a number of stages. We will describe each stage separately, beginning with interphase.

1) Interphase: This phase is called the resting stage. However, the cell is "resting" only with respect to the visible events of division in later phases. During this phase, the nucleus is metabolically very active and chromosomal

duplication is occurring. During interphase, the chromosomes appear as vague, dispersed thread-like structures, and are referred to as chromatin material.

2) Prophase: Prophase begins when the chromatin threads begin to condense and appear as a tangled mass of threads within the nucleus. Each prophase chromosome is composed of two identical members resulting from duplication in interphase. Each member of the pair is called a chromatid. The two chromatids are held together at a dark, constricted area called the centromere. At this point the centromere is a single structure.

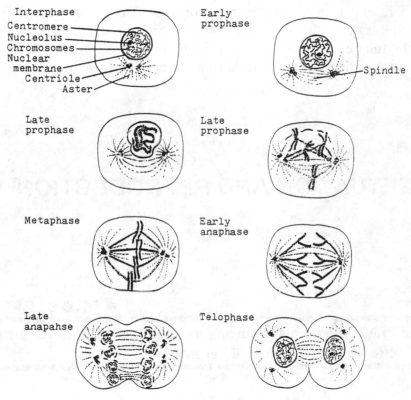

Figure 1. The stages of mitosis in a cell with a diploid number of 4.

The above events occur in the nucleus of the cell. In the cytoplasm, the centriole (a cytoplasmic structure involved in division) divides and the two daughter centrioles migrate to opposite sides of the cell. From each centriole there extends a cluster of raylike filaments called an aster. Between the separating centrioles, a mitotic spindle forms, composed of protein fibrils with contractile properties. In late prophase the chromosomes are fully contracted and appear as short, rod-like bodies. At this point individual chromosomes can be distinguished by their characteristic shapes and sizes. They then begin to migrate and line up along the equatorial plane of the spindle. Each doubled chromosome appears to be attached to the spindle at its centromere. The nucleolus (spherical body within the nucleus while RNA synthesis is believed to occur) has been undergoing dissolution during prophase. In addition, the nuclear envelope breaks down, and its disintegration marks the end of prophase.

3) Metaphase: When the chromosomes have all lined up along the equatorial plane, the dividing cell is in metaphase. At this time, the centromere divides and the chromatids become completely separate daughter chromosomes. The division of the centromeres occurs simultaneously in all the chromosomes.

4) Anaphase: The beginning of anaphase is marked by the movement of the separated chromatids (or daughter chromosomes) to opposite poles of the cell. It is thought that the chromosomes are pulled as a result of contraction of the spindle fibers in the presence of ATP. The chromosomes moving toward the poles usually assume a V shape, with the centromere at the apex pointing toward the pole.

5) Telophase: When the chromosomes reach the poles, telophase begins. The chromosomes relax, elongate, and return to the resting condition in which only chromatin threads are visible. A nuclear membrane forms around each new daughter nucleus. This completes karyokinesis, and cytokinesis follows.

The cytoplasmic division of animal cells is accomplished by the formation of furrow in the equatorial plane. The furrow gradually deepens and separates the cytoplasm into daughter cells, each with a nucleus. In plants, this division occurs by the formation of a cell plate, a partition which forms in the center of the spindle and grows laterally outwards to the cell wall. After the cell plate is completed, a cellulose cell wall is laid down on either side of the plate, and two complete plant cells form.

Meiosis

● **PROBLEM 4-23**

Outline briefly the events occurring in each stage of meiosis. Illustrate your discussion with diagrams if necessary.

SOLUTION:

Meiosis is the process by which diploid organisms (having two sets of chromosomes) produce haploid gametes (having only one set of chromosomes). When two gametes fuse in fertilization, the zygote formed will thus have the full diploid chromosomal complement.

Meiosis consists of two cell divisions, the first (Meiosis I) called a reduction division, and the second (Meiosis II) a mitotic type division.

Interphase I: This phase is similar to mitotic interphase. The cell appears
inactive in reference to cell division; but it is during interphase that chromosome duplication occurs.

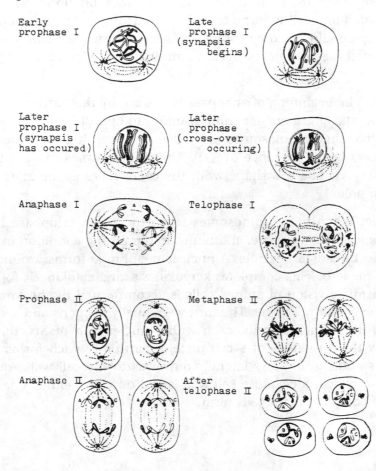

Figure 1. The stages of meiosis in a cell with a diploid number of 6.

Prophase I: The chromosomes become thicker and more visible. While they
are still long thin threads, an attractive force (as yet not identified) causes
homologous chromosomes to come together in pairs, a process known as
synapsis. This is the stage during which cross-over between homologous
chromosomes will occur.

After synapsis, the chromosomes continue to shorten and thicken; their
double nature becomes visible, so that each homologous pair appears as a
bundle of four chromatids called a tetrad. Each tetrad is composed of two
doubled homologous chromosomes. The number of tetrads is thus equal to
the haploid number. The centromeres of homologous chromosomes are connected, and there are thus two centromeres for the four chromatids.

88

While these events are occurring, the centrioles migrate to opposite poles, the spindle begins to form between them, and the nucleolus and nuclear membrane dissolve. The tetrads move to the equatorial plane of the spindle.

Metaphase I: Migration to the equatorial plane is complete, and the nuclear membrane and nucleolus have dissolved.

Anaphase I: At this point the homologous chromosomes that had paired in prophase separate and move to opposite poles of the cell. Each is still composed of two identical daughter chromatids joined at the centromere. Thus the number of chromosome types in each resultant cell is therefore reduced to the haploid number.

Telophase I: Cytoplasmic division occurs as in mitosis. Meiosis I concludes and meiosis II begins. There is no definable interphase between the two series of divisions. The chromosomes do not separate or duplicate, nor do they form chromatin threads.

Prophase II: The centrioles that had migrated to each pole of the parental cell, now incorporated in each haploid daughter cell, divide, and a new spindle forms in each cell. The chromosomes move to the equator.

Metaphase II: The chromosomes are lined up at the equator of the new spindle, which is at right angles to the old spindle.

Anaphase II: The centromeres divide and the daughter chromatids, now chromosomes, separate and move to opposite poles.

Telophase II: Cytoplasmic division occurs. The chromosomes gradually return to the dispersed form and a nuclear membrane forms.

The two meiotic divisions yield four cells, each carrying only one member of each homologous pair of chromosomes. These cells are for this reason called haploid cells.

● **PROBLEM 4-24**

Compare the events of mitosis with the events of meiosis, consider chromosome duplication, centromere duplication, cytoplasmic division, and homologous chromosomes in making the comparisons.

SOLUTION:

In mitosis, the chromosomes are duplicated once, and the cytoplasm divides once. In this way, two identical daughter cells are formed, each with the same chromosome number as the mother cell. In meiosis, however, the chromosomes are duplicated once, but the cytoplasm divides two times, resulting in four daughter cells having only half the diploid chromosomal complement. This difference arises in the fact that there is no real interphase, and thus no duplication of chromosomal material, between the two meiotic divisions.

In mitosis, there is no pairing of homologous chromosomes in prophase as there is in meiosis. Identical chromatids joined by their centromere are separated when the centromere divides. In meiosis, duplicated homologous chromosomes pair, forming tetrads. The daughter chromatids of each homolog are joined by a centromere as in mitosis, but it does not split in the first meiotic division. The centromeres of each duplicated member of the homologous pair are joined in the tetrad, and it is these centromeres which separate from one another in anaphase of meiosis I. Thus the first meiotic division results in two haploid daughter cells, each having chromosomes composed of two identical chromatids. Only in meiosis II, after the reduction division has already occurred, does the centromere joining daughter chromatids split as in mitosis, thus separating identical chromosomes.

Asexual and Sexual Reproduction

● **PROBLEM 4-25**

Define and compare asexual reproduction with sexual reproduction in animals. Give examples.

SOLUTION:

The fundamental difference between asexual reproduction and sexual reproduction is the number of parents involved in the production of offspring. In asexual reproduction only a single parent is needed. Offspring identical to the parent are produced when the parent splits, buds, or fragments. Asexual reproduction typically occurs in animals such as euglena, paramecium, amoeba, hydra, flatworms, and starfish.

Two parents are usually involved in sexual reproduction. A fertilized egg is produced through the union of specialized sex cells (egg and sperm) from each parent. Instead of having traits identical to a parent, the offspring possess a variety of recombined traits inherited from both parents. In higher animals such as man, sexual reproduction is the most common form.

It must be noted that in some cases, sexual reproduction can take place with a single parent. In the hermaphroditic worms, such as the earthworm and the fluke, both male and female sex organs occur in the same individual. Whereas self-fertilization is avoided in the earthworm by certain adaptive mechanisms, it does take place in the parasitic fluke. This is an exception to the general observation that sexual reproduction involves two parents.

Differentiate between fission, budding, and fragmentation as means of asexual reproduction.

SOLUTION:

Most protozoans reproduce asexually by fission, which is the simplest form of asexual reproduction. Fission involves the splitting of the body of the parent into two approximately equal parts, each of which becomes an entire, new, independent organism. In this case, the cell division involved is mitotic.

Hydras and yeasts reproduce by budding, a process in which a small part of the parent's body separates from the rest and develops into a new individual. It may split away from the parent and take up an independent existence or it may remain attached and maintain an independent yet colonial existence.

Lizards, starfish, and crabs can grow a new tail, leg, or arm if the original one is lost. In some cases, this ability to regenerate a missing part occurs to such an extent that it becomes a method of reproduction. The body of the parent may break into several pieces, after which each piece regenerates its respective missing parts and develops into a whole animal. Such reproduction by fragmentation is common among the flatworms, such as the planaria.

METABOLISM AND ENERGY PRODUCTION

Anaerobic Respiration

● PROBLEM 4-27

How does a facultative anaerobe differ from an obligatory anaerobe?

SOLUTION:

Organisms that can live anaerobically are divided into two groups. The obligatory, or strict, anaerobe cannot use oxygen and dies in the presence of oxygen. These include denitrifying bacteria of the soil, which are responsible for reducing nitrate to nitrogen, and methane-forming bacteria, which produce marsh gas. Some obligatory anaerobes are pathogenic to man; these include *Clostridium botulinum,* responsible for botulism, a fatal form of food poisoning; *Clostridium perfringens,* which causes gas gangrene in wound infections; and *Clostridium tetani,* which causes the disease tetanus.

The facultative anaerobes can live either in the presence or absence of oxygen. Under anaerobic conditions, they obtain energy from a fermentation process; under aerobic conditions, they continue to degrade their energy source anaerobically (via glycolysis) and then oxidize the products of fermentation using oxygen as the final electron acceptor. Yeast will grow rapidly under aerobic conditions but will still continue to live when oxygen is removed. It reproduces more slowly but maintains itself by fermentation. Winemakers take advantage of this behavior by first aerating crushed grapes to allow the yeasts to grow rapidly. They then let the mixture stand in closed vats while the yeasts convert the grape sugar anaerobically to ethanol.

Glycolysis

● PROBLEM 4-28

Explain the events which take place during glycolysis.

SOLUTION:

Glycolysis is the series of metabolic reactions by which glucose is converted to pyruvate, with the concurrent formation of ATP. Glycolysis occurs in the cytoplasm of the cell, and the presence of oxygen is unnecessary. Glucose is first "activated," or phosphorylated by a high-energy phosphate from ATP (See reaction 1). The product, glucose-6-phosphate, undergoes rearrangement to fructose-6-phospate, which is subsequently phosphorylated by another ATP to yield fructose-1, 6-diphosphate (reactions 2 and 3). This hexose is then split into two three-carbon sugars, glyceraldehyde-3-phosphate (also called PGAL), dihydroxyacetone, and phosphate (see reaction 4). Only PGAL can be directly degraded in glycolysis; dihydroxyacetone phosphate is reversibly converted into PGAL by enzyme action (reaction 4a).

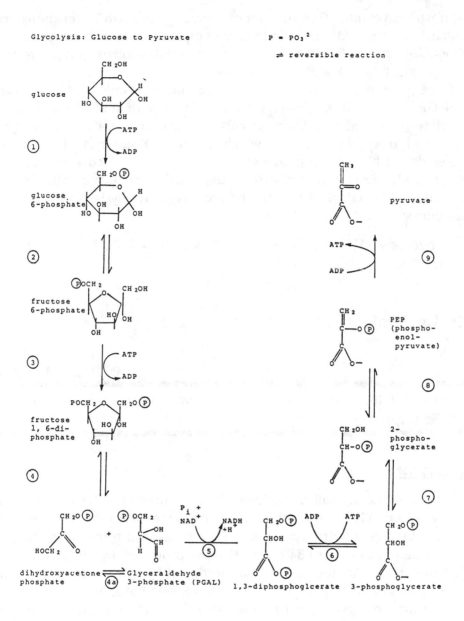

Glycolysis: Glucose to Pyruvate $P = PO_3^{2}$

$\rightleftharpoons$ reversible reaction

Since two molecules of PGAL are thus produced per molecule of glucose oxidized, the products of the subsequent reactions can be considered "doubled" in amount

$$1 \text{ glucose} \rightarrow 2 \text{ PGAL}$$

PGAL gets oxidized and phosphorylated. NAD⁺, the coenzyme in the dehydrogenase enzyme which catalyzed this step, gets reduced to NADH, and 1,3-diphosphoglycerate is formed (reaction 5). The energy-rich phosphate at carbon 1 of 1,3 diphosphoglycerate reacts with ADP to form ATP and

93

3-phosphoglycerate. This undergoes rearrangement to 2-phosphoglycerate, which is subsequently dehydrated, forming an energy-rich phosphate: phosphoenolpyruvate (PEP) (reaction 8). Finally, this phosphate group is transferred to ADP, yielding ATP and pyruvate (reaction 9).

Since two molecules of PGAL are formed per molecule of glucose, four ATP molecules are produced during glycolysis. The net yield of ATP is only 2, since 2 ATP were utilized in initiating glycolysis (reactions 1 and 3). Pyruvate is then converted to acetyl coenzyme A which enters the Krebs cycle. In addition, two molecules of NADH are produced per molecule of glucose. Hence, the net result of glycolysis is that glucose is degraded to pyruvate with the net formation of of 2 ATP and 2 NADH. The process of glycolysis can be summarized as follows:

$$\text{glucose} + 2ADP + 2Pi + 2NAD^+ \rightarrow 2 \text{ pyruvate} + 2ATP + 2NADH + 2H^+$$

Krebs Cycle

What structural advantages enable mitochondria to be efficient metabolic organelles?

SOLUTION:

Mitochondria are called the "powerhouses" of the cell because they are the major sites of ATP production in the cell. They contain the enzymes involved in both the Krebs (citric acid) cycle and the electron transport system, which work together to furnish 34 of the 36 ATPs produced by the complete oxidation of glucose. Another 2 ATPs are produced by glycolysis, which occurs in the cytoplasm, making the total 36 ATPs /oxidized glucose.

Pyruvate from glycolysis traverses both the outer and inner mitochondrial membranes easily because the membranes are totally permeable to pyruvate. Once inside the mitochondrion's matrix (see Figure 1) pyruvate is converted by the enzyme pyruvate dehydrogenase to acetyl coenzyme A. The coenzyme can then enter the Krebs cycle which occurs in the matrix where all the enzymes that catalyze the cycle's reactions are present (except succinic dehydrogenase which is located on the inner membrane). Conveniently bound to the surface of the cristae, the greatly folded inner membrane of the mitochondria, are the enzymes of the electron transport system. Since the cristae jut into the matrix, the distance needed to travel by $FADH_2$ and NADH, generated by the TCA cycle, to the enzymes of the electron transport system is reduced, and, since the surface area of the inner membrane is so greatly enhanced by its cristae, the probabilities of NADH and $FADH_2$ encountering the electron transport system's enzymes which are concerned with ATP production become sharply increased. Also contributing to the efficiency of this organelle's ATP producing ability is the nature of the cristae's enzymes: they are actually multi-enzyme complexes which group together a number of sequentially acting enzymes responsible for electron transport and oxidative phosphorylation. These assemblies enhance the efficiency of respiration, since the product of one reaction is located near the enzyme of the subsequent reaction.

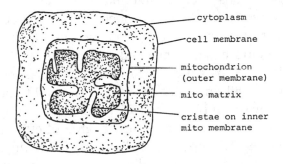

Figure 1. The mitochondrion in the cell.

● **PROBLEM 4-30**

Discuss feedback control involved in glycolysis and the TCA cycle.

SOLUTION:

Glycolysis and the TCA cycle are both regulated by means of allosteric control of the enzymes involved. Allostery involves regulation of the activity of an enzyme by the binding of a molecule at a site other than the active site. The molecule that is bound changes the conformation of the enzyme, thereby changing its activity. If the molecule regulates an enzymatic reaction involved in its own synthesis, this regulation is called feedback control.

In glycolysis, one control point occurs at the conversion of fructose-6-phosphate to fructose 1,6-diphosphate, catalyzed by the enzyme phosphofructokinase. This enzyme can be allosterically inhibited by either ATP or citrate. This explains why the rate of glycolysis decreases as soon as aerobic respiration begins in yeast; once the electron transport chain begins to operate, much more ATP is formed per glucose molecule. This causes an accumulation of ATP in more than sufficient amounts for cellular metabolism. This large amount of ATP inhibits phosphofructokinase and therefore inhibits glycolysis. Since glycolysis is inhibited, so is ATP production, for the end products of glycolysis would normally enter the Krebs cycle in order to produce more ATP. This makes sense, since the cell no longer needs to utilize glucose at such a high rate in order to generate sufficient energy. The cell needs only to allow glycolysis to proceed at a rate such that the amount of glycolytic products entering the Krebs cycle will yield an appropriate supply of ATP. Feedback inhibition provides the mechanism for this control. The inhibition by citrate, a Krebs cycle intermediate, works much the same way.

In the Krebs cycle, a major control point occurs at the conversion of isocitrate to $\propto$-ketoglutarate, catalyzed by the enzyme isocitrate dehydrogenase. This enzyme is allosterically inhibited by either ATP or NADH. If too much ATP is being synthesized, or too much NADH is produced to be oxidized by the electron transport chain, the reaction is blocked and the whole cycle ceases. Some citrate is accumulated which acts to allosterically inhibit phosphofructokinase, thus shutting down glycolysis as well. With glycolysis shut down, pyruvate will not build up or be converted to lactate or ethanol (which would normally occur if only the TCA cycle were stopped).

Allosteric control allows for a high degree of efficiency and cooperation in glycolysis and the TCA cycle. In addition, there are other control points in both these pathways and in other pathways as well, all serving to keep the cell's metabolic processes in balance.

ATP Production

● PROBLEM 4-31

Discuss the various ways in which energy is expended within the human body.

SOLUTION:

Energy is primarily expended during the anabolic reactions of the cell; that is, energy is required for the synthesis of macromolecules. Some organisms ingest simple chemical substances and combine them to form the complex molecules needed for the building of new protoplasm. Others, the higher organisms, ingest complex organic materials, degrade them, and use the simple products to synthesize the complex organic compounds that they need. In both cases, growth results.

Energy is also expended during motion. Motion includes the contraction of muscle tissue, which allows an animal to either move itself (locomotion) or part of its body (the bending of a limb). Muscle contraction also occurs in the diaphragm during breathing, in the heart, and in the walls of the digestive organs.

Energy is also required during movement of materials across the cell membrane. During active transport, molecules move from a region of low concentration to one of high concentration, a process which requires energy. Active transport is thought to involve a carrier molecule driven by the hydrolysis of ATP, the energy-releasing source.

Another energy-requiring process is heat production. During metabolic activity, the heat given off is important to "warm-blooded" animals (homeotherms) in keeping body temperature constant despite changes in environmental temperatures. Even "cold-blooded" animals (poikilotherms) whose body temperature is determined by the environmental temperature, must release heat in order to survive extremely cold conditions. Homeotherms, which include birds and mammals, generally eat more food per body weight than do poikilotherms, which include fish, amphibians, reptiles, and invertebrates. This fact reflects the need to furnish more energy to maintain body temperature.

Both anabolism and muscle contraction require the energy obtained from the splitting of the energy-rich terminal phosphate group of ATP, which has the structure:

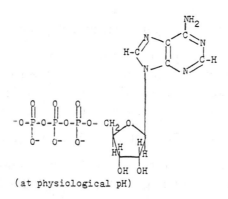

(at physiological pH)

ATP is produced during oxidative phosphorylation — the process by which the flow of electrons in the electron transport system of respiration transfers the released energy to be stored in ATP. However, certain compounds, such as the hormone thyroxine, can uncouple phosphorylation from the electron flow so that the energy is not trapped as ATP, but is released as heat. This mechanism is important when more heat is needed by an organism than is provided by its normal metabolic activity.

What are the roles of ATP in the cell? How is ~P produced, stored, and utilized?

SOLUTION:

One of the roles of ATP in the cell is to drive all of the energy-requiring reactions of cellular metabolism. Indeed, ATP is often referred to as the "energy currency" of the cell. The hydrolysis of one mole of ATP yields 7 kcal of energy:

$$ATP \xrightarrow{H_2O} ADP + Pi \quad \Delta G^{o1} = -7 \text{ kcal/mole}$$

Because of their larger free energies of hydrolysis, the first and second bonds broken in ATP are called high energy phosphate bonds and can be written:

$$adenosine - P \sim P \sim P.$$

A second role of ATP is to activate a compound prior to its entry into a particular reaction. For example, the biosynthesis of sucrose has the following equation:

$$Glucose + fructose \rightleftharpoons sucrose + H_2O$$

The forward reaction is very unfavorable in a plant cell because of a preponderance of H_2O compared to glucose and fructose (recall Le Chatelier's principle). A great deal of energy would be needed to help the forward reaction occur. The cell alleviates this problem by first activating glucose with ATP:

$$glucose + ATP \rightarrow glucose -1- phosphate + ADP$$

The phosphate bond attached to glucose is a high energy bond; the cleavage of this bond yields enough energy to enable the following reaction to proceed with the formation of sucrose:

$$glucose -1- phosphate + fructose \rightarrow sucrose + phosphate$$

This series of reactions shows how activation by ATP permits a thermodynamically unfavored anabolic process to occur.

To produce energy-rich phosphate groups (~P), energy from the complete oxidation of glucose in the process of respiration is utilized. The energy is used to add inorganic phosphate (P_i) to ADP to form ATP. The energy-rich phosphate groups are stored in the form of ATP. They are utilized during the hydrolysis of ATP to ADP and P_i. This energy-yielding reaction is coupled to energy-requiring reactions, allowing the latter to occur.

The amount of ATP present in a cell is usually small, so muscle cells, which require much energy during a brief period of time (during contraction), may run short of it. Therefore, an additional substance, creatine phosphate, serves as a reservoir of ~P. The terminal phosphate of ATP is transferred by an enzyme to creatine to yield creatine phosphate and ADP. The phosphate bond is also high energy but the ~P must be transferred back to ADP to form ATP in order for it to be used in an energy-requiring reaction. That is, creatine phosphate replenishes the cell's ATP supply by donating its ~P to ADP.

Photosynthesis

● **PROBLEM 4-33**

What pigments may be present in plant cells? What are the functions of these pigments?

SOLUTION:

Chlorophyll *a* occurs in all photosynthetic eucaryotic cells and is considered to be essential for photosynthesis of the type carried out by plants. It functions in the capture of light energy by either directly absorbing it or receiving it in the form of high energy electrons from the accessory pigments. These accessory pigments, such as chlorophyll *b*, are found in vascular plants, bryophytes, green algae, and euglenoid algae. Chlorophyll *b* differs from chlorophyll *a* structurally and in its absorption spectra. Chlorophyll *b* shares with chlorophyll *a* the ability to absorb light energy and produce in the molecule some sort of excited state. The excited chlorophyll *b* molecule transfers light energy via high energy electrons to a chlorophyll *a* molecule, which then proceeds to transform it into chemical energy. Since chlorophyll *b* absorbs light of wavelengths that are different from chlorophyll *a*, it extends the range of light that the plant can use for photosynthesis. Chlorophyll *c* or *d* takes the place of chlorophyll *b* in some algae and plant-like protists.

The carotenoids are another class of accessory pigments. Carotenoids are red, orange, or yellow fat-soluble pigments found in almost all chloroplasts. Carotenoids that do not contain oxygen are called carotenes, and are deep orange in color; those that contain oxygen are called xanthophylls, and are yellowish. Like the chlorophylls, the carotenoids are bound to proteins within the lamellae of the chloroplast. In the green leaf, the color of the carotenoids is masked by the much more abundant chlorophylls. In some tissues, such as those of a ripe red tomato or the petals of a yellow flower, the carotenoids predominate. As accessory pigments, the carotenoids function in absorbing light not usable by the chlorophylls and in transferring the absorbed energy to chlorophyll *a*.

Another pigment that may be found in plants is the light-sensitive, blue phytochrome. Phytochromes play a fundamental role in the circadian rhythms of plants; they allow the plant to detect whether it is in a light or dark environment.

Describe the light reactions of photosynthesis. What are the products of these reactions?

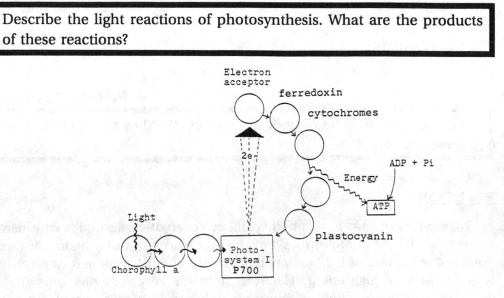

Figure 1. Cyclic photophosphorylation.

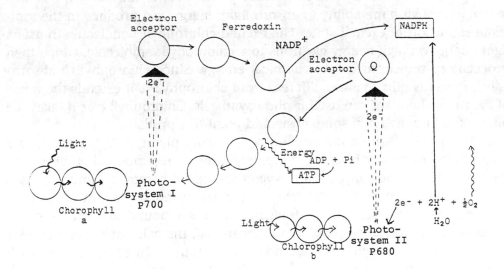

Figure 2. Noncyclic photophosphorylation.

SOLUTION:

The essential requirements for the energy-requiring dark reactions of photosynthesis are ATP and NADPH$_2$. These molecules are produced via the light reactions of photosynthesis, which occur entirely within the chloroplasts. This was proven by Daniel Arnon in 1954 who showed that intact chloroplasts carefully isolated from spinach leaves were able to carry out the complete photosynthetic reaction.

Scientists now agree that there are two reaction pathways occurring in the chloroplasts which generate ATP molecules from light energy, one of the pathways being designated cyclic photophosphorylation, the other noncyclic photophosphorylation. Both reactions require the presence of light. Each pathway is a photosystem. A photosystem is an energy-trapping center which receives packets of energy from excited chlorophyll molecules and converts them into a stream of high-energy electrons which can then travel down the electron transport chain. Photosystem I is called P700 due to the wavelength at which chlorophyll a absorbs light (700 nm). Photosystem II is similarly designated P680 due to the response by chlorophyll b.

In cyclic photophosphorylation, light striking a chlorophyll a molecule excites one of the electrons to an energy level high enough to allow it to leave the molecule. The chlorophyll a^+ molecule, having lost an electron, is now ready to serve as an electron acceptor because of its net positive charge. However, the ejected electron does not return to its ground state and the chlorophyll a^+ molecule directly; instead it is taken up by ferredoxin and passed along an electron transport chain. As the electron passes from ferredoxin to the cytochromes, to plastocyanin and finally back to chlorophyll a^+, two ATP molecules are produced. In this way, light energy is converted into chemical bond energy, and not lost as heat as it would have been had the excited electron returned directly to its ground state.

In noncyclic photophosphorylation, oxygen is produced by the photolysis of water. NADPH and ATP molecules are formed. The excitation of chlorophyll a by light at Photosystem I ejects high energy electrons. These electrons pass to ferredoxin and then to NADP$^+$, reducing it to NADPH. To restore chlorophyll $a+$ to its original state, another set of chlorophyll molecules known as chlorophyll b come into play at Photosystem II. When light energy is absorbed by chlorophyll b, it also ejects high energy electrons. These pass to an electron acceptor called Q and then via plastoquinone, cytochromes, and plastocyanin to chlorophyll a^+. During these steps, ADP is phosphorylated to ATP. The electrons necessary to restore chlorophyll b^+ to its ground level come from the splitting of water due to the high affinity that chlorophyll b^+ has for electrons. The water molecule is thus split into component protons, electrons, and oxygen. The oxygen, after combining with another oxygen atom, is released in gaseous form as O$_2$. The two electrons are picked up by cytochrome b and the hydrogen ions are used in the conversion of NADP$^+$ to NADPH.

Discuss the sequence of reactions that constitute the "dark reactions" of photosynthesis. What are the products of these reactions?

SOLUTION:

The dark reactions of photosynthesis, in which carbohydrates are synthesized, occur in a cyclic sequence of three phases — the carboxylative, reductive, and regenerative phases. These dark reactions do not require the presence of sunlight.

In the carboxylative phase, a five-carbon sugar, ribulose-5-phosphate, is phosphorylated by ATP to yield ribulose diphosphate (see Figure 1). Ribulose diphosphate is then carboxylated (that is, CO_2 is added), presumably yielding a six-carbon intermediate, which is split immediately by the addition of water to give two molecules of phosphoglyceric acid. The three-carbon phosphoglyceric acid is reduced by NADPH in an enzymatic reaction in the reductive phase, utilizing energy from ATP. The product of this reduction is phosphoglyceraldehyde, another triose. Two molecules of phosphoglyceraldehyde can then condense in the regenerative phase to form one hexose molecule, fructose diphosphate. This is subsequently converted to a glucose-6-phosphate molecule and finally transformed into starch.

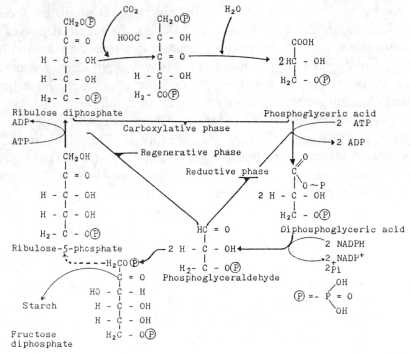

Figure 1. The "dark" reactions of carbohydrate synthesis by which carbon dioxide is incorporated into sugars. The dotted line from fructose diphosphate to ribulose-5-phosphate indicates several reactions of the pentose phosphate pathway.

102

Ribulose-5-phosphate, the cycle-initiating reactant, can be regenerated from fructose diphosphate via certain reactions of the pentose phosphate pathway. Some scientists tend to believe that the ribulose molecule is regenerated from phosphoglyceraldehyde by a complicated series of reactions. However, the cyclicity of the dark reactions is a well established and universally accepted fact.

The materials consumed in the production of one hexose molecule are one molecule each of CO_2 and H_2O, three ATP molecules, and four H atoms (from two molecules of $NADPH_2$). Ribulose-5-phosphate is not consumed but generated at some point in the cycle. The glucose-6-phosphate produced can either be polymerized into starch and stored, or broken down to yield energy for work.

SHORT ANSWER QUESTIONS FOR REVIEW

Choose the correct answer.

1. The nucleolus is an organelle that functions in (a) protein synthesis. (b) the production of ribosomal RNA. (c) formation of the mitotic spindle. (d) secretion.

2. Unlike plant cells, animal cells possess (a) a cell wall. (b) centrioles. (c) chloroplasts. (d) a nuclear membrane.

3. A great deal of rough endoplasmic reticulum is observed in a cell. This would lead one to conclude that the cell is actively involved in (a) chromosomal replication. (b) triglyceride metabolism. (c) protein synthesis. (d) pinocytosis.

4. The Golgi apparatus primarily functions in (a) packaging protein for secretion. (b) synthesizing protein for secretion. (c) packaging protein for hydrolysis. (d) both **a** and **b**

5. In animal cells, centrioles play an important role in (a) mitosis. (b) thrombosis. (c) pinocytosis. (d) protein synthesis.

6. Intercellular protoplasmic channels in plant cells are known as (a) cellulose. (b) gap junctions. (c) plasmodesmata. (d) desmosomes.

7. Sperm cells are highly motile cells and require a great deal of energy to maintain their activity. An organelle that would be found in great abun-

dance in this cell is the (a) mitochondrion. (b) ribosome. (c) lysosome.
(d) testosterone.

8. The chloroplasts in green plants (a) are energy producers. (b) are energy
transducers. (c) synthesize ATP from carbon dioxide. (d) result in ADP
formation only in the presence of light.

9. The proteins that comprise microfilaments include: (a) tubulin. (b)
pseudopods. (c) myosin. (d) actin.

10. Gene duplication takes place during (a) telophase. (b) anaphase. (c) interphase. (d) metaphase.

11. Which statement is true concerning asexual and sexual reproduction? (a)
Asexual reproduction involves one or more parents. (b) Asexual reproduction rarely results in identical offspring. (c) Sexual reproduction is
predominant amongst the flatworms and starfish. (d) Two parents are
usually involved in sexual reproduction. (e) Sexual reproduction never
involves only one parent.

12. Which of the following contributes to the "powerhouse" properties of the
mitochondria? (a) the presence on the mitochondria's inner membrane
of the enzymes necessary for the functioning of the electron transport
system (b) the presence of cristae, which increase the surface area of the
mitochondria's inner membrane (c) the ease with which pyruvate can
travel through the outer and inner membrane into the mitochondria's
inner matrix (d) All of the above

13. Which of the following is *incorrect* concerning feedback regulation? (a) In
the same way that high quantities of ATP and NADH are inhibitors of the
Krebs cycle, high quantities of ADP and NAD^+ are stimulators of the Krebs
cycle. (b) Control of feedback regulation in both the glycolytic pathway
and the Krebs cycle is due to the presence of allosteric enzymes. (c) Since
many more ATPs are produced by the Krebs cycle and electron transport
system than in glycolysis, once the former begin to function, they will
inhibit the latter. (d) The only control point in the glycolytic pathway is
at the conversion of fructose-6-phosphate to fructose-1,6 diphosphate by
the enzyme phosphofructokinase. It is inhibited by high quantities of
ATP.

14. Which of the following is *incorrect* concerning the production and use of
ATP? (a) ATP can be produced by either oxidative or substrate phosphorylation. Inorganic phosphate must be available for either of these reactions to occur. (b) The energy released upon hydrolysis of the terminal

phosphate group is enough to drive many endergonic metabolic reactions, the use of an intermediate compound (one with a phosphate attached to it) never being necessary. (c) Not only does the terminal phosphate bond of ATP contain much energy, but both the terminal and second phosphate bonds can be used to drive endergonic reactions. (d) In the reaction forming sucrose from glucose and fructose, the energy needed originally comes from ATP, but must pass through a phosphorylated intermediate before it can ultimately be used.

15. If a metabolic reaction requires 5000 calories of energy in order to occur, will the hydrolysis of the terminal phosphate bond of ATP supply enough energy to drive the reaction? Will there be any energy left over? (a) No, the hydrolysis will not supply enough energy. (b) Yes, hydrolysis will supply exactly the energy needed. (c) Yes, the hydrolysis will supply the energy needed, plus some will be left over. (d) None of the above

16. Which of the following pigments absorb radiant energy and ultimately transfer it to chlorophyll a as high energy electrons? (a) chlorophyll b (b) carotene (c) xanthophyll (d) All of the above (e) None of the above

17. During the light reactions of photosyntheses, which is not produced? (a) ATP (b) NADPH (c) O_2 gas (d) NADP (e) all are produced

18. What is the final electron acceptor during cyclic phosphorylation? (Light reaction) (a) chlorophyll a (b) ferredoxin (c) plastoquinone (d) cytochromes (e) oxygen

Fill in the blanks.

19. The middle lamella is an intercellular layer in plants, and is mainly composed of _____, a complex polysaccharide.

20. The analogue of plasmolysis in animal cells is _____.

21. The pores of the nuclear membrane allow communication between the _____ and _____.

22. The type of enzymes that lysosomes possess are called _____.

23. The inner membrane of a chloroplast is composed of flattened sacs called _____; collectively these sacs are termed _____.

24. The _____ is part of the cell duplication in animal cells but not in plant cells.

105

25. In _____, the chromosomes are duplicated once, the cytoplasm divides once, and two identical daughter cells are formed.

26. Chromosomes line up along the equatorial plate during the _____ stage of mitosis.

27. A process during which a part of the parent organism separates from the rest and develops into a new individual is known as _____.

28. In the process of winemaking, the fact that yeast is a _____, allows it to first grow in the presence of oxygen; when the oxygen is removed, it will produce ethanol by the process of _____.

29. The sequence of the glycolytic pathway is as follows: glucose→ _____, using 1 molecule of ATP, → fructose-6-phosphate→ _____, with use of another molecule of ATP; → glyceraldehyde-3-phosphate + _____→ 2 (_____) → 2 (phosphoglyceric acid), with electrons being accepted by a molecule of _____; → 2 (1,3 diphosphoglyceric acid), with the new phosphate groups coming from _____ and the electrons being accepted by a molecule of _____; → 2 (3-phosphoglyceric acid), the lost phosphate groups combining with _____ to form _____; → 2 (_____) → 2 (phosphoenol pyruvic acid), → 2 (pyruvic acid), the lost phosphate groups combining with _____ to form _____.

30. The excited _____ molecule transfers light energy via high energy electrons to a chlorophyll *a* molecule.

31. Carotenoids that do not contain oxygen are called _____ and are deep orange in color, those that contain oxygen are called _____ and are yellowish.

32. _____ allows the plant to discern whether it is in a dark or light environment.

33. The three phases of the dark reactions of photosynthesis are the _____, _____, and _____ phases.

34. _____ serve as cytoskeletal elements in that they give support and shape to the cell.

35. The inner membrane of the mitochondria has a series of folds called _____.

Determine whether the following statements are true or false.

36. Turgor pressure will increase when a plant cell is placed in a hypertonic solution.

37. It is believed that smooth endoplasmic reticulum is involved in lipid synthesis as well as ATP production.

38. Lysosomes and peroxisomes are similar in that they contain enzymes that function in cellular transport.

39. Microfilaments are involved in the cytoplasmic streaming of plant cells.

40. The basal body of a cilium is composed of microtubules.

41. Centromere duplication takes place during anaphase.

42. Karyokinesis defines mitosis in its strictest sense referring only to the division of nuclear material.

43. In muscle, creatine phosphate is used as storage form for the high-energy phosphate bond. The energy derived from the hydrolysis of this bond is used directly to drive energy-requiring reactions in muscle.

44. The energy stored in a molecule of ATP can be used in only 3 ways; by cleavage of the terminal phosphate and its subsequent attachment to a compound, by cleavage of the last two phosphates and their subsequent attachment to a compound, and by cleavage of the last two phosphates and the subsequent attachment of the remaining AMP molecule to a compound.

ANSWER KEY

1. b	2. b	3. c
4. a	5. a	6. c
7. a	8. b	9. d
10. c	11. d	12. d

13. d   14. b   15. c

16. d   17. d   18. a

19. pectin   20. crenation

21. nucleus, cytoplasm   22. acid hydrolases   23. thylakoids, grana

24. cleavage furrow   25. mitosis   26. metaphase

27. budding   28. facultative anaerobe, fermentation

29. glucose-6-phosphate; fructose-1,6-diphosphate; dihydroxy acetone phos-
    phate; glyceraldehyde-3-phosphate; inorganic phosphate; NAD$^+$; ADP;
    ATP, 2-phosphoglyceric acid; ADP; ATP

30. chlorophyll *b*   31. carotenes, xanthophylls

32. Phytochrome   33. carboxylative, reductive, regenerative

34. Microtubules   35. cristae   36. False

37. False   38. False   39. True

40. True   41. False   42. True

43. False   44. False

CHAPTER 5

MENDELIAN GENETICS

Mendel's Laws

What are Mendel's Laws and how did he formulate his hypothesis?

Figure 1. Gregor Johann Mendel

SOLUTION:

Gregor Mendel was able to formulate his laws on the basis of his work with the garden pea. He chose to work with garden peas because they were readily hybridized and had well defined traits. Mendel studied seven garden pea traits that appeared in one form or another without blending to produce intermediate traits (see Figure 2). The traits he studied included round vs. wrinkled seeds, yellow vs. green seeds, and tall vs. dwarf plants.

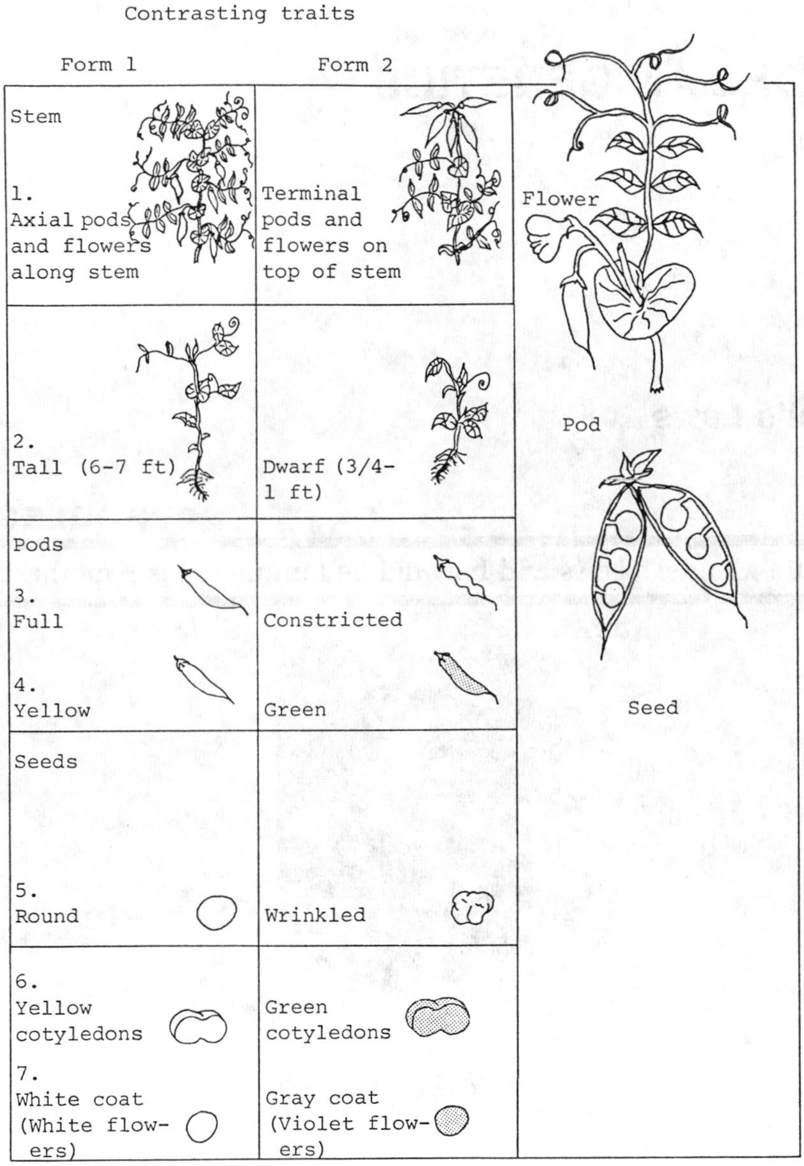

Figure 2. Seven traits of the garden pea.

After many crosses, Mendel was able to demonstrate that the seven traits each behaved in mathematically precise and predictable ways. When tall plants that had come from a line of tall parents were self-fertilized, they produced only tall offspring. The same held true for dwarf plants, which produced only dwarf offspring. Mendel also found that when the tall plants were crossed with dwarf plants, the first generation plants, the F_1 generation, were all tall. However, when these tall hybrids were allowed to self-fertilize, the next (F_2) generation was composed of 787 tall plants and 277 short plants, roughly a 3:1 ratio. When the F_2 generation was self-fertilized, Mendel found that all of the short plants produced only short offspring. On the other hand, 1/3 of the F_2 tall plants produced only tall offspring while the other 2/3 produced both tall and short plants in, roughly, a 3:1 ratio.

From these results Mendel was able to theorize that the determinants of heredity (called "factors" by Mendel, but now known as genes) occur in pairs, and that they segregate in the formation of gametes, allowing only one of each pair to be transmitted to a gamete. The double number is restored when the gametes come together to form the zygote. This principle is known as the Law of Segregation.

Mendel also noted that the pattern of inheritance in his peas featured a dominant and recessive relationship between alternate forms of each trait. For example, the tall trait is shown to be dominant over the dwarfness trait because hybrids between tall and short strains produce only tall plants, even though the hybrid contains genes for both tallness and dwarfness. Mendel designated dominant factors with capital letters and recessive ones with corresponding lower case letters. Thus, a pure tall plant would be designated *DD*, and a dwarf plant *dd*. A hybrid tall would be designated *Dd*.

In addition to the single factor crosses, Mendel made several hybridizations in which he studied two or three pairs of factors simultaneously. For example, one cross involved plants producing round yellow seeds with those producing wrinkled green seeds. The seeds from the first generation were all round and yellow, since these are the dominant traits. When these plants were self-fertilized, four types of seeds resulted in the F_2 generation. They were found in proportions of 9/16 round and yellow, 3/16 wrinkled and yellow, 3/16 round and green, and 1/16 wrinkled and green, a 9:3:3:1 ratio. Mendel recognized that this 9:3:3:1 ratio resulted from the independent assortment of two single factor crosses. The segregation of both factors was occurring independently for both factors. The ratio resulting from this cross could be predicted from results for each pair when crossed individually. When only looking at seed color, a 3:1 yellow to green ratio occurred. A 3:1 round to wrinkled ratio is seen when shape is considered individually. Multiplying these together:

3(yellow) + 1(green)
× 3(round) + 1(wrinkled)
_____

9(yellow, round) + 3(yellow, wrinkled) + 3(green, round) + 1(green, wrinkled)

yields the ratio expected, based on what Mendel found in his cross involving two simultaneous factors. This is called the Law of Independent Assortment. Each factor in the cross segregates independently of the other factors involved. The principle makes it easy to predict the results of crosses involving multiple pairs of factors by merely multiplying together the results for each pair considered individually.

● **PROBLEM 5-2**

Suppose pure line lima bean plants having green pods were crossed with pure line plants having yellow pods. If all the F_1 plants had green pods and were allowed to interbreed, 580 F_2 plants, 435 with green pods and 145 with yellow pods would be obtained. Which characteristic is dominant and which is recessive? Of the F_2 plants, how many are homozygous recessive, homozygous dominant, and heterozygous? Using G to represent the dominant gene and g to represent the recessive gene, write out a plan showing the segregation of genes from the parents to the F_2 plants.

SOLUTION:

This example is used to illustrate the basic concepts of genetics and the methods of solving genetic problems. First, some definitions:

a) chromosomes — filamentous or rod-shaped bodies in the cell nucleus which contain the hereditary units, the genes.

b) gene — the part of a chromosome which codes for a certain hereditary trait.

c) genotype — the genetic makeup of an organism, or the set of genes which it possesses.

d) phenotype — the outward, visible expression of the hereditary constitution of an organism.

e) homologous chromosomes — chromosomes bearing genes for the same characters.

f) homozygote — an organism possessing an identical pair of alleles on homologous chromosomes for a given character or for all given characters.

g) heterozygote — an organism possessing different alleles on homologous chromosomes for a given character or for all given characters.

In solving genetic problems, one uses letters to represent the genotype of

112

the organism. For example, *a* represents the gene for blue color and *A* represents the gene for red color. A capital letter is used for a dominant gene; that is, the phenotype of that gene will be expressed in a heterozygous state. For example, if the genotype *Aa* is expressed as red, then *A* is the dominant gene. Small letter *a* represents the recessive gene; that is, one whose phenotype will be expressed only in the homozygous state. Therefore, *aa* would be expressed as blue.

To solve a genetic problem, one writes down the genotypes of the two parents in the cross. Mendel's First Law tells us what to do. This law, also known as the Law of Independent Segregation, states that genes, the units of heredity, exist in individuals in pairs. In the formation of sex cells or gametes, the two genes separate and pass independent of one another into different gametes, so that each gamete has one, and only one, member of each pair. During fertilization, the gamete of one parent fuses with that of the other parent. Fusion brings the genes from each parent together, giving rise to off-spring with paired genes. Now we will illustrate the Law of Segregation as it applies to the problem given. Let *G* represent the gene for green pod color and *g* represent the gene for yellow pod color. Since the parents come from pure lines, meaning that the two members of each gene pair are identical, we write the genotype of the parent plant with green pods as *GG*, and that of the parent plant with yellow pods as *gg*. Each gamete from the first parent will have one *G* and each gamete from the second will have one *g*. (Recall the Law of Independent Segregation.)

Writing out a schematic cross, we have:

P (Parent)	*GG* ×	*gg*
Gametes formed	*G* ↓	*g*
F_1 (first filial) generation	*Gg*	

The genotype of the F_1 generation is written as *Gg* because it results from the fusion of the two gametes.

We are told that all the F_1 generation from the above cross are green, and we observe that they are all heterozygous. Therefore *G*, which stands for the gene with green pods, must be dominant (by definition), and *g*, which stands for the gene with yellow pods, must be recessive.

To determine the possible genotypes of the F_1 plants, or the second generation offspring, we mate two F_2 plants. The possible gametes derived from the parents are again obtained using Mendel's First Law. But now we obtain two types of gametes, *G* and *g*, from each parent, because either gene can come from the parental genotype of *Gg*.

Schematically, then:

P	*Gg* ×	*Gg*
	↓	
gametes	G_1 *g*	G_1 *g*

113

It is easier to determine the F_2 generation using the Punnet square. The square is constructed as follows:

	G	g	possible gametes from male parent
G	GG	Gg	
g	Gg	gg	

possible gametes from female parent →

It gives all possible combinations of the parental gametes, so in F_2 we have genotypically:

1 *GG*: 2 *Gg*: 1 *gg*

Phenotypically:

GG is homozygous dominant and green because *G* is dominant;
Gg is heterozygous and green because *G* is dominant; and
gg is homozygous recessive and yellow because *g* is recessive.

It is important to note that we cannot observe the genotype itself because it lies in the constitution of the gene. Our observations come only from what we actually see, that is, the phenotypic differences.

We know from the Punnet square that in the F_2 generation the ratio of homozygous dominant to the entire progeny is 1/4; the ratio of heterozygous is 2/4 or 1/2 and the ratio of homozygous recessive is 1/4. Therefore, the number of homozygous dominant (*GG*) plants is

1/4 × 580 or 145,

the number of heterozygote (*Gg*) plants is

1/2 × 580 or 290

and the number of homozygous recessive (*gg*) plants is

1/4 × 580 or 145.

When added together, they total 580, the number of F_2 plants.

Soon after the Mendelian laws became firmly established, numerous exceptions to Mendel's second law, the Law of Independent Segregation, were demonstrated by experiments. Parental non-allelic gene combinations were found to occur with much greater frequencies in offspring than were the non-parental combinations. How can this be explained?

SOLUTION:

The Law of Independent Segregation states that when two or more pairs of genes are involved in a cross, the members of one pair segregate independently of the members of all other pairs. This law was substantiated by Mendel's experiments with pea plants. However, in Mendel's time, the physical nature of genes was not known, nor was it known how they are carried. When it was learned that chromosomes are the bearers of genes, the reasons why Mendel's law was both supported by some experiments and negated by others became obvious.

It was seen that the chromosomes are relatively few in number. For example, Drosophila have only four pairs of chromosomes. Man has twenty-three pairs. In comparison, however, the number of genes possessed by each species is very large, often in the thousands. Since there are so many more genes than chromosomes, and the chromosomes carry the genes, it follows that there must be many genes on each chromosome. And since it is now known that it is whole chromosomes which segregate independently during meiosis, gene separation can only be independent if the genes in question are on different chromosomes. Genes located on the same chromosomes are physically forced to move together during meiosis. Such genes are said to show linkage.

When genetic experiments are performed using genes that are linked, very different ratios from the expected Mendelian ratios are obtained. Genes that were linked together on parental chromosomes tend to remain together in the gametes, and so occur in conjuction with one another more frequently in the offspring than they would if they had segregated independently.

Exactly how linkage produces these variant ratios will be dealt with in later problems. At the present we can see that linkage explains how exceptions to the Law of Independent Segregation could possibly occur.

In *Drosophilia*, black body and vestigial wings are both recessive traits, while gray body and normal wings are dominant. How would you determine if the genes for black body and vestigial wings are on the same chromosome? Show the expected results if they are on the same chromosome, and the results if they are on different chromosomes.

SOLUTION:

To determine whether or not the genes for body color and wing type are on the same chromosome, we can do a testcross between an individual heterozygous for both traits and a double recessive individual. A testcross with a double recessive allows the genotype of the other parent to be expressed in the offspring in the same proportions as the gametes produced by that parent. This is because the double recessive parent has no genes that will obscure the genotype of the other parent. We use a heterozygote to determine if linkage is present because such a parent carries all the genes involved. If the offspring of the testcross give a 1:1:1:1 phenotypic ratio, then the genes have assorted independently and are not linked. If they give some other ratio, then linkage is indicated, and they are probably located on the same chromosome. This can best be illustrated by doing the crosses.

Let G be the gene for gray body, g be the gene for black body, N be the gene for normal wings, and n be the gene for vestigial wings. We can obtain the heterozygote by crossing a known homozygous dominant with a homozygous recessive. Then we do the test cross. If the genes are not linked we have:

P $GgNn$ × $ggnn$
Gametes GN Gn gN gn ↓ gn
F$_2$

	GN	Gn	gN	gn
gn	$GgNn$	$Ggnn$	$ggNn$	$ggnn$

Phenotypically:

$GgNn$ is gray-normal,

$Ggnn$ is gray-vestigial,

$ggNn$ is black-normal, and

$ggnn$ is black-vestigial.

According to the Law of Independent Segregation, the gametes formed from the $GgNn$ parent (GN, Gn, gN, gn) are in equal numbers. Thus the proportion

116

of different F_2 offspring are equal; that is, 1:1:1:1.

If the genes are located on the same chromosome, GN the heterozygous parent will have the genotype $\underline{\underline{GN}}$.
$$\text{gn}$$

(Note: the genes are written on a bar $\underline{\underline{GN}}$ to show linkage). Since the genes are linked, there is a chance that crossover will occur between them during meiosis. The heterozygous parent can thus form four kinds of gametes in the following manner:

$$
\begin{array}{lll}
G\,N & & G\,N \ - \ \text{parental type} \\
G\,N & & G\,n \ - \ \text{recombinant} \\
g\,n & \longrightarrow & g\,N \ - \ \text{recombinant} \\
g\,n & & g\,n \ - \ \text{parental type}
\end{array}
$$

Note that since their presence in the gametic population depends on the occurrence of a crossover event, the frequency of the recombinants (those arising from crossover) will be lower than that of the parental types (those having the same gene combination as the parent).

In the test cross we obtain:

| P | | $\dfrac{G\,N}{g\,n}$ | $\times$ | $\dfrac{g\,n}{g\,n}$ | ♀ |

| | Gametes | $\begin{array}{c} G\,N \\ G\,n \\ g\,N \\ g\,n \end{array}$ | | $g\,n$ | |

F_2

	$G\,N$	$G\,n$	$g\,N$	$g\,n$
	$G\,N$	$G\,n$	$g\,N$	$g\,n$
$g\,n$	$G\,N$	$G\,n$	$g\,N$	$g\,n$
	$g\,n$	$g\,n$	$g\,n$	$g\,n$

Phenotypically:

$\dfrac{G\,N}{g\,n}$ is gray-normal,

$\dfrac{G\,n}{g\,n}$ is gray-vestigial,

$\dfrac{g\,N}{g\,n}$ is black-normal, and

$\dfrac{g\,n}{g\,n}$ is black-vestigial.

Although the same phenotypes are produced in this cross as in the cross between genes on separate chromosomes, the ratios will not be the same. Because their frequency as gametes is much higher than the recombinant types, the parental types (gray-normal and black-vestigial) will occur with much higher frequency in the offspring. The frequency of the recombinant types will depend on the distance between the two genes. If the genes are far apart, there is more chance of a crossover event between them, and the occurrence of recombinants will be higher than if the genes were very close together on the chromosome. Also, since the formation of one recombinant type necessitates that the other type also be formed (refer to the diagram of the crossover), their frequencies will be about equal, as will the frequencies of the two parental types.

Thus whenever the observed ratio in a test cross varies from the predicted Mendelian ratio, and resembles the ratios outlined above, linkage is usually indicated.

● PROBLEM 5-5

Two long-winged flies were mated. The offspring consisted of 77 with long wings and 24 with short wings. Is the short-winged condition dominant or recessive? What are the genotypes of the parents?

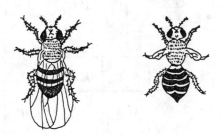

Figure 1. Fruit flies (enlarged)

SOLUTION:

When we are not told which of the characteristics is dominant and which is recessive, we can deduce it from the ratio of phenotypes in the progeny. We know that 77 flies have long wings and 24 have short wings. This gives us an approximate ratio of 3 long-winged flies to every 1 short-winged fly.

$$\frac{77}{24} \sim \frac{3}{1}$$

As previously noted, the three-to-one ratio signifies that dominant and recessive characteristics are most likely involved. Moreover, because there are three long-winged flies to every short-winged one, it suggests that short-wingedness

118

is the recessive characteristic, and long-wingedness is dominant.

We cannot immediately conclude that both the long-winged parents are homozygous. In fact they are not, because if they were, no short-winged offspring could have resulted in the cross. So the presence of short-winged flies (homozygous recessive) in the progeny suggests that both parents carry the recessive gene and are thus heterozygotes.

Let L be the gene for long wings in flies and l be the gene for short wings in flies. In the cross between two long-winged heterozygous parents:

P		Ll	$\times$	L_1
Gametes		$L;l$	$\downarrow$	$L;l$
F_1		1 LL: 2 Ll:	1 ll	
		long wing	short wing	

The phenotypes of the F_1 show the three-to-one ratio of long-winged flies to short-winged flies, which concurs with the data given. Therefore, the genotypes of the parents are the same, both being heterozygous (Ll).

● PROBLEM 5-6

Predict the genotypic and phenotypic results from each of the following crosses in garden peas:
(a) a tall (homozygous dominant) plant crossed with a dwarf plant;
(b) the progeny of (a) when self-pollinated;
(c) the progeny of (a) crossed with a homozygous tall plant;
(d) the progeny of (a) crossed with a dwarf plant.

SOLUTION:

(a) D — tall
     d — dwarf

   DD — homozygous tall
   Dd — heterozygous tall
   dd — homozygous dwarf

	D	D
d	Dd	Dd
d	Dd	Dd

Genotypic results: All Dd.
Phenotypic results: All tall.

(b) This part asks for a cross between two F₁ individuals:

Dd × *Dd*

	D	d
D	DD	Dd
d	Dd	dd

There are 4 different progeny. Of these 4, 1 is homozygous dominant, or *DD*; hence the fraction 1/4. The remaining fractions were obtained in a similar fashion.

Genotypic results: 1/4 *DD*; 1/2 *Dd*; 1/4 *dd*.
Phenotypic results: 3/4 tall; 1/4 dwarf.

(c) This part of the problem asks for the following cross:

Dd × *DD*.

	D	d
D	DD	Dd
D	DD	Dd

Genotypic results: 1/2 *DD*; 1/2 *Dd*.
Phenotypic results: All tall.

(d) This final part asks for a *Dd* × *dd* cross.

	D	d
d	Dd	dd
d	Dd	dd

Genotypic results: 1/2 *Dd*; 1/2 *dd*.
Phenotypic results: 1/2 tall; 1/2 dwarf.

From these results it can be seen that in order for a dwarf variety to be produced, both of the parents must carry the recessive allele, *d*.

If two fruit flies, heterozygous for genes of one allelic pair, were bred together and had 200 offspring a) about how many would have the dominant phenotype? b) of these offspring, some will be homozygous dominant and some heterozygous. How is it possible to establish which is which?

SOLUTION:

Let A be the dominant gene and a be the recessive gene. Since the flies are heterozygous, each must therefore be Aa.

a) In the cross, we have:

P Aa × Aa

Gametes $A; a$ ↓ $A; a$

F_1

	A	a
A	AA	Aa
a	Aa	aa

1 AA : 2 Aa : 1 aa

homozygous dominant: heterozygous: homozygous recessive

The proportion of offspring expressing the dominant phenotype is $1/4 + 2/4 = 3/4$. Therefore, the expected number with the dominant phenotype is $3/4$ x 200 or 150.

b) To establish which of the dominant phenotypes are homozygous and which are heterozygous, we have to perform a test cross; i.e., crossing one fly whose genotype is to be determined with a homozygous recessive fly. If the test fly is homozygous dominant:

P_2 AA × aa

Gamete A ↓ a

F_2 100% Aa

All the progeny will show the dominant phenotype. This implies that the test fly is homozygous dominant.

If the test fly is heterozygous, then in the back cross:

P_2 Aa × aa

Gamete A, a ↓ a

F_2 Aa ; aa

So half the progeny will show dominant phenotype and the other half will show recessive phenotype. This indicates that the test fly was heterozygous.

Therefore, by performing a test cross between a fly whose genotype we do not know and homozygous recessive fly, we can determine if the fly is homozygous or heterozygous by looking at the phenotypes of the progeny.

●PROBLEM 5-8

The checkered pattern of pigeons is controlled by a dominant gene C; plain color is determined by the recessive allele c. Red color is controlled by a dominant gene B, and brown color by the recessive allele b. Complete a Punnett square for a dihybrid cross involving a homozygous checkered red bird and a plain brown bird. For this cross, show the expected phenotypes, genotypes, genotypic frequencies, and phenotypic ratios for the F_2 generation.

P: CCBB × ccbb

Gametes: CB   cb

$F_1 × F_1$:   CcBb × CcBb

Gametes	CB	Cb	cB	cb
CB	CCBB	CCBb	CcBB	CcBb
Cb	CCBb	CCbb	CcBb	Ccbb
cB	CcBB	CcBb	ccBB	ccBb
cb	CcBb	Ccbb	ccBb	ccbb

SOLUTION:

This problem involves the Law of Independent Assortment — Mendel's Second Law. The law states that any pair of genes will segregate independently of all other pairs. Because of this, the results of an experiment involving several sets of characters may be obtained by multiplying the proportions expected for each factor when considered individually. The cross would result in the following:

Summary of F_2:

Phenotypes	Genotypes	Genotypic frequency	Phenotypic ratio
checkered red	CCBB	1	9
	CCBb	2	
	CcBB	2	
	CcBb	4	
checkered brown	CCbb	1	3
	Ccbb	2	
plain red	ccBB	1	3
	ccBb	2	
plain brown	ccbb	1	1

Normal-length fur in rabbits is controlled by the dominant allele R, and a short type of fur, called "rex," is determined by the recessive allele r. The dominant allele B controls black fur color; the recessive allele b controls brown.

(a) Diagram a dihybrid cross between a homozygous rabbit with normal-length black fur and a rex rabbit with brown fur. What are the phenotypic ratios resulting from this cross?

(b) What proportion of the normal, black rabbits in the F_2 generation of this cross can be expected to be homozygous for both pairs of genes?

(c) What would be the expected phenotypic and genotypic results of a backcross between a member of the F_1 generation and a fully recessive rex, brown parent?

P: BBRR   ×   bbrr

Gametes: BR   br

F_1:   BbRr

$F_1 \times F_1$:   BbRr   ×   BbRr

Gametes	BR	Br	bR	br
BR	BBRR	BBRr	BbRR	BbRr
Br	BBRr	BBrr	BbRr	Bbrr
bR	BbRR	BbRr	bbRR	bbRr
br	BbRr	Bbrr	bbRr	bbrr

Figure 1. Summary of F_2 phenotypes: 9 black, long: 3 black, rex: 3 brown, long: 1 brown, rex.

SOLUTION:

(a) This is an example of a typical dihybrid cross. Assuming the genotype of the homozygous black rabbit with normal length fur is $BBRR$ and that the genotype of the homozygous brown rex rabbit is $bbrr$, the results of the cross are shown in Figure 1. This 9:3:3:1 ratio is expected from all dihybrid crosses involving simple dominance.

(b) By scanning the above diagram, one counts 9 normal-furred black F_2 rabbits (either BB or Bb for fur color, and either RR or Rr for fur length, since normal-length fur and black color are dominant traits); of these, only one is homozygous for both traits — $BBRR$.

Total number of normal, black F_2 rabbits expected = 9
Number of these expected to be homozygous for both traits = 1
Ratio = 1/9
The proportion of normal, black rabbits that can be expected to be double homozygous is thus 1/9.
(c) Genotype of F_1 member — *BbRr*
Genotype of brown, rex parent — *bbrr*
The genotypic and phenotypic results of this back cross are:

BbRr x bbrr

Gametes	BR	Br	bR	br
br	BbRr	Bbrr	bbRr	bbrr

Figure 2. Summary of back cross results: 1 black, long: 1 black, rex: 1 brown, long: 1 brown rex.

● PROBLEM 5-10

In the common garden pea, *Pisum sativuum*, the alleles for tall plants, yellow seeds and round seeds — D, G, and W, respectively — are all dominant over the alleles for dwarf plants, green seeds, and wrinkled seeds — d, g, and w.
(a) A homozygous tall, yellow round plant and a dwarf, green, wrinkled plant are mated. Show all possible gametes from each parent and the F_1 generation.
(b) Using the forked line method, show a cross between two F_1 plants.
(c) Show the results of a cross between an F_1 plant and a dwarf, green, wrinkled parent by using the forked line method again. Give results for the phenotypes, the genotypes, the genotypic frequency, and the phenotypic ratio.

SOLUTION:

Virtually no two cross-fertilizing plants have the exact same combination of alleles. These plants usually differ in more than one or two pairs of alleles, and mating in natural breeding populations usually involves new combinations of many genes. Crosses between parents that differ at three gene loci — trihybrid crosses — are a combination of three monohybrid crosses operating together:

Tall — D; Dwarf — d
Yellow seed — G; Green seed — g
Round seed — W; Wrinkled seed — w

genotype of homozygous tall, yellow, round parent:
> *DDGGWW*

genotype of dwarf, green, wrinkled parent:
> *ddggww*

(a) A cross between a tall, yellow, round-seeded parent and a dwarf, green wrinkle-seeded parent is shown in Figure 1.

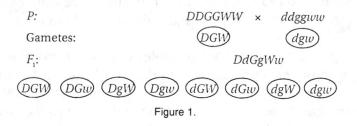

Figure 1.

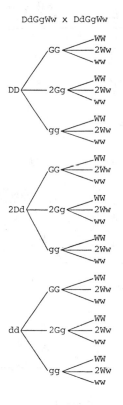

Summary of F_2 phenotypes:

27 tall, yellow, round
9 tall, yellow, wrinkled
9 tall, green, round
9 dwarf, yellow, round
3 tall, green, wrinkled
3 dwarf, yellow, wrinkled
3 dwarf, green, round
1 dwarf, green, wrinkled

Figure 2.

(b) The forked-line method is used here to visualize the segregation of alleles. All combinations are obtained by starting with one trait. For instance, by starting with the trait *Dd*, a cross of these parents would be *Dd* × *Dd*. The result of this could be *DD*, *Dd* or *dd*. Looking at only the next trait, the cross is *Gg* × *Gg*. This results in the genotypes *GG*, *Gg*, and *gg* in a 1:2:1 ratio. As shown in the diagram, each of these is connected to the first allele by a line, hence the name forked-line method. Each of the succeeding traits work in a similar manner until all are completed. This can be done for any number of traits.

By following a line from one set of alleles out to the end, the entire genotype can be determined. For example, starting at *DD* follow the line to *GG* and then to *WW*. The genotype of this pea plant would be *DDGGWW*. By following a different line from *GG*, we could get the genotype *DDGGww*. All the possible genotype combinations can then be found.

DdGgWw x ddggww
Summary of backcross results:

	Phenotypes	Genotypes	Genotypic frequency	Phenotypic ratio
Gg — Ww	tall, yellow, round	DdGgWw	1	1
Gg — ww	tall, yellow, wrinkled	DdGgww	1	1
gg — Ww	tall, green, round	DdggWw	1	1
gg — ww	tall, green, wrinkled	Ddggww	1	1
Gg — Ww	dwarf, yellow, round	ddGgWw	1	1
Gg — ww	dwarf, yellow, wrinkled	ddGgww	1	1
gg — Ww	dwarf, green, round	ddggWw	1	1
gg — ww	dwarf, green, wrinkled	ddggww	1	1

(Dd — top four rows; dd — bottom four rows)

Figure 3.

126

What are the possible gametes that can be formed from the following genotypes, assuming all the gene pairs segregate independently? What are the gamete frequencies?

(a) *AaBBCc*

(b) *DdEEffGg*

(c) *MmNnOo*

SOLUTION:

Mendel recognized quite early that the segregation of one pair of alleles is independent of the segregation of other pairs of alleles. Using the Law of Independent Assortment discussed in previous problems, let us consider an example: Let *AaBb* be a diploid double hybrid parent. *Aa* and *Bb* are separate pairs of alleles that will segregate to separate gametes independently of each other. Each gamete will get one allele for each trait, making it haploid. Four combinations are possible, see Figure 1.

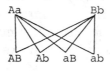

Figure 1.

These gametes occur in the following frequencies:

1/4 *AB*: 1/4 *Ab*: 1/4 *aB*: 1/4 *ab*

The gamete frequencies of all the genotypes given in the problem can be obtained similarly.

(a) The parental genotype is *AaBBCc*. If only the *A* and *B* loci are examined, *AB* and *aB* are possible in equal frequencies. One half the gametes will contain *AB* and one half will contain *aB*. Since the third locus also contains two different alleles, *C* and *c*, they will segregate so that 1/2 the gametes will have *C* and the other 1/2 *c*. There is a 50 percent change that any one gamete will contain *C*, and a 50 percent chance that it will contain *c*. Both types of gametes can combine with either *AB* or *aB*. The gamete frequencies for all three loci can be calculated by multiplying the chances of each individual frequency:

1/2 *AB* × 1/2 *C* → 1/4 *ABC*

1/2 *AB* × 1/2 *c* → 1/4 *ABc*

1/2 *aB* × 1/2 *C* → 1/4 *aBC*

1/2 *aB* × 1/2 *c* → 1/4 *aBc*

Each of the gamete types occurs 1/4 of the time, so there is a 25 percent chance of one gamete containing one of the four combinations of alleles.

(b) Since the parent contains homozygous genotypes of both *EE* and *ff*, the *Dd* trait is the only one that varies in segregation. There is a 50 percent chance of *D* segregating with *Ef* and a 50 percent chance of *d* segregating with *Ef*. But *E* has to segregate with *f* in both instances since both traits are homozygous. With this information, the following results are obtained:

Parent — *DdEEffGg*

1/2 *DEf*
  1/2 *G* → 1/4 *DEfG*
  1/2 *g* → 1/4 *DEfg*

1/2 *dEf*
  1/2 *G* → 1/4 *dEfG*
  1/2 *g* → 1/4 *dEfg*

The various gametes and frequencies would be:

1/4 *DEfG* : 1/4 *DEfg* : 1/4 *dEfG* : 1/4 *dEfg*

(c) This problem is slightly different since all three traits have heterozygous genotypes. Because of this there are more possible allele combinations. By drawing a diagram similar to that used in previous parts of this problem, but incorporating the third varying trait into it, we obtain the following:

Parent — *MnNnOo*

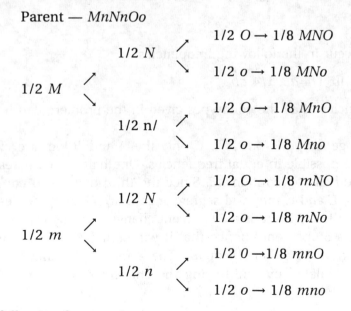

the following frequencies occur:

1/8 *MNO*; 1/8 *MNo*; 1/8 *MnO*; 1/8 *Mno*; 1/8 *MNO*; 1/8 *mNo*; 1/8 *mnO*; 1/8 *mno*.

Linking and Crossing Over

In snapdragons, plants homozygous for red have red flowers; those homozygous for white have white flowers, and those which are heterozygous have pink. If a pink flowered snapdragon is crossed with a white flowered plant, what will be the expected phenotypic results in the progeny?

SOLUTION:

This is a case of incomplete dominance. Red (R), White (R') Heterozygous pink individuals are RR'.

	Pink flowered		White flowered
Genotypes	RR'	×	$R'R'$
Types of gametes:	R R'		R' R'

Types of gametes

	R	R'
R'	RR'	$R'R'$
R'	RR'	$R'R'$

Phenotypic results:

1/2 $R'R$ pink

1/2 $R'R'$ white

Mendel believed that hereditary factors were always either dominant or recessive. How might he have altered this view had he performed the following cross? When pure line sweet peas with red flowers are crossed with pure line plants having white flowers, all the F_1 plants have pink flowers.

SOLUTION:

Let R be the gene for red color and W be the gene for white color. In the cross:

P	RR	×	WW
Gametes	R	↓	W
F₁		RW	
		pink	

After observing such a cross, Mendel could not have proposed the concepts of dominance or recessiveness, because there is evidence for neither in the results. It is possible that he might have proposed the idea of "blending"; saying that the heterozygous genotype is the result of a genotypic blending of the two alleles. This would be erroneous however, because the two alleles still act and separate independently. This could be evidenced if a cross between two F_1 plants were done:

P_2	RW	×	RW
Gametes	R; W	↓	R; W
	1 RR : 2 RW : 1 WW		

Two pink flowered plants have produced not only pink offspring, but also offspring having the red and white homozygous traits. Therefore the genes are still separating independently in the heterozygotes.

Mendel could have proposed that the two genes products interacted to form some sort of phenotypically blended product, but this is not exactly what occurs. If one looked closely at the pink flowers of the heterozygote, the independent action of each of the alleles is obvious. The pink color is not the result of some sort of blending to produce pink pigment, but results from the independent expressions of the red and the white pigments in the flower. The flower appears pink because of the interspersion of the red and white pigment granules in the petal.

The two alleles are said to be codominant. In such a case, neither allele is expressed in preference to the other. Each allele is capable of some degree of expression of its own trait in the heterozygous state.

●PROBLEM 5-14

What is epistasis? Distinguish between the terms epistasis and dominance.

SOLUTION:

Several genes are usually required to specify the enzymes involved in metabolic pathways leading to phenotypic expression. Each step in the pathway is catalyzed by different enzymes specified by different wild-type genes. Genetic interaction occurs whenever two or more genes specify enzymes involved in a common pathway. If any one of the genes is mutant, the pathway is blocked and genes after it in the pathway cannot have any phenotypic effect. We normally say that the mutant gene is *epistatic* to the suppressed gene.

Genotypes	A_B_	A_bb	aaB_	aabb
Classical ratio	9	3	3	1
Dominant epistasis	12		3	1
Recessive epistasis	9	3	4	
Duplicate genes with cumulative effect	9	6		1
Duplicate dominant genes	15			1
Duplicate recessive genes	9	7		
Dominant and recessive interaction	13		3	

When epistasis is involved in a dihybrid cross, the classical 9:3:3:1 ratio is modified into ratios which are various combinations of the classical groupings, resulting in less than four phenotypes. Six types of epistatic ratios are commonly recognized. A summary of them appears in the table.

Epistasis can involve any of these ratios. Examples of them will be shown in following problems.

Dominance involves *intra-allelic* gene suppression, where masking effects are seen between alleles at the same locus. Epistasis involves *inter-allelic* gene suppression between genes of different loci.

●PROBLEM 5-15

Two independently assorting loci, (c) and (a), control coat color in mice. Mice which are homozygous for recessive (c) cannot synthesize pigment, and thus have white hair (albino). Mice which are homozygous for (a) have completely black hair. It is thought that the (a) locus is involved in pigment placement, because in the case of (aa), melanin is distributed throughout the hair; but, when the dominant allele A is present, the melanin only goes to parts of the hair, resulting in a grayish coat called "agouti." Of course, this color cannot occur when the mice have the albino alleles, (cc), no matter what (a) alleles are present. Consider a cross between black with (CCaa) genotypes and white mice carrying (ccAA) genes. What are the phenotypic ratios for the F$_1$ and F$_2$ generations?

P: | black | × | albino

CCaa   ccAA

(Ca)   (cA)

F₁: agouti × agouti

CcAa   CcAa

F₂:

	(CA)	(Ca)	(cA)	(ca)
(CA)	CCAA agouti	CCAa agouti	CcAA agouti	CcAa agouti
(Ca)	CCAa agouti	CCaa black	CcAa agouti	Ccaa black
(cA)	CcAA agouti	CcAa agouti	ccAA albino	ccAa albino
(ca)	CcAa agouti	Ccaa black	ccAa albino	ccaa albino

Summary: 9/16 agouti, 3/16 black, 4/16 albino

SOLUTION:

When genes exhibit epistasis, the genotypes are exactly the same as in other multihybrid crosses. Only the phenotypic ratios are different. The Punnett square for the cross is shown in the diagram.

The F₁ progeny are all (CcAa). They express the agouti pattern because (Aa) is producing the pigment and (Cc) is distributing it to parts of the hairs.

F₂ progeny were classified as 9 agouti, 3 colored, and 4 albino. This is a recessive epistasis ratio. cc is epistatic to A_ in this case. The pigment-distributing gene (A) cannot be expressed because there is no pigment to distribute. (A_) is masked when (cc) is present and results in the same phenotype as (ccaa) does. This produces the 9:3:4 ratio.

●PROBLEM 5-16

Height in a certain plant species is controlled by two pairs of independently assorting alleles, with each participating allele A or B adding 5 cm to a base height of 5 cm. A cross is made between parents with genotype AABB and aabb. Disregarding environmental influences,
(a) What are the heights of each parent?
(b) What is the expected height of the members of the F₁ generation?
(c) What are the expected phenotypic ratios in the F₂ generation?

132

SOLUTION:

Base height = 5 cm
Since each allele contributes an additional 5 cm, we use the following formula:

Total height = (each effective allele × 5 cm) + base height

(a) Height of $AABB$ = (4 × 5 cm) + 5 cm

Height of $AABB$ = 25 cm

Height of $aabb$ = 0 + 5 cm

Height of $aabb$ = 5 cm

(b)   P: $AABB$ × $aabb$

Gametes: AB × ab

F_1: $AaBb$

Height of $AaBb$ = (2 × 5) + 5

= 15

(c) The possible F_2 progeny are:

	AB	Ab	aB	ab
AB	AABB	AABb	AaBB	AaBb
Ab	AABb	AAbb	AaBb	Aabb
aB	AaBB	AaBb	aaBB	aaBb
ab	AaBb	Aabb	aaBb	aabb

The genotypes and phenotypes of the F_2 can be arranged in tabular form.

Genotype	Number of Genes for Height	Fraction of F_2	Height
AABB	4	1/16	25
AABb, AaBB	3	4/16	20
AAbb, aaBB, AaBb	2	6/16	15
aaBb, Aabb	1	4/16	10
aabb	0	1/16	5

133

CHROMOSOMES

Structure

Describe the structure of a chromosome. What methods are used to study chromosomes?

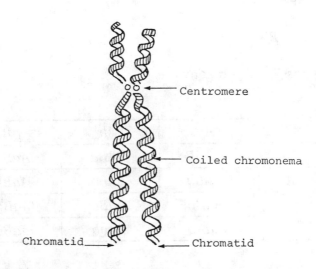

Figure 1. Chromsome structure

SOLUTION:

Chromosomes contain DNA, histone proteins, a small amount of RNA and the enzymes necessary for DNA and RNA synthesis. These chromosomes reside in the nucleus of cells in numbers and morphologies that are characteristic of each species. Humans have 23 pairs of chromosomes: two of these chromosomes determine the sex of the individual and are hence called sex chromosomes. The remaining 44 (or 22 pairs) are called autosomes. The structures of the chromosomes have been studied by various techniques including chemical analysis, X-ray diffraction, electron microscopy, and autoradiography. Individual chromosomes have also been studied by karyotype and banding techniques.

Chromosomes owe their linear structure to the linear nature of DNA. Each eukaryotic chromosome contains one DNA duplex molecule. This molecule twists and coils to produce the compact shape of the chromosomes seen during mitosis and meiosis. A chromosome also contains histone proteins. The

DNA complexes to a group of eight histone proteins (an octamer). The DNA winds around this bundle of protein to form a structure called a nucleosome. Electron micrographs have been produced that show these repeating structures to look like a string of beads if the chromosome is artificially stretched out. These protein complexes help to protect the DNA from degradation by nucleases in the nuclei.

The centromere region, described in a previous question, is the area of spindle fiber attachment (and possibly formation). See Figure 1. The centromere is necessary for chromosome transport towards a pole during nuclear division. Little is known about the chemical composition of the centromere since no method exists which is sensitive to the centromere region alone.

Further characteristics of chromosomal structure can be described through cytogenetic analysis. Chromosomes can be studied by karyotype technique and through various staining techniques. The karyotype technique permits the study of the complete chromosome set of a cell. Figure 2 shows this technique. Blood cells are first placed in a solution that stimulates mitosis. Colchicine is then added to stop mitosis at metaphase (colchicine disrupts the microtubules of the mitotic spindle). The white blood cells are separated and collected from the culture medium by centrifugation. A hypotonic solution (distilled water) is added to disperse the chromosomes and the cells are then fixed and spread on a slide. The slide is stained with various dyes and a selected cell is photo-

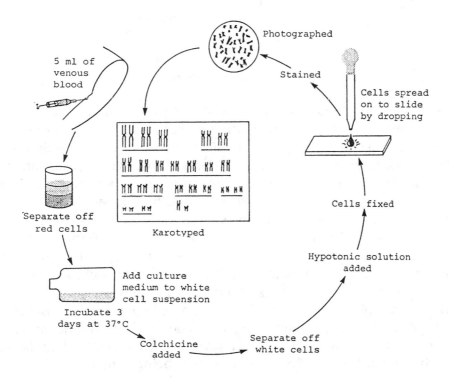

Figure 2. Preparation of a karyotype

135

graphed through a microscope. Each chromosome is then cut out and arranged by size, shape, and banding pattern. Karyotypes can be used to analyze abnormal chromosomal patterns and to correlate these patterns with clinical symptoms.

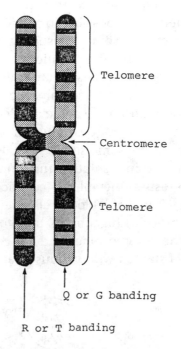

Figure 3. Chromosome banding

Karyotype analysis usually involves staining or banding techniques. Each chromosome produces a unique pattern of dark and light bands when stained with certain reagents. One reagent is Giemsa reagent. Giemsa stain reveals G-bands. G-bands have patterns almost identical to Q-bands which are a result of staining with quinacridine. Quinacridine inserts itself into the DNA duplex and produces fluorescent bands when excited by ultraviolet light. R- and T-banding techniques produce bands where G- and Q-banding techniques do not, see Figure 3. Thus, since G- and Q-bands do not form at the ends of chromosomes, R- and T-banding techniques can be used to detect terminal deletions. Through these banding techniques abnormal chromosomes of an individual can be detected. These banding techniques have also been used to study chromosomes comparatively. Differences between chromosomes of related species can be determined to aid in studies of an evolutionary nature.

Chromosomes have been analyzed in ways that reveal structural differences. In addition, the DNA of the chromosomes is being studied in detail. Eventually a correlation between DNA sequences and chromosome structure may be established. But there is much more research that has to be done before anything conclusive is accomplished.

●PROBLEM 5-18

What are the effects, if any, of changes in chromosomal structure? What are the various structural changes that can occur?

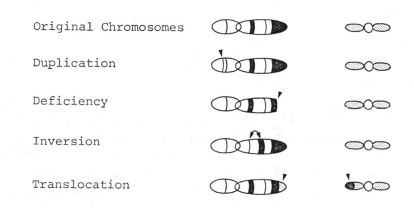

SOLUTION:

There are several events that result in a change in chromosomal structure. These changes are generally harmful and result in many debilitating syndromes in humans. The various structural changes that can occur are: duplications, deficiencies, inversions, and translocations.

I. Duplication
A duplication is the presence of an extra copy of a piece of chromosomal material. The duplication may be a result of unequal crossing over; such a cross-over would result in one chromosome with a duplication and one with a deficiency. Down's syndrome manifests itself only if one band of chromosome 21 is present in triplicate. Down's syndrome results in mongolism and a low resistance to disease.

II. Deficiency
A deficiency (or deletion) is the loss of a piece of genetic information. As mentioned earlier, deficiencies most commonly arise from unequal crossing over (see Figure 1). If there is a deficiency in the short arm of chromosome 5 in humans, cri-du-chat syndrome results. This syndrome includes severe mental retardation and a very cat-like cry in young infants.

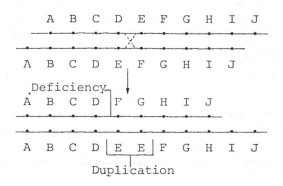

Deficiency for "E"
Duplication for "E

Figure 1.

III. Inversions

In inversions, the arrangement of the chromosomal material is changed, rather than the amount, as in duplications and deficiencies. Inversions occur when a chromosome is broken and the broken piece is reversed and reinserted. (See Figure 2.) Paracentric inversions are those which do not involve the centromere. Pericentric inversions do involve the centromere, and thus alter the morphology of the chromosome with respect to the location of the centromere. The karyotype has presumably evolved by such chromosomal changes.

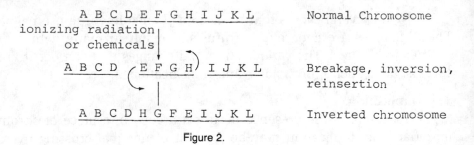

Figure 2.

IV. Translocations

Translocations involve the rearrangement of genetic material between nonhomologous chromosomes. Such exchanges are usually reciprocal, meaning that each chromosome both donates and receives a piece of chromosome. A person who carries a translocation could have one normal chromosome 14 and one normal chromosome 21 but also a chromosome that is a result of a fusion between chromosomes 14 and 21. This translocated chromosome is designated *t*(14; 21). This person may be phenotypically normal since he carries the full diploid set of chromosomes. When meiosis occurs however, some gametes will contain 14 but not 21 or 21 and *t*(14;21). Translocation Down's syndrome can appear in one of this person's offspring if a gamete 21 + *t*(14;21) fuses with a normal gamete containing 14 and 21 since there will be 3 copies of chromosome 21.

These chromosomal aberrations are not always deleterious. For instance, small duplications may become advantageous. Resistance to pesticides and antibiotics may arise by duplications of the genes that produce the gene products that are susceptible to the substance. Duplications are also important substrates through which mutations can occur. Since the cell contains a complete genetic complement plus a duplication, a mutation in the duplication will not adversely affect the organism's survival. Mutations of these types are a means through which evolution can occur.

●PROBLEM 5-19

How are chromosomal breaks produced? What factors modify these breaks?

SOLUTION:

Energy is required to disrupt the relatively stable chromosome. Any form of high energy radiation can provide sufficient energy to break a chromosome. Factors such as radiation frequency, ion density, length of exposure, and chromosome state can determine how effectively a chromosome is broken.

The effective power depends on the frequency of the radiation. Higher frequency radiation, such as ultraviolet light, is more effective than the lower frequency visible light. X-rays and gamma rays, having even higher frequencies than ultraviolet rays, are much more effective chromosome breakers.

Another factor that influences the breakage is the length and density of the ion track which varies according to the type of ionizing radiation. Ions break the chromosome by breaking bonds between atoms. Molecules are formed by shared atomic electrons. Ionizing radiation knocks out the electrons, thus ionizing the affected atom. If the electrons that are knocked out are those that are shared in a molecule, then the molecule will no longer hold together. Thus, the more concentrated the track of ions, the more harmful the radiation is to chromosomal molecules. Ion clusters can also produce more than one break in a chromosome by attacking it in separate, independent tracks. Such rearrangements show a breakage frequency that is faster than the dosage; these are non-linear relationships. These rearrangements also show a threshold dose.

When chromosomes are broken by radiation, "sticky" ends are produced. These ends are capable of rejoining. If the rejoining of ends can take place so that normal chromosomes are reformed (this is known as restitutional union), prolonging the delivery of the radiation will reduce the frequency of such rejoinings. Thus, when irradiated for longer stretches of time, the chromosomes are unable to rejoin properly resulting in more abnormal chromosomes.

The physio-chemical state of the chromosomes and other cellular structures also modifies the frequency of breakage. The type of structural change depends on the mass of chromosomal material present in the nucleus and upon the numbers and sizes of the chromosomes.

Polyploidy and Aneuploidy

●PROBLEM 5-20

What are the terms that describe variations in the number of chromosomes?

SOLUTION:

Variations in chromosome number are described by the terms euploidy and aneuploidy. Euploidy describes the existence of the entire set of chromosomes in multiples. Aneuploidy describes additions and deletions of only parts of the chromosomal set.

I. Euploidy
The following is a list of the different types of euploidy:

Euploidy type	Chromosome sets
1. Haploid	One (n)
2. Diploid	Two (2n)
3. Polyploid	More than two
a. Triploid	Three (3n)
b. Tetraploid	Four (4n)
c. Pentaploid	Five (5n)
d. Hexaploid	Six (6n)

Haploidy is the normal state of gametes. Diploidy is the state of zygotes, higher plants, and animals. Polyploidy is of agricultural importance since polyploid plants have greater vigor, larger flowers, and larger fruits than diploid plants. Polyploidy in animals usually results in sterility since animals contain differentiated sex chromosomes. Fertility seems to depend on a delicate balance between the numbers of sex chromosomes and the numbers of autosomes — polyploidy upsets this balance.

There are two types of polyploidy: autopolyploidy and allopolyploidy. Autopolyploidy refers to polyploidy when all of the chromosome sets are homologous. Allopolyploidy refers to nonhomologous chromosome sets that arise from different species. Figure 1 shows two ways that autopolyploidy is produced: the first case is when two or more sperm fertilize an egg; the second case is when mitosis fails to separate chromosomes.

140

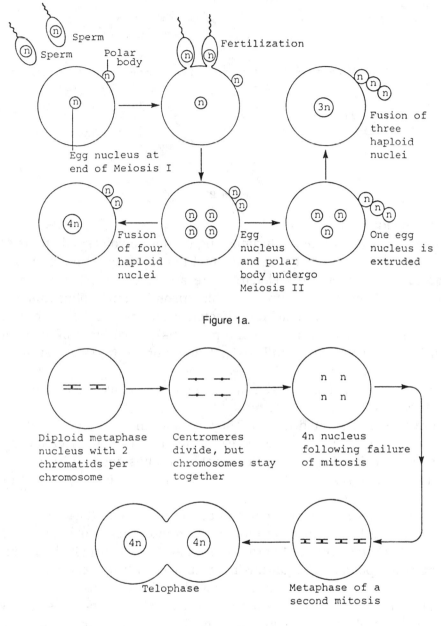

Figure 1a.

Figure 1b.

Allopolyploidy describes nonhomologous chromosome sets that are contributed by different species. Since the chromosomes of different species are essentially nonhomologous, chromosome pairing in meiosis is absent. The chromosomes are distributed randomly to the gametes. This leads to sterility. But, if a mitotic failure producing tetraploidy (4n) occurs, meiosis will proceed normally since each chromosome has something to pair with. Figure 2 shows a summary of allopolyploidy.

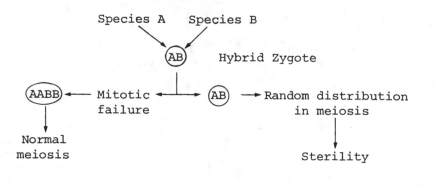

Figure 2.

II. Aneuploidy

Another type of variance in chromosome number involves only parts of the chromosome set. This is called aneuploidy. In aneuploidy some chromosomes are copied while others are deleted. There are several types of aneuploidy: monosomic, trisomic, tetrasomic, double trisomic, and nullosomic. These names refer to the number of the affected chromosome. Monosomics are diploids missing one chromosome of a pair $(2n-1)$. Two types of gametes are formed by monosomics: (n) and $(n-1)$. The abnormal $(n-1)$ gametes usually do not function in plants.

In animals $(n-1)$ gametes result in a genetic imbalance which shows itself through reduced fertility or high mortality.

Trisomics are designated $(2n+1)$. They contain an extra copy of one chromosome. They can create (n) and $(n+1)$ gametes. The $(n+1)$ gametes have various phenotypic effects depending on the chromosome that is in triplicate. In humans, this may be deleterious; Down's syndrome is a result of an extra copy of chromosome 21.

Tetrasomics have two extra copies of one chromosome $(2n+2)$. Double trisomics $(2n+1+1)$ have two extra different chromosomes. Nullosomics $(2n-2)$ have completely lost a pair of chromosomes and this is usually lethal in diploids; however, polyploid organisms may survive, with reduced vitality, when nullosomic. Their survival is due to their additional chromosome copies.

Variance in chromosome number is a way in which organisms can evolve genetic and, therefore, phenotypic changes. Thus, these changes can result in increased adaptability of the organism.

What is the genetic basis of Down's syndrome?

SOLUTION:

Down's syndrome occurs in approximately one of every 600 live births, and the syndrome increases in frequency as the age of the mother at parturition increases. Usually, the syndrome is a result of trisomy of chromosome 21. The relationship between maternal age and incidence of Down's syndrome suggests that nondisjunction occurs more often in older egg cells. Recall that the human egg cell remains in a diplotene state from the fetal stage onward. It is possible that egg cells in older women are simply more prone to mechanical difficulties.

About 10 percent of the cases of Down's syndrome are caused by a translocation. The translocation chromosome arises as a fusion between chromosomes 14 and 21. A woman who has such a translocation has a normal chromosome 14 and a normal chromosome 21. She also has the translocated chromosome which is designated $t(14;21)$. She will be phenotypically normal since she has a full diploid set of chromosomes. However, in meiosis, synaptic pairing is asymmetric and hence the orientation of the spindle can become abnormal. Such a woman may produce eggs that have chromosome 14 but not chromosome 21, 21 but not 14, 21 and $t(14;21)$ or 14 and $t(14;21)$. If an egg with the constitution 21 and $t(14;21)$ is fertilized by a normal sperm containing both chromosomes 14 and 21, Down's syndrome will be the result. The child will have the 3 copies of chromosome 21 necessary to display Down's syndrome.

● **PROBLEM 5-22**

What is the F_1 phenotypic ratio in the jimson weed, *Datura stramonium,* when a purple female (*PPp*) is crossed with a purple male (*PPp*)?

PPp ♀ x PPp ♂

gametes: P, P, Pp, Pp, PP, p   P, P, p

Female gametes

		2P	2Pp	PP	P
Male gametes	2P	PP 4	PPp 4	PPP 2	Pp 2
	p	Pp 2	Ppp 2	PPp 1	pp 1

143

This problem involves a cross between two individuals that have three alleles for the color of their flowers. Since they have three alleles, they probably have the rest of the chromosomes to go with them. They are, therefore, trisomic. Jimson weed plants that are trisomic in their flower color allele have an extra copy of chromosome 9. In this gene purple is dominant over white. But since these are trisomics, the alleles will not segregate in the usual 3:1 Mendelian ratio, as will be seen.

The female plant produces P, Pp, PP, and p megaspores. The male, on the other hand, only produces functional P and p pollen; pollen with more or less than the normal 12 chromosomes will be nonfunctional.

The cross is shown above.

By counting the numbers of similar progeny, a genotypic ratio of $4PP:4Pp:5PPp:2Ppp:2PPP:1pp$ is obtained. The presence of one or more P alleles is expressed phenotypically as purple flowers. White flowers are only expressed in plants homozygous for the recessive p allele. Thus, the phenotypic ratio is 17 purple:1 white.

SEX DETERMINATION AND SEX LINKAGE

Sex Determination

●PROBLEM 5-23

Explain the mechanism of the genetic determination of sex in man.

SOLUTION:

The sex chromosomes are an exception to the general rule that the members of a pair of chromosomes are identical in size and shape and carry allelic pairs. The sex chromosomes are not homologous chromosomes. In man, the cells of females contain two identical sex chromosomes, or X chromosomes. In males there is only one X chromosome and a smaller Y chromosome with which the X pairs during meiotic synapsis. Men have 22 pairs of ordinary chromosomes (autosomes), plus one X and one Y chromosome, and women have 22 pairs of autosomes plus two X chromosomes.

Thus, it is the presence of the Y chromosome which determines that an individual will be male. Although the mechanism is quite complex, we know that the presence of the Y chromosome stimulates the gonadal medulla, or sex organ, forming a portion of the egg to develop into male gonads, or sex organs. In the absence of the Y chromosome, and in the presence of two X chromosomes, the medulla develops into female gametes. (Note: a full complement of two X chromosomes is needed for normal female development.)

In man, since the male has one X and one Y chromosome, two types of sperm, or male gametes, are produced during spermatogenesis (the process of sperm formation, which includes meiosis). One half of the sperm population contains an X chromosome and the other half contains a Y chromosome. Each egg, or female gamete, contains a single X chromosome. This is because a female has only X chromosomes, and meiosis produces only gametes with X chromosomes. Fertilization of the X-bearing egg by an X-bearing sperm results in an XX, or female offspring. The fertilization of an X-bearing egg by a Y-bearing sperm results in an XY, or male offspring. Since there are approximately equal numbers of X- and Y-bearing sperm, the numbers of males and females born in a population are nearly equal.

●PROBLEM 5-24

How do chromosomal variations influence sex determination in humans?

SOLUTION:

Chromosomal variations in humans result in intermediate sex individuals. Most of the variants are associated with chromosomal abnormalities involving either an excess or a deficiency of sex chromosomes. With modern techniques it is possible to observe and count human chromosomes accurately. Numbers above and below the usual 46 can be detected. One in every 200 newborns has been shown to have a numerical chromosome irregularity.

The most common sex chromosome anomalies are Turner's syndrome and Klinefelter's syndrome. Turner's syndrome occurs in one out of every 2,000 births. These individuals have 45 chromosomes, and are monosomic for the X chromosome; they are XO. They are short in stature and usually have webbed necks. They are sexually infantile, and often have primary amenorrhea in addition to a failure to develop signs of puberty. Plasma concentrations of follicle stimulating hormone (FSH) and luteinizing hormone (LH) are elevated. The patients lack ovaries, accounting for the failure to develop sexually. Since they have only one X chromosome, buccal smears show no Barr bodies. Therefore, they cannot be distinguished from the cell prepara-

145

tion of a male.

A person with Klinefelter's syndrome has an XXY karyotype and shows male characteristics even though his cells contain Barr bodies. It is sometimes difficult to distinguish these individuals from normal males, although they usually have small testes and are below normal in intelligence. Pubic hair and fat distribution may also follow a female pattern. They are usually sterile.

Other chromosomal variations influencing sex determination have been reported. Males with XXXY, XXYY, and XXXXXY chromosomes are known to exist, as are females with XXX, XXXX, and XXXXX chromosomes. The presence of a Y chromosome is usually linked with "maleness"; the absence of it will lead to an individual with female characteristics.

● PROBLEM 5-25

Chromosomes in which one arm has been deleted and replaced by a piece identical to the remaining arm are called isochromosomes.
(a) Explain how this might occur.
(b) What are the consequences of carrying one normal X chromosome and either the long-arm isochromosome of $X(X^L.X^L)$ or the short-arm isochromosome of $X(X^S. X^S)$?
(c) What are the consequences of carrying one normal X and the isochromosome $Y^L.Y^L$ or $Y^S.Y^S$?

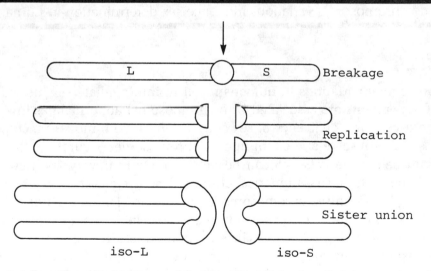

Figure 1. Formation of isochromosomes following centromeric breakage and chromosome replication

146

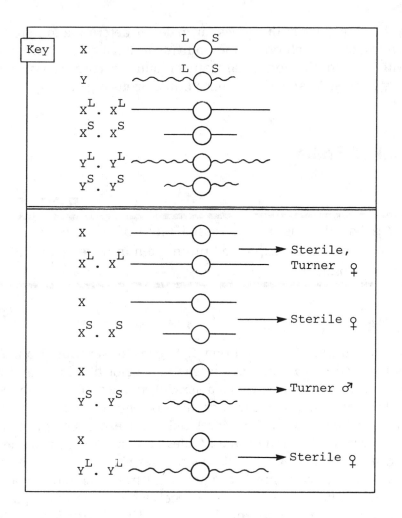

Figure 2.

SOLUTION:

(a) Chromosomes can undergo any one of several types of breakage rearrangement. If breakage occurs near or within the centromere, and sister ends fuse after replication, isochromosomes (chromosomes made up of identical lengthwise halves) are made. This process is shown in Figure 1.

(b) Persons who carry either $X^L.X^L$ or $X^S.X^S$ isochromosomes (Figure 2) along with a normal X chromosome are sterile females. X^LX^L individuals appear to have typical Turner's syndrome, while X^SX^S females do not have the nonsexual features of Turner's syndrome, such as the neck webbing and short stature. Because of this, the nonsexual features of Turner's syndrome have been attributed to the loss of genetic material in X^S.

(c) Phenotypic females result when the $Y^L.Y^L$ isochromosome is accompanied by a normal X. Because no nonsexual features of Turner's syndrome are

147

present, it is thought that the genes for male sex determination are mainly in the short-arm of the Y chromosome. Individuals having XYˢ.Yˢ are phenotypic males with many of the nonsexual features found in Turner's syndrome. This is possibly because Y^L and X^s may have homologous regions.

Sex-Linked Traits

Some sex-linked traits are expressed more often in females than in males, while others are expressed more often in males than in females. How is this possible?

SOLUTION:

The X chromosome carries not only the genes for sex, but also many other genes not related to sex, such as the gene for color blindness and the gene for hemophilia. Such genes are called sex-linked, because they are located on the sex chromosome. The Y chromosome does not carry any genes that we know of other than those which are related to the expression of the male sex.

Females have two X chromosomes. Males have one X chromosome and one Y chromosome. Each individual inherits one sex chromosome from each parent; thus, a female gets one X chromosome from her mother and one X chromosome from her father. A male receives an X chromosome from his mother and a Y chromosome from his father. (His mother cannot give him a Y chromosome since she only has X chromosomes to give.)

Since the genes for sex-linked traits are carried only in the X chromosome, it follows that a female would have twice the chance of receiving a sex-linked gene than would a male, because she receives two X chromosomes, while a male receives only one. Thus, a female has a chance to receive a sex-linked gene if either of her parents carry that gene. A male, however, could only receive such a gene from his mother, even if his father carried that gene on his X chromosome.

Although a female has a greater chance than a male of receiving a sex-linked gene, the chance that either of them will express the trait coded for by that gene varies according to the dominant, or recessive, nature of the gene.

For example, if the gene for sex-linked trait is dominant, that trait would be more commonly expressed in females than in males. Because it is dominant, only one copy of the gene is necessary for its expression. Since females have a greater chance of receiving a copy of a sex-linked gene, they have a greater chance of expressing its trait.

148

If a sex-linked trait is recessive, a male would have a greater chance of expressing the trait. In order for a female to express that trait, she would have to have two copies of the recessive gene, because its expression would be masked by the presence of a normal X chromosome or one with a dominant allele. Thus, both her parents would have to carry the gene. A male, however, need only have one copy of the gene in order to express its trait, because his Y chromosome does not carry any genes that would mask the recessive gene. So only his mother need carry the gene. The chances of this happening are much greater than the chance that two people carrying the gene will mate and have a female, so the trait is more commonly expressed in males.

It is important to note that females still have a greater chance of receiving a single copy of a recessive gene, although they may not express it. Such individuals are called carriers, and their frequency in the population is greater than that of individuals expressing the trait, be they male or female.

●PROBLEM 5-27

Vitamin D-resistant rickets is produced by an X-linked dominant allele. Two recessive alleles together will lead to normal bone development. What are the expected results from the following crosses?
(a) A normal woman and a man with Vitamin D-resistant rickets.
(b) A normal man and a woman with the condition who has a normal father.

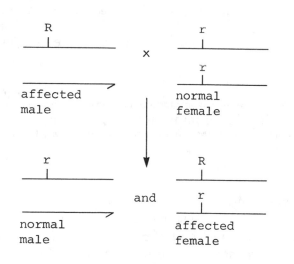

SOLUTION:

The common form of rickets usually occurs in infants or children because of low levels of Vitamin D. Vitamin D-resistant rickets, caused by a mutant

X-linked dominant allele, is resistant to normal treatment. Exceptionally large amounts of calcium and Vitamin D must be given to treat it.

Mutant X-linked traits which are dominant are seen in both males and females whenever they carry the mutant allele. Affected females will transmit the allele to 1/2 of all their offspring while affected males can only give the alleles to their daughters.

(a) Letting R represent the mutant allele and r the recessive normal allele, the diagram on the previous page would result.

In this type of problem, _____ represents a Y chromosome. __R__ stands for X chromosome with the rickets disorder and __r__ stands for an X chromosome with a normal allele. All of the males from this cross would be normal, and all of the females would have the disorder.

(b) Similarly, the solution for question (b) is:

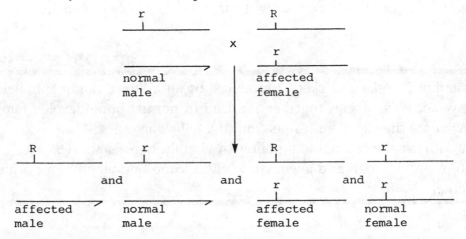

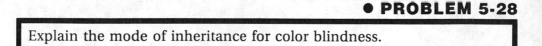

Fifty percent of the males and fifty percent of the females will be affected.

● PROBLEM 5-28

Explain the mode of inheritance for color blindness.

SOLUTION:

Color blindness is one of the most common genetic disorders that occurs in the human race. About eight percent of males in the U.S. are red-green color defective. The trait for color blindness is caused by a recessive gene located on the X chromosome. Since the Y chromosome does not contain an allele for this gene, men are hemizygous for either the normal allele or the color-defective one. Because of this, the usual "dominant" and "recessive" terms do not apply in males. Whichever allele is present is expressed. The terms can be used in females since they have two X chromosomes. Because it is a recessive gene, a woman heterozygous for the trait will be phenotypically normal.

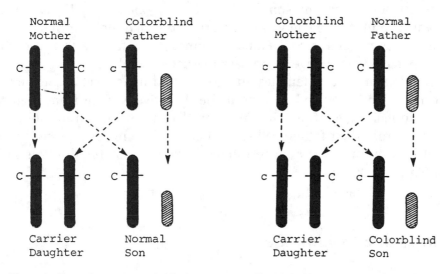

Figure 1. Normal woman × colorblind man

Figure 2. Normal woman × normal man

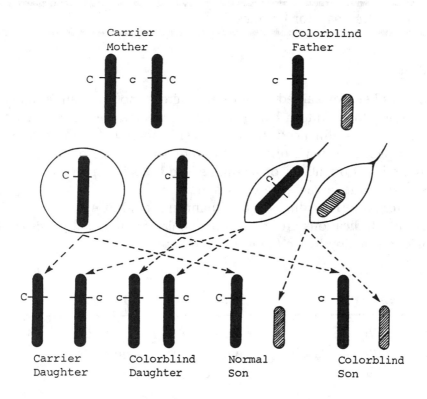

Figure 2. Carrier woman × colorblind man

Females heterozygous for color blindness will pass the mutant gene on to 1/2 of their children. Males who get this allele will be color blind because, possessing only one X chromosome, this is the only allele they have. Female children with the mutant allele will be heterozygous like their mother as long as the father has normal vision. Females homozygous for the trait are rare, since both parents would have to possess the defective allele.

The daughters of normal females and color blind males will all be carriers with normal vision. They will all inherit the defective X gene from their father and a normal X gene from their mother. Because males do not inherit X chromosomes from their fathers, all sons of color blind males and normal females will have normal vision. The transmission of color blindness is illustrated in Figures 1, 2, and 3.

Variations of Sex Linkage

Is there a genetic basis for baldness?

SOLUTION:

Baldness has been explained by several different modes of inheritance by different investigators. Pattern baldness appears to be a sex-influenced trait. Genes governing sex-influenced traits may reside on any of the autosomes or on the homologous portions of the sex chromosomes. The dominant or recessive properties of the alleles of sex-influenced traits is dependent upon the sex of the bearer, due largely to sex hormones.

The gene for pattern baldness is dominant in men, but exhibits recessiveness in women. Indications are that a single pair of autosomal genes control pattern baldness, acting in the following fashion:

Genotype	Male	Female
BB	bald	bald
Bb	bald	nonbald
bb	nonbald	nonbald

The allele seems to exert its effect only in the presence of testosterone.

In *Drosophila melanogaster*, the gene for white eyes, w, is recessive and X-linked. Red eyes result from the wild-type allele at this locus.

(a) On chromosomes, symbolize the genotypes of a white-eyed male, a red-eyed female (both possible types), and a white-eyed female.

(b) Diagram a cross between a homozygous red-eyed female and white-eyed male. Carry this to the F_2 generation and give phenotype ratios for each sex.

(c) Show a cross between an F_1 female and white-eyed male. Give phenotype ratios.

(d) Show a cross between an F_1 female and wild-type male. Also give ratios.

(a) $\dfrac{w}{\longrightarrow}$, $\dfrac{w^+}{\longrightarrow}$, $\dfrac{w^+}{w^+}$, and $\dfrac{w^+}{w}$, $\dfrac{w}{w}$.

(b) $\dfrac{w^+}{w^+} \times \dfrac{w}{\longrightarrow}$ P

$\dfrac{w^+}{\quad}$ $\dfrac{w}{\quad}$ $\dfrac{}{\longrightarrow}$ gametes

$\dfrac{w}{w^+}$ $\dfrac{w^+}{\longrightarrow}$ $F^1 \times F^1$ (all red-eyed)

$\dfrac{w}{\quad}$ $\dfrac{w^+}{\quad}$ $\dfrac{w^+}{\quad}$ $\dfrac{}{\longrightarrow} F^2$ gametes

$\dfrac{w}{w^+}$ $\dfrac{w^+}{w^+}$ F^2 females, all red-eyed

$\dfrac{w}{\longrightarrow}$ $\dfrac{w^+}{\longrightarrow}$ F males, 1/2 red, 1/2 white

(c) $\dfrac{w}{w^+} \times \dfrac{w}{\longrightarrow}$ females, 1/2 red, 1/2 white; males, 1/2 red, 1/2 white

(d) $\dfrac{w}{w^+} \times \dfrac{w^+}{\longrightarrow}$ females, all red males, 1/2 red, 1/2 white

SOLUTION:

X-chromosomes are usually represented by a "——" and Y chromosomes by a "——→". Since only X chromosomes carry this gene, letters symbolizing the eye color gene are only on the "——". Crosses are then completed in the usual way.

SHORT ANSWER QUESTIONS FOR REVIEW

Choose the correct answer.

1. Two mice with long tails were mated. The offspring consisted of 32 mice with long tails and 9 mice with short tails. We can determine that _____ is the dominant trait, and given L represents long tail and L represents short tails the genotype of each parent was _____. (a) short tails, LL (b) long tails, LL (c) short tails, Ll (d) long tails, Ll

2. A cross between a homozygous dominant tall pea plant and a homozygous recessive dwarf pea plant would yield (a) $4DD$ (b) $1DD$, $2Dd$, $1dd$ (c) $4Dd$ (d) $3Dd$, $1DD$.

3. A phenotypic ratio of 9:3:3:1 can be expected when crossing (a) any parental strains. (b) $F_1 \times F_1$ heterozygotes with two pairs of factors being determined. (c) $F_2 \times F_1$ heterozygotes with two pairs of factors being determined. (d) $P \times F_2$ with three pairs of factors being determined.

4. In lima beans, green color is dominant over yellow color. A cross between a pure green bean and a pure yellow bean yields 40 hybrid beans. A cross between two of these hybrid beans yielded 80 F_2 beans. How many of these F_2 beans should be green? (a) 40 (b) 50 (c) 60 (d) 80

5. A cross between a homozygous tall pea plant (DD) and a heterozygous tall pea plant (Dd) should yield (a) one homozygous tall, two heterozygous tall, one homozygous dwarf. (b) two homozygous tall, two heterozygous tall. (c) one homozygous tall, three heterozygous tall. (d) four heterozygous tall.

6. If a hybrid purple radish plant of genotype RR' is crossed with another hybrid plant of identical genotype, the observed phenotypic ratio is one red : two pink : one white. What can be concluded from this ratio? (a) There was no crossing over. (b) Genes assort independently. (c) A mutation in the gene locus for color produced red and white flowers. (d) None of the above.

7. Mice with the genotypes *BB* and *Bb* are black, and those with the genotype *bb* are brown. At another locus the genotypes *CC* and *cc* code for color while the homozygous recessive genotype *cc* codes for albinism. What phenotypic ratio would be expected from a cross between two mice with the genotype *BbCc*? (a) 9 black : 3 brown : 4 albino (b) 12 black : 3 brown : 1 albino (c) 9 black : 6 brown : 1 albino (d) 9 black : 0 brown : 7 albino

8. A 15:1 phenotypic ratio is observed in an F_2 generation. This ratio is characteristic of (a) duplicate recessive epistasis. (b) recessive epistasis. (c) duplicate dominant epistasis. (d) both **a** and **b** (e) None of the above

9. Chromosomes lack which of the following items? (a) DNA (b) centrioles (c) histones (d) RNA

10. Of the 23 pairs of chromosomes present in humans, what is the number of autosomal pairs? (a) 20 (b) 21 (c) 22 (d) 23

11. Ions break chromosomes by (a) causing them to fracture during replication. (b) allowing disjunction of certain genes. (c) adding electrons to the chromosomes to increase the charge. (d) breaking bonds between atoms.

12. Which of the following terms represents the euploidy state of gametes? (a) diploid (b) haploid (c) polyploid (d) tetraploid

13. Autopolyploidy refers to (a) polyploidy when all chromosomes are homologous. (b) polyploidy with non-homologous chromosomes from different species. (c) the normal state of human gametes. (d) None of the above

14. An advantage to creating polyploid and diploid nuclei in plants is (a) creating sterile hybrids. (b) producing a larger quantity of less desirable mutations. (c) producing more desirable phenotypes. (d) decreasing the economic value of products grown on these plants.

15. Down's syndrome is usually the result of (a) nullosomy of chromosome 14. (b) tetrasomy of chromosome 21. (c) double trisomy of chromosomes 14 and 21. (d) trisomy of chromosome 21.

16. In the jimson weed, purple flower color is dominant over white. If a purple male of genotype *PPp* is crossed with a female of the same genotype, what would be the phenotypic ratio of the progeny? (a) 3 purple : 1 white (b) 1 purple : 3 white (c) 17 purple : 1 white (d) 1 purple : 17 white

17. Which one of the following statements does not apply to human sex chromosomes? Human sex chromosomes (a) carry allelic pairs. (b) determine individual sex. (c) are identical in women. (d) are identical in men. (e) both **a** and **d**

18. The Y chromosome determines that an individual will be male by (a) stimulating the sex organs to become male gonads. (b) stimulating the brain to secrete male hormones. (c) inducing the X chromosome to cease estrogen production. (d) destroying one X chromosome.

19. Barr bodies result from (a) inactivation of one X chromosome by the Y chromosome. (b) a third X chromosome. (c) inactivation of one X chromosome for dosage compensation. (d) both **b** and **c**

20. A man and a woman are both affected by vitamin D resistant rickets which is a dominant sex-linked allele. All of the female offspring of these people are affected with rickets, but some of the males are not. What are the possible genotypes of the parents? (a) Both are homozygous for the trait. (b) The woman is heterozygous and the man is homozygous. (c) The woman is homozygous, and the man is heterozygous. (d) None of the above.

21. Pseudohypertrophic muscular dystrophy is a disease determined by a sex-linked recessive allele. What are the possible genotypes of a woman and man whose offspring are all affected with this disease? (a) Woman is homozygous dominant and man is heterozygous. (b) Woman is homozygous recessive and man is homozygous dominant. (c) Woman is homozygous recessive and man is heterozygous recessive. (d) None of the above.

22. The fly *Drosophila melanogaster* has the gene that codes for white eyes as recessive and X-linked. Red eyes result from the wild type allele at the same locus. A cross between a heterozygous red eyed female and a white eyed male would produce (a) all red eyed progeny. (b) all white eyed males and all red eyed females. (c) one red eyed male and one white eyed male. (d) one red eyed female and one white eyed female. (e) Both **c** and **d**

23. The gene for pattern baldness is dominant in men, but exhibits recessiveness in women. The difference in expression results from (a) the gene for baldness being X-linked. (b) the gene for baldness being Y-linked. (c) the expression of the gene depending upon the hormonal balance of the individual. (d) Both **a** and **c** (e) None of the above

Fill in the blanks.

24. The ratio of 12:3:1 obtained from a dihybrid cross is indicative of the presence of _____ epistatic genes.

25. The ratio of 9:3:4 expresses a _____ epistatic interaction.

26. In an epistatic interaction between two gene loci, the number of phenotypes that would be expressed is less than _____.

27. Using the _____ technique, the complete set of chromosomes of a cell can be studied.

28. _____ is required to cause a break in the structure of the relatively stable chromosome.

Determine whether the following statements are true or false.

29. Epistatic genotypes are exactly the same as the genotypes produced in multiple hybrid crosses.

30. If an allele is not dominant then it must be recessive.

31. Higher frequency radiation, such as x-ray, is less effective than radiation of a lower frequency in disrupting the structure of the chromosome.

32. When a chromosome is broken, the ends are incapable of rejoining.

33. Since two X ova are produced for every Y sperm, the number of females born in a population is twice the number of males born.

34. Barr bodies are found in all tissues of a female mammal that has two or more X-chromosomes.

35. A person with Klinefelter's Syndrome has an XXY karyotype and is usually a phenotypically sterile male.

36. Sex-linked traits are carried mostly on the X chromosome. Since females have two X chromosomes, they have twice the chance of expressing a recessive sex-linked trait.

37. Color blindness is an inherited disorder produced by a sex-linked recessive allele.

ANSWER KEY

1. d	2. c	3. b
4. c	5. b	6. d
7. a	8. c	9. b
10. c	11. d	12. b
13. a	14. c	15. d
16. c	17. e	18. a
19. c	20. b	21. c
22. e	23. c	24. dominant
25. recessive	26. four	27. karyotype
28. Energy	29. True	30. False
31. False	32. False	33. False
34. True	35. True	36. False
37. True		

CHAPTER 6

HEREDITY

The Gene

What experimental evidence indicates that genes control the amino acid sequences in proteins?

SOLUTION:

In 1953, the first amino acid sequence of a protein was completed. After six years, Frederick Sanger had succeeded in sequencing the amino acid sequence of a relatively small protein, insulin. He used different proteolytic enzymes to cleave the protein molecule into fragments that could be sequenced more easily than the large molecule. Many of the fragments had overlapping sequences, so the linear order of the whole insulin molecule could be pieced together. This showed that the amino acid sequence is what individualizes proteins. Insulin is insulin because of its specific amino acid sequence.

Vernon Ingram chose a well-studied inherited disorder, sickle-cell anemia. In 1957, he sequenced normal hemoglobin (HbA) and sickled hemoglobin (HbS). He compared the amino acid sequences and found a difference of one amino acid. This connected the abnormal amino acid sequence of a protein to an inherited, and hence, genetic disorder.

Ingram's discovery was proof that a mutation in a gene resulted in an abnormal amino acid sequence in a protein. But, as in almost all experimentation, he had to use techniques pioneered by others. The sequencing technique developed by Sanger was very important in the determination of a link between genes and amino acid sequences in proteins.

Give the following sequence of nucleotides for a single strand of DNA:
5'——A A A T C G A T T G C G C T A T C G——3'
Construct the complementary sequence that would be incorporated
during replication to complete the double helix of DNA molecule.

SOLUTION:

Since there is specific complementary pairing between A-T or T-A and between G-C or C-G, the complementary sequence of nucleotides will be:
3'——T T T A G C T A A C G C G A T A G C——5'

A DNA molecule has 180 base pairs and is 20 percent adenine. How
many cytosine nucleotides are present in this molecule of DNA?

SOLUTION:

In DNA, the complementary pairing between bases is always A-T (T-A) and
G-C (C-G). Thus, if 20 percent of the nucleotides are adenine, then the total
composition of A-T will be 40 percent, and the total composition of G-C will
be 60 percent. The amount of cytosine will be 30 percent, or 108 nucleotides
$(360 \times .30 = 108)$.

Given the following molecule of DNA:
strand 1——A A A T C G A T T G G C A C A——
strand 2——T T T A G C T A A C C G T G T——
Assuming that strand 1 will serve as the transcription template, construct the molecule of mRNA that will be transcribed.

SOLUTION:

Since RNA has U instead of T, the complementary pairing that will occur
in transcription is A of DNA with U of RNA and T of DNA with A of RNA.
Thus, the mRNA molecule that will be transcribed from the above DNA strand
1 will be:
——U U U A G C U A A C C G U G U——

Would you expect the transfer RNA molecules and the messenger RNA molecules to be the same in the cells of a horse as in similar human cells? Give reasons for your answer in each case.

SOLUTION:

All tRNA and mRNA molecules are composed of the same chemical constituents, regardless of what species they come from. That is, they all contain the bases adenine, thymine, uracil and cytosine, ribose and phosphate (tRNA may have other bases in addition).

Observations from biochemical experiments aimed at elucidating the sequence and chemical composition of tRNA from different species have demonstrated that between species the different types of tRNA molecules have basically the same nucleotide sequence and the same three-dimensional configuration (cloverleaf-shaped). The reason for this lies in the fact that the function of tRNA is to transfer the amino acids to their correct positions specified by the mRNA. Since all organisms make use of the same 20 amino acids to make their proteins, the tRNA used to transfer these amino acids are basically the same for different species.

Unlike tRNA, mRNA molecules do not have a strict function. Their purpose is to provide the protein-synthesizing machinery with the information needed for protein production. The different mRNA molecules made by the cells of the same animal differ considerably in length. Different proteins are of different lengths and, therefore, there is a corresponding difference in lengths of the mRNA.

When we compare the mRNA from different species, such as man and horse, we have to bear in mind that there exist both equivalent and contrasting systems in the two species. Equivalent systems such as the Krebs cycle and electron transport system, which are almost universal among higher organisms utilize similar enzymes. The digestive system is an example of a contrasting system. The horse is a herbivore, whereas man is an omnivore. Because of the different modes of nutrition some very different enzymes are involved.

We know that enzymes, which are protein molecules, are the products of translation of mRNA. When translated, different mRNA molecules will give rise to different enzymes. Because horses and men rely on different enzymes — at least for digestion — we would infer that the mRNA from the two animals is different. However, we must not forget that both animals also use similar enzymes, as in Krebs cycle and electron transport system. Therefore they would also possess some similar, if not identical, mRNA.

In summary, we have determined that tRNA from cells of horse and man are basically the same, whereas the mRNA from the cells of these two animals would show much more difference.

Explain what difficulties would arise if messenger RNA molecules were not destroyed after they had produced some polypeptide chains.

SOLUTION:

Upon translation, mRNA molecules give rise to polypeptide chains. Normally, mRNA molecules are short-lived and are broken down by RNAase after a few translations. If an mRNA molecule were not destroyed, it would continue to synthesize its protein, and soon there would be an excess of this protein in the cell. This condition leads to some important implications for the cell.

The continual translation of mRNA into proteins would entail a serious depletion of the energy store in the cell. For example, before an amino acid can attach to a tRNA molecule, it has to be activated. Activation is brought about by the hydrolysis of one molecule of ATP. So for each amino acid in the polypeptide chain, one molecule of ATP molecules would be consumed and the energy supply in the cell would be depleted.

In addition, the cell would accumulate proteins that it may not need. This use of large amounts of energy to produce unneeded protein would be a wasteful process. Indeed the excessive accumulation of a protein may even be harmful to the cell or organism. For example, given the right environment, a protease such as pepsin, if present in more than sufficient amounts, will eat away the wall of the stomach, forming an ulcer.

The degradation of mRNA molecules allows a cell to control its metabolic activity. This control is important to the proper functioning of the cell.

The Central Dogma

The central dogma of biochemical genetics is the basic relationship between DNA, RNA, and protein. DNA serves as a template for both its own replication and for the synthesis of RNA, and RNA serves as a template for protein synthesis. How do viruses provide an exception to this flow scheme for genetic information?

SOLUTION:

The central dogma of biochemical genetics can be summarized in the following diagram

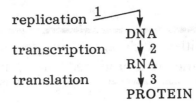

replication ¹

DNA

transcription ↓ 2

RNA

translation ↓ 3

PROTEIN

Arrow 1 signifies that DNA is the template for its self-replication. Arrow 2 signifies that all cellular RNA molecules are made on DNA templates. All amino acid sequences in proteins are determined by RNA templates (arrow 3). However, in the viral infection of a cell, RNA sometimes acts as a template for DNA, providing an exception to the unidirectionality of the scheme involving replication, transcription, and translation. The agents involved are certain RNA viruses. For example, an RNA tumor virus undergoes a life cycle in which it becomes a prophage integrated into the DNA of a host chromosome. But how can a single-stranded RNA molecule become incorporated into the double-helical structure of the host DNA? It actually does not.

An RNA tumor virus first absorbs to the surface of susceptible host cell, then penetrates the cell by a pinocytotic (engulfment) process, so that the whole virus particle is within the host cell. There, the particle loses its protein coat (probably by the action of cellular proteolytic enzymes). In the cytoplasm, the RNA molecule becomes transcribed into a complementary DNA strand. The enzyme mediating this reaction is called reverse transcriptase and is only found in viruses. (Thus, cells do not have the capacity to transcribe DNA from an RNA template; a virus is not a true cell.) Cellular DNA polymerase then converts the virally produced single stranded DNA into a double-stranded molecule. This viral DNA forms a circle and then integrates into the host chromosome, where it is transcribed into RNA needed for new viral RNA and also for viral-specific protein synthesis. The RNA molecules and protein coats assemble, and these newly made RNA tumor viruses are enveloped by sections of the cell's outer membrane and detach from the cell surface to infect other cells. The release of the new virions does not require the lysis of the host cell and is accomplished by an evagination of the outer membrane. Other cells are infected through the fusion of the envelope and the potential host cell's outer membrane, thereby releasing the virus particle into the cytoplasm. Unlike the λ phage infection of an *E. coli* cell, the RNA tumor virus does not necessarily interfere with normal cellular processes and cause death.

The mechanism of the action of reverse transcriptase is somewhat like other DNA polymerases. It synthesizes DNA in the 5' to 3' direction and needs a primer. The primer is a noncovalently bound tRNA molecule that was picked up by the RNA viral genome from the host during the previous round of replication. Since retroviruses have single-stranded linear RNA genomes, they encounter a problem during replication: the newly formed RNA molecules are

incomplete because, when the primer was degraded, there was no complement to act as a template strand. The solution to this problem is that there
are initially two molecules of RNA, hydrogen bonded to each other near their
5' ends. Each of these molecules has an identical sequence of the 5' and 3'
ends:

5' ABCDE —— WXYZABC 3'

When new RNA strands are replicated they form concatamers because the
single-stranded tails are complementary to each other.

3′	5′
a	A
b	B
c	C
x	X
y	Y
	Z
a	A
b	B
c	
d	D
e	E
f	F
a	A
b	B
3′	5′

The gaps can be filled since the 3' end of one duplex forms as a primer to fill
in the missing nucleotides at the 5' end of the adjoining molecule.
   Thus, the enzyme reverse transcriptase of RNA viruses provides the basis
for the single known exception to the standard relationship between DNA,
RNA, and proteins by catalyzing the transcription of DNA from RNA.

Transcription

●PROBLEM 6-8

What is the relationship between transcription and translation in the
production of polypeptides?

SOLUTION:

The genetic information that is stored in the nucleotide sequence of DNA is not directly used to make polypeptides. An RNA intermediate is used. This messenger RNA (mRNA) can be synthesized and degraded very rapidly. With the existence of this intermediate, the stable DNA acts simply as a blueprint of information, while the RNA can move away from the chromosome to the cytoplasm where the protein synthesizing machinery awaits. The actual protein producers are the RNAs: mRNA, rRNA, and tRNA.

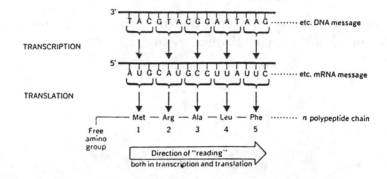

Figure 1. Schematic showing the relation between transcription and translation to produce polypeptides.

The formation of the mRNA from DNA is termed transcription. DNA-dependent RNA polymerase catalyzes the initiation and elongation of the RNA chain. The production of RNA is halted when the RNA polymerase reaches a string of thymine residues in an A-T rich region and an inverted repeat in a G-C rich region of the DNA. These sequences signal termination and the mRNA dissociates from the DNA template.

The genetic information can now move to the ribosomes in the cytoplasm in a form that the rRNA and the tRNA recognize. The codons in the mRNA are recognized by the anticodons of the tRNA molecules who transfer their amino acid to the growing polypeptide chain.

So, the relationship between transcription and translation is merely that of steps in the production of the final amino acid sequence of a polypeptide from the original nucleotide sequence of the chromosomal DNA.

●PROBLEM 6-9

What do the codons AUG, UAG, UAA, and UGA code for?

SOLUTION:

These four codons are special since they can either signal the beginning or the end of a polypeptide chain. When strategically placed at the 5' end of the mRNA, AUG codes for methionine (which is formulated in prokaryotes but not in eukaryotes) and signals the start of protein synthesis. At other places in the mRNA, AUG codes for the amino acid methionine. The other codons, UAG, UAA, and UGA, are terminator (or nonsense) codons. They code for no amino acids and signal the end of a polypeptide chain. They have been given the names amber (UAG), ochre (UAA), and opal (UGA).

The terminator codons occur naturally in a cell's mRNA to signal the termination of the polypeptide chain. However, mutations that change the reading frame or substitute wrong bases can create terminator codons in the middle of an mRNA chain. Such nonsense mutations result in the production of incomplete polypeptides. These polypeptides are not usable by the cell. The protein's activity can be restored if a second mutation, a suppressor mutation, occurred. A mutation in the anticodon region of a tRNA is a suppressor mutation. If the tRNA's codon became AUC, ACC, or ACU, it would be complementary to the nonsense codons. Thus, the tRNA could bind to the mRNA, donating its amino acid to the polypeptide chain. The resulting polypeptide will contain one wrong amino acid, but that usually does not affect its activity drastically. The protein will function more effectively than the incomplete fragment produced by the nonsense mutation.

● PROBLEM 6-10

What is the wobble hypothesis?

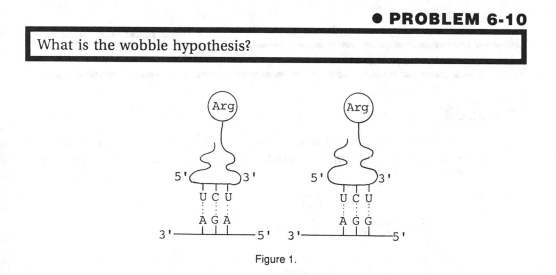

Figure 1.

SOLUTION:

Many amino acids are coded by more than one codon. Some examples of this degeneracy are UUU and UUC which code for phenylalanine, GAA and GAG which code for glutamate, and CUA, CUC, CUG, and CUU which all code for leucine. The wobble hypothesis helps to explain this degeneracy.

Francis Crick developed the wobble hypothesis to explain some experimental evidence. Some experiments showed that highly purified tRNA species could recognize several different codons. Also, another anticodon base, inosine, was found. Inosine is similar to guanine and will normally pair with cytosine. Crick hypothesized that the base at the 5' end of the anticodon was not as rigidly fixed as the other two bases and it could hydrogen bond to several bases at the 3' end of the coding. The pairing is restricted to the combinations shown below:

Base in Anticodon	Base in Codon
G	U or C
C	G
A	U
U	A or G
I	A, U, or C

An example of the pairing that is permitted by this hypothesis is shown in Figure 1.

Translation

●PROBLEM 6-11

How is protein synthesis initiated?

SOLUTION:

Messenger RNA molecules are translated to proteins at the ribosomes. At their 5' ends, the mRNAs have a leader sequence. This "cap" contains a

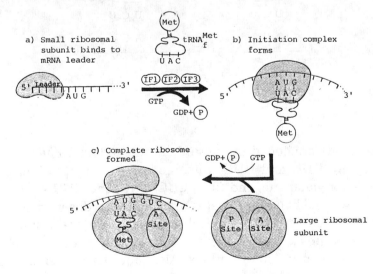

methyl-guanosyl triphosphate group which binds to the small ribosomal sub-unit. In eukaryotes, the association of ribosome, mRNA, and tRNA requires three protein factors called initiation factors — IF-1, IF-2, and IF-3. IF-3 is necessary for the binding of the ribosome to mRNA. Once bound, the other two initiation factors and the hydrolysis of GTP is required for the binding of the first codon of the mRNA to the small ribosome. When the initiation factors are released, the large ribosomal subunit attaches. The complete ribosome has two sites for tRNA molecules, the peptidyl (P) site and the aminoacyl (A) site. The mRNA codons are held near these spots so the tRNAs can bind. The initiation is complete and the machinery is poised for elongation of the polypeptide chain.

● PROBLEM 6-12

How is the peptide chain elongated during protein synthesis?

SOLUTION:

Peptide elongation is the next step in the synthesis of a polypeptide. The alignment of the initiator codon (AUG) with the P site leaves the A site aligned with the next codon. In *E. coli*, the association of the next mRNA codon with its tRNA anticodon requires the hydrolysis of GTP and the association of two protein elongation factors, EF-1 and EF-2. A displacement occurs to allow the peptide bond to form between the two amino acid residues. This reaction is catalyzed by peptidyl transferase. The next event, translocation, involves the movement of the tRNA from the A site to the P site and the movement of the whole ribosome three nucleotides. These simultaneous events result in the alignment of a new codon in the A site and the previous codon in the P site. This process is repeated until a termination signal is recognized.

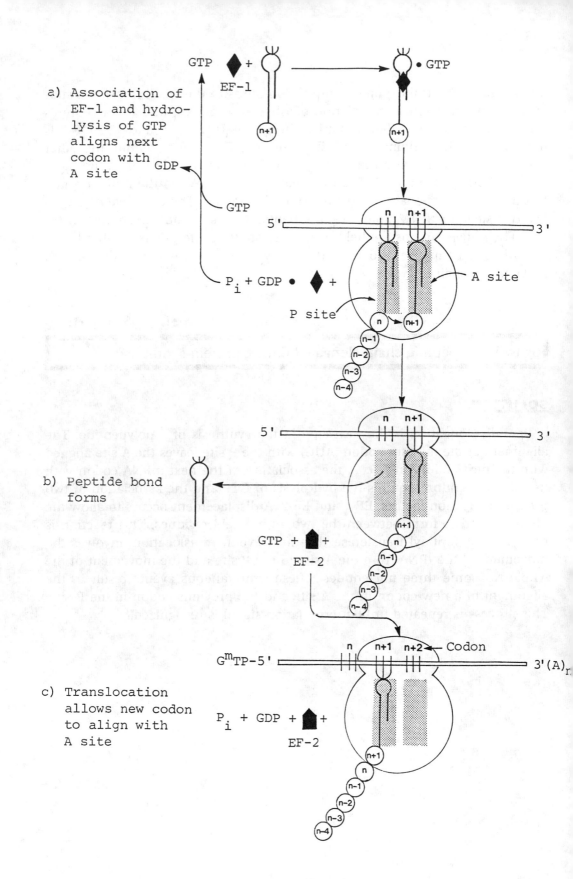

a) Association of EF-1 and hydrolysis of GTP aligns next codon with A site

b) Peptide bond forms

c) Translocation allows new codon to align with A site

How is protein synthesis terminated?

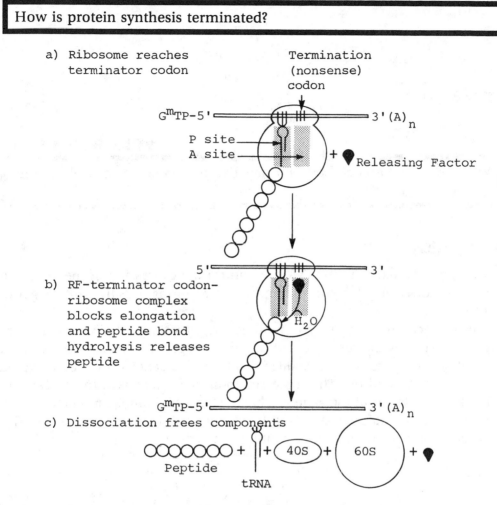

a) Ribosome reaches terminator codon

Termination (nonsense) codon

b) RF-terminator codon-ribosome complex blocks elongation and peptide bond hydrolysis releases peptide

c) Dissociation frees components

SOLUTION:

When a ribosome reaches a terminator codon in the mRNA, the peptide elongation halts. The terminator codons, UAA, UGA, and UAG, are not recognized by any naturally occurring aminoacyl tRNAs. The terminator (or stop) codon in the A site prevents the further addition of amino acids to the polypeptide chain. There are two release factors in *E. coli* that interact with specific terminator codons: RF-1 recognizes UAA or UAG and RF-2 recognizes UAA or UGA. This interaction forms an RF-terminator codon-ribosome complex which clogs the A site and blocks further elongation. Another releasing factor hydrolyzes the bond between the peptide and the tRNA in the P site. This releases the protein and tRNA from the ribosome. The ribosome then dissociates into its two subunits, free to form new initiation complexes to begin another round of peptide synthesis.

171

GENE REGULATION

Prokaryotes

What is the difference between negative and positive control of gene expression?

SOLUTION:

Compounds that bind to DNA can control the expression of the genes on that piece of DNA. This control can take two forms: positive and negative control.

Negative control is operative in some prokaryotic catabolic systems, see Figure 1. The *lac* operon of *E. coli* is under negative control. This form of control utilizes repressors and inducers to turn off a genetic system that would otherwise be turned on. The repressor molecule interacts with the DNA to inhibit the synthesis of the gene products. This inhibition is terminated when the inducer, the molecule that is to be catabolized, is present. Thus negative control involves substances that inhibit gene activity.

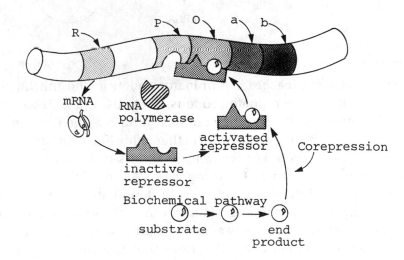

Figure 1. Negative control in a repressible operon.

Positive control is found in biosynthetic as well as catabolic systems. The *lac* operon is under positive control as well as negative control. Positive control occurs when components enhance gene activity. Hormones, special proteins such as the catabolite activator protein (CAP), and cyclic AMP can act to enhance the transcription of genes, see Figure 2.

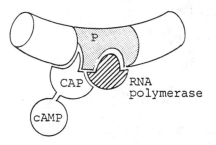

Figure 2. Positive control by the cAMP-CAP complex.

Genes can be controlled by positive and /or negative control. Catabolic systems, such as the breakdown of lactose, utilize negative control since the genes need to be expressed only in the presence of the compound to be degraded. Biosynthetic systems, such as tryptophan biosynthesis, use positive control since they synthesize a product. There is still much to learn about the regulation of gene activity. But it seems that different forms of regulation are needed for different types of gene expression.

Given the lactose operon in the bacterium, *Escherichia coli:*

i		p	o	z	y	a

where i = regulator gene

   p = promoter site

   o = operator site

   z = structural gene for ß-galactosidase

   y = structural gene for ß-galactoside permease

   a = structural gene for thiogalactoside transacetylase

Assuming that the inducer molecule, lactose, is present, what would be the result in terms of enzyme synthesis if the following mutational events took place:

a) mutation of i such that a defective repressor results that does not recognize o

b) mutation of i such that a "superrepressor" results which does not recognize lactose

c) mutation of o such that repressor will not recognize o

d) mutation of p.

SOLUTION:

Jacob and Monod first described the *lac* operon as a model to explain mutations such as these. Studies of mutations are an extremely important component of genetic analyses.

a) Since a defective repressor is produced, the normal repression of o will not occur; thus, there will be constitutive synthesis of the structural gene products regardless of the presence of an inducer molecule.

b) Since the product that results does not recognize the inducer molecule, the system will be permanently shut off, and no structural enzymes will be produced.

c) With the mutation of o resulting in nonrecognition by the repressor, no repression will occur regardless of the presence or absence of the inducer; thus, constitutive synthesis of all structural gene products will occur.

d) With a mutation at p, the most likely result is nonrecognition either by the mRNA polymerase, the CAP-cAMP (catabolite activator protein — cyclic AMP) or both; thus, no structural gene products will result.

Eukaryotes

●PROBLEM 6-16

How can the expression of eukaryotic genes be regulated?

SOLUTION:

Eukaryotic organisms are decidedly more complex than prokaryotes. They have diploid rather than haploid genomes. They can surpass the one-celled state of most prokaryotes and grow into multicellular organisms whose numerous cells are highly specialized. This complexity complicates the study of eukaryotic regulation. But many forms of genetic regulation can be related to the processes of the expression of the genetic information. The genome can be regulated by DNA modification and through transcriptional, post-transcriptional, and translational control.

DNA can be modified by the methylation of its cytosine residues. Specific methylation patterns exist, for example, the cytosine residues that are methylated are usually next to guanine residues. These patterns are not random; they are tissue specific and clonally inherited. Under methylation of DNA is correlated with active gene expression. Conversely, methylation is correlated with nonexpression.

Control of transcription can account for the differential gene activity that occurs during development. Ovalbumin transcription can be initiated by the steroid hormone estrogen in immature chicken oviduct cells.

The separation of the genetic material in the nucleus from the translation apparatus in the cytoplasm introduces post-transcriptional control.

The RNA molecule that is produced in the nucleus is different from the one that is translated at the ribosomes. The nuclear RNA (hnRNA) contains sequences called introns or intervening sequences that are excised and never translated. The RNA that reaches the ribosomes (mRNA) is considerably shorter than the hnRNA. The hnRNA of different types of cells is similar even though their mRNAs are different. The processing of the hnRNA to create the specific mRNAs may be involved in the control of gene expression. The introns that are spliced out of the hnRNA may have a role in the regulation of some genes. This has been shown in the virus SV40 but not in prokaryotic or eukaryotic cells.

Other mechanisms of regulation of eukaryotic gene expression may occur during translation. Translation may be modulated by one or more factors that are involved in protein synthesis. For instance, in the unfertilized sea urchin egg, there is a lot of masked mRNA which may be inactive for months. Once the egg is fertilized, the masked mRNA is translated into protein. The gene products are produced when they are needed.

Eukaryotic gene regulation is not a well-defined area of genetics. Much of the information is speculative and has been derived from other experimental systems. Eventually these theories will be genetically analyzed in the eukaryotic system.

●PROBLEM 6-17

How can some hormones regulate gene action?

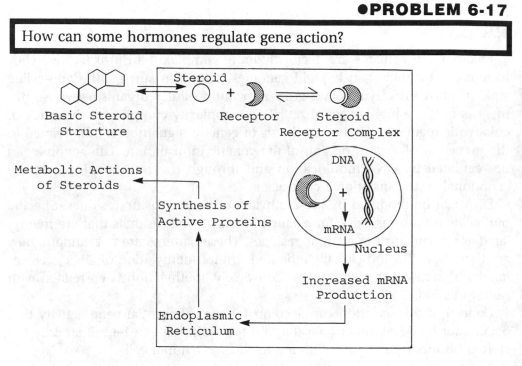

Figure 1.

SOLUTION:

Hormones are control chemicals produced by cells in both plants and animals. They are produced in small amounts in specialized cells that are far removed from their sites of action. In higher plants, they are transported via the vascular system and in animals they are carried by the blood. They are effective in small concentrations, so they probably influence the synthesis or activity of enzymes. Some hormones that influence genetic activity are gibberellic acid, abscisic acid, ecdysone, and estrogen.

Gibberellic acid and abscisic acid are plant hormones that are involved in plant growth and development. Gibberellic acid has a role in controlling the early phases of growth. It activates stem lengthening, stimulates pollen germination, induces flower formation, and stimulates seed germination. The stimulation of seed germination is a very important function. Just prior to germination, the seed embryo secretes gibberellins which induce the production of the enzyme α-amylase. This enzyme hydrolyzes stored starch and activates the other enzymes of the seed. An inhibitor of RNA synthesis, actinomycin D, effectively inhibits the synthesis of α-amylase. This suggests that gibberellic acid initiates the transcription of α-amylase. Somehow it interacts with genetic material to induce its expression. Abscisic acid inhibits the production of α-amylase. It may bind to the DNA or interact with gibberellic acid in such a way that the transcription is turned off.

Ecdysone is one of the hormones involved in insect maturation. Ecdysone is a steroid hormone that acts as shown in Figure 1. When small amounts of ecdysone are injected into *Drosophila*, chromosome puffs are observed at certain sites. Chromosome puffs are visible in the salivary glands since they have very large (polytene) chromosomes. Chromosome puff formation is an indication of the activation of certain genes or sets of genes. Thus, ecdysone activates gene expression in *Drosophila*.

Estrogen is another steroid hormone. Estrogen is produced by the ovaries in mammals. It stimulates the development and maintenance of female reproductive structures and secondary sexual characteristics and it stimulates the growth of the uterine lining. Estrogen increases the transcription in uterine tissue.

These are only a few of the many hormones that exist. Many other hormones probably act in similar ways.

●PROBLEM 6-18

Do histones control gene activity?

SOLUTION:

Histones are the proteins that complex with eukaryotic DNA to form chromosomes. Histones are very similar from cell to cell and from organism to organism; therefore, they cannot be responsible for specific gene regulation. However, they do bind to the DNA so they can insulate it from transcription.

As shown in Figure 1, histones can repress the transcription of DNA. They can physically block the polymerases and other enzymes from interacting with the DNA. This repression may be overcome by the action of RNA. RNA may hybridize to the nontranscribing (antisense) strand of the DNA, thus freeing the sense strand for transcription. This occurs in a restricted area of the genome; only a few selected genes are open for transcription.

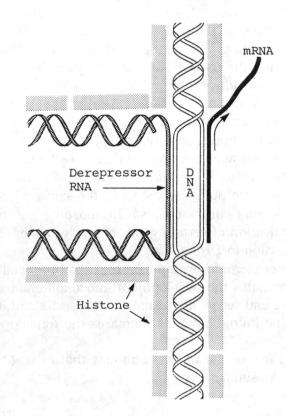

Figure 1. Model for gene repression and selective derepression by histones.

Thus, histones have a physical role in the regulation of gene expression. They protect the DNA from transcription enzymes until a signal arrives to initiate proper transcription. The specific regulation may be carried out by the other proteins found in chromosomes: the nonhistone proteins.

Virus

Explain how gene expression is regulated during phage λ infection.

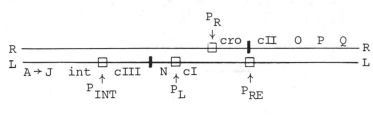

Figure 1.

SOLUTION:

The phage λ has a system of operons and regulatory proteins that regulate whether it will undergo lysis or lysogeny when it infects a host. Whether the virus undergoes lysis or lysogeny depends on environmental stimuli which affects gene expression. The genes that are involved in this regulation are ordered strategically on the λ chromosome. Contrary to most chromosomes, each strand of DNA is used as a sense strand — one is read towards the right and the other is transcribed towards the left. A linear representation of the λ chromosome is shown in Figure 1.

There are three phases that regulate λ's lytic cycle. They are the immediate-early, delayed-early, and -late phases. The immediate-early phase begins immediately after the phage infects a cell. The host's polymerases bind to a promoter region (P_R) of the phage genome. P_R directs transcription on the R strand in the rightward direction. The second immediate-early transcript begins at the leftward promoter (P_L) which transcribes to the left. The transcription that begins at P_R leads to the production of Cro protein, and the transcription that begins at P_L leads to the production of N protein. N protein is an antiterminator. It enables the RNA polymerase to get over the chain terminating sequences that are denoted by black bars in Figure 1. N protein also stimulates the transcription of the delayed-early phase. The delayed-early genes are cII and cIII, which are used only in lysogeny; genes O and P, which are needed for the replication of the phage chromosome; and gene Q which is needed for the stimulation of the next phase. When the Q gene has been transcribed, the Q protein, another antiterminator, stimulates the late-phase genes. These genes, denoted A → J in Figure 1, encode the head and tail proteins of the phage. Once these proteins are made, the replicated phage chromosomes are packaged inside protein coats and the host cell is lysed. Figure 2 shows the three lytic phases. The genome is actually circular, so the third phase is not actually split as it appears in the diagram.

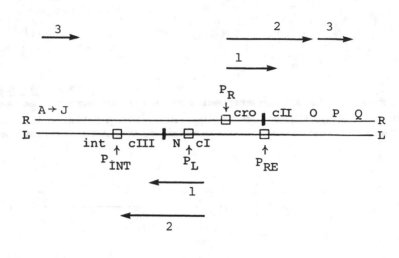

Figure 2.

Lysogeny requires two events: the repressor protein, cI, must be synthesized to turn off the lytic cycle by binding to operator regions near the promoters, P_R and P_L, and the Int protein must be synthesized to mediate λ's integration into the bacterial host's genome. In order for cI to be transcribed, a polymerase must bind to the P_{RE} promoter. P_{INT} must be recognized by a polymerase for the Int protein to be transcribed. Both promoters are recognized by RNA polymerase only in the presence of cII and cIII proteins. The cII protein acts as an activator protein; it stimulates polymerase to bind to promoters.

The race between lysis and lysogeny pivots on the levels of Cro protein and cI. Cro protein can act as a repressor by binding to the operators that cI can bind. It is not as stable as cI, nor does it bind as strongly. Thus, when it binds it slows down but does not stop, the expression of N, cIII, cro, cII, O, P, and Q genes. When there is a lot of Cro protein, little cII and cIII is transcribed, and thus no cI is made. When there is no cI, there is no strong repression of the lytic cycle phases, so the phage lyses the cell. When there is a small amount of cro, the cII and cIII levels are high because cro is not slowing their synthesis. These proteins are necessary for cI transcription, so cI is produced. The cI protein strongly inhibits the lytic cycle genes and the phage undergoes lysogeny.

The state of the phage is influenced by the levels of the proteins that are produced. Cro protein levels are affected by temperature, the metabolic state of the host, the genotype of the host, and the genotype of the infecting phage. The lytic cycle will be followed when the conditions are optimal for the survival of the phage's progeny. Otherwise, the lysogenic cycle will be followed.

What are the two types of bacteriophage infection?

SOLUTION:

Bacteriophage are viral particles that infect bacteria. The bacteriophage, or phage, like all viruses, cannot self-replicate. They are made of nucleic acid surrounded by a coat of protein. Their nucleic acid contains genes for the construction of new viruses but they have little or none of the necessary machinery, such as ribosomes and enzymes. They must use the apparatus of their host if they are to replicate.

Once a phage infects a cell it can follow one of two paths; lysis or lysogeny. Some phages are restricted to the lytic cycle. The lytic cycle causes the release of many viral particles and the death of the host cell. The phages T2, T4, T3, and T7 can only conduct infection through the lytic cycle. The lysogenic cycle does not lead to the immediate death of the host cell. Temperate phages can undergo either lysis or lysogeny depending on the conditions.

The lytic cycle begins when the phage makes contact with the host cell and injects its nucleic acid into the cell. In the case of T2 infection of *E. coli*, three sets of genes are expressed. They are the early gene that inhibits *E. coli* RNA synthesis; the DNA metabolism gene products which are enzymes that replicate the phage chromosome; nuclei that degrade the bacterial chromosome so the nucleotides are free for use by the phages; and the late gene products which include the phage proteins necessary to package the newly synthesized chromosomes into mature phage particles. One of the last gene products is lysozyme which digests the bacterial cell wall releasing as many as 250 phage particles. These viruses are free to find their own hosts to begin the cycle all over again.

The lysogenic infection cycle, Figure 1, occurs in temperate phages such as λ and φ 80. These phages can eventually lyse their host by following the lytic cycle. Under certain conditions the infection of a bacterial cell by a temperate phage does not cause lysis. The viral chromosome dictates the synthesis of a repressor molecule that inhibits the expression of the lytic genes. The chromosome inserts into a special region of the host chromosome where it is replicated along with the bacterial chromosome for many generations. The phage in this state is called a prophage. The viral genome, once incorporated, may produce phenotypic changes in the bacterial cell. For instance, the diphtheria bacteria, *Corynebacterium diphtheriae*, can produce the toxin that causes the disease only when it carries a certain prophage. The viral genes also give the bacteria immunity to further infection by the same type of virus. A drop in the level of the repressor molecules releases the viral producing genes from repression, thus initiating the lytic cycle. This can be induced experimentally by irradiation with ultraviolet light or by the exposure to certain chemicals such as nitrogen mustard or organic peroxides.

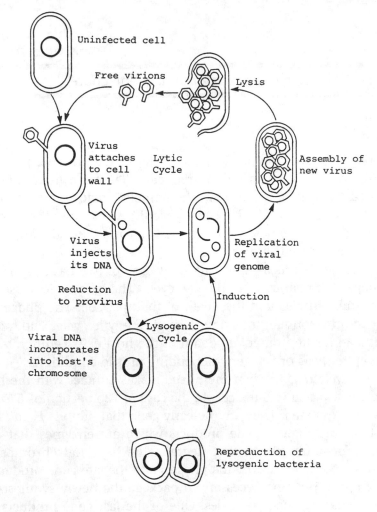

Figure 1.

Bacteriophage, although relatively simple physically, have very effective means for reproducing even without their own equipment. Nature has once again designed very elegant solutions to problematic situations.

Mutations

● **PROBLEM 6-21**

a) How are mutations detected?
b) How are potential mutagens tested?

SOLUTION:

Since mutations are changes in the DNA, they can be detected as abnormalities among a population of organisms. The study of mutations is very important to the study of genetics because it is through a comparison of these abnormalities that many conclusions regarding gene structure, function, and regulation have been reached. Mutations can be observed through visible phenotypic differences and through altered nutritional requirements. Mutagens are agents that can induce mutations. Using bacteria with a specific mutation, the Ames test can detect chemical mutagens.

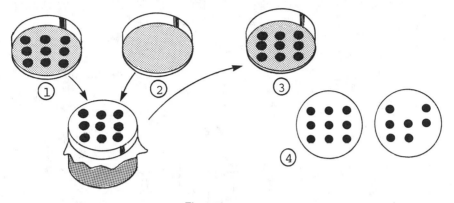

Figure 1.

(a) Different mutations manifest themselves in different ways. Mutations in structural genes can lead to visible phenotypic differences in an individual. Mutations in genes used in metabolic or catabolic pathways may lead to changes in nutritional requirement. *Drosophila* has been used extensively to study how mutations that produce visible alterations, such as wing structure or eye color, are inherited. Mutations that affect biochemical pathways have been studied in *E. coli* and other bacteria. Specific clones of cells can be followed through a technique called replica plating as shown in Figure 1.

In replica plating, a plate of cells growing on normal medium (1) is pressed onto a velveteen-covered block. Cells from each colony stick to the velveteen when plate (1) is removed. Plate (2), with a special medium, such as a medium lacking one nutrient, is now pressed onto the velveteen. When this plate is removed it has the colonies in the same places as the original, (3). Step (4) shows a comparison of the original plate to that of the plate with a deficient medium. The colonies that grow on the original, but not on the deficient medium, are those clones that contain a mutation. This technique can be used to test other types of mutations, such as those leading to antibiotic resistance.

(b) A very powerful way to test potential mutagens is by the Ames test. This procedure involves subjecting a strain of *Salmonella typhimurium*, that has a specific frameshift or base pair mutation that makes it His⁻, to chemicals. Those chemicals that can mutate the bacteria to His⁺ are mutagenic. Some chemicals become mutagenic only when a liver extract, S-9, is added to the medium. This extract oxidizes the chemicals to a mutagenic form much as the mammalian system inadvertently does. The Ames test has proven to be a useful primary test to screen for potential mutagens and carcinogens. The chemicals can be further tested in more expensive animal tests.

How does ultraviolet light damage DNA?

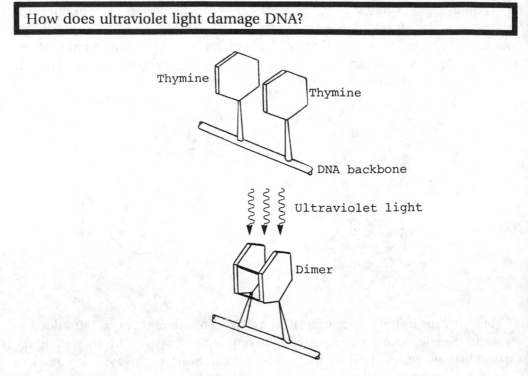

Figure 1. Thymine dimerization between adjacent thymine bases in a single strand of DNA.

SOLUTION:

Ultraviolet light is a nonionizing form of radiation. It has several effects on DNA, but the major damage of DNA, induced by UV light, is the production of thymine dimers. Thymine dimers are chemical bonds between two adjacent thymine residues as shown in Figure 1. These dimers distort the DNA helix by interrupting the hydrogen bonding between the thymine residues and their complementary adenine residues on the other strand. This interferes with strand replication and leads to mutation or cell death.

Fortunately, thymine dimers are recognized by certain enzymes. The dimers can be made into thymine monomers by photoreactivating enzymes which need a photon of visible light to perform the reaction. Dimers are also recognized by an endonuclease that cuts the helix near the dimer. An exonuclease can then digest the portion of the strand containing the dimer, thus leaving a gap. The gap is filled by a DNA polymerase that uses the complementary strand as a template. Ligase seals the remaining nick. This process is called excision repair.

Most of the dimers induced by UV light are repaired. A faulty excision repair system has been implicated in humans who have xeroderma pigmentosum. Such individuals are homozygous for the mutant allele and are very sensitive to the UV light of sunlight.

How is the DNA damaged by ultraviolet light repaired?

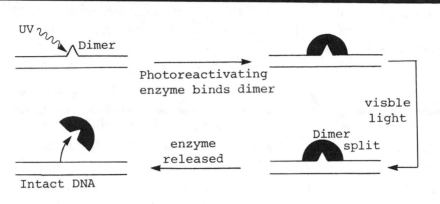

Figure 1. Photoreactivation

SOLUTION:

The solution to the previous question mentioned two repair systems in the bacterial cell which can remove the dimers formed by UV light. These systems are photoreactivation and excision repair.

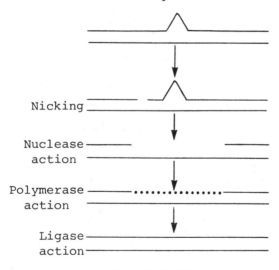

Figure 2. Excision repair

Photoreactivation can only occur when a photon of visible light is absorbed by the photoreactivation enzyme. This enzyme can bind to a dimer and split it leaving an intact strand of DNA, see Figure 1.

Excision repair is a more complex process because it does not simply break the covalent bond in the dimer. This repair system uses four enzymes to remove the dimer entirely and then to fill in the resulting gap. Figure 2 shows the process. An endonuclease is needed to make a single-stranded nick in the dimer-bearing strand. An exonuclease then digests a length along the strand, including the dimer. A DNA polymerase uses the complementary strand as a template to fill in the missing piece. Ligase then binds the newly copied piece to the original. Base pair substitutions may occur when the DNA polymerase resynthesizes the strand. Such substitutions, however, are not as immediately harmful as the dimers.

●PROBLEM 6-24

Photoreactivation and excision repair are two efficient repair mechanisms available to a cell which has undergone UV irradiation. However, extremely high doses of UV elicit a third type of repair system that greatly increases the rate of mutation. What is this system and why does it increase the mutation rate?

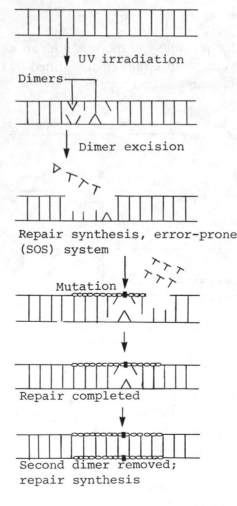

Figure 1.

SOLUTION:

A cell that has been severely damaged by the dimerization of its thymine residues may resort to the SOS repair system. This repair system is highly error-prone so it leads to a high mutation rate.

The SOS system promotes cell survival by allowing DNA synthesis past the pyrimidine dimers during replication. This leaves gaps to be filled in where the dimers originally were. These gaps are filled in by any base regardless of the sequence of the other strand of DNA. These incorrect bases increase the mutations of the cell. However, at least the cell is able to pass some information on to the next generation. A mutated genome is a small step above a genome that is unable to be replicated at all.

Alleles

Distinguish between penetrance and expressivity.

SOLUTION:

A recessive gene produces a given trait when it is present in the homozygous state. A dominant gene produces its effect in both the homozygous and heterozygous states. Geneticists, however, have found that many genes do not always produce their phenotypes when they should. Genes that always produce the expected phenotype in individuals who carry the gene in an expressible combination are said to have complete penetrance. If only 70 percent of such individuals express the character phenotypically, then the gene is said to have 70 percent penetrance. Penetrance is thus defined as the percentage of individuals in a population who carry a gene in the correct combination for its expression (homozygous for recessive, homozygous or heterozygous for dominant) and who express the gene phenotypically.

Some genes that are expressed may show wide variations in the appearance of the character. Fruit flies homozygous for the recessive gene producing shortening of the wings exhibit variations in the degree of shortening. Expressivity is defined as the degree of effect or the extent to which a gene expresses itself in different individuals. If it exhibits the expected trait fully then the gene is said to be completely expressed. If the expected trait is not expressed fully, the gene shows incomplete expressivity.

The difference between the two terms — penetrance and expressivity — lies in the fact that the former is a function of the gene at the population level, while the latter varies on an individual level. Thus, a given gene having a certain penetrance within a population may have varying expressivity in individuals of that population who express it.

Both penetrance and expressivity are functions of the interaction of a given genotype with the environment. Changes in environmental conditions can change both the penetrance and expressivity of a gene. For example, a given gene may code for an enzyme required for the synthesis of a given metabolite in bacteria. If that metabolite is provided in the organism's nutrient environment, the organism might not produce the enzymes needed for its synthesis and the gene will not be expressed. If, however, the nutrient is depleted from the media, the organism will begin to manufacture the enzyme and thus express the gene. In humans, it is thought that allergy is caused by a single dominant gene; the different types of allergies are due to the varying expressivity of the gene, as a result of the interaction of the gene with both the environment and a given individual's genetic and physical makeup.

●PROBLEM 6-26

What are multiple alleles and how do they originate?

SOLUTION:

Multiple alleles are three or more genes that control a single trait. They presumably have arisen from mutations in the same gene of different individuals. Most series of multiple alleles are associated with gradation in a phenotype. For instance, *Drosophila* has a series of mutations in eye color that vary from the wild-type red to the mutant white. Mutants can have apricot, buff, eosin, coral, honey, pearl, or blood colored eyes. In humans, the blood type locus has multiple alleles.

If a person with O type blood marries a person with AB type blood what will be the expected results in the progeny?

SOLUTION:

Blood types	Genotypes
A	AA or Aa
B	$A^B A^B$ or $A^B a$
AB	AA^B
O	aa

	O type		**AB type**
Phenotypes			
Genotypes	aa	×	AA^B
	↓ ↓		↓ ↓
Types of gametes	a a		A A^B

	a	a
A	Aa	Aa
A^B	$A^B a$	$A^B a$

1/2 Aa A type
1/2 $A^B a$ B type

BACTERIAL GENETICS

Gene Transfer and Conjugation

How are genes transferred in bacteria?

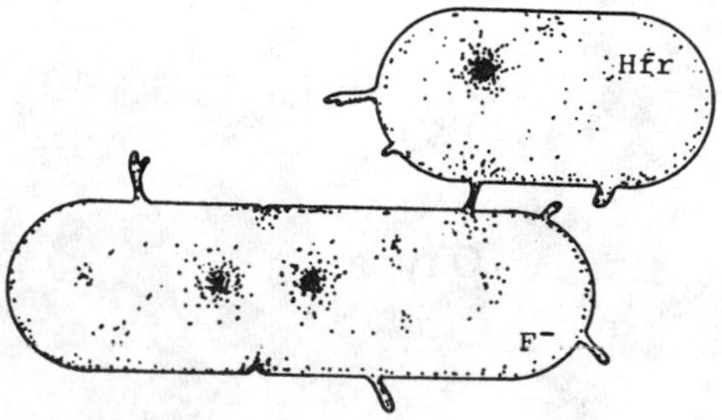

Figure 1. Conjugation between two E. coli cells

SOLUTION:

Bacteria, unlike eukaryotic organisms, can only pass genes in a one-way transfer; there is no reciprocal exchange of genetic information. Thus, in bacteria the genetic information travels from a donor to a recipient cell. There are three main ways this can occur: conjugation, transformation, and transduction.

Conjugation involves the transmission of the genetic material through a specialized sex pilus, see Figures 1 and 2. Bacterial cells which can make a pilus are said to have the F factor. The F factor contains at least 15 genes which include those that control the F pili. F⁺ cells will only establish contact with cells without the F factor (F⁻). The F pilus probably serves as a channel between the two cells. Usually only a single copy of the F factor is transferred.

Transformation, Figure 3, is the process in which genes enter the recipient in fragments. Certain strains of bacteria, *Streptococcus pneumoniae* and *Bacillus subtilis*, undergo transformation readily. Other strains, such as *E. coli*, have to be made competent by special laboratory conditions. Once the single-stranded pieces of DNA have been pulled into a cell, they can incorporate themselves into homologous regions of the host chromosome.

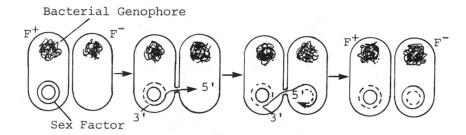

Figure 2. Transfer of the sex factor from an F⁺ donor to an F⁻ recipient by conjugation. Dotted lines indicate replication of the sex factor.

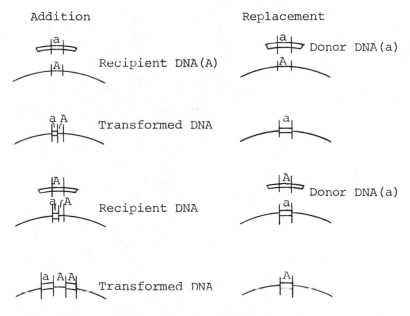

Figure 3. Two explanations of transformation in Pneumococcus.

Transduction, Figure 4, is the process in which a bacteriophage picks up some genes from one bacteria and carries the information to another bacteria. In the recipient bacteria, the DNA fragment may become incorporated as in transformation.

Thus, there are several ways that bacterial genes can move from one bacterium to another. These are methods of introducing variety in haploid organisms that cannot induce variety through the means employed by diploid organisms.

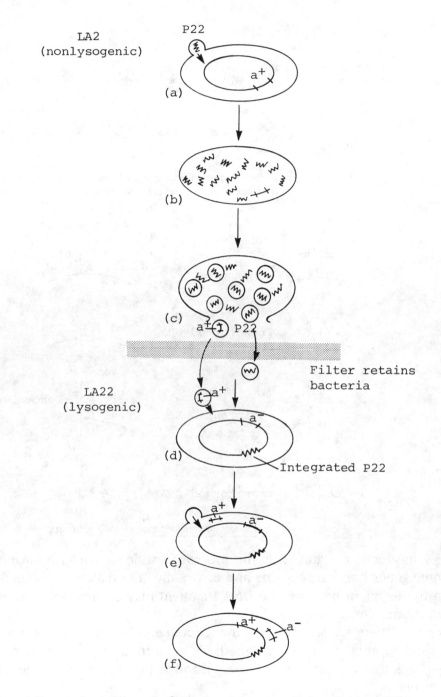

Figure 4. Transduction in Salmonella. Strain is nonlysogenic and is lysed by phage P22. Strain LA22 is lysogenic and allows integration of P22 into its genome.

A male bacterium conjugates with a female bacterium. After conjugation, the female becomes a male. Account for this "sex change."

SOLUTION:

Conjugation occurs between bacterial cells of different mating types. Maleness in bacteria is determined by the presence of a small, extra piece of DNA, the sex factor, which can replicate itself and exist autonomously (independent of the larger chromosome) in the cytoplasm. Male bacteria having the sex factor, also known as the F factor, are termed F$^+$ if the sex factor exists extrachromosomally. F$^+$ bacteria can only conjugate with F$^-$ the female counterparts, which do not possess the F factor. Genes on the F factor determine the formation of hairlike projections on the surface of the F$^+$ bacterium, called F or sex pili. The pili form cytoplasmic bridges through which genetic material is transferred and aids the male bacterium in adhering to the female during conjugation. During conjugation of an F$^+$ with an F$^-$ bacterium, the DNA that is the most likely to be transferred to the female is the F factor. Prior to transfer, the F factor undergoes replication. The female thus becomes a male by receiving one copy of the F factor, and the male retains its sex by holding on to the other copy. The DNA of the male chromosome is very rarely transferred in this type of conjugation.

If this were the only type of genetic exchange in conjugation, all bacteria would become males and conjugation would cease. However, in F$^+$ bacterial cultures, a few bacteria can be isolated which have the F factor incorporated into their chromosomes. These male bacteria that conjugate with F$^-$ cells are called Hfr (high frequency of recombination) bacteria. They do not transfer the F factor to the female cells during conjugation, but they frequently transfer portions of their chromosomes. This process is unidirectional, and no genetic material from the F$^-$ cell is transferred to the Hfr cell.

●PROBLEM 6-30

How do bacteria develop drug resistance?

SOLUTION:

Most antibiotic resistant bacteria result from genetic changes and subsequent selection. The genetic changes may be due to chromosomal mutations or to the introduction of extra chromosomal elements.

Spontaneous mutations in a bacterial chromosome can cause antibiotic resistance in several forms. The mutation may make the cell impermeable to the drug by changing the shape of the receptor molecule. The mutation may create an enzyme that inactivates the drug once it enters the cell. The mutation may make the drug's intercellular targets resistant to the drug. Streptomycin, which inhibits the binding of formyl-methionyl tRNA to the ribosomes, may be blocked if the ribosome was changed so that the interaction was prevented.

Antibiotic resistance may also arise extrachromosomally. Conjugal plasmids, such as R plasmids, contain genes which mediate their genetic transmission. R plasmids carry genes conferring antibiotic resistance. Thus, R^+ cells can pass the genes for resistance to R^- cells by conjugation.

Once a bacterial cell strain has become resistant to an antibiotic, the presence of that antibiotic in the environment favors the cells that contain the resistance element. Cells without the resistance will be killed by the antibiotic; those that have the resistance will flourish.

Transformation

●PROBLEM 6-31

What is transformation?

SOLUTION:

Transformation is a means by which genetic information is passed in bacterial cells. The recipient cell takes up the DNA that has been released by the donor cell. This occurs naturally in some species; however, it is usually performed as part of an experimental procedure. The DNA is extracted from the donor cell and mixed with recipient cells. *Hemophilus influenzae* and *Bacillus subtilis* are naturally competent; they are capable of taking up high molecular weight DNA from the medium. Competent cells have a surface protein called competence factor, which binds DNA to the cell surface. Other cells, such as *E. coli,* cannot readily undergo transformation. They will only pick up extracellular DNA under special laboratory conditions. The cells must have mutations that stop exonuclease I and V activity. The cells must be treated with high $CaCl_2$ concentrations to make their membranes permeable to the DNA. The donor DNA must be present in very high concentrations.

The DNA that is picked up by the recipient cell must be double-stranded. As it enters the cell, an intracellular DNAase degrades one of the strands. This hydrolysis provides the energy needed to pull the rest of the DNA into the cell. Once inside the cell, the now single-stranded DNA can insert into homologous regions of the recipients' chromosome. When the donor DNA and recipient DNA have genetic mutations that act as markers, genetic linkage can be established through transformation experiments.

●PROBLEM 6-32

Using a virus, how can one transform *E. coli* bacteria unable to utilize galactose (gal⁻ mutants) into those that can utilize galactose (gal⁺).

SOLUTION:

E. coli are usually able to utilize galactose, a monosaccharide, as a carbon and energy source. However, mutations arise which affect an enzyme necessary for galactose utilization. These *E. coli* mutants are unable to utilize this sugar and are called gal⁻ mutants. To transform some of these gal⁻ mutants into the wild-type, gal⁺, one can use a lysogenic virus such as the λ (lambda) bacteriophage.

One can infect a culture of prototrophic *E. coli* (gal⁺) with the lysogenic phages. The viruses will inject their DNA into the bacterial cells. In the host the viral DNA molecule changes from a linear structure to a circular one. At a specific attachment site on the bacterial chromosome the viral DNA pairs with the bacterial chromosome and integrates into it after recombination. The viral DNA, now called a prophage, remains incorporated within the *E. coli* chromosome until conditions are favorable for the excision of the prophage and its induction to a vegetative virus which replicates and lyses the cell.

The gene necessary for galactose utilization is very near the incorporated prophage. In the case of the phage its proximity to the bacterial gal⁺ gene allows rare errors to occur in which excision of the prophage includes the gal⁺ gene. The λ prophage may coil in such a way that the recombination event leading to excision of the circular viral DNA includes the gal gene. To remain approximately the same size, the circular viral DNA leaves behind some if its own genes, which were replaced by the substituted bacterial region. Since it now lacks some necessary genes, the virus, now called a transducing particle or λ gal, is considered to be defective. These transducing particles can lyse the bacterial cell, but they cannot establish a lysogenic relationship with, or cause lysis of, subsequent bacterial cells. The excision of the prophage which has the incorporated gal⁺ gene can be illustrated as shown in the figure below.

One can then harvest these transducing particles and add them to a culture of gal⁻ *E. coli* mutants. These phages attach to the mutant bacteria and inject their DNA (containing the gal⁺ gene). The gal⁺ region of the viral DNA may then recombine with the gal⁻ region of the bacterial chromosome. The gal⁺ gene may be incorporated into the *E. coli* through the recombination process, transforming them to the wild-type, which are able to utilize galactose. The whole viral DNA rarely becomes incorporated, since the transducing phage lacks a complete genome. The viral chromosome, containing the gal⁻ gene, cannot be inserted into the bacterial chromosome and so is lost.

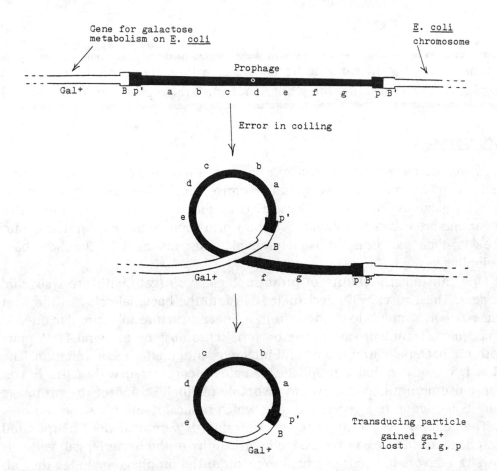

This process by which a virus transfers genes from one bacterial cell to another is called transduction. In specialized transduction, as opposed to generalized transduction, only one gene is transferred. Transduction thus serves as a mechanism for recombination in bacteria.

Transduction

●PROBLEM 6-33

What is transduction?

SOLUTION:

Transduction is a phage-mediated transfer of genetic material between two bacteria. There are three types of transduction: generalized, specialized, and f-mediated.

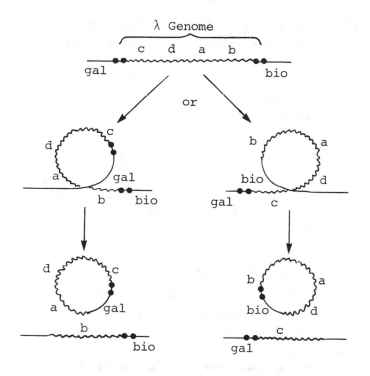

Figure 1. Specialized transducing phages produced by the improper excision of λ from the bacterial genome.

Generalized transduction occurs when a piece of bacterial chromosome becomes incorporated in a phage head and is transferred to a recipient bacteria. It can become incorporated in the recipient by recombination at the homologous region of the chromosomal DNA. The bacterial DNA becomes incorporated at the end of the phage's lytic cycle. The phages that can accomplish this are not as selective towards the DNA fragments that they incorporate as those which cannot transduce. But the incorporation of bacterial DNA is not always so simple. For example, in phage P22 a gene can recognize particular signals in the *Salmonella* chromosome. The gene is responsible for cutting up the DNA into sizes appropriate for the head protein. The signals that the gene recognizes may be certain base sequences and, as a result, certain *Salmonella* markers are transduced more frequently than others.

Specialized transduction, Figure 1, results in restricted parts of the bacterial chromosome being incorporated into the phage particle. This happens when the original transducing particle is produced by a faulty outlooping of the prophage. The phage thus formed is defective since some of its genes remain in the bacteria replaced by some of the bacterial genes.

F-mediated sexduction is the third form of transduction. An F element that contains extra bacterial genes is called an F' element. By conjugation, the F' element can be transferred to a bacterial cell that is mutant in the extra genes on the F' element. Cells are then selected for those that have the F element

197

integrated next to where a phage has integrated. When the prophage is induced, the phage that results will probably contain the genes from the F element. This virus is then used as the vector to transfer the bacterial genes to another bacterial cell.

These viral-mediated gene transfer mechanisms have been exploited by geneticists to map bacterial chromosomes. Very detailed maps that are continuously being revised are the result.

●PROBLEM 6-34

A bacterial strain is unable to synthesize the amino acids methionine and histidine and is also unable to ferment arabinose. It is transduced by a phage with the wild-type genome, met$^+$ his$^+$ ara$^+$. Recombinants are selected for by growth on plates supplemented with histidine. The colonies that grew on his+ plates were placed on plates containing arabinose. A total of 320 colonies grew on histidine supplemented plates and 150 of these could also ferment arabinose. What is the amount of recombination between met and ara?

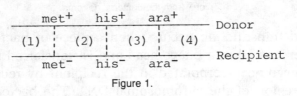

Figure 1.

SOLUTION:

Transduction is the process whereby bacterial DNA is transferred from one cell to another via a phage vector. The phenotype of the recipient bacteria will be altered to that of the donor if recombination occurs between the incoming and the native DNA. Figure 1 shows how the homologous areas of DNA could line up and where crossing over could occur.

Crossing-over in the different regions produces different recombinants. Since the original plates were supplemented with histidine, both his$^+$ and his$^-$ cells will be able to grow; crossing-over in regions (2) and (3) are thus not accounted for in the selected colonies. Crossing-over in regions (1) and either (2) or (3) produce prototrophic mutants (met$^+$ara$^-$) that can grow on unsupplemented medium. The frequency with which recombination occurs between met and ara can be found by dividing the number of met$^+$ara$^-$ prototrophs by the total number of recombinants.

recombination ratio = $\dfrac{\text{\# of met}^+\text{ara}^-}{\text{\# of met}^+\text{ara}^+}$

$$= \frac{320-150}{320}$$

$$= 0.531 \text{ or } 53.1 \text{ percent}$$

POPULATION GENETICS

Hardy-Weinberg Principle and Gene Frequency

●PROBLEM 6-35

What are the implications of the Hardy-Weinberg Law?

SOLUTION:

The Hardy-Weinberg Law states that in a population at equilibrium both gene and genotype frequencies remain constant from generation to generation. An equilibrium population refers to a large interbreeding population in which mating is random and no selection or other factor which tends to change gene frequencies occurs.

The Hardy-Weinberg Law is a mathematical formulation which resolves the puzzle of why recessive genes do not disappear in a population over time. To illustrate the principle, let us look at the distribution in a population of a single gene pair, *A* and *a*. Any member of the population will have the genotype *AA*, *Aa*, or *aa*. If these genotypes are present in the population in the ratio of 1/4 *AA* : 1/2 *Aa* : 1/4 *aa*, we can show that, given random mating and comparable viability of progeny in each cross, the genotypes and gene frequencies should remain the same in the next generation. Figure 1 below shows how the genotypic frequencies of *AA*, *Aa*, and *aa* compare in the population and among the offspring.

| Mating | | Frequency | Offspring |
Male	Female		
AA × AA		1/4 × 1/4	1/16 AA
AA × Aa		1/4 × 1/2	1/16 AA + 1/16 Aa
AA × aa		1/4 × 1/4	1/16 Aa
Aa × AA		1/2 × 1/4	1/16 AA + 1/16 Aa
Aa × Aa		1/2 × 1/2	1/16 AA + 1/8 Aa + 1/16aa
Aa × aa		1/2 × 1/4	1/16 Aa + 1/16aa
aa × AA		1/4 × 1/4	1/16 Aa
aa × Aa		1/4 × 1/2	1/16 Aa + 1/16aa
aa × aa		1/4 × 1/4	1/16aa
			Sum:4/16 AA + 8/16 Aa + 4/16aa

Figure 1. The offspring of the random mating of a population composed of
1/4 *AA*, 1/2 *Aa*, and 1/4 *aa* individuals.

Since the genotype frequencies are identical, it follows that the gene frequencies are also the same.

It is very important to realize that the Hardy-Weinberg Law is theoretical in nature and holds true only when factors which tend to change gene frequencies are absent. Examples of such factors are natural selection, mutation, migration, and genetic drift.

●PROBLEM 6-36

Contrast the meanings of the terms "gene pool" and "genotype."

SOLUTION:

A gene pool is the total genetic information possessed by all the reproductive members of a population of sexually reproducing organisms. As such, it comprises every gene that any organism in that population could possibly carry. The genotype is the genetic constitution of a given individual in a population. It includes only those alleles which that individual actually carries. In a normal diploid organism, there is a maximum of two alleles for any one given locus. In the gene pool, however, there can be any number of alleles for a given locus. For example, human blood type is determined by three alleles, I^A, I^B, and i. The gene pool contains copies of all three alleles, since all these are found throughout the entire population. Any given individual in the population, however, can have at the most two of the three alleles, the combination of which will determine his blood type.

Can complete equilibrium in a gene pool exist in real situations?

SOLUTION:

Of the four conditions necessary for the genetic equilibrium described by the Hardy-Weinberg Law, the first, large population size is met reasonably often; the second, absence of mutations, is never met; the third, no migration, is met sometimes; and the fourth, random reproduction, is rarely met in real situations. Therefore it follows that complete equilibrium in a gene pool is not expected.

With regard to the first condition, many natural populations are large enough so that chance alone is not likely to cause any appreciable alteration in gene frequencies in their gene pools. Any breeding population with more than 10,000 members of breeding age is probably not significantly affected by random changes.

The second condition for genetic equilibrium, the absence of mutations, is never met in any population because spontaneous mutations are always occurring. Most genes probably undergo mutation once in every 50,000 to 1,000,000 duplications, with the rate of mutation for different genes varying greatly. However, since the rate of spontaneous mutation is usually low, it is usually insignificant in altering the gene frequencies in a large population.

The third condition for genetic equilibrium, implies that a gene pool cannot exchange its genes with the outside. Immigration or emigration of individuals would change the gene frequencies in the gene pool. A high percentage of natural populations, however, experience some amount of migration. This factor, which enhances variation, tends to upset Hardy-Weinberg equilibrium.

The fourth condition, random reproduction, refers not only to the indiscriminate selection of a mate but also to a host of other requirements that contribute to success in propagating the viable offspring. Such factors include the fertility of the mating pair, and the survival of the young to reproductive age. An organism's genotype actually influences its selection of a mate, the physical efficiency and frequency of its mating, its fertility, and so on. Thus entirely random reproduction in reality is not possible.

We can conclude, therefore, that if any of the conditions of the Hardy-Weinberg Law are not met, then the gene pool of a population will not be in equilibrium and there will be an accompanying change in gene frequency for that population. Since it is virtually impossible to have a population existing in genetic equilibrium, even with animals under laboratory conditions, there must then be a continuous process of changing genetic constitutions in all populations. This is ultimately related to evolution in that evolutionary change is not usually automatic, but occurs only when something disturbs the genetic equilibrium.

Why are genetic ratios more reliable when there are large numbers of offspring? Discuss the above with a reference to one inherited character in human beings.

SOLUTION:

Genetic ratios are often misunderstood. When we say that a certain type of cross yields a 3:1 ratio, this does not mean that for every four offspring, there will always be three of one type and one of another. A ratio is worked out on the basis of mathematical probability and will be approached when large numbers are considered.

In tossing a coin there is an equal probability of obtaining either a head or a tail, and the ratio of heads to tails would be 1:1. This is because each toss or event is independent of, and therefore not influenced by, the results of any preceding or subsequent tosses. The 50 percent chance of obtaining either side of the coin is the probability within which each individual event operates, and does not change, regardless of the number of times the event occurs. However, when the event takes place a large number of times, the results do tend to average out to the expected probability, and the actual ratio approaches the anticipated ratio of 1/2.

The same is true for certain genetic events. For instance, the cross between a heterozygous brown-eyed man (Bb) and a blue-eyed woman (bb) would be depicted as the following:

P		bb	×	Bb	
gametes		b		B ; b	

F_1		B	b
	b	Bb	bb
	b	Bb	bb

Each offspring produced has a 1/2 chance of being brown eyed and a 1/2 chance of being blue eyed. Thus, the expected ratios are; 1 Bb : 1 bb; or phenotypically, 1 brown : 1 blue. We might expect then, a 1:1 ratio in eye color among their offspring. But suppose their first child had blue eyes. This does not automatically mean that their second child must have brown eyes. That child has, like the first child, an equal probability of being either brown or blue eyed; either outcome is equally probable regardless of what eye color the first child has. This is because the separation of alleles in gamate formation is, like a coin toss, a purely random event, not effected by preceding events.

So, while we know that in this case the egg can only be carrying the gene for blue eyes, (because the female in this case is homozygous for blue eyes), the gene carried by the sperm that will fertilize the egg has an equal chance of being brown or blue, and we cannot predict which it will be because of the randomness of gene segregation. Therefore, though we might expect a 1:1 ratio for brown-eyed and blue-eyed offspring, the actual ratio may deviate from expected entirely by chance.

However — and this is the important point — if we were to tabulate the eye color of thousands of children from many families of parents having the same genotypic combinations as this couple, we would indeed find that close to one half of them will have blue eyes and the other half will have brown eyes. As was the case for the coin toss, the larger our sampling population, the closer our ratio approaches 1:1, the expected ratio. Our actual ratio approaches the probable ratio, and our results become more reliable.

Pedigree Analysis

●PROBLEM 6-39

Using the pedigree below, fill in the genotype of each individual. Assume the trait is recessive and an individual who marries into the family and does not exhibit a trait does not carry the recessive gene for it.

Left-handedness

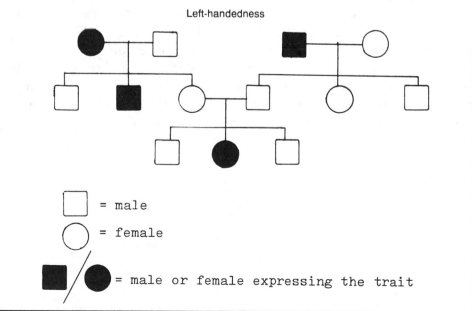

$\square$ = male

$\bigcirc$ = female

$\blacksquare$ / $\bullet$ = male or female expressing the trait

SOLUTION:

For simplicity and conciseness, we shall use the following system to refer to any one of the members in the pedigree:

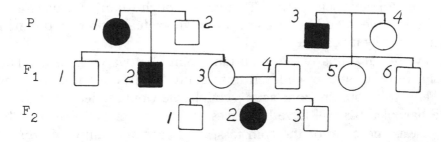

Let the allele for left-handedness be a and the allele for right-handedness be A. Consider P_1 (that is, the first member of the Parental generation). Since she expresses the trait, her genotype is aa. To determine the genotype of P_2, we look at the progeny, F_1 (first generation). From the diagram, we see that $F_{1,2}$ is left-handed; hence his genetic make-up is aa. This means that he must have received a copy of a from each of his parents. Therefore we know that P_2 carries a copy of the recessive gene. But since P_2 is phenotypically normal, his genotype must be Aa. $F_{1,1}$ and $F_{1,3}$ are right-handed. Yet they must have received an a allele from P_1 since she has only a alleles to transmit. Therefore their genotype of $F_{1,1}$ and $F_{1,3}$ is Aa.

Consider the cross between P_3 and P_4. We know P_3 is aa (because he is left-handed) and P_4 can be AA or Aa (since she is right-handed). Since all the offspring are right-handed, it seems probable that P_4 is AA; however, we cannot be entirely certain of this, since both genotypes AA and Aa are compatible with the phenotypes of the offspring. We know, however, that $F_{1,4}$, $F_{1,5}$, and $F_{1,6}$ must all have the genotype Aa since they carry an a allele donated by P_3.

In the F_2 generation, we see that $F_{2,2}$ is left-handed, and therefore her genotype is aa. This is compatible with what we have determined to be the genotypes of the parents ($F_{1,3}$ and $F_{1,4}$) namely Aa. $F_{2,1}$ and $F_{2,3}$ are both right-handed, and are either AA or Aa. Since both parents are Aa, either genotype is possible, though Aa is more probable.

Using the pedigree below, determine the method of inheritance of the trait and, as far as possible, fill in the genotypes of each individual. Assume that the trait is recessive.

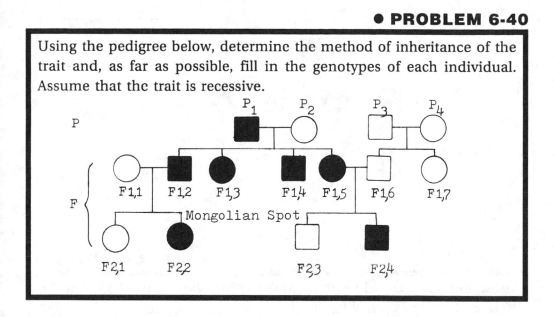

SOLUTION:

Let B represent the normal allele and b represent the allele for Mongolian spot. Using the system established in the previous question, we can say that P_1, $F_{1,2}$, $F_{1,3}$, $F_{1,4}$, $F_{1,5}$, $F_{2,2}$ and $F_{2,4}$ (see pedigree) are genotypically bb, because they all express the recessive Mongolian spot trait. Since all of the progeny of P_1 and P_2 carry the trait, the genetic make-up of P_2 who does not express the trait but must carry the recessive gene, is Bb. In the cross between $F_{1,1}$ and $F_{1,2}$, we see that one of their children ($F_{2,2}$) shows the trait. Since $F_{1,2}$ must have contributed one recessive gene, the other recessive gene must have come from $F_{1,1}$. But $F_{1,1}$ is normal, so her genotype must be Bb. $F_{2,1}$ is also Bb.

To determine the genotypes of P_3 and P_4, we have to examine the cross between $F_{1,5}$ and $F_{1,6}$. One of the offspring in this cross ($F_{2,4}$) shows Mongolian spots. This implies that both parents must have a copy of b. We already know that $F_{1,5}$ is bb. Therefore $F_{1,6}$ must be Bb, since he is normal. $F_{2,3}$ is also Bb because he can receive only the recessive allele from $F_{1,5}$. Since $F_{1,6}$ is heterozygous, one of his parents must have allele b. We cannot assume which parent carries the b allele, because the information is not available for us to be certain. Conceivably, both parents can be Bb, the number of their progeny being too small to necessarily include a homozygous recessive. Or one parent may be BB, in which case all their offspring would show the normal phenotype. The genotype of $F_{1,7}$ can thus be either BB or Bb.

We can summarize the genotypes of the individuals in the following diagram:

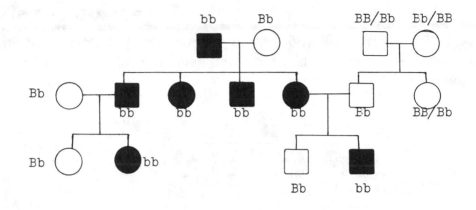

●PROBLEM 6-41

Using the pedigree below, determine the method of inheritance of the trait, and as far as possible, fill in the genotypes of each individual.

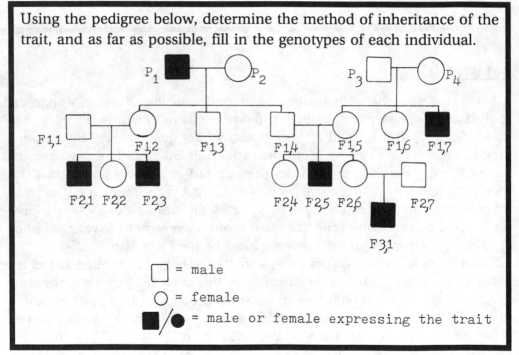

☐ = male

○ = female

■/● = male or female expressing the trait

SOLUTION:

One should immediately note that the trait is only exhibited by male members of the family. Although the number of individuals is small enough that this could have been a chance occurrence, it strongly suggests that the trait is sex-linked. Proceeding on this assumption, we can deduce the possible genotype of each member.

Letting r represent the recessive, sex-linked allele, we can assign the genotype X^rY to P_1, $F_{1,7}$, $F_{2,1}$, $F_{2,3}$, $F_{2,5}$, and $F_{3,1}$, since all are males expressing the trait. Since $F_{2,7}$, a male, does not express the trait, and therefore does not carry the

r allele, his genotype is X^RY, where R represents the normal allele. We know that $F_{3,1}$ must have received the r allele from his mother, $F_{2,6}$, since to a male offspring, the mother contributes the X while the father contributes the Y chromosome. The genotype of $F_{2,6}$ is then X^RX^r, since she does not express the trait. $F_{1,5}$ must also be a carrier (X^RX^r) since $F_{2,6}$ is a carrier, $F_{2,5}$ expresses the trait, and $F_{1,4}$, who must be X^RY, could not have donated the recessive allele to his offspring. Since we have no information concerning the offspring of $F_{2,4}$, her genotype could be either X^RX^R or X^RX^r, depending on whether she received a dominant or recessive allele from $F_{1,5}$. Since $F_{1,5}$ is a carrier, and her father P_3, who does not express the trait, is X^RY, we can assign P_4 the genotype X^RX^r, which shows that she is also a carrier. $F_{1,6}$ can be either X^RX^R or X^RX^r, one dominant allele in either case being necessarily donated by P_3.

$F_{1,3}$ a male not expressing the trait, is X^RY. Since no male offspring of P_1 and P_2 express the trait, it is likely though not necessary, that P_2 is not a carrier. Her possible genotypes are X^RX^R and X^RX^r. $F_{1,2}$ must have received the recessive allele from P_1 and be a carrier (X^RX^r). $F_{1,1}$ must be X^RY since he does not express the trait. $F_{2,2}$ could be either X^RX^R or X^RX^r.

Summarizing, we can see that our assumption of sex linkage is consistent with the inheritance pattern of the trait:

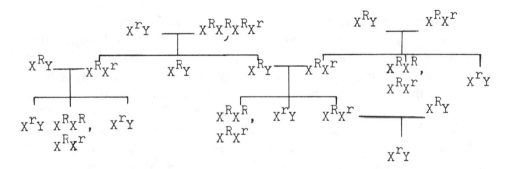

Populations

In a plant breeding experiment, cross-fertilization can cause a marked increase in the yield and height of the plants. Explain.

SOLUTION:

In cross-breeding experiments the progeny are very often more vigorous than the parents. This is called heterosis. Heterosis has been explained by two theories. The first is called the dominance hypothesis. This assumes that in the course of selecting for certain desirable traits the breeder has created strains with somewhat deleterious recessive genes in other places along the genome. The hybrid formed between two inbred strains would be heterozygous at these loci and hence would show vigor that the parents did not show.

The second hypothesis regarding heterosis is called the overdominance hypothesis. This theory says that the hybrid is more vigorous because it is more heterozygous. Heterozygotes may be more flexible than homozygotes since they have two different alleles for their heterozygous genes. The heterozygote may be better able to survive fluctuations in its environment since it has two versions of its heterozygous genes and hence, two versions of the gene products.

Heterosis has been used to increase crop yields and disease resistance in some plants such as corn and sorghum wheat.

●PROBLEM 6-43

What is polymorphism? What are some advantages of polymorphism?

SOLUTION:

A polymorphic locus has one or more alleles, in addition to the most common allele, present in more than one percent of the population. Polymorphism is extensive in natural populations. Its existence may offer flexibility of a species to a changing environment. An allele that was previously deleterious may, with the proper environmental climate, become beneficial. Alternatively, some mutant genes may be advantageous in the heterozygous state but deleterious in the homozygous state. Sickle-cell anemia, for instance, is a result of a mutant form of hemoglobin, HbS. In its heterozygous form, this trait offers a protection against malaria. In its homozygous form it is lethal.

Another hypothesis regarding the advantages of polymorphism in a population is that the allozymes (the slightly different enzyme products that arise from alleles at the same gene locus) may persist due to natural selection. For example, a population of isopod crustaceans, *Asellus aquaticus,* was found to have two allozymes for the enzyme that breaks down starch-amylase. One allozyme was better able to digest beech leaves and the other was better at digesting willow leaves. The pond where this population of isopods lived had a group of willows at one end and a group of beeches at the other. The isopods with the beech-digesting amylase lived near the beech trees and those with the willow-digesting allozyme lived nearer to the willow trees. This population was shown to interbreed, so it is not composed of separate populations with different allelic frequencies.

These examples show how polymorphism can be advantageous to different populations. Polymorphism, in these cases, enhances the survival of populations in potentially pernicious environments.

SHORT ANSWER QUESTIONS FOR REVIEW

Choose the correct answer.

1. A DNA molecule with 200 base pairs that consists of guanine will contain _____ thymine nucleotides. (a) 40 (b) 80 (c) 120 (d) 160

2. The complete ribosome has _____ spots for tRNA molecules. (a) 4 (b) 3 (c) 2 (d) 1

3. Which one of the following codons cannot signal the beginning or end of a polypeptide chain? (a) GAU (b) UAA (c) UGA (d) AUG

4. In essence, negative gene control is a mechanism by which (a) inducer genes are used to turn on a genetic system. (b) inducer genes are used to turn off a mutated genetic system. (c) inducer genes are used to turn off a genetic system that would otherwise be turned on. (d) repressor genes are used to turn off the action of an enzyme.

5. Hormones which influence genetic activity are (a) gibberellic acid. (b) abscisic acid. (c) ecdysone. (d) all of the above.

6. Histones directly influence genes by (a) physically blocking the polymerase from interacting with DNA. (b) transcribing antisense codons on the DNA strand. (c) transcribing sense codons on the DNA strand. (d) None of the above

7. The two ways thymine dimers can repair themselves are (a) photoreactivation and endonucleation. (b) endonucleation and ligation. (c) photoreactivation and incision repair. (d) photoreactivation and excision repair.

8. The most rarely used system of repair a cell can use when it has been severely radiated by ultraviolet light is the (a) ligation system. (b) SOS system. (c) base lipidization system. (d) spindle system.

9. A man with type A blood marries a woman with type AB blood. What are the different blood types their children could have? (a) A only (b) AB only (c) A and AB (d) A, B, and AB

10. Which of the following choices is not a way bacteria can donate genetic material? (a) transformation (b) transduction (c) meiosis (d) conjugation

11. R plasmids carry (a) genes for antibiotic resistance. (b) only mutant genes. (c) only phenotypic information. (d) both **a** and **b**

12. Specialized transduction (a) has only restricted parts of the bacterial chromosome incorporated into the phage. (b) varies according to the size of the chromosome. (c) does not occur in human cells. (d) can only occur in gametes.

13. Bacteriophages are (a) viral particles in general. (b) viral particles that infect bacteria. (c) bacteria in general. (d) bacteria that infect viruses.

14. Viruses contain (a) RNA only. (b) DNA only. (c) both RNA and DNA. (d) either RNA or DNA.

15. In which of the following ways can a mutation cause an organism to be resistant to an antibiotic? (a) By changing the shape of the receptor molecule (b) By creating an enzyme that inactivates the drug (c) By acting on the drug's intracellular targets (d) All of the above

16. For the Hardy-Weinberg Law to hold in a population, which one of the following is not necessary? (a) large interbreeding population (b) high mutation rates (c) random mating (d) no natural selection

17. An advantage of a polymorphic trait is that it (a) allows separate species to coexist in a given territory. (b) produces variations in a trait. (c) confers greater vigor in the crossbred progeny. (d) All of the above.

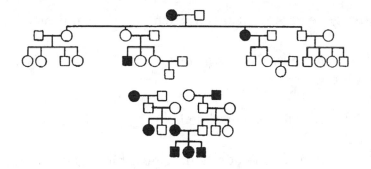

The following questions refer to the family pedigree shown above, in which an abnormal trait is inherited as simple recessive. Colored squares and circles represent expressions of the trait. Unless there is evidence to the contrary, individuals who have married into the family do not carry the recessive gene.

18. The best explanation for the offspring of the cross between F_{1-3} and F_{1-4} is that (a) both parents are carriers. (b) a mutation has occurred. (c) F_{1-4} has brought a dominant allele for the trait into the family. (d) F_{1-3} has a mutant phenotype which can be attributed to her parents.

19. If F_{2-1} and F_{2-9} should marry, the probability of the trait appearing in a given offspring is: (a) 1/16 (b) 1/4 (c) 1/2 (d) 1/8

Fill in the blanks.

20. The complimentary sequence of the DNA strand
3'—GCGTCGAAAATT—5' is _____.

21. Sanger's work with insulin helped to prove that _____ control the amino acid sequence in proteins.

22. _____ is the formation of mRNA from DNA.

23. The _____ hypothesis helps to explain why many amino acids are coded by more than one codon.

24. A repressor molecule interacts with the _____ molecule of a given gene to inhibit its enzyme synthesis.

211

25. Negative gene control occurs in such _____ organisms as *E. coli.*

26. In eukaryotic cells, DNA can be modified by the methylation of its _____ residues.

27. Methylation of DNA is correlated with _____ of genes.

28. The _____ involves the addition of possible chemical mutagens to a specific strain of *Salmonella typhimurium.*

29. In order for photoreactivation to occur, at least one _____ must be present.

30. Penetrance differs from expressivity in that penetrance deals with the function of the gene at the _____ level, while expressivity deals with the function of each gene _____ .

31. Both penetrance and expressivity are functions of the interactions of a given _____ with the environment.

32. During conjugation, genetic material is transmitted through a _____.

33. In real situations, Hardy-Weinberg equilibrium _____ exist in a gene pool.

34. Mating of heterozygotes which yields a progeny of greater vigor than the parents is termed _____.

35. _____ is the presence of three or more alleles in a given locus.

Determine whether the following statements are true or false.

36. The tRNA from the cells of cows is similar to that from human cells.

37. Three or more factors are responsible for elongation of the peptide chain during protein synthesis.

38. mRNA molecules are short lived and are broken down after only a few translations.

39. Positive gene control utilizes components such as hormones and special proteins to augment gene activity.

40. Negative gene control involves the production of repressor molecules which interact with the enzyme produced by a given gene.

41. The only way to detect a mutation is through visible differences.

42. Multiple alleles are three or more genes that control a certain trait.

43. During transformation, genes enter the recipient in fragments.

44. After conjugation, a female bacterium can become a male.

45. Spontaneous mutations in a bacterial chromosome cannot cause antibiotic resistance.

46. The lysogenic cycle leads to the immediate deterioration of the host cell.

47. Lysogenic phages can cause beneficial mutations.

48. It only takes one generation to bring a population initially in disequilibrium to equilibrium if the conditions for Hardy-Weinberg Law exist.

ANSWER KEY

1. a	2. c	3. a
4. c	5. d	6. a
7. d	8. b	9. d
10. c	11. a	12.a
13. b	14. d	15. d
16. b	17. b	18. a
19. d	20. 5'—CGCAGCTTTTAA—3'	
21. genes	22. Transcription	23. wobbble
24. DNA	25. prokaryotic	26. cytosine
27. non-expression	28. Ames test	29. photon
30. population, individually		31. genotype
32. sex pilus	33. does not	34. heterosis
35. Polymorphism	36. True	37. False
38. True	39. True	40. False
41. False	42. True	43. True
44. True	45. False	46. False
47. True	48. True	

CHAPTER 7

KINGDOM PROTISTA AND KINGDOM FUNGI

SECTION I: KINGDOM PROTISTA

The Protozoans

What are the chief characteristics of the protozoans?

SOLUTION:

The protozoans are a heterogeneous assemblage of a large number of species, which are almost exclusively microscopic organisms.

In the past, protozoans had been grouped into the phylum Protozoa within the Animal Kingdom, although this classification was considered controversial. Most biologists now accept that the protozoans have more in common with the Kingdom Protista. Protozoa live either singly or in colonies. These organisms are usually said to be unicellular. Therefore they contain no tissue or organs, which are defined as aggregations of differentiated cells. Instead of organs, they have functionally equivalent subcellular structures called organelles. These organelles do show a great deal of functional differentiation for the purposes of locomotion, food procurement, sensory reception, response, protection, and water regulation. Certain protozoans have interesting plant-like characteristics in both structure and physiology.

Reproduction among the protozoans is variable. An individual may divide into two, usually equal halves, after which each grows to the original size and form. This form of reproduction is called binary fission and can be seen in the flagellates, among the ciliates, and in organisms such as the amoeba. Multiple fission, or sporulation, where the nucleus divides repeatedly and the cytoplasm becomes differentiated simultaneously around each nucleus resulting in the production of a number of offspring, is also seen among the protozoans. Other types of reproduction characteristics of the protozoans are plasmotomy, which is the cytoplasmic division of a multinucleate protozoan without nuclear division, resulting in smaller multinucleate products.

Budding is another reproductive process by which a new individual arises as an outgrowth from the parent organism differentiating before or after it becomes free. All the reproductory mechanisms thus far mentioned illustrate asexual means of reproduction. Sexual reproduction may also occur by the fusion of two cells, called gametes, to form a new individual, or by the temporary contact and nuclear exchange (conjugation) of two protozoans (for example, two paramecia). The result of conjugation may be "hybrid vigor," defined as the superior qualities of a hybrid organism over either of its parental lines. Some species have both sexual and asexual stages in their life cycles.

With regard to their ecology, protozoans are found in a great variety of habitats, including the sea, fresh water, soil, and the bodies of other organisms. Some protozoans are free-living; meaning that they are free-moving or free-floating, whereas others have sessile organisms. Some live in or upon other organisms in either a commensalistic, mutualistic, or parasitic relationship.

The mechanisms for the acquisition of nutrition is also variable among the protozoans. Some are holozoic, meaning that solid foods such as bacteria, yeasts, algae, protozoans, and small metazoans or multicellular organisms, are ingested. Others may be saprozoic, wherein dissolved nutrients are absorbed directly; holophytic, wherein manufacture of food takes place by photosynthesis; or mixotrophic, which use both the saprozoic and holophytic methods.

It should be pointed out that the unicellular level of organization is the only characteristic by which the phylum Protozoa can be described. In all other respects, such as symmetry and specialization of organelles, the phylum displays extreme diversity.

> What problems had scientists faced in referring to the many forms of protozoans as belonging to a single animal phylum vs. a kingdom?

SOLUTION:

The first problem was that the unicellular level of organization was the only characteristic by which the phylum could be described; in all other respects the phylum displayed extreme diversity. Protozoans exhibit all types of symmetry, a great range of structural complexity, and adaptations for all types of environmental conditions. Although all of them have remained at the unicellular level, they have evolved along numerous lines through the specialization of the protoplasm. Specialization has occurred through the evolution of an array of subcellular organelles. A second problem involved taxonomic organization.

As is true of any taxonomic category, a phylum should contain members which are derived from a common ancestral form. In the classification of the protozoans, virtually all motile unicellular organisms had been grouped into a single phylum, with very little regard to evolutionary relationships. It is among the flagellate protozoans that the concept of a single subphylum produced the greatest aberration. Most unicellular free-living flagellates are organisms which, when assembled, constitute a collection of largely unrelated forms.

A third problem was with the possession of certain plant-like features, such as autotrophism and the presence of chloroplasts. In fact, certain green flagellate "protozoans" appear to be rather closely related to unicellular green algae which belong to the Kingdom Plantae. Thus, not only was the concept of a single phylum questionable, there was the additional problem of whether the Protozoa should be a true animal phylum.

Sarcodina (The Amoeba)

●PROBLEM 7-3

> The amoeba has no mouth for ingestion of food, but can take food in at any part of the cell. Explain this method of ingestion. What occurs following ingestion?

SOLUTION:

In the amoeba, pseudopodia (false feet) are used for nutrient procurement. These are temporary projections of cytoplasm which extend around the prey in a cup-like fashion eventually enveloping it completely. These pseudopodia can form anywhere on the surface of the amoeba. The enclosing of the captured organism by cytoplasm results in the formation of a food vacuole within the amoeba. Usually, the pseudopodia are not in intimate contact with the prey during engulfment and a considerable amount of water is enclosed within the food vacuole along with the captured organism. Engulfment may also involve complete contact with the surface of the prey, and the resulting vacuole is then completely filled by food. Death of the prey takes from 3 to 60 minutes and results primarily from a lack of oxygen.

Digestion occurs within the food vacuole. In amoeba, as in man, digestion is controlled by enzymes, and different enzymes act at definite hydrogen-ion concentrations. The enzymes that function in the vacuoles of an amoeba enter by fusion of the vacuoles with lysosomes. The enzymes hydrolyze the proteins into amino acids, fats into fatty acids and glycerol, and carbohydrates into simple sugars. These end products of digestion are absorbed by the rest of the organism through the vacuolar membrane. The food vacuole is not stationary within the organism but circulates in the fluid cytoplasm. Undigested material is egested from the cytoplasm. Like that of ingestion, the point of egestion is not fixed; food vacuoles containing undigested material may break through the surface at any point.

●PROBLEM 7-4

Describe locomotion in the amoeba.

SOLUTION:

The locomotion of amoeba is considered to be the simplest type of animal locomotion. A moving amoeba sends out a projection, termed a pseudopodium. Following this, the organism advances as the inner, granular, gel-like endoplasm flows into the pseudopodium. Two or three pseudopodia may be formed simultaneously but ultimately one will become dominant for a time. As new pseudopodia are formed, the old ones withdraw into the general body region. In its locomotion the amoeba often changes its course in response to environmental stimulation, by forming a new dominant pseudopodium on the opposite side, thus moving in a very irregular fashion.

Currently there is no fully complete explanation for the changes, both physical and chemical, which are involved in amoeboid movement. The theory accepted by zoologists at the present time is based on changes in the texture of the cytoplasm. As a result of some initial stimulus, ectoplasm, the outer clear, thin layer of the organism, undergoes a liquefaction and becomes endoplasm, which is gel-like. As a result of this change, internal pressure builds up and causes the endoplasm to flow out at this point, forming a pseudopodium. In the interior of the pseudopodium, the endoplasm flows forward along the line of progression; around the periphery, endoplasm is converted to ectoplasm, thereby building up and extending the sides of the pseudopodium like a sleeve. At the posterior of the body, ectoplasm is assumed to be undergoing conversion to endoplasm. During this entire process, energy consumption is known to have taken place.

●PROBLEM 7-5

What is the function of the contractile vacuole?

SOLUTION:

Unicellular and simple multicellular organisms lack special excretory structures for the elimination of nitrogenous wastes. In these organisms, wastes are simply excreted across the general cell membranes. Some protozoans do, however, have a special excretory organelle called the contractile vacuole. It appears that this organelle eliminates water from the cell but not nitrogenous wastes. These organelles are more common in fresh water protozoans than in marine forms. This is because, in fresh water forms, the concentration of solutes is greater in the cytoplasm than in the surrounding water, and water passively flows into the cell through the cell membrane. The fresh water protozoan is said to live in a hypotonic environment. This inflow of water would cause a fatal bloating if the water were not removed by the contractile vacuole. The vacuole swells and shrinks in a steady cycle, slowly ballooning as water collects in it, then rapidly contracting as it expels its contents, and then slowly ballooning again. The exact process of how the cell pumps water out of the vacuole is still unclear, but it is believed that the process is an energy consuming one.

Mastigophora (The Flagellates)

●PROBLEM 7-6

Euglena is a common green flagellate protozoan found in freshwater ponds. Describe briefly the method of locomotion, nutrition, and asexual reproduction in this organism.

SOLUTION:

Normally, locomotion in Euglena is produced by undulating movements of the flagellum. These movements of the flagellum draw the organism after it in a characteristic spiral path. Actually, Euglena has two flagella, but only one extends from the body and is used for locomotion.

With regard to nutrition, Euglena carries on autotrophic nutrition, as do green plants, synthesizing food from inorganic substances in the presence of light. However, under condition of total darkness for long periods of time, in a medium containing necessary nutrients, Euglena will shift to a heterotrophic mode of nutrition. Under these conditions the chloroplasts, the organelles which carry on photosynthesis, disappear, and the organisms live by absorbing the necessary nutrients from the surrounding medium through their cell membranes. When returned to the light environment, the chloroplasts reappear, and the autotrophic mode of living is resumed. This behavior is one of the reasons why Euglena is said to be both plant-like and animal-like.

The life cycle of Euglena involves both an active phase, during which the organism moves about, and an encysted phase, during which the organism is rounded up with a protective cyst membrane surrounding it. Asexual reproduction can occur in both stages. The division is typically a longitudinal binary fission. The nucleus divides by mitosis, and then the cytoplasm divides, forming two cells each with a nucleus.

Ciliophora (The Ciliates)

●PROBLEM 7-7

Unlike Amoeba, Paramecium has a permanent structure, or organelle, that functions in feeding. Describe this organelle and the method of feeding and digestion in Paramecium.

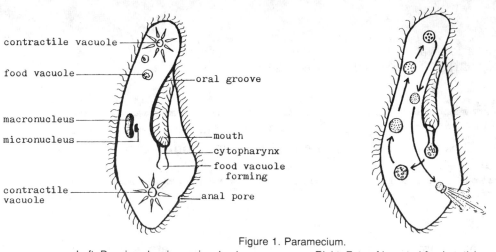

Figure 1. Paramecium.
Left: Drawing showing major structures.   Right: Fate of ingested food particles.

SOLUTION:

The feeding organelle in Paramecium begins with an oral groove. This oral groove is a ciliated channel located on one side of the organism. Food particles are swept into the oral groove by water currents produced by the beating cilia, and are carried down the groove to a point called the cytostome, which can be thought of as the mouth. Food is carried through the cytostome into the cytopharynx, which is also lined with cilia. As food accumulates at the lower end of the cytopharynx, a food vacuole forms around it. The vacuole eventually breaks away and begins to move toward the anterior of the cell. Lysosomes fuse with the food vacuole and secrete digestive enzymes into the vacuole. As digestion proceeds, the end products, such as sugars and amino acids, diffuse across the membrane of the vacuole into the surrounding cytoplasm, and the vacuole begins to move toward the posterior end of the cell. When at the posterior end of the cell, the vacuole fuses with a structure there called the anal pore. Undigested material in the vacuole is expelled to the outside through the anal pore. In addition to serving as the digestive organ, the food vacuole also serves, by its movement, to distribute the products of digestion to all parts of the cell.

●PROBLEM 7-8

The ciliates are the fastest moving protozoans. Explain ciliary movement in a ciliate. What other function is served by the cilia?

SOLUTION:

Ciliary movement consists of an effective and a recovery stroke. As depicted in Figure 1, during the effective (power) stroke, the cilium is outstretched and moves from a forward to a backward position. During the recovery stroke, the cilium, bent over to the right against the body when viewed from above and looking anteriorly, is brought back to the forward position in a counterclockwise movement. The recovery position offers less water resistance. The beating of the cilia is synchronized and waves of ciliary beat progress down the length of the body from anterior to posterior. The direction of the waves is slightly oblique, which causes the ciliate to swim in a spiral course and at the same time to rotate on its longitudinal axis.

The beating of the cilia can be reversed in direction, and the animal can move backwards. The so-called "avoidance reaction" is associated with the backward movement of the ciliate. When the organism comes in contact with some undesirable object, the ciliary beat is reversed. It moves backward a short distance, turns, and moves forward again. This avoidance reaction can be repeated.

Detection of external stimuli is another function of the cilia and though perhaps all of the cilia can act as sensory receptors in this respect, there are certain long, stiff cilia that play no role in movement and are probably exclusively sensory. The two functions, then, of the cilia are locomotion and sensory reception.

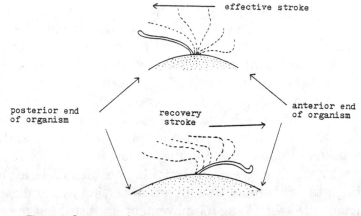

Figure 1. One cycle of ciliary movement. Only one cilium is shown.
Result of cycle is that animal moves forward.

●PROBLEM 7-9

What results would you expect if the macronucleus were removed from a paramecium?

SOLUTION:

Ciliates differ from all other animals in possessing two distinct types of nuclei — a large macronucleus and one or more smaller micronuclei. The macronucleus is sometimes called the vegetative nucleus, since it is not critical in sexual reproduction, as are the micronuclei. The macronucleus is essential for normal metabolism, for mitotic division, and for the control of cellular differentiation. The macronucleus is considered to participate actively in the synthesis of RNA, which is used in cell metabolism. Removal of the macronucleus from a ciliate causes cell death, even if a micronucleus is present.

Sporozoans (The Spore Producers)

Name an organism which produces spores in its life cycle and explain how this aids in its proliferation.

SOLUTION:

While spores are primarily used as a means of reproduction in plants, there is one class of protozoans (the Sporozoa) which produces spores. These spores are highly resistant forms of the organism which can withstand extreme environmental conditions and are specialized for asexual reproduction.

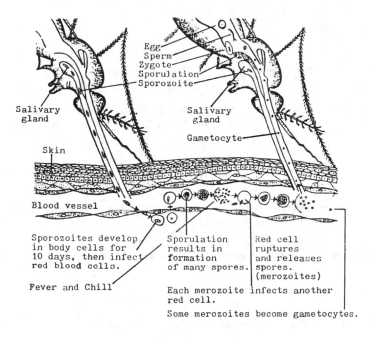

Figure 1. The life cycle of the malaria parasite, Plasmodium.

The sporozoan *Plasmodium* is a spore-forming protozoan that causes the disease malaria. *Plasmodium* spores are produced initially by sexual reproduction in the body of a mosquito (see Figure 1) which has sucked the blood of an individual infected with the organism. These spores (sporozoites) may now be injected into another individual's bloodstream when the mosquito bites the new host. After invading the red blood cells, the spores reproduce asexually, producing many spores (merozoites) within each invaded cell. This causes the cell to burst, releasing the spores. Each is able to invade another red blood cell. It is thus through repeated sporulation that the organism proliferates in the bloodstream of the infected individual. Some merozoites develop into male and female gametocytes. It is these gametocytes which a mosquito sucks up when she bites. In the mosquito the gametocytes develop into gametes. By sexual reproduction, the gametes fuse into zygotes which become sporozoites and the cycle repeats.

The Algae

●PROBLEM 7-11

Describe the kingdoms within which algae are classified.

SOLUTION:

Algae fall into the Plant, Protistan, and Moneran Kingdoms. The three phyla divisions of the Thallophytes (a major plant division) includes the Chlorophyta (green algae), Rhodophyta (red algae), and Phaeophyta (brown algae). The Protistan algae include the Euglenophyta (photosynthetic flagellates), Chrysophyta (golden algae and diatoms), and the Pyrrophyta (dinoflagellates). The Moneran Kingdom includes the Cyanophyta (blue-green algae).

●PROBLEM 7-12

All of the algae have the green pigment chlorophyll, yet the different phyla of algae show a great variety of colors. Explain.

SOLUTION:

The pigments found in the different algae phyla are extremely varied, and their concentrations result in different colors. The earliest classifications of algae were based on color. Fortunately, later study of algae showed that algae of similar pigmentation also shared other important characteristics and that the older classifications were still valid.

In addition to the green pigment chlorophyll, most algae possess pigments of other colors called accessory pigments. The accessory pigments may play a role in absorbing light of various wavelengths. The energy of these light wavelengths is then passed on to chlorophyll. This absorption widens the range of wavelengths of light that can be used for photosynthesis.

The accessory pigments phycocyanin and phycoerythrin serve this function in the red algae, the Rhodophyta. These pigments give the Rhodophyta their characteristic red color, although occasionally, they may be black. The red algae often live at great depths in the ocean. The wavelengths absorbed by chlorophyll *a* do not penetrate to the depths at which the red algae grow. The wavelengths that do penetrate deep enough are mostly those of the central portion of the color spectrum. These wavelengths are readily absorbed by phycoerythrin and phycocyanin. The energy trapped by these pigments is then passed on to chlorophyll *a*, which utilizes this energy for photosynthesis.

In the green algae, the Chlorophyta, the chlorophyll pigments predominate over the yellow and orange carotene and xanthophyll pigments. The predominance of carotene pigments imparts a yellow color to the golden algae, members of the phylum Chrysophyta. The diatoms, the other important class of Chrysophyta, possess the brown pigment fucoxanthin. The Pyrrophyta (dinoflagellates) are yellow-green or brown, due to the presence of fucoxanthin and carotenes. Some red dinoflagellates are poisonous, containing a powerful nerve toxin. The blooming of these algae are responsible for the "red tides" that kill millions of fish.

The brown algae, the Phaeophyta, have a predominance of fucoxanthin. These algae range in color from golden brown to dark brown or black. The procaryotic cyanophyta (blue-green algae) have the blue pigment phycocyanin as well as phycoerythrin, xanthophyll, and carotene. The Euglenophyta contain chlorophyll *a* and *b* and some carotenoids.

●PROBLEM 7-13

List the structural characteristics of the blue-green algae. Where may they be found?

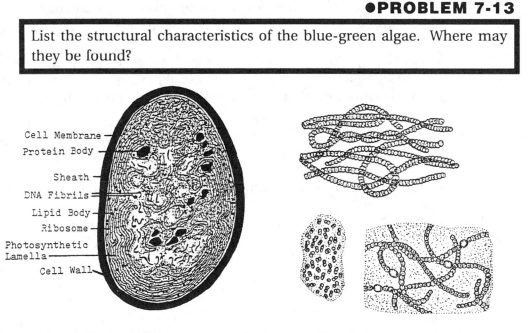

Figure 1. Structure of a blue-green algal cell as seen under the electron microscope. Note its similarity to bacterial cell structure.

Figure 2. Some common species of blue-green algae.

225

SOLUTION:

The blue-green algae, (Cyanophyta or cyanobacteria) are prokaryotic unicellular or filamentous organisms. The filamentous forms are strings of individual cells held together by fused walls (See Figure 1). In most species, there are no protoplasmic connections, such as plasmodesmata, between the adjacent cells. The unicellular forms exist as either single rods or spheres, and each individual cell is capable of carrying out all necessary life processes.

The Cyanophyta are the most primitive chlorophyll containing autotrophic organisms now living. The Cyanophyta are quite different from other algae, being structurally similar to bacteria. These similarities have formed the basis for grouping them with the bacteria in the kingdom Monera.

All blue-green algae possess photosynthetic pigments, which are located in folds or convolutions of the cell membrane extending into the interior of the cell. These photosynthetic pigments are chlorophyll *a*, carotenoids, phycocyanin (blue pigment), and sometimes phycoerythrin (red pigment). Like the bacteria, the blue-green algae lack mitochondria, Golgi apparatus, a nuclear membrane, endoplasmic reticulum, and the large cell vacuole characteristic of higher plants. Ribosomes are present along with many proteinaceous granules and granules of a stored carbohydrate material known as cyanophycean starch, which is very similar to glycogen. The nuclear region consists of a single circular chromosome composed of double-stranded DNA.

The cell walls of blue-green algae contain some muramic acid and cellulose. Outside this cell wall is a sticky gelatinous sheath composed of pectic materials. It covers the entire cell. The cytoplasm of blue-green algae is unusually viscous, being composed of a very dense colloidal material.

Cell division in blue-green algae is accomplished by binary fission. Reproduction also occurs frequently by fragmentation of filaments. Sexual reproduction has never been observed in the Cyanophyta but is thought to occur infrequently.

No blue-green algae possess flagella, yet many species are capable of movement. The filamentous forms exhibit a peculiar slow gliding or oscillatory motion.

The blue-green algae are found in many varied habitats. Most are found in fresh water pools and ponds. A few species are found in hot springs, at temperatures up to 85°C. Some species are marine while others are common in soils, the banks of trees, and the sides of damp rocks. Some species of blue-green algae exhibit a symbiosis with fungi, in which both act together to form a lichen.

What are the importance of desmids, diatoms, and dinoflagellates to humans?

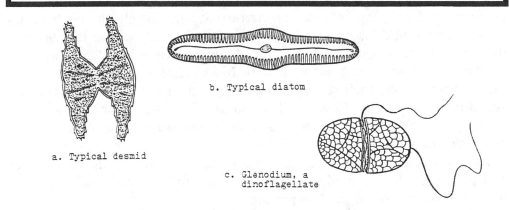

a. Typical desmid

b. Typical diatom

c. Glenodium, a dinoflagellate

SOLUTION:

Desmids, diatoms, and dinoflagellates are all unicellular algae. Desmids are nonmotile, freshwater green algae, commonly found in lakes and rivers. Desmids have symmetrical, curved, spiny, or lacy bodies with a constriction in the middle of the cell. Under the microscope they look like snowflakes. Diatoms, members of Chrysophyta, are found in fresh and salt water. They have two shelled, siliceous cell walls and store food as leucosin and oil. The cell walls are ornamented with fine ridges, lines, and pores that are either radially symmetrical or bilaterally symmetrical along the long axis of the cell. Diatoms lack flagella, but are capable of slow, gliding motion. Dinoflagellates, the majority of the Pyrrophyta, are surrounded by a shell consisting of thick, interlocking plates. All are motile and have two flagella. A number of species lack chlorophyll. These are the heterotrophs which feed on particulate organic matter. Dinoflagellates are mainly marine organisms.

All of these organisms play extremely important roles in aquatic food webs. Plankton is defined as small aquatic organisms floating or drifting near the surface. Phytoplankton are photosynthetic autotrophs and the zooplankton are heterotrophs. Desmids are important freshwater phytoplankton. Diatoms are the most abundant component of marine plankton (a gallon of sea water often contains one or two million diatoms). Diatoms are also found in abundance in many rivers. Dinoflagellates are second only to the diatoms as primary producers of organic matter in the marine environment. Probably three quarters of all the organic matter in the world is synthesized by diatoms and dinoflagellates. In addition to the production of organic material, these algae have the primary responsibility for the continued production of molecular oxygen via photosynthesis. Respiration by animals utilizes oxygen. If the supply were not constantly being replenished, the oxygen on earth would be exhausted.

Phytoplankton are essential to aquatic food chains; they are eaten by zooplankton, by invertebrates, and by some fish. The organisms which eat phytoplankton are in turn eaten by other organisms. Ultimately all aquatic life depends on the phytoplankton. Since terrestrial animals rely ultimately on the oceans, rivers, and lakes for a large part of their food source, the desmids, diatoms, and dinoflagellates are of crucial importance to land life as well.

Diatoms are also important to humans by virtue of their glasslike cell walls. When the cells die, their silica-impregnated shells sink to the bottom of the sea, and do not decay. These shells accumulate in large quantities and geologic uplifts bring the diatomaceous earth to the surface, where it is mined and used commercially.

Diatomaceous earth is used as a fine abrasive in detergents, toothpastes, and polishes. It is also used as a filtering agent, and as a component in insulating bricks and soundproofing products.

Diatoms utilize oils as reserve material, and it is widely believed that petroleum is derived from the oil of diatoms that lived in past geologic ages.

SECTION II – KINGDOM FUNGI

General Characteristics

● **PROBLEM 7-15**

How are fungi important to man?

SOLUTION:

Fungi are divided into four groups: Oomycetes (Oomycota) – the egg fungi, Zygomycetes (Zygomycota) – Zygo-spore-forming fungi, Ascomycetes (Ascomycota) – the sac fungi, and Basidiomycetes (Basidiomycota) – the club fungi.

Fungi are both beneficial and detrimental to man. Beneficial fungi are of great importance commercially. Ascomycetes, or sac fungi, are used routinely in food production. Yeasts, members of this group, are utilized in liquor and bread manufacture. All alcohol production relies on the ability of yeasts to degrade glucose to ethanol and carbon dioxide, when they are grown in the absence of oxygen. Yeasts used in alcohol production continue to grow until the ethanol concentration reaches about 13 percent. Wine, champagne, and beer are not concentrated any further. However, liquors such as whiskey or vodka are then distilled, so that the ethanol concentration reaches 40 to 50 percent. The different types of yeasts used in wine production are in part responsible for the distinctive flavors of different wines. Bread baking relies on CO_2 produced by the yeasts which causes the dough to rise. Yeasts used in baking and in the brewing of beer are cultivated yeasts, and are carefully kept as pure strains to prevent contamination. Sac fungi of genus Penicillium are used in cheese production. They are responsible for the unique flavor of cheeses such as Roquefort and Camembert. The medically important antibiotic penicillin is also produced by members of this genus. Certain Ascomycetes are edible. These include the delicious morels and truffles.

The club fungi, or Basidiomycetes, are of agricultural importance. Mushrooms are members of this group. About 200 species of mushrooms are edible while a small number are poisonous. The cultivated mushroom, *Agaricus campestris*, differs from its wild relatives, and is grown commercially.

Fungi are often of agricultural significance in that they can seriously damage crops. Members of the Oomycetes, also known as water molds, cause plant seedling diseases, downy mildew of grapes, and potato blight (this was the cause of the Irish potato famine). Mildew is a water mold that grows parasitically on damp, shaded areas.

Rhizopus stolonifer, a member of the Zygomycetes, is known as black bread mold. Once very common, it is now controlled by refrigeration and by additives that inhibit mold growth. The Aascomycete *Claviceps purpurea* causes the disease ergot, which occurs in rye and other cereal plants and results in ergot poisoning of humans and livestock. This type of poisoning may be fatal. The disease caused in humans is called St. Vitus's dance. Visual hallucinations are a common symptom of this disease. Lysergic acid is a constituent of ergot and is an intermediate in the synthesis of LSD. The "dance macabre" of the Middle Ages is now believed to have been caused by ergot poisoning.

Basidiomycetes are also responsible for agricultural damage. Certain club fungi are known as smuts and rusts. Smuts damage crops such as corn, and rusts damage cereal crops such as wheat. Bracket fungi, another type of club fungi, cause enormous economic losses by damaging wood of both living trees and stored lumber.

Fungi are also important to man because of the diseases they cause in man and livestock. *Candida albicans* causes a throat and mouth disease, "thrush," and also infects the mucous membranes of the lungs and genital organs. Many skin diseases are caused by fungi, including ringworm and athlete's foot.

What advantages and disadvantages do the fungi have in comparison with chlorophyll-bearing plants in terms of survival?

SOLUTION:

The chlorophyll-bearing plants require no organic food source. Their sole needs are light, carbon dioxide, water, and inorganic minerals. Plants are able to grow in any environment where these needs are met. The ocean is a habitat very favorable to green plants (e.g., the green algae), but not to fungi. Since fungi do not photosynthesize, they are able to grow in the dark. Green plants cannot do this. Fungi do not require light penetration and they can survive with very thick, tough cell walls. The cell walls of fungi sometimes contain cellulose, but chitin is usually their most important constituent. Chitin, a polysaccharide of acetyl glucosamine, is also the principal constituent of the exoskeleton of arthropods-insects, lobsters, shrimp, and crabs. The strong cell wall of fungi permits them to grow in environments where no plants or other organisms can grow. Certain fungi are extremely resistant to plasmolysis (cell shrinkage in hypertonic medium), and can grow in concentrated salt solutions and sugar solutions. Certain fungi are able to withstand high concentrations of toxic substances. An example is the ethanol-producing yeasts, which grow at extremely high concentrations of ethanol. Other organisms are killed at these ethanol concentrations.

Fungi are less adept at surviving than green plants in that fungi require an organic food source, and are only able to grow where large quantities of foodstuffs are present. Fungi cannot capture their food, they must obtain nutrition by growing directly on or within their food source. For these reasons, they are not commonly found in ocean habitats.

What is the difference between a hypha and a mycelium and between an ascus and a basidium?

SOLUTION:

A few fungi are unicellular, but most have multicellular bodies made up of tubular branching filaments called hyphae. A mass of hyphae is called a mycelium. The hyphae of the algai fungi, or Phycomycetes (which contain the Oomycetes and the Zygomycetes), are not divided by cross walls between adjacent nuclei — they are coenocytic hyphae. These fungi are thus multinucleate. The Ascomycetes and Basidiomycetes have hyphae divided by cross walls

— they are septate; these fungi are multicellular. The mycelium may appear as a cobweb-like mass of fibers, as in bread mold, or may be fleshy and compact, as in truffles.

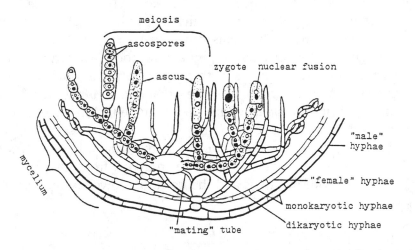

Figure 1. Sexual reproduction in the Ascomycetes. The "male" hyphae fuse with the "female" hyphae to produce dikaryotic hyphae, from which an ascus is produced. Meiosis occurs within the ascus to produce ascospores.

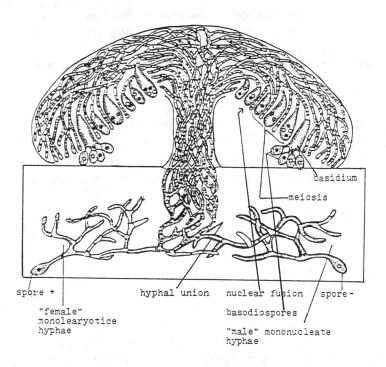

Figure 2. Sexual reproduction in the Basidiomycetes.
Diagram of section through a mushroom. Hyphae from two uninucleate mycelia — one of the plus, the other of the minus, mating type — unite and give rise to binucleate hyphae, which then develop into the above-ground part of the mushroom. The entire stalk and cap are composed of these hyphae tightly packed together. Spores are produced by basidia on the lower surface of the cap.

A basidium and an ascus are both reproductive structures. Ascus is Latin for sac, and fungi whose life cycle includes an ascus are termed sac fungi or ascomycetes. The ascus is formed from a single parent cell. The zygote is an elongated cell, and its nucleus divides meiotically to produce four haploid spores. These usually divide mitotically to produce eight small spore cells. Spores are released when the ascus ruptures.

The basidiomycetes, or club fungi, have reproductive structures called basidia. Mushrooms are members of this group. The basidium differs from the ascus in that spores are formed on the outside of the parent cell rather than within it. The zygote nucleus within the elongated, club-shaped basidium divides meiotically to produce four haploid nuclei. These nuclei migrate to protuberances which develop at the tip of the basidium. Each protuberance then buds off to form a spore. The spores may fall from the basidium or they may be ejected. Both the ascus and the basidium develop from a single zygote.

Myxomycophyta

●PROBLEM 7-18

In what ways are slime molds like true fungi? In what ways do they resemble animals?

SOLUTION:

Both cellular slime molds (acrasiomycota) and true slime molds (myxomycota) have unusual life cycles containing fungus-like and animal-like stages. Slime molds have membrane-bound nuclei, are heterotrophic, ingest food, lack cell walls, and produce fruiting bodies. They belong to the kingdom Protista in the phylum Gymnomycota.

The true slime mold's adult vegetative stage is decidedly animal-like. At this stage, the slime mold is a large, diploid, multinucleated amoeboid mass called a plasmodium. It moves about slowly and feeds on organic material by phagocytosis. Plasmodium growth continues as long as an adequate food supply and moisture are available. When these run short, the plasmodium becomes stationary and develops organs specialized to produce haploid spores, known as the fruiting bodies. At this stage, the true slime mold is similar to the fungi. Meiosis occurs in the fruiting body, and spores with cellulose cell walls are released. Spores are a resistant and dormant form of a slime mold. When the spores germinate, they lose their cell walls and become flagellated gametes. Gametes fuse to become zygotes. The zygotes lose their flagella, become amoeboid, and grow into multinucleated plasmodial slime molds.

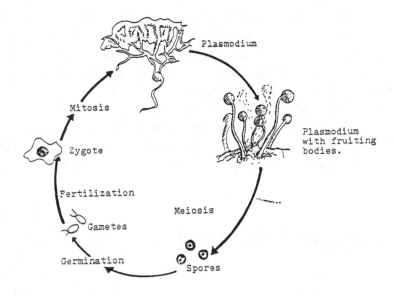

Figure 1. Life cycle of the true slime mold.

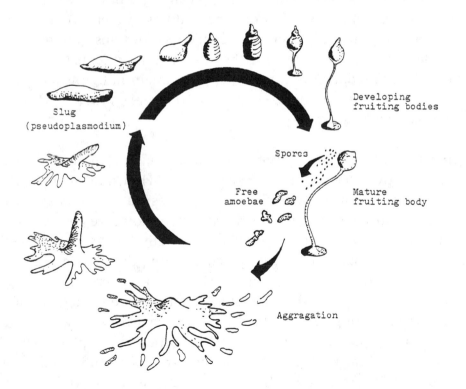

Figure 2. Life cycle of the cellular slime mold.

Cellular slime molds differ from the true (acellular) slime molds in being haploid and in that the amoeboid cells, on swarming together, retain their identity as individual cells. The cellular slime molds resemble amoebas throughout most of their life cycle: they lack cell walls, move about, and ingest particulate matter. Under certain conditions, the amoebas aggregate to form a multicellular pseudoplasmodium, called a slug. The pseudoplasmodium becomes stationary and fruiting bodies are formed. Spores are not produced by cellular division, but by the formation of cell walls around the individual amoeboid cells. Each spore becomes a new amoeboid cell when it germinates. Cellular slime molds are haploid throughout their life cycles. The formation of a fruiting, spore-forming body is characteristic of fungi.

SHORT ANSWER QUESTIONS FOR REVIEW

Choose the correct answer.

1. Which of the following is incorrect concerning protozoans? (a) Protozoans are usually only found on land and fresh water. (b) Protozoans can take part in parasitic or mutualistic relationships. (c) Protozoans can feed holozoically, meaning they can ingest nutrients like bacteria directly, or holophytically, meaning they obtain nutrients via photosynthesis. (d) Because their shapes are so diverse, protozoans cannot be classified by symmetry.

2. In reference to the life cycle of the euglena, what is meant by the terms "active phase" and "encysted phase"? How and when does reproduction occur in relation to these phases? (a) The "active phase" refers to movement of the euglena without a protective coat, while the "encysted phase" is movement with a protective coat surrounding the euglena. Reproduction can only occur during the "active phase" by plamotomy. (b) The "active phase" refers to movement of the euglena at times other than while digesting, while the "encysted phase" is movement during feeding, the protective coat necessary for proper digestion. Reproduction can take place during either phase sexually by conjugation. (c) The "active phase" refers to the portion of a euglena's life cycle in which it is free to move about, while the "encysted phase" is the portion of the cycle when the euglena is covered by a protective coat, not free to move about. Reproduction can take place in either phase and occurs asexually via binary fission. (d) None of the above

3. Which of the following best explains the probable mechanism of amoeboid movement? (a) The simultaneous conversion of both ectoplasm and endoplasm to a gel-like mass causes the formation of a pseudopodia. This acts as a foot-like device, as the amoeba uses it to move around. (b) The simultaneous conversion of both ectoplasm and endoplasm to a liquid-like mass causes pressure to build up on the rim of the amoeba, forming a pseudopodia. The amoeba then uses the pseudopodia to move around. (c) Neither ectoplasm nor endoplasm change their original consistency. A pseudopodia is formed due to a change in internal pressure inside the interior of the amoeba. The pseudopodia is then used by the amoeba to move around. (d) Ectoplasm moves from outside to inside along the periphery of the cell, causing pressure to build up inside the amoeba. This causes the endoplasm to move out to the periphery, causing the formation of a pseudopodia. The endoplasm then continues flowing outward, until its flow is fountain-like, moving back towards the cell interior. The process then begins again.

4. Which of the following is *incorrect* concerning the method of feeding of a paramecium? (a) Food is taken into the organism via water currents by way of the oral groove. From there, it moves into the cytostome, the so-called mouth of the organism. (b) The nutriments are transported around the paramecium by a food vacuole. (c) Undigested material leaves the paramecium when the food vacuole fuses with the cell membrane. (d) Digestive enzymes are secreted by lysosomes that fuse with the food vacuole.

5. Which of the following best describes ciliary movement in a paramecium? (a) simple back and forth movement (b) movement similar to a rowing motion (c) a highly coordinated motion consisting of a power stroke and a recovery stroke (d) movement that begins at the tip of the cilia and moves downward in a wave-like motion

6. In the life cycle of the sporozoan which causes malaria, which is the animal that is the vector of the disease? (a) man (b) *Anopheles* mosquito (c) *Plasmodium* (d) All of the above (e) None of the above

Fill in the blanks.

7. Once a pseudopod has surrounded its prey, the amoeba takes in the food via a _____. The nutriment is then broken down, as in man, by _____. Any unwanted material is egested from the cytoplasm via _____ also, at _____ point along the cell membrane.

8. The protozoan *Plasmodium* is the organism responsible for the disease malaria. It is one of the rare cases in which an animal reproduces by means of _____.

9. Chlorophyta have a larger quantity of the green pigment _____ than other pigments, so they appear green. Chrysophyta, on the other hand, have a predominance of the pigment _____ giving them a yellowish color.

10. The difference between phytoplankton and zooplankton is that the former are _____, while the latter are _____. Among the important jobs performed by these organisms is the production of _____. They also serve as the main _____ source for many invertebrates and fish in our oceans.

11. Blue-green algae are associated with bacteria for a number of reasons. They both _____ mitochondria and have _____ nuclear membrane. They are thus both _____, while other algae and fungi are _____.

12. Yeast, a member of the fungi class _____, is used in the production of _____. Another member of this class is used in the production of the antibiotic _____.

13. The cell wall of fungi is usually composed of one of two substances; one of them is _____, the most abundant constituent of all plant cell walls, and the other is _____, the same constituent that makes the _____ of some insects, all lobsters, and shrimp.

14. In its animal-like stage, a true slime mold is a diploid, amoeboid-like mass called a _____. It feeds via _____. When its food supply runs short, it reproduces by haploid spores contained in a _____. This type of reproduction is similar to that of _____. Cellular slime molds differ

236

from the animal-like stage of true slime molds only in the fact that the former are _____.

Determine whether the following statements are true or false.

15. Although there are a number of methods by which protozoa reproduce asexually, sexual reproduction does not occur in protozoa.

16. The function of a contractile vacuole in protozoans is strictly limited to the elimination of nitrogenous waste materials.

17. In Ciliates, such as the paramecium, both the micronucleus and the macronucleus are necessary for sexual reproduction.

18. Cilia serve no other function other than locomotion, and in that capacity, can only move in one direction.

19. After diatoms die, their shells form a sediment near ocean's bottom that serve no purpose and can, if in excess, become a nuisance.

20. Some fungi possess the unique characteristic of causing disease, while others can prevent disease.

21. Fungi that are multicellular are made up of branching filaments called hyphae. A mass of these filaments together is called a mycelium.

22. An example of a "fruiting body" is a mushroom. Once it is formed, it detaches completely from the non-reproductive part of the basidiomycetes.

ANSWER KEY

1. a   2. c   3. d

4. c   5. c   6. b

7. food vacuole, digestive enzymes, food vacuoles, any

8. spores   9. chlorophyll, carotene

10. autotrophs, heterotrophs, molecular oxygen, food

11. lack, no, prokaryotes, eukaryotes

12. Ascomycetes, alcohol, penicillin

13. cellulose, chitin, exoskeleton

14. plasmodium, phagocytosis, fruiting body, fungi, haploid

15. False   16. False   17. False

18. False   19. False   20. True

21. False   22. False

CHAPTER 8

PLANT KINGDOM

Anatomical Survey (Angiosperm)

Describe the parts of a typical flower. What are their functions?

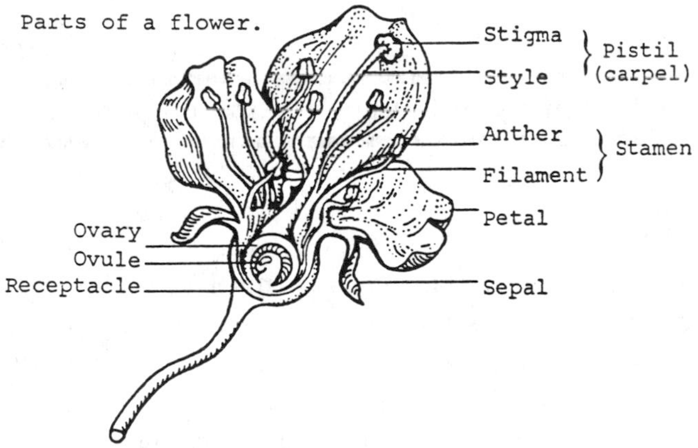

Parts of a flower.

Stigma ⎫ Pistil
Style ⎭ (carpel)

Anther ⎫ Stamen
Filament ⎭

Ovary
Ovule
Receptacle

Petal

Sepal

Figure 1. Parts of a flower.

SOLUTION:

The flower of an angiosperm is a modified stem on which concentric rings of modified leaves are attached. A typical flower consists of four such rings of structures borne on the receptacle, the expanded end of the flower stalk. The stalk of the flower is also known as the pedicel. The outermost ring, usually green and most like ordinary leaves, is composed of sepals. These enclose and protect the flower bud until it is ready to open. Collectively, the sepals are known as the calyx. Internal to the calyx are the petals, which are often brilliantly colored in order to attract those insects or birds which promote pollination. Flowers which are pollinated by the wind need not be attractive to birds and insects, and so their petals tend to be less showy, and may even be absent.

Inside the corolla lie the stamens, the male reproductive organs of the flower. Each stamen consists of a slender stalk called the filament, which supports an expanded anther at the tip. The immature anther is composed primarily of pollen sacs. After reaching maturity, the anther contains numerous pollen grains, which produce haploid male gametes upon germination. In the center of the flower is a pistil (carpel) or pistils, the female reproductive organ. Each pistil is composed of a swollen portion, the ovary, at its base; a long, slender stalk which rises from the ovary, the style; and on top of this, an enlarged flattened crown called the stigma. The ovary contains one or more ovules, which are the future seeds of the angiosperm. The stigma's function is to secrete a moist, sticky substance to which the pollen grains will adhere. The style provides a lubricated pathway through which the pollen tube of the germinated pollen grain can grow on its way towards the egg cell.

Plant Tissues

●PROBLEM 8-2

What are the difficulties in the classification of tissues of higher plants?

SOLUTION:

The characteristics of plant cells themselves make it difficult for botanists to agree on any one classification system. The different types of cells intergrade and a given cell can change from one type to another during the course of its life. As a result, the tissues formed from such cells also intergrade and can share functional and structural characteristics. Some plant tissues contain cells of one type while others consist of a variety of cell types. Plant tissues cannot be fully characterized or distinguished on the basis of any one single factor such as location, function, structure, or evolutionary heritage. Plant tissues can be divided into two major categories: meristematic tissues, which are composed of immature cells and are regions of active cell division; and permanent tissues, which are composed of more mature, differentiated cells. Permanent tissues can be subdivided into three classes of tissues — surface, fundamental, and vascular. However, the classification of plant tissues into categories based purely on their maturity runs into some difficulties. Some permanent tissues may change to meristematic activity under certain conditions. Therefore, this classification is not absolutely reliable.

●PROBLEM 8-3

Plant tissues that are neither considered surface tissues nor vascular tissues, are referred to as fundamental tissue. Describe the various types of fundamental tissues.

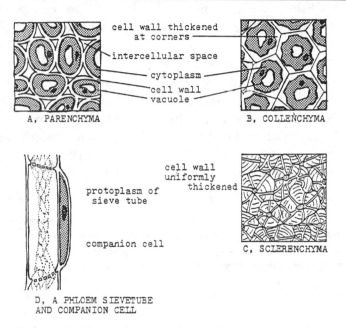

Figure 1. Some types of plant tissues: parenchyma, collenchyma, sclerenchyma, and endodermis.

SOLUTION:

Fundamental tissues make up most of the plant body. Examples include the soft parts of the leaf, the pith (central core of stems and roots), the cortex (outer area of stems and roots), and the soft parts of flowers and fruits. The chief functions of the fundamental tissues are the production and storage of food. Some fundamental tissues may also function in physical support of the plant body. There are four types of fundamental tissues, each composed of a single type of cell.

One type is parenchyma tissue, which occurs in roots, stems, and leaves. Parenchyma consists of small cells with a thin cell wall and a thin layer of cytoplasm surrounding a large vacuole. The cells are loosely packed, resulting in abundant spaces in the tissue for gas and nutrient exchange. Most of the chloroplasts of leaves are found in these cells.

A second type is collenchyma tissue. It contains cells that are generally more elongate and their cell walls are irregularly thickened compared to the cell walls of parenchyma. The corners of their cell walls are thickened to provide the plant with support. These tissues occur just beneath the epidermis of stems and leaf stalks.

Sclerenchyma tissue, a third type, also functions in support. Most mature cells of this tissue are dead. They have very thick cells walls to provide support and mechanical strength. The cell wall is usually impregnated with an additional tough substance called lignin. The cell wall may be so thick that the internal space of the cell is nearly obliterated. Sclerenchyma is found in many stems and roots. Sclerenchyma cells are divided into two categories, fibers and sclereids. Fibers are elongate cells with tapered ends. Fiber cells are tough and strong, but flexible. Sclereids are more irregularly shaped cells. Stone cells are rounded sclereids. They are found in the hard shells of nuts and in seeds.

Endodermis, the fourth type of fundamental tissue, occurs in a layer surrounding the vascular core of roots. Endodermal cells have cell walls thickened with lignin and suberin which are chemical substances that make the cells waterproof. The endodermal layer is one cell thick, and the cells are compactly arranged. This cell layer is called the Casparian strip. The Casparian strip regulates the entry of water into the vascular tissues of roots.

●PROBLEM 8-4

In plants, which tissue is responsible for new growth?

SOLUTION:

Meristematic tissue is responsible for new growth in plants. There are several regions in a growing plant where meristematic tissues are found. The apical meristem near the tips of roots, the stem, and branches is important in the growth and differentiation in these areas of a plant. The meristems in the buds of a stem are responsible for outgrowths of the stem. Another meristematic tissue is found in the cambium; this tissue, called the vascular cambium, is where thickening of the stem occurs.

The cells of the meristematic tissue are often small, thin-walled, more or less rounded, each with a large nucleus and few or no vacuoles. Furthermore, meristematic cells generally are closely packed together, and thus few intercellular spaces are found. These cells are embryonic, relatively undifferentiated cells that are capable of rapid cell division. The resultant new cells grow and transform into specific types of plant tissue. The meristem of the root, for example, gives rise to cells that eventually differentiate into all of the cell types present in the root.

A plant embryo is composed entirely of meristematic cells and consequently is capable of rapid growth. As the plant develops, most of the meristem undergoes changes and differentiates into specific tissues. Some of the meristem continues to function in certain parts of the adult plant, and thus provides for continued growth. This gives some plants such as the perennials, the unique ability to continue growth throughout their lives.

●PROBLEM 8-5

Which tissue of plants most resembles, in function, the skin of animals?

SOLUTION:

Surface tissues form the protective outer covering of the plant body. The epidermis is the principal surface tissue of roots, stems, and leaves. It resembles the skin of animals in having a protective function. This tissue can be one cell thick, although some plants that live in very dry habitats, where protein from water loss is critical, have a thick epidermis consisting of many layers of cells. Most epidermal cells are relatively flat and contain a very large vacuole with only a thin layer of cytoplasm. Their outer walls are thicker than their inner walls. Epidermal cells often secrete a waxy, water-resistant substance, called cutin, on their outer surface. The thick outer cell wall and the cuticle aid in protection of the plant against loss of water.

Some epidermal cells on the surface of the leaves are specialized as guard cells. These regulate the size of small holes in the epidermis, the stomata, through which gases can move into or out of the leaf interior. Epidermal cells of roots have no cuticle which may interfere with their function of absorption. They are, however, characterized by hair-like outgrowths, called root hairs, that increase the absorptive surface for the intake of water and dissolved minerals from the soil.

Periderm is the surface tissue that constitutes the corky outer bark of tree trunks or the outer cork layer of large roots. Cork cells are dead when they are mature, and their cell walls contain another waterproof material, suberin, for additional protection.

The Stem

●PROBLEM 8-6

What are the functions of the stem? How are stems and roots differentiated?

The stem is the connecting link between the roots, where water and minerals enter the plant, and the leaves, where organic foodstuffs are synthesized. The vascular tissues of the stem are continuous with those of the root and the leaves and provide a pathway for the transport of materials between these parts. The stem and its branches support the leaves so that each leaf is exposed to as much sunlight as is possible. The stem of a flowering plant also supports flowers in the proper orientation to enhance reproduction and later, seed dispersal. Along the stem are growing points where the primordia of leaves and flowers originate. Some stems have cells which carry out photosynthesis, others have cells specialized for the storage of starch and other nutrients.

Roots and stems are structurally quite different. Stems have an epidermis covered with a protective layer of cutin while the epidermis of roots has no cutin but gives rise to hairlike projections called the root hairs. Stems, but not roots, have nodes, which are junctions where leaves arise. Stems may have lenticels for "breathing" while roots do not. The tip of a root is always covered by a root cap whereas the tip of a stem is naked unless it terminates in a bud. The dicot stem typically contains separate rings of xylem and phloem, with the xylem central to the phloem, whereas in the roots, phloem tubes lie between the arms of the star-shaped xylem tissues.

●PROBLEM 8-7

Describe the functions of the structures of the stem.

SOLUTION:

The stem is covered on the outside by a layer of rectangular cells, known as the epidermis. Just inside the epidermis is the cortex. The cortical cells are photosynthetic. An outer layer of thick walled collenchymal cells serve as supportive tissue for the stem. Inside the ring of the cortex is a one celled thick layer called the endodermis. The endodermis is interrupted at some points by passage cells through which water and minerals can pass. Immediately adjacent to the endodermis is another layer known as the pericycle. The pericycle of the stem has thick walled cells for the purpose of support. On the inner border of the pericycle is the vascular system, composed of xylem and phloem tissues. The xylem and phloem tissues are arranged in scattered bundles in the monocots or arranged in a ring in the dicots. The stem contains a central axial core of tissue, called the pith, which is composed of colorless parenchymal cells that serve in the function of nutrient storage.

Woody and Herbaceous Plants

Differentiate between herbaceous and woody plants and between annual, biennial, and perennial plants. How do the stem of woody plants increase in diameter?

SOLUTION:

Plants are generally differentiated into two types based on the nature of their stems. Herbaceous plants have a supple, green, rather thin stem, woody plants have a thick, tough stem or trunk, covered with a layer of cork. This cork is derived from the cork cambium, a layer of meristematic cells in the outer cortex of woody stems. Herbaceous plants are typically annuals or biennials. Annual plants start from seed, develop flower, and produce seeds within a single growing season, and die before the following winter. Biennial plants characteristically have two-season growing cycles. During the first season, while the plant is growing, food is stored in the root. Then the top of the plant dies and is replaced in the second growing season by a second top which produces seeds. Carrots and beets are examples of biennials. Woody plants, exemplified by a wide variety of trees and shrubs, are usually perennial plants, which live longer than two years. Perennials have been found that live hundreds or even thousands of years. They produce seeds yearly.

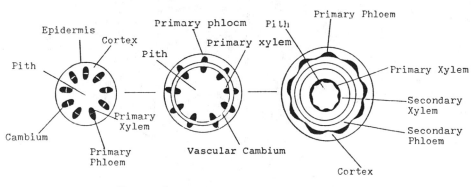

Figure 1. Stages of growth in a woody stem.

The stems of woody plants resemble herbaceous ones during their first year of growth, with each containing an epidermis, a cortex, an endodermis, a pericycle, vascular bundles, and a pith. But by the end of the first growing season, a cambium layer has taken a form which extends as a continuous ring between the primary xylem and phloem, pushing the phloem to the periphery of the stem and keeping the xylem toward the pith (see Figure 1). This

245

cambium layer, called the vascular cambium, is a region of rapid cell division, that is, the cambium is meristemic. In each successive year, this ring of meristem divides to form two types of cells: those inside the ring differentiate into the secondary xylem elements, and those outside the ring become the secondary phloem cells. The yearly deposits of xylem form the annual rings. Addition of a new ring to the old ones each year causes the stem of a woody plant to increase in diameter. Monocotyledons and some dicotyledons have herbaceous stems, while all gymnosperms and some dicotyledons have woody stems.

●PROBLEM 8-9

Differentiate between sapwood and heartwood and between spring wood and summer wood. What are the vascular rays?

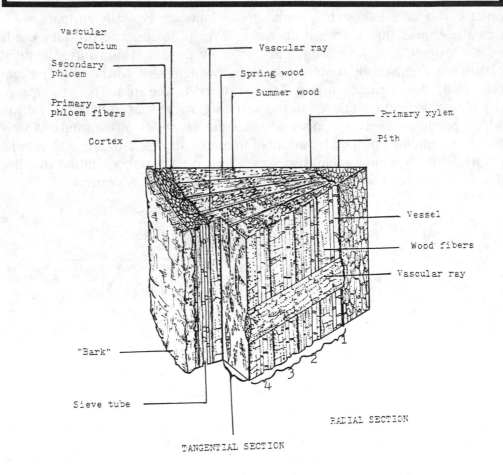

Figure 1. Diagram of a four year old woody stem.

SOLUTION:

The sapwood is the youngest, outermost portion of the xylem in a woody plant. It contains tracheids and vessels which function in carrying water and minerals from the root to the leaves. The heartwood is the older, inner portion of the xylem whose tracheids and vessels have lost the ability of conduction. The heartwood serves to increase the strength of the stem, and to support the increasing load of foliage as the tree grows.

The spring wood and summer wood together make up the secondary xylem ring (see Figure 1) of each growing season. They account chiefly for the increase in diameter of a woody tree trunk. They are derived from the vascular cambium, which also gives rise to the secondary phloem. At the beginning of each growing season, the cambial cells divide to produce relatively large, thin-walled xylem cells, which make up the spring wood (early wood). Toward the end of each season, the xylem cells produced are smaller and have thicker walls. These smaller cells constitute the summer wood (late wood). Ordinarily, there is only one growth season per year and abrupt change in cell size between the spring wood and summer wood clearly marks off distinct alternate circular zones called annual rings. The number of annual rings found in the cross-section of a woody trunk is now used as an indicator of the age of the tree. In addition, because the width of the annual rings varies according to the climatic conditions prevailing when ring was formed, it is possible to infer what the climate was at a particular time by examining the rings of old trees.

The vascular rays are rows of small, parenchymal cells that lie at right angles to the long axis of the stem or root, reaching radially from the secondary xylem to the secondary phloem. They are, like the secondary xylem and phloem, derived from the vascular cambium, and extend in length as the plant increases in girth. The vascular rays conduct water and minerals from the secondary xylem to the vascular cambium, the secondary phloem, and the cortical cells. Nutrients form the secondary phloem are channeled to the vascular cambium, the living cells of the secondary xylem, and the cells of the pith (if living).

● PROBLEM 8-10

What are the functions of (a) the vascular cambium, (b) stomata, (c) heartwood, (d) lenticels, (e) abscission layer, and (f) cutin?

SOLUTION:

The vascular cambium is a meristemic region found in the stem. Sometimes it is found in the roots of higher plants. It exists as a continuous ring of cells extending between the cluster of phloem cells and xylem cells. The cambium produces these two types of cells during periods of active mitotic cell division. The ones facing the center of the stem differentiate into xylem cells; and the ones facing the periphery become phloem cells.

The stomata are small specialized pores scattered over the epidermal surfaces of leaves and some stems. These pores are found mainly on the lower surface of the leaves. The stomata are delineated by a pair of cells called the guard cells. The guard cells, by changing their shape (due to changes in their turgor pressure), regulate the size of the stomatal aperture. An open stoma permits the escape of water and the exchange of gases.

The heartwood is the inner layer of the xylem in a woody plant. They are composed of dead, thick-walled xylem cells which have lost the ability to conduct water and minerals. Instead it has become tough supporting fibers. The heartwood increases the strength of the stem, and accommodates the increasing load of foliage as the tree grows.

Lenticels are masses of cells which rupture the epidermis and form swellings. These masses of cells are formed from cells of the cork cambium which divide repeatedly and rupture the epidermis lying above. Lenticels represent a continuation of the inner plant tissues with the external environment, and permits a direct diffusion of gases into and out of the stem or twig. Such direct passages are necessary because the cork cambium forms a complete sheath around the vascular bundles and effectively obstructs the ventilation of the vascular bundles.

An abcission layer is a sheet of thin-walled cells, loosely joined together, which extends across the base of the petiole. The formation of the abscission layer separates and loosens the point of attachment of the petiole to the stem. After the abscission layer is formed, the petiole is held on only by the epidermis and the fragile vascular bundles, so that wind or other mechanical disturbances will cause the leaf to fall off. This is the mechanism that accounts for the fall of leaves during autumn.

Cutin is a waxy organic substance secreted by the epidermal cells of the stems and leaves, but not the roots. Its waterproof property retards evaporative water loss to the atmosphere.

Leaf and Gas Exchange

●PROBLEM 8-11

What is the function of the leaves? Describe the structures of a typical dicot leaf.

SOLUTION:

The leaf is a specialized nutritive organ of the plant. Its function is to carry out photosynthesis, a process requiring a continuous supply of carbon dioxide, water, and radiant energy.

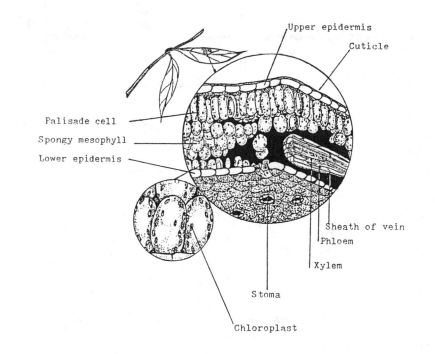

Figure 1. The microscopic structure of a leaf.

The leaf of a typical dicot consists of a stalk, called the petiole, attached to the stem, and a broad blade, which may be simple or compound. The petiole, like a stem in cross-section, contains vascular bundles. Within the blade, the vascular bundles fork repeatedly and form a network of veins. A cross-section of the leaf shows that it is composed of several types of cells. The outer cells, lining both the top and bottom surfaces of the leaf, make up the epidermis which secretes a protective, waterproof cutin covering. Distributed throughout the epidermal surface are many small, specialized pores, the stomata, each surrounded by two guard cells. There are many more stomata on the lower surface than the upper surface of the leaf in most species. The chloroplast containing guard cells regulate the size of the stomata by changing their turgor pressure and thus their shape. The stomata allow oxygen to diffuse out and carbon dioxide to diffuse into the leaf. Most of the space between the upper and lower epidermal layers is filled with thin-walled cells, called mesophyll, which are full of chloroplasts. The mesophyll layer near the upper epidermis is usually made of cylindrical palisade cells, closely packed together with their long axes perpendicular to the epidermal surface. The rest of the mesophyll cells are very loosely packed together, with large air spaces between them. These loosely-packed cells form the spongy layer of the leaf. The cells of the palisade layer, containing abundant chloroplasts, are chiefly responsible for the photosynthetic functioning of the leaf, while the air spaces between the mesophyll of the spongy layer hold moisture and gases. These air spaces are continuous with the stomata where exchange of gases takes place.

Discuss the mechanism by which the guard cells regulate the opening and closing of a stoma.

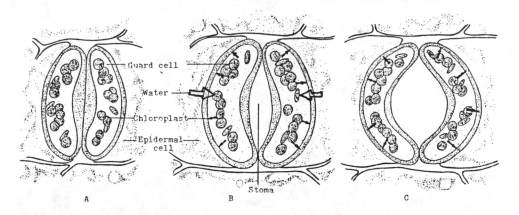

Figure 1. Diagrams illustrating the regulation of the size of the stoma by the guard cells.

SOLUTION:

The opening and closing of a stoma is regulated by changes in the turgor pressure within the two guard cells that surround the stomatal opening. Each bean-shaped guard cell has a thicker wall on the side toward the stoma called the inner wall, and a thinner wall on the side away from the stomatal opening called the outer wall. Increased turgor pressure causes the cells to bulge. Since the outer walls are thinner than the inner walls, the former stretch more than the latter, causing the cells to bow in and the stoma to open. When the turgor pressure in the guard cells decreases, the inner walls regain their original shape and the cells unbend, closing the stoma as a result.

Thus the opening and closing of a stoma depends on a mechanism which varies the turgor pressure within the guard cells. This variation of turgor involves in part the production of glucose and other osmotically active substances in the guard cells themselves. It is believed that light initiates a sequence of enzymatic reactions that lead to the conversion of starch stored in the guard cells into osmotically active glucose molecules, thus increasing the turgor pressure of the guard cells. As light increases the rate of photosynthesis, carbon dioxide is utilized and the decrease in carbon dioxide concentration, increases the pH of the guard cells (remember that guard cells contain chloroplasts and so they are able to undergo photosynthesis). This increased basicity stimulates the enzyme phosphorylase to convert starch to glucose-1-phosphate. The glucose-1-phosphate is subsequently converted to glucose, increasing the concentration of glucose in the guard cells and causing the influx of water into the cells by osmosis. (Another osmotically active solute may be K^+—potassium ions—which are pumped into the guard cell from the epidermal cell as CO_2 levels decrease.) This phenomenon raises the turgor pressure in the guard cells and causes the stoma to open (see Figure 1). In the dark the process is reversed. Thus, under normal conditions, the stomata in many species open regularly in the morning and close in the evening.

●PROBLEM 8-13

Explain why the stomata of a leaf tend to open up during the day and to close at night. What advantage is there in this?

SOLUTION:

During the day, the plant undergoes photosynthesis, a process which converts carbon dioxide and water into carbohydrates. This results in a drop of the carbon dioxide content of the cell as carbon dioxide is used up. When this happens, the acidity of the cell decreases, promoting the conversion of the insoluble starch to the soluble glucose. This can be explained by the fact that the cellular enzymes that catalyze the conversion of starch to glucose do not function in acidic surroundings. During the night hours, production of carbon dioxide occurs during respiration. In addition, no carbon dioxide is depleted by photosynthesis which occurs only during the day. This results in a high carbon dioxide level in the cells. When its levels are high, carbon dioxide will combine with water to form carbonic acid. This will inhibit the conversion of starch to sugar, due to a decrease in the pH. When the carbon dioxide level in the cell is as low as it is during the daytime when photosynthesis occurs, much of the carbonic acid is reconverted to carbon dioxide and water, increasing the alkalinity of the cell and thus raising the pH. The greater alkalinity of the plant cells during the day brings about a higher cellular glucose concentration with the reverse true at night.

During the day, the high cellular concentration of glucose causes water to enter the guard cells by osmosis, rendering them turgid. The turgor of the guard cells cause them to bend, opening the stoma as a result. At night, the acidity of the cell inhibits the breakdown of starch. Since starch is insoluble in the cell sap, it does not exert an osmotic pressure. In the absence of osmotic pressure, the guard cells lose their turgor, causing them to collapse and close the stoma.

What then is the purpose of having the stoma open in the day and closed at night? In the daytime, when the leaves are photosynthesizing, the carbon dioxide supply in the cell is constantly being depleted and its supply must be replenished in order to maintain photosynthesis. Thus, it is highly advantageous to have the stomata open during the day, in order for carbon dioxide molecules to enter the leaf from the atmosphere through the stomata. Open stomata also result in continuous transpiration, hence the air spaces of the leaf are always kept moist for carbon dioxide to dissolve in. This is important since carbon dioxide must first dissolve in water before it can enter the cell. At night when photosynthesis ceases, an external supply of carbon dioxide is not required. The stomata close to retard water loss by transpiration which may occur rapidly if the night is dry or the temperature is high.

Transport

●PROBLEM 8-14

What is the role of transpiration in plants? Describe the mechanism of transpiration.

SOLUTION:

The leaves of a plant exposed to the air will lose moisture by evaporation unless the air is saturated with water vapor. This loss of water by evaporation, mainly from the leaves (but also from the stems) is called transpiration. Transpiration plays a very important role in water transport in plants. It directs the upward movement of water and minerals from the soil to the leaves, keeps the air spaces of leaves moist for carbon dioxide to dissolve in, concentrates initially dilute leaf cell solutions of minerals that have been absorbed by the roots, and contributes to the cooling of the plant body by removing heat during the vaporization of water (540 calories of heat are needed to convert each gram of water to water vapor).

Transpiration is responsible for the great amount of water that passes through a plant body per day. About 98 percent of the water absorbed by the roots is lost as vapor. As water is lost by evaporation from the surface of a mesophyll cell, the concentration of solutes in the cell sap increases, causing water to pass into it from neighboring cells that contain more water, that is, lower solute concentration. These neighboring cells in turn receive water from the tracheids and vessels of the leaf veins, which ultimately obtain water from the soil via root hair cells. Thus, during transpiration, water passes from the soil via the xylem system of the roots, stem, and leaf veins, and through the intervening cells, to the mesophyll and finally into air spaces in the leaves, where most of it vaporizes and escapes.

How do transpiration and the theory of water cohesion explain the process of water transport in plants? When does root pressure become important in water transport?

SOLUTION:

Water transport in plants can be explained by transpiration and the theory of cohesion-tension. When a leaf transpires, water is lost from the leaf cells, molecule by molecule. As a consequence of the water loss, the osmolarity of the leaf cells increases and water molecules enter these cells by osmosis from adjacent cells with a lower osmolarity. These adjacent leaf cells in turn receive water from neighboring leaf cells and so on, which all ultimately get their water from the xylem cells in the vascular tissue.

Since water molecules are linked to each other by hydrogen bonds into continuous columns within the xylem vessels right down to the root tip, a molecule leaving a xylem cell to enter a mesophyll cell of the leaf will necessarily tug this entire column of water along behind it. Because water has sufficient tensile strength, the column does not snap when being pulled. The upward movement of this column causes a negative pressure to develop within the xylem. This negative pressure is similar to the suction produced while sucking a drink through a straw. This draws water molecules from the root tip cells into the vessels. This theory of water movement in the xylem is known as the cohesion-tension theory. In the root tip, water molecules from the soil pass down a gradient through the root hairs to the cells that have just lost water to the xylem. In this way, the upward stream of water is continuous. In short, while transpiration provides a pull at the top of the plant, the strong tendency of water molecules to stick together attributed to hydrogen bonds (cohesive force of water molecules) transmits this force through the length of the stem and roots and results in the movement of the entire water column up the xylem.

In the spring, before leaves are formed and transpiration becomes important, root pressure is probably the major force bringing about the rise of sap. In addition, under conditions of high humidity, still air currents, or extremely low temperatures, root pressure may become important in raising water to the leaves of some plants. Thus root pressure may contribute to the upward movement of water under some conditions, but it probably is not the principal force causing water to rise in the xylem of most plants most of the time.

What is meant by translocation? What theories have been advanced to explain translocation in plants? Discuss the value and weakness of each.

SOLUTION:

Translocation is the movement of nutrients from the leaves where they are synthesized to other parts of the plant body where they are needed for a wide variety of metabolic activities. Translocation takes place through the sieve tubes of the phloem.

Experimental data indicates that the high rate at which translocation occurs cannot be attributed to simple diffusion. Three theories have been offered to explain the mechanism of translocation. Each of them has its own value and weakness, but the first one presented (pressure-flow theory) holds the most support.

The pressure-flow theory, which had been widely accepted in the past, proposes that the nutrient sap moves as a result of differences in turgor pressure.

Sieve tubes of the phloem in the leaf contain a high concentration of sugars, which results in high osmotic pressure into the cells. This osmotic pressure causes an influx of water, and build up of turgor pressure against the walls of the sieve tube cells.

In the roots however, sugars are constantly being removed. Here, a lower concentration of solute is present resulting in a lowering of the osmotic pressure. There is consequently a lower turgor pressure exerted against the sieve tube walls of the root as compared to the leaf. This difference in turgor pressure along the different regions at the phloem is believed to bring about the mass flow of nutrients from a region of high turgor pressure — such as the leaves (where photosynthesis produces osmotically-active substances like glucose) — to regions of lower turgor pressure — such as the stem and roots. The fluid containing the nutrients is pushed by adjacent cells, along the gradient of decreasing turgor, from the leaves to the roots. This theory predicts that the sap should be under pressure as it moves down the phloem, and this is experimentally verified. But there are problems with this hypothesis. Under some conditions, sugar is clearly transported from cells of lesser turgor to cells of greater turgor. In addition, this theory fails to explain how two substances can flow along the phloem in different directions at the same time, a situation observed to occur by some investigators.

Another theory proposes that cyclosis, the streaming movement evident in many plant cells, is responsible for translocation. According to this theory, materials pass into one end of a sieve tube through the sieve plate and are picked up by the cytoplasm which streams up one side of the cell and down the other. At the other end of the sieve tube, the material passes across the sieve plate to the next adjacent sieve tube by diffusion or active transport. This theory is able to account for the simultaneous flowing of nutrient saps in different directions. However, it is attacked by some investigators on the basis that cyclosis has not been observed in mature sieve cells.

A third theory proposes that adjacent sieve-tube cells are connected by cytoplasmic tubules, in which sugars and other substances pass from cell to cell. The movement of these substances is powered by the ATP from the mitochondria-like particles that are believed to lie within these connecting tubules. This theory is, however, weak since it is supported by few experimental findings and much of its content is based on speculation.

●PROBLEM 8-17

If a ring is cut through the bark all the way around a tree, down to the wood, the tree will live for a while, then die. Explain why.

SOLUTION:

When a ring is cut through the bark down to the wood of a tree, the vascular system is being separated into two halves. Water moves continuously upward in the xylem in response to osmotic pressure buildup in the roots, transpiration, and capillary action. Severing the xylem will prevent the upper region of the tree from obtaining water from the roots by the processes mentioned. The upper half of the tree, deprived of further supply of water could however continue to carry on photosynthesis using as much of the remaining water and minerals as it has stored in the upper half of the bisected xylem.

It will inevitably suffer rapid water loss as a result of evaporation at the surface of the leaves. As a consequence of the water loss at the leaf surface and the failure to receive water from the roots, the cells in the upper half of the tree gradually lose their turgor. This reduced turgidity causes the guard cells to collapse, closing the stomata in an attempt to prevent further water loss through the stomata.

What this indicates is that even though photosynthesis could theoretically be maintained in the upper region temporarily on stored nutrients and water, this usually does not occur. Photosynthesis is suspended as the stomata close to avoid desiccation.

Since the phloem is also discontinued at the cut, organic substances traveling down the phloem ooze out of the cut, and cannot be delivered to the lower portion of the tree. The lower half of the stem and the root system can nevertheless sustain a low level of respiration for a short while, using the food reserve, such as starch, stored in the cells. They will reduce their energy expenditure by reducing cell division and enlargement, which are energy requiring processes.

Thus, after the cut, the tree will strive to survive with minimal growth for a while. But once the water supply is exhausted in the upper half of the tree, and the food reserve is used up in the lower half, both halves cannot generate any more ATP to carry out the vital biological activities, and the tree will eventually die.

Roots

What are the functions of roots? What are the two types of root systems?

SOLUTION:

Roots serve two important functions: one is to anchor the plant in the soil and hold it in an upright position; the second and biologically more important function is to absorb water and minerals from the soil and conduct them to the stem. To perform these two functions, roots branch and rebranch extensively through the soil resulting in an enormous total surface area which usually exceeds that of the stem's. Roots can be classified as a taproot system (i.e., carrots, beets) in which the primary (first) root increases in diameter and length and functions as a storage place for large quantities of food. A fibrous root system is composed of many thin main roots of equal size with smaller branches.

Additional roots that grow from the stem or leaf, or any structure other than the primary root or one of its branches are termed adventitious roots. Adventitious roots of climbing plants such as the ivy and other vines attach the plant body to a wall or a tree. Adventitious roots will arise from the stems of many plants when the main root system is removed. This accounts for the ease of vegetative propagation of plants that are able to produce adventitious roots.

●PROBLEM 8-19

Describe the growth zones of a typical root.

SOLUTION:

The tip of each root is covered by a protective root cap, a thimble-shaped group of cells. This root cap protects the rapidly growing meristemic region

256

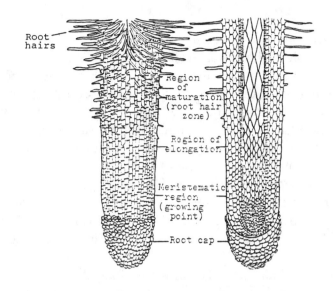

Figure 1. Longitudinal section of a root.

of the root tip. The outer part of the root cap is rough and uneven because its cells are constantly being worn away as the root pushes its way through the soil. The meristem, protected by the root cap, consists of actively dividing cells from which all the other tissues of the root are formed. It also gives rise to new root cap cells to replace the ones that are sloughed off. Immediately behind the meristem is the zone of elongation. The cells of this zone remain undifferentiated but grow rapidly in length by taking in large amounts of water. The meristematic region and the zone of elongation together account for the increase in length. In the zone of maturation (or differentiation) of the root cells differentiate into the permanent tissues of the root, for example, the xylem and the phloem tissues. Present in this region too, are slender, elongated, hairlike projections called root hairs that arise laterally. There is one root hair to each epidermal cell. Root hairs greatly increase the surface area of the root and enhance the absorption of the water and minerals into the root. As the root elongates, the delicate, short-lived root hairs wither and die, and are replaced by the ones newly formed by the meristematic region. Root hairs occur only in a short lower segment of the zone of maturation, usually only 1 to 6 cm long.

●PROBLEM 8-20

Describe the processes by which a root absorbs water and salts from the surrounding soil.

SOLUTION:

The movement of water from the soil into the root can be explained by purely physical principles. The water available to plants is present as a thin film loosely held to the soil particles and is called capillary water. The capillary water usually contains some dissolved inorganic salts and perhaps some organic compounds, but the concentration of these solutes in capillary water is lower than that inside the cells of the root. The cell sap in the root hair of the epidermal cells has a fairly high concentration of glucose and other organic compounds. Since the plasma membrane of this cell is semi-permeable (it is permeable to water but not to glucose and other organic molecules), water tends to diffuse through the membrane from a region of higher concentration (the capillary water of the soil) to a region of lower concentration (the cell sap of the root hair). This movement of water is controlled by a process called osmosis.

As an epidermal (root hair) cell takes in water, its cell sap now has a lower solute concentration than that of the adjacent cortical cell. By the same process of osmosis, water passes from the root hair to the cortical cell. Because of the osmotic gradient, water will continue to diffuse inward toward the center of the root. In this way, water finally reaches the xylem and from there, water is transported upwards to the stem and leaves by a combination of root pressure and transpiration pull.

Reproduction

●PROBLEM 8-21

Describe the process of gamete formation and fertilization in the angiosperms.

SOLUTION:

Reproduction in the flowering plants begins with the development of the gametes. The female gametes, or megaspores, develop within the ovules of the ovary, each ovule being attached to the ovary by a stalk. Embedded deep within the ovule is one cell, called a megasporangium, which enlarges to become the megaspore mother cell (see Figure 1), from which the gametes will be formed. The megaspore mother cell undergoes meiosis to form four megaspores. In most species, three of these disintegrate, leaving one functioning megaspore. This surviving cell then undergoes three mitotic divisions, producing eight nuclei which migrate so that three position themselves at the far end of the now enlarged megaspore and form the antipodal cells; three move towards the micropyle and form the egg and synergid cells. The synergid and antipodal cells are short-lived; their function is obscure. The remaining two central nuclei are the polar nuclei. The entire mature structure is termed the embryo sac, and becomes enclosed by the integument, layers of cells which develop from the megasporangia surrounding the megaspore mother cell.

The development of the sperm or microgametophytes begins within the tissues of the anther. Each anther typically contains four pollen sacs or microsporangia (see Figure 2). Early in its development, accelerated cell division in the microsporangia produces numerous microspore mother cells. Each of these microspore mother cells undergoes meiosis, resulting in a tetrad of four microspores. Each microspore then undergoes a mitotic division to form a

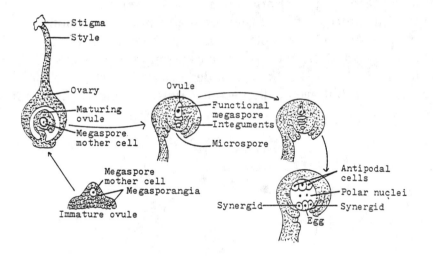

Figure 1. Megagametophyte development in angiosperms.

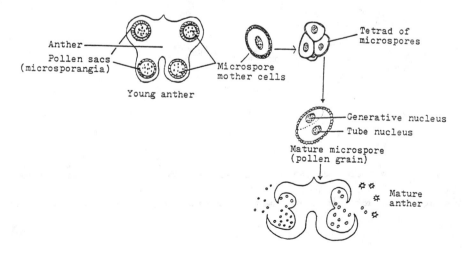

Figure 2. Microgametophyte development in angiosperms.

tube nucleus and a generative nucleus. At this point the structure is termed a pollen grain. When the pollen is mature, the anthers split open and shed the many pollen grains produced. Pollination may now occur by any one of various methods, resulting in the deposition of the pollen onto the stigma of either the same flower (self-pollination) or another flower (cross-pollination).

Upon successful pollination, the pollen produces a pollen tube which digests its way from the stigma down through the style (see Figure 3) to the ovule. If it has not done so already, the generative nucleus will divide to form two functioning sperm during the journey down the pollen tube to the embryo sac, where they will be released. One sperm will fertilize the egg; the other will migrate and fuse with the two polar nuclei to form the triploid endosperm nucleus. The number of polar nuclei, however, may vary between species, with a consequent variation in the chromosome number of the endosperm. This process of the fusion of sperm nuclei with both the egg and polar nuclei is known as double fertilization. The fertilized egg will develop into the embryo, and the endosperm nucleus into the endosperm, or nutritive tissue for the embryo. The embryo undergoes its first stages of development within the ovary, but eventually becomes dormant and is shed with its surrounding tissues as a seed.

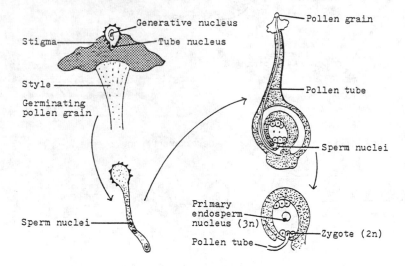

Figure 3. Fertilization in angiosperms.

●**PROBLEM 8-22**

Describe some of the methods which insure cross-pollination.

SOLUTION:

Cross-pollination involves pollen transfer between plants having different genetic constitutions. Since land plants are immobile, they must evolve spe-

260

cialized features to allow them to mate over distances. The seed plants have evolved structures which promote cross-pollination by wind, insects, bats, birds, and other animals.

Wind-pollination is common in plants having inconspicuous flowers, such as grasses and sedges. Flowers of grasses are dull-looking, and most of them lack both odor and nectar, making them unattractive to insects. Moreover, their pollen is light, dry, and easily carried by the wind. Their stigmas are feathery and expose a large surface area to catch pollen. Their stamens are well exposed to the action of the wind. Wind-pollinated flowers, such as those of the grasses, probably represent a special adaptation to colder climates, where insects are less prevalent.

Insect-pollination is the method of pollen dispersal in plants with colorful, showy flowers. These flowers also produce a sweet nectar and volatile compounds having unique odors which attract insects. As an insect approaches a flower, floral architecture ensures transfer of pollen onto the insect's body. In this way, pollen of one flower is carried to the stigma of another as the insect goes from flower to flower.

Flower-visiting bats are also an agent of cross-pollination. Bats are attracted to the flowers largely through their sense of smell. Bat-pollinated flowers characteristically have very strong fermenting or fruit-like odors. Bats fly from plant to plant, eat floral parts, and carry pollen on their fur. Birds may also serve as pollinators. Birds have keen vision, and most bird-pollinated flowers are colorful. Some birds regularly visit these flowers to feed on nectar, floral parts, and flower-inhabiting insects. Pollen transfer is also aided by other animals with fur as they pass from plant to plant.

Certain species of plants are monoecious, meaning they have both sexes contained within the same plant. In order to effect cross-pollination and avoid inbreeding within the same plant, specific tactics have been devised. In some species, such as the goldenrod (Solidago), the male and female organs of the same plant mature at slightly different times, making self-pollination unlikely. In some other species, the pollen is unable to germinate on the same plant. In plants such as these, bisexuality has an advantage in that a pollinator can both pick up and deliver pollen at the same time.

●PROBLEM 8-23

What is a fruit? What roles do fruits play in the dispersion of the seeds?

SOLUTION:

The ovary of an angiosperm is the basal part of the pistil. The ovary contains the ovules which will become the seeds after fertilization. Concomitant with the development of the zygote into an embryo, the ovary enlarges to form the fruit. A fruit therefore can be defined as a matured ovary, containing the matured ovules. A true fruit is one developed solely from the ovary. An accessory fruit is one developed from sepals, petals, or the receptacle as well as the ovary. The apple, for example, is mostly an enlarged receptacle; only the core is derived from the ovary. All angiosperms have fruits, either true or accessory. This characteristic makes them unique among living things.

Fruits represent an adaptation for the dispersal of the seeds by various means, and they may be classified according to this criterion as wind-borne fruits, water-borne fruits, or animal-borne fruits.

Wind-borne fruits are light and dry so that they can easily be carried by wind. In the tumbleweeds, the whole plant, or fruiting structure, is blown by the wind and scatters seeds as it goes. Other wind-borne fruits, such as the maple, have evolved wing-like structures. Still others, such as the dandelion, develop a plume-like pappus which keeps the light fruits aloft.

Water-borne fruits are adapted for floating, either because air is trapped in some part of the fruit, or because the fruit contains corky tissue. The coconut fruit has an outer coat especially adapted for carriage by ocean currents. Rain is another means of fruit dispersal by water, and is particularly important for plants living on hillsides or mountain slopes.

Animal-borne fruits are mostly fleshy. This makes them appetizing to vertebrates. When fleshy fruits ripen, they undergo a series of characteristic changes, mediated by the hormone ethylene. Among these are a rise in sugar content, a general softening of the fruit through the breakdown of pectic substances, and often a change in color to conspicuous bright red, yellow, blue, or black. When such fruits are eaten by birds or animals, they spread the seeds that lie within them either passing them unharmed through their digestive tracts or carrying them as adherent passengers on their fur or feathers. Some fruits are further equipped with prickles, hooks, hairs, or sticky coverings, and so can be transported for long distances by animals. The modifications of seeds for dispersal by animals illustrate an evolutionary adaptation to the coexistence of plant and animal forms.

●PROBLEM 8-24

What exactly is a seed? What tissues are present and what are their respective functions?

SOLUTION:

A seed is actually a matured ovule, and consists of a seed coat surrounding a core of nutritive tissue in which the embryo is embedded. The seed is an interesting structure in that it is composed of tissues from three generations. The embryo consisting of 2n cells derived from the fusion of egg and sperm, is the new sporophyte generation and functions in the continuation of the species by developing into a new reproducing plant. The nutritive tissue, or endosperm, is derived from the female gametophyte. In gymnosperms it is haploid, but in angiosperms it is triploid, resulting from the fusion of both polar bodies with the sperm. Its high starch content provides a source of nourishment for the growing embryo. The seed coat differentiates from the outer layer of the ovule, known as the integument, and as such is 2n and belongs to the old sporophyte generation. The seed coat encloses the endosperm and embryo, and owing to its tough, resistant properties, protects the seed from heat, cold, desiccation, and parasites.

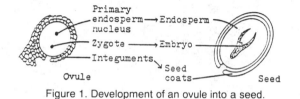

Figure 1. Development of an ovule into a seed.

●PROBLEM 8-25

Describe the development of the seed.

SOLUTION:

After fertilization, the zygote undergoes a number of divisions and develops into a multicellular embryo. The triploid endosperm nucleus also undergoes a number of divisions and forms a mass of endosperm cells carrying a high content of nutrients. This endospermal mass fills the space around the embryo and provides it with nourishment. The sepals, petals, stamens, stigma, and style usually wither and fall off after fertilization. The ovule with its contained embryo and endosperm becomes the seed; its wall, or integument, thickens to form the tough outer covering of the seed. The seed has an adaptive importance in dispersing the species to new locations and in enabling it to survive periods of unfavorable environmental conditions. This insures that germination will occur only when favorable growth is possible.

Monocots and Dicots

Discuss the early development of the angiosperm embryo. What primary structures form and what does each become in the seedling?

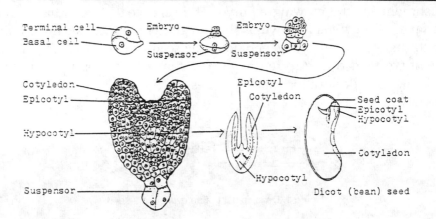

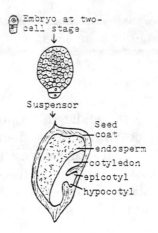

Figure 1a. Dicot embryonic development.

Figure 1b. Monocot embryonic development.

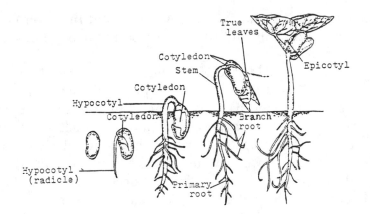

Figure 2a. Germination and early development of a dicot.

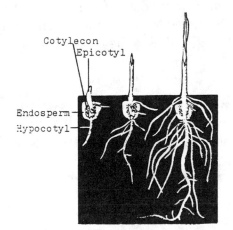

Figure 2b. Germination and early development of a monocot.

SOLUTION:

The first cell division that the zygote undergoes following fertilization produces a basal cell and a terminal cell. The basal cell develops into the suspensor, a filament of cells serving as a point of attachment for the embryo within the seed. The suspensor will eventually disintegrate as development of the embryo proceeds. The embryo will develop from the terminal cell, and as the cell undergoes successive divisions, the characteristic structures of the embryo begin to take shape (see Figures 1a and 1b). The most obvious of these are the cotyledons, or primary leaves. Dicots develop two such leaves, monocots only one. In dicots, the cotyledons can serve to either absorb or to both store and absorb food from the endosperm while within the seed. In the monocots, the single cotyledon serves primarily to absorb, rather than store, the endosperm tissue. The portion of the embryo lying along the central axis below the point of attachment of the cotyledons is called the hypocotyl and

265

the part above is called the epicotyl. At this point in its development, the embryo becomes dormant, and will remain so until conditions are favorable for its germination.

Upon germination, the hypocotyl elongates and emerges from the seed coat (see Figures 2a and 2b). It gives rise to the primitive root or radicle. Since the radicle is strongly and positively geotropic, it grows directly downward into the soil. The arching of the hypocotyl in the seed pulls the cotyledons and epicotyl out of the seed coat. The epicotyl, being negatively geotropic, grows upward out of the soil. It will develop into the stem and leaves.

In most dicots, by the time germination occurs, the cotyledons will have completely absorbed the endosperm. They now serve as reserves of food for the growing seedling until it has developed enough chlorophyll to become independent, at which point they shrivel and fall off. In some dicots, the cotyledons do not store nutrient material, but become photosynthetic foliage leaves upon germination. In monocots, the endosperm usually persists even after germination, and the cotyledon continues to absorb the nutrient material for the seedling until it can synthesize its own nutrients.

●PROBLEM 8-27

What are the differences between the growth patterns of dicots that use their cotyledons as an absorption organ and those that use them for both storage and absorption?

SOLUTION:

In the dicots, the cotyledons can either serve as only an absorption organ or as both an absorption and storage organ. When the cotyledons function only in absorption, the embryo remains relatively small and is surrounded by endosperm. The cotyledons of these plants absorb the stored food of the endosperm. After the seed germinates, and the endosperm has been depleted, these cotyledons develop into leaf-like photosynthetic organs. In other dicots, such as beans and peas, the cotyledons function in storage as well as absorption of nutrients. The embryo grows until all of the endosperm is absorbed by the cotyledons. Subsequently the cotyledons undertake the function of food reserve, resulting in their appearance as enlarged, thickened structures, which are not photosynthetic in function. In these dicots, the endosperm is usually completely absorbed before the seed germinates. The cotyledons remain as a food supply until the seedling is capable of photosynthesis, at which point they shrivel and fall off.

Differentiate between the monocots and dicots.

SOLUTION:

The two classes of angiosperms, the monocotyledons and dicotyledons, differ in eight respects. First, the monocot embryo has one cotyledon (seed leaf) while the dicot has two. The cotyledon of the monocots functions generally in food absorption while that of the dicots can function both in absorption and storage.

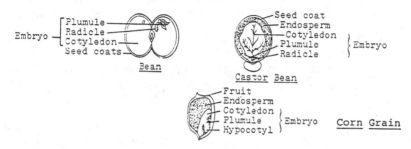

Figure 1. Sections through the seeds of three species with large seeds.
All the endosperm of the bean used up before it matured, so only the embryo is found inside the seed coats. Note that the outer layer of a corn grain is fruit, not seed coats.

Second, the endosperm typically persists in the mature seed of the monocots, while it is usually absent from the mature seed of the dicots.

Third, the leaves of the monocots have parallel veins and smooth edges; dicot leaves have net-like veins and lobed or indented edges.

Fourth, cambium or meristematic cork and vascular tissue is usually present in the stems of dicots but absent in the monocots.

Fifth, the vascular bundles of xylem and phloem are scattered throughout the stem of monocots. In the dicots they occur either as a single solid mass in the center of the stem or as a ring between the cortex and pith.

Sixth, the flowering parts of monocots — petals, sepals, stamens, and pistils — exist in threes or multiples of three, whereas dicot floral parts usually occur in fours, fives, or multiples thereof.

Seventh, the monocots are mostly herbaceous plants while many dicots are woody plants.

Finally, the roots of monocots are typically fibrous and adventitious (outgrowths of the stem) whereas the root system of dicots usually consist of one or more primary tap roots and numerous secondary roots.

Bryophyta (Mosses and Liverworts)

Why must mosses and liverworts (phylum *Bryophyta*) always live in close association with the water?

SOLUTION:

The bryophytes are generally considered to be primitive land plants because they are relatively ill-adapted to the terrestrial environment compared to the higher land plants. Mosses, for instance, are found frequently on stream banks or moist roadsides.

Liverworts, lacking a cuticle, are not as well protected against desiccation as are the mosses, and are even more restricted in their distribution — the majority of them grow in moist, shady localities, and some are even true aquatic plants.

The fact that mosses and liverworts always live in close association with water can be explained by their anatomical structures and reproductive mechanism. They have rhizoids which are simple filaments of cells or cellular projections performing the function of water absorption. The rhizoids are, however, not efficient absorbers and in relatively dry areas cannot withdraw adequate materials from the ground. In addition, mosses and liverworts lack vascular tissues to conduct water, minerals, and organic substances to different parts of the plant. Therefore transport of materials in the mosses and liverworts depends to a great extent on simple diffusion and active transport through the leaves and plant axis. Furthermore, mosses and liverworts are small plants with a high surface to volume ratio. This means that evaporation can cause a rapid dehydration of inner as well as outer tissues. These disadvantages can be avoided in a moist habitat where evaporation by the atmosphere is slower and sufficient water is available through diffusion to compensate for water lost through the surface.

A moist habitat also favors the reproductive process of the bryophytes. The gametophyte plant produces flagellated sperm which can swim to the egg only when water is present. In order to reproduce successfully, mosses and liverworts must grow in close proximity to water.

In what ways do mosses and liverworts resemble and differ from each other?

Mosses and liverworts are two classes of bryophytes. Being in the same phylum, they resemble each other in several respects. First, they share an ability to live and reproduce on land. Second, they have evolved similar structures to help them survive on land: an epidermis to prevent excessive evaporation, pores on the surface to effect gaseous exchange, rootlike projections called rhizoids for anchorage, and small green leaflets to manufacture food. Third, the two classes have a similar life cycle in which the gametophyte is the dominant generation and the sporophyte is partially dependent upon the gametophyte for water, minerals, and anchorage. Fourth, both produce their sex cells in multicellular sex organs (called an antheridium in the male and an archegonium in the female) and have flagellated sperm requiring a moist medium for transport. Last, the embryos of both develop protected within the archegonia.

However, the mosses and liverworts have certain structural differences which separate them into these two distinct classes. First, the moss plants have an erect stem supporting spirally-arranged leaves. The more primitive liverworts are simply flat, sometimes branched, ribbonlike structures that lie on the ground, attached to the soil by numerous rhizoids. Second, the rhizoids of the liverworts are specialized, unicellular projections extending downward from the leaf-like plant body (thallus). The rhizoids of the mosses, on the other hand, are composed of filaments of cells extending from the base of the stem. Third, the liverworts' thallus, unlike the leaflets of the moss, is more than one cell layer thick and bear scales, frequently brown or red, on its lower, ground-facing surface. On the opposite, upper surface are small cups, known as gemmae cups. These form oval structures, the gemmae, which when detached from the parent plant give rise asexually to new gametophyte individuals. Finally, whereas in the mosses, the sex organs are borne at the tip of the stem, in the liverworts they are embedded in deep, lengthwise depressions or furrows in the dorsal surface of the thallus.

● PROBLEM 8-31

How does asexual reproduction take place in the bryophytes?

SOLUTION:

The mosses and liverworts carry out asexual as well as sexual reproduction. The young gametophyte of the moss, the protonema, is derived from a single spore but may give rise to many moss shoots simply by budding, a process of asexual reproduction. Some liverworts, such as Marchantia, form gemmae cups on the upper surface of the thallus. Small disks of green tissue, called gemmae, are produced within these cups. The mature gemmae are broken off and splashed out by the rain and scattered in the vicinity of the parent thallus where they grow into new plants.

Describe sexual reproduction in the mosses.

SOLUTION:

The moss plant has a life cycle characterized by a marked alternation between the sexual and asexual generations. The sexual gametophyte generation is the familiar, small, green, leafy plant with an erect stem held to the ground by numerous rhizoids. When the gametophyte has attained full growth, sex organs develop at the tip of the stem, in the middle of a circle of leaves and sterile hairs called paraphyses. The male organs are sausage-shaped structures, called the antheridia. Each antheridium produces a large number of slender, spirally-coiled swimming sperm, each equipped with two flagellae. After a rain or in heavy dew, the sperm are released and swim through a film of mois-

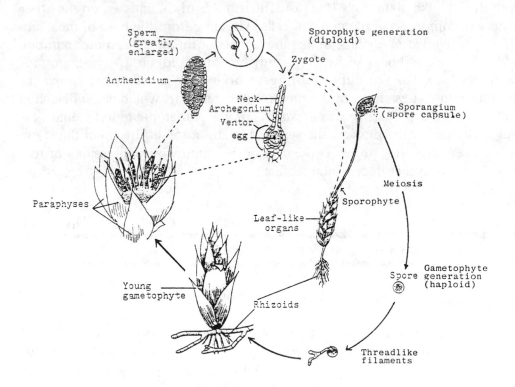

Figure 1. The life cycle of a moss plant.

270

ture to a neighboring female organ, either on the same plant or on a different one. The female organ, the archegonium, is shaped like a flask and has one large egg at its broad base, the ventor. The archegonium releases a chemical substance that attracts the sperm and guides them in swimming down the archegonium to the ventor. Here one sperm fertilizes the egg. The resulting zygote is the beginning of the diploid, asexual sporophyte generation.

The mature sporophyte is composed of a foot embedded in the archegonium and a leafless, spindle-like stalk or seta which rises above the gametophyte. The sporophyte is nutritionally dependent on the gametophyte, absorbing water and nutrients from the archegonium via the tissues of the foot. A sporangium, called the capsule, forms at the upper end of the stalk. Within the capsule each diploid spore mother cell undergoes meiotic division to form four haploid spores. These spores are the beginning of the next gametophyte generation.

When the capsule matures, it opens and releases spores under favorable conditions in a mechanism specific to its kind. In the Sphagnum, for example, the mature capsule shrinks, bursts, pushes away the lid, and exposes the spores to the wind. If a spore drops in a suitable place, it germinates and develops into a protonema, a green, creeping, filamentous structure. The protonema buds and produces several leafy gametophytes, thereby completing the moss life cycle.

Tracheophyta

● **PROBLEM 8-33**

What features enable the ferns to grow to a much larger size than the mosses?

SOLUTION:

The ferns (Division Pterophyta) are placed higher up on the evolutionary ladder than the mosses. One obvious difference between the two lies in their sizes. While the mosses rarely grow beyond 15 cm in height, ferns have been found that reach a height of 16 meters, larger by a factor of 100. Ferns are able to attain these heights because of the presence of both more efficient roots and a vascular system. The root of a fern is much more advanced than the rhizoid of a moss. It is elaborated into tissues and varying zones of maturity. From the bottom up, it is composed of a protective cap, an apical region of rapid cell division, a zone of elongation, and above it, a zone of maturation. To increase the total surface area for absorption, the primary root branches and rebranches to form many smaller roots. This well-developed root system of the ferns, in contrast to the simple rhizoids of mosses which are merely filaments of cells, allows for firmer anchorage and more efficient absorption of materials as demanded by a larger plant. The absorbed water and minerals are then conducted up the stem and leaf petioles of the fern to the leaves by the xylem of the vascular system. In addition to xylem, there is the phloem, which transports organic products synthesized in the leaves down to the stem and roots. The xylem and phloem tissues, present in the ferns but not the mosses, make possible long-distance transport of the essential materials required by a big plant. Since the vascular system serves also as supportive tissue, it adds strength and rigidity to a fern plant, enabling it to grow to a large size.

In summary, because of the presence of an elaborate root system and a vascular system, the ferns are able to grow to a much larger size than are the mosses.

●PROBLEM 8-34

In what ways do ferns resemble seed plants? In what respects do they differ from them?

SOLUTION:

The Pterophyte (ferns) and the Spermophyte (seed plants — gymnosperms and angiosperms) are alike in a number of respects. They are both terrestrial plants and as such have adapted certain similar anatomical structures. The roots, of both plants are differentiated into root cap, an apical meristem, a zone of elongation and a zone of maturation. Their stems have a protective epidermis, supporting, and vascular tissues: and their leaves have veins, chlorenchyma with chlorophylls, a protective epidermis and stomatae. The ferns also resemble the seed plants in that the sporophyte is the dominant generation.

The characteristics that distinguish ferns from the seed plants include the structure of the vascular system, the location of the sporangia, the absence of seeds, the structure and transport of sperm, and the patterns of reproduction and development. Unlike the seed plants, ferns have only tracheids in their xylem and no vessels. They bear their sporangia in clusters on their leaves (fronds), in contrast to the seed plants which carry their sporangia on specialized, non-photosynthetic organs, such as the cone scales of a gymnosperm. The ferns produce no seeds and the embryo develops directly into the new sporophyte without passing through any protected dormant stage as seen in the seed plants. The ferns retain flagellated sperm and require moisture for their transport and subsequent fertilization. The seed plants, on the other hand, have evolved a mechanism of gametic fusion by pollination, i.e., the growth of a pollen tube. The pollen tube eliminates the need for moisture and provides a means for the direct union of sex cells.

The ferns also differ from the seed plants in their life cycle. While in both, the sporophyte is the dominant generation, the fern gametophyte is an independent photosynthetic organism whereas the seed plant's gametophyte, bearing no chlorophyll, is parasitic upon the sporophyte. Also, the gametophyte of the seed plant is highly reduced in structure. The cycad (a gymnosperm) male gametophyte, for instance, consists of only three cells. The ferns, furthermore, are unlike the seed plants in being homosporous, that is, producing only one kind of spore. The seed plants, on the contrary, have two types of spores, the larger, female spores and the smaller, male spores.

●PROBLEM 8-35

Describe the life cycle of a typical fern plant.

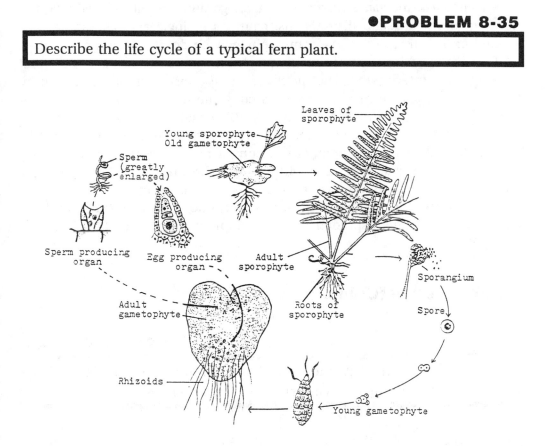

SOLUTION:

The fern plant, like other vascular plants, has a life cycle in which the sporophyte generation is dominant. The sporophyte generation is the relatively large, leafy green plant we recognize as the fern plant growing in both the tropics and temperate regions. The sporophyte consists of a horizontal stem, or rhizome, lying at or just under the surface of the soil and bearing fibrous roots. From the rhizome grows several leaves or fronds, usually finely divided into pinnae. On the under surfaces of certain pinnae develop small, brown sori. A sorus is a cluster of sporangia or spore cases in which haploid spores are formed. Most modern ferns are homosporous, that is, all their spores are alike. When mature and proper conditions, the spores are shed. After germination, each spore develops into a gametophyte which is typically tiny, thin, and often heartshaped. Small and obscure as it is, the fern gametophyte, also called a prothallus, is an independent photosynthetic organism. It grows in moist, shady places, especially on decaying logs and on moist soil and rocks. A number of rhizoids grow from the gametophyte into the substrate, anchoring it and absorbing water and salts.

The male and female sex organs (antheridia and archegonia) develop on the under-surface of the gametophyte. Each archegonium, usually located near the notch of the heart-shaped prothallus, contains a single egg. The antheridia, located at the other end of the gametophyte, each develop a number of flagellated sperm, which are ovoid in shape and have many flagellae on a spiral band at their anterior end. The sperm, released after a rain and attracted by a chemical substance released by the archegonium, swim through a film of moisture to the egg. Although the fern plant is usually monoecious (that is, it possesses both the male and female sex organs), the sperm of one plant usually fertilizes the egg of another, thus accomplishing cross-fertilization.

The zygote begins to develop within the archegonium into a sporophyte embryo. At first the sporophyte develops as a parasite on the gametophyte, but it soon acquires its own roots, stems, and photosynthetic leaves and becomes an independent sporophyte, thus completing the life cycle.

Gymnosperms (Conifers)

● **PROBLEM 8-36**

What do the words "gymnosperm" and "angiosperm" mean? What characteristics distinguish conifers from flowering plants?

SOLUTION:

The term gymnosperm means "naked seeds" and the term angiosperm means "enclosed seeds." The gymnosperms and angiosperms are both seed-producing plants which differ in the degree of protective covering provided to the seeds by the structures producing them. The seeds of angiosperms are formed inside a fruit, and the seed covering is developed from the wall of the ovule of the flower. The seeds of gymnosperms are borne in various ways, usually on cones, but they are never really enclosed as are angiosperm seeds. Although embedded in the cone, the seeds lie open to the outside on the cone scales, and are not contained within any modified protective tissue.

Conifers are classified as members of the group gymnosperm, while flowering plants are classified as angiosperms. An easy way to distinguish conifers from flowering plants is to compare the gross anatomy of their leaves. Needle-like leaves having a heavily cutinized epidermis are peculiar to the conifers. Due to their small amount of surface area (as compared to the broad, flat leaves of angiosperms) and their waxy coat, these leaves enable the conifers to survive hot summers and cold winters and to withstand the mechanical abrasions of storms. Most angiosperms cannot. Both conifers and angiosperms utilize xylem for the transport of water. The two types of xylem cells through which water is conducted are tracheids and vessel elements. If we cut open the trunk of a conifer, we will find that its xylem consists almost entirely of tracheids with bordered pits. On the other hand, the xylem of many flowering plants are composed of both tracheids and vessel elements, although the vessel elements predominate. Conifers can also be distinguished from flowering plants by their reproductive structures. Whereas angiosperms produce flowers and fruits, conifers produce cones which are formed from spirally arranged scale-like leaves bearing either seeds or pollen on the inner surfaces. Seed-bearing cones are referred to as female or ovulate cones; pollen-bearing cones are called male or pollen cones. The method of fertilization differs in these two groups as well. The flower of the angiosperm has its pistil constructed in such a way that the germinating pollen tube must grow through both the stigma and the style in order to reach the egg. In the conifers, pollen lands on the surface of the ovule and its tube grows directly into the ovule. Moreover, there is the phenomenon of double fertilization in flowering plants, which gives rise to a diploid zygote and a triploid endosperm. Since fertilization is a single process in the conifers, the endosperm consists of the haploid tissue of the female gametophyte and is thus quite different from the triploid endosperm cells of the angiosperms.

●PROBLEM 8-37

What is a cone? Describe its structure.

SOLUTION:

Cones are the typical reproductive structures of the gymnosperms. A cone or strobilus is a spiral aggregation of modified leaves called cone scales (see Figure 1, problem 8-38). These cone scales are the sporophylls, and each scale bears on its surface the sporangia. In most gymnosperms, the microsporangia and megasporangia are borne on separate cones. In the conifers, both male and female cones are borne on the same plants. It would thus appear that self-fertilization occurs. However, the male cones are borne on the lower branches of the conifers, while the female cones are borne on the higher branches. Thus, self-fertilization is essentially prevented. The ovulate, or female cones, are larger. In these cones, the megasporangia are enclosed by enveloping integuments to form structures called ovules. Each scale bears two ovules; each ovule is composed of the outer integuments and the inner nucellus (megasporangium) and has a small opening at one end known as the micropyle, through which the pollen grains will enter. It is from the tissue of the nucellus, that the megaspore mother cell will be produced. It is of interest to note that the megaspore, which gives rise to the megagametophyte, is never released from the megasporangium. It remains embedded in the sporangium, which is enclosed to form the ovule. It is the ovule, which when mature, constitutes the naked seed of the gymnosperms.

Male or staminate cones are smaller and bear the microsporangia on their scales. The number of microsporangia produced by each microsporophyll varies among gymnosperms; in conifers, two is the usual number, while cycads have many microsporangia scattered on the lower surface of each scale. Each microsporangium will produce the microspore mother cell, which will give rise to numerous microgametes or pollen grains.

● **PROBLEM 8-38**

Describe the life cycle of a pine tree.

SOLUTION:

The pine tree, being a conifer, produces both male and female cones on the same plant. Each cone bears two sporangia on its surface. Within each ovule of the female cone, the nucellus, or megasporangia, contains a single megaspore mother cell. This cell divides by meiosis to form four haploid megaspores. Three of the megaspores disintegrate, leaving one functional megaspore which divides mitotically to form a multicellular haploid megagametophyte. The megagametophyte will form two to five archegonia (female sex organs) each containing a single large egg.

A similar process of gamete production occurs in the staminate (male) cone. Within each microsporangium are many microspore mother cells, each of which undergoes meiosis to form four haploid microspores. While still within the microsporangium, the microspores divide mitotically to form a four-celled microgametophyte or pollen grain. Upon maturity, the microsporangia burst open and the pollen grains are released and carried by the wind. When a

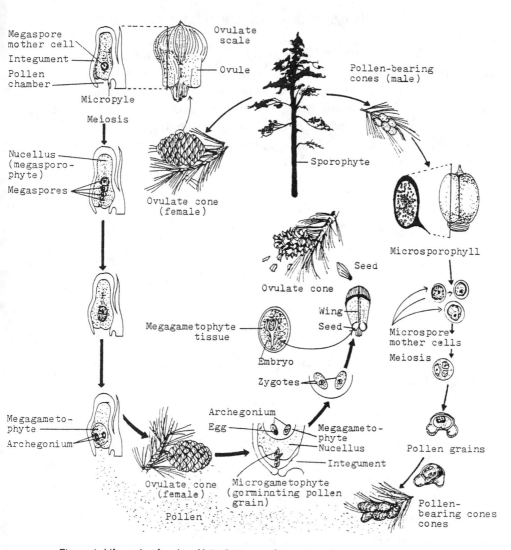

Figure 1. Life cycle of a pine. Note that more than one archegonia may be present and be fertilized within an ovule. However, only one embryo will survive and develop within the seed.

pollen grain reaches an ovulate cone it may sift down between the scales and land on the region of the ovule near the micropyle, which is sticky due to a secretion from the nucellus. As the sticky secretion dries, the pollen grain is pulled through the micropyle. The integument swells and closes around the micropyle. Once inside the micropyle, the pollen grain comes in contact with the end of the nucellus. At this point, one cell of the four-celled pollen grain elongates into a pollen tube, which grows through the nucellus toward the megagametophyte. This cell is known as the tube nucleus. A second cell, known as the generative cell, enters the pollen tube and undergoes a mitotic division. Only one of the daughter nuclei is functional, and undergoes division to form two sperm nuclei. When the end of the pollen tube reaches the neck of an archegonia, it bursts open and discharges its sperm nuclei near the egg.

One sperm fuses with the egg to form the diploid nucleus, and the other disintegrates.

After fertilization, the zygote, the surrounding megagametophyte tissue, the nucellus, and the integument develop into the seed. The haploid endosperm is derived from megagametophytic tissue. It will nourish the embryo during its early growth and development, in which several leaflike cotyledons, an epicotyl and a hypocotyl form. The embryo then remains dormant until the seed is shed and germinates. Upon germination, it will develop into a mature sporophyte, which is the pine tree.

SHORT ANSWER QUESTIONS FOR REVIEW

Choose the correct answer.

1. Unlike collenchyma and sclerenchyma tissues, parenchyma tissue does not function in (a) support. (b) gas exchange. (c) nutrient exchange. (d) **b** and **c**

2. The apical meristem is responsible for growth and differentiation in the (a) vascular cambium. (b) stem, root tips, and branches. (c) stem, sepal, and root tips. (d) blastula.

3. The following are all characteristics of the meristemic region except: (a) it differentiates into the permanent tissues of the root. (b) it is composed of actively dividing cells. (c) it gives rise to new root cap cells as old ones are being sloughed off. (d) all other tissues of the root are formed from its cells.

4. Turgor pressure and thus the opening and closing of the stomata depends on all of the following except: (a) a change in the amount of carbon dioxide taken up. (b) a change in the amount of oxygen taken up. (c) the conversion of starch to glucose by a light initiated reaction. (d) a change in the pH of the guard cells.

5. Transpiration (a) helps cool the plant body. (b) keeps the air spaces of the leaves moist. (c) directs the upward movement of water and minerals to the leaves. (d) All of the above

6. The gymnosperms and angiosperms differ from the rest of the vascular plants in that (a) they have an independent gametophyte generation. (b) they have flagellated sperm. (c) they are heterosporous. (d) embryo development occurs within the female gametophyte.

7. Double fertilization refers to the fact that (a) two eggs are fertilized by a single sperm. (b) two eggs are fertilized by two sperm. (c) one sperm fuses with the egg; the other fuses with the polar nuclei. (d) one sperm fuses with the egg; the other fuses with the vegetative nucleus.

8. In the gymnosperms, the megaspore mother cell is produced from the tissue of (a) the integument. (b) the nucellus. (c) the microsporangia. (d) the endosperm.

9. Which of the following characteristics of the angiosperms shows them to be more advanced than the gymnosperms? (a) covered seeds (b) broad, flat leaves (c) pollen tube (d) double fertilization

10. In monocots, the cotyledons, or embryonic leaves, function primarily (a) as photosynthetic organs. (b) as protective coverings for the seed. (c) in food storage. (d) in nutrient absorption.

11. If a plant produces flowers that are the same color as its leaves, then it is likely that pollination of that plant occurs by (a) birds. (b) wind. (c) insects. (d) animals.

12. The young gametophyte of the moss which asexually reproduces many new moss shoots is called the: (a) gemmae. (b) antheridia. (c) strobilus. (d) protenema.

13. Although mosses and liverworts are both bryophytes, they differ in some respects. In the following list, if the trait is characteristic of mosses label it I, if it is characteristic of liverworts label it II, if it is characteristic of both label it III. (a) gemmae cups (b) the gametophyte is the dominant generation (c) fertilization must take place in a moist environment (d) the sex organs are located at the tip of the stem (e) erect stem (f) the thallus bears scales and is more than one layer thick (g) epidermis (h) the protenema is responsible for asexual reproduction

Fill in the blanks.

14. _____ is the surface tissue that comprises the outer bark of a tree.

15. The vascular system on the inner border of the pericycle is composed of _____ and _____ tissues.

16. Mary took a clipping from one of her plants and placed it in water. After some time passed, roots grew out of the stem allowing her to place this clipping into soil. It was now able to grow into a full, new plant. The roots that developed from the stem are called _____ roots.

17. There are various types of woody tissues. _____ is the youngest, outermost portion of the xylem in a woody plant, _____ is the older, inner portion of the xylem which has lost the ability to conduct. The secondary xylem is composed of _____ and _____.

18. Nutrients are moved from the _____ where they are synthesized to other parts of the plant where they are needed by _____. This takes place in the _____ cells of the _____.

19. Upon germination, one cell of the pollen grain, called the _____, elongates to form the pollen tube. The _____ then enters the pollen tube and undergoes mitosis to form two sperm nuclei.

20. A cone is a spiral aggregation of modified _____ called cone scales or _____.

21. The term gymnosperm means _____. The term angiosperm means _____.

22. The fern has a dominant _____ generation which produces _____ from the cells within the _____ by the process of _____. At the proper time the _____ are released, fall to the ground and develop into _____.

Determine whether the following statements are true or false.

23. The Casparian strip is an endodermal plant cell layer which regulates the entrance of water into the vascular tissues of roots.

24. The cuticle of a plant cell helps prevent the loss of cytoplasm.

25. Guard cells regulate the size of the stomata in order to control the amount of gas exchange.

26. Water is moved up through the xylem by transpiration and cohesion tension. The upward movement of the column of water causes a positive pressure to develop in the xylem.

27. As sap moves down through the phloem, pressure is exerted on it.

28. The seed coat of a gymnosperm is analogous to the fruit of an angiosperm.

29. The endosperm of dicots is usually completely absorbed by the time the seed germinates.

30. The stem contains a central axial core of tissue, the pith, which is composed of colorless parenchymal cells that serve in the function of nutrient storage.

ANSWER KEY

1. a   2. b   3. a

4. b   5. d   6. c

7. c   8. b   9. a

10. d   11. b   12. d

13. a) II, b) III, c) III, d) I, e) I, f) II, g) III, h) I

14. Periderm   15. xylem, phloem   16. adventitous

17. Sapwood, heartwood, spring wood, summer wood

18. leaves, translocation, sieve tube, phloem

19. tube nucleus, generative nucleus

20. leaves, sporophylls   21. naked seed, enclosed seed

22. sporophyte, spores, spore mother, sporangia, meiosis, spores, gametophytes

23. True   24. False   25. True

26. False   27. True   28. False

29. True   30. True

CHAPTER 9

ANIMAL KINGDOM — THE INVERTEBRATES

Porifera (Sponges)

What is the structure of a sponge? How do sponges obtain food and water?

SOLUTION:

The most primitive metazoans belong to the phylum Porifera and are commonly called the sponges. Sponges may be radially symmetrical, but more commonly they are asymmetrical animals, consisting of loose aggregations of cells which are poorly arranged into tissues.

The surface of a sponge is perforated by small openings, or incurrent pores, which open into the interior cavity, the atrium or spongocoel. The atrium opens to the outside by a large opening at the top of the tube-shaped sponge, called the osculum. There is a constant stream of water passing through the incurrent pores into the atrium, and out through the osculum.

The body wall is relatively simple. The outer surface is covered by flattened polygonal cells called pinacocytes. The pores are guarded by cells called porocytes, which are modified pinacocytes, and are shaped like tubes extending from the outside of the sponge to the spongocoel. The pore, or ostium, can be regulated by contractions in the outer end of the porocyte.

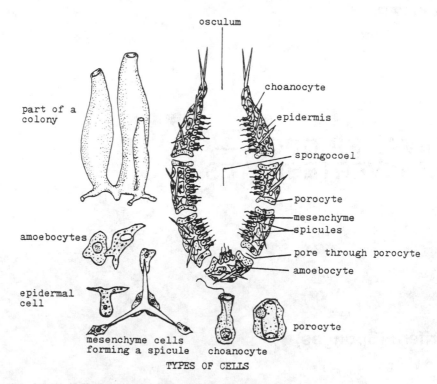

osculum

choanocyte

epidermis

spongocoel

porocyte

mesenchyme
spicules

pore through porocyte

amoebocyte

part of a
colony

amoebocytes

epidermal
cell

mesenchyme cells
forming a spicule

choanocyte

porocyte

TYPES OF CELLS

Figure 1. Sponges. Upper left, sketch of part of a colony of sponges.
Upper right, diagram of a section through a simple sponge showing its cellular organization.
Lower, sketches of the types of cells found in a sponge.

The mesophyl, a layer consisting of a gelatinous protein matrix, contains skeletal material and amoeboid cells, and lies directly beneath the pinacoderm. The skeletal material may be calcareous or siliceous spicules, or protein spongin fibers, or a combination of the last two. The composition, size, and shape of these spicules form the basis for the classification of species of sponges. Though the spicules are located in the mesophyl, they frequently project through the pinacoderm. The skeleton, whether composed of spicules or spongin fibers, is secreted by amoebocytes called sclerocytes. Amoeboid cells in the mesophyl include the archaeocytes. These cells are capable of forming other types of cells that are needed by the sponge.

Coelenterata

●**PROBLEM 9-2**

Describe the body plan of a hydra.

SOLUTION:

Hydra belong to the animal phylum called the Coelenterata (or Cnidaria). This phylum also includes such animals as the jelly fish, sea anemones, and corals. Most are marine except for hydra which is freshwater. These animals display radial symmetry, a digestive cavity, which opens into a mouth, and a circle of tentacles surrounding the mouth. The body wall consists of three basic layers: an outer epidermis; an inner layer of cells lining the digestive cavity or gastrovascular cavity called the gastrodermis; and between these two, a layer called the mesoglea. This last layer is usually devoid of cells, containing rather a gelatinous matrix.

Though all coelenterates are basically tentaculate and radially symmetrical, two different structural types are encountered within the phylum. One type which is sessile, is known as the polyp. The other form is free-swimming and is called the medusa. The hydra exists only in the polypoid stage.

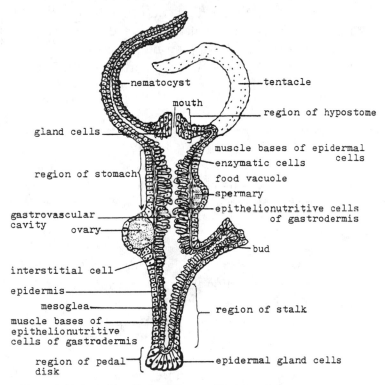

Figure 1. Hydra cut longitudinally to reveal its internal structure.

The body of the hydra is divided into several specialized regions (see Figure 1). The first region is called the hypostome, or manubrium. This is a conical elevation located at the oral end of the body, the apex of which is the mouth. Surrounding the hypostome is a second region composed of tentacles. In the hydra, there are usually five or six hollow and highly extensile tentacles.

285

Along the arms of the tentacles are located batteries of stinging cells called cnidocytes. These specialized cells, which are unique to and characteristic of all coelenterates, contain stinging structures called nematocysts. Nematocysts need not be restricted to the tentacles but may be found elsewhere in the hydra. A combination of physical and chemical stimuli causes the release of the nematocyst to take place. Undifferentiated cells in the epidermal layer, called interstitial cells, become modified to form the cnidocyte cells. These interstitial cells may also form generative cells, resulting in germ cell-producing bodies as well as buds.

The body of the hydra is in the shape of a cylindrical tube. The tube is more or less divided into a stomach or gastric region and a stalk region that terminates in the region of the pedal disk. The gastrodermis in the gastric region contains enzyme-secreting gland cells in addition to flagellated, amoeba-like cells. The cells in the stalk region do not produce enzymes, but are highly vacuolated, indicating intracellular absorption.

The pedal disk marks the attaching end of the body. An adhesive substance for attaching the body to some object is secreted by the epidermal cells. These cells can also produce a gas forming a bubble inside the adhesive secretion, which allows the organism to float to the surface of the water.

●PROBLEM 9-3

Mesoglea and mesoderm are two terms used to describe the middle tissue layer of an organism. What distinction can be made between the two and in what organisms can each be found?

SOLUTION:

Mesoglea is the term used to describe the layer between the outer epidermis and the inner layer of cells lining the gastrovascular cavity. It is found in adult Coelenterates (Cnidarians) such as hydra, Obelia, and Portuguese man-of-war (Physalia). The mesoglea consists of either a thin non-cellular membrane or thick, fibrous, jellylike, mucoid material with or without cells.

The term mesoderm is used to describe the middle of the three embryonic tissue layers first delineated during an early developmental stage of the embryo. This layer gives rise to the skeleton, circulatory system, muscles, excretory system, and most of the reproductive system. It is found in higher invertebrates, the insects, and all vertebrate groups.

The mesoderm is always a cellular layer and always refers to an embryonic layer. Mesoglea, on the other hand, is usually acellular and merely denotes the middle layer of the body wall of an organism.

The tentacles of hydra are armed with stinging cells. What is the structure of these cells, how are the stingers fired, and of what value are they to the animal?

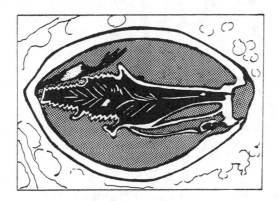

Figure 1. Sagittal section of an undischarged nematocyst of hydra

SOLUTION:

The stinging cells of hydra are called cnidocytes and are located throughout the epidermis. These cells contain stinging structures called nematocysts (see Figure 1). A cnidocyte is a rounded or ovoid cell with a short, stiff, bristle-like process, called a cnidocil, at one end. The cnidocil is exposed to the surface. The interior of the cell is filled by a capsule containing the nematocyst, which is a coiled tube, and the end of the capsule that is directed toward the outside is covered by a cap or lid. Supporting rods run the length of the cnidocyte.

The nematocysts are discharged from the cnidocyte and are used for anchorage, for defense, and for capture of prey. The discharge mechanism apparently involves a change in the permeability of the capsule wall. Under the combined influence of mechanical and chemical stimuli, which are initially received and conducted by the cnidocil, the lid of the nematocyst opens. Water pressure within the capsule everts the tube, and the entire nematocyst explodes to the outside. A discharged nematocyst consists of a bulb representing the old capsule, and a thread-like tube of varying length, which may be spiked.

From a functional standpoint, nematocysts can be divided into three major types. The first, called a volvent, is used to entangle prey. When discharged, the volvents wrap around the prey animal. The second type is called a penetrant. The tube of a penetrant is open at the tip and frequently armed with barbs and spines. At discharge, the tube penetrates into the tissues of the prey and injects a protein toxin that has a paralyzing action. The nematocysts of

287

hydra do not have this effect on man; but the larger marine Cnidaria can produce a very severe burning sensation and irritation. The third type of nematocyst is a glutinant, in which the tube is open and sticky and is used in anchoring the animal under certain conditions.

The cnidocyte degenerates following discharge of its nematocyst, and new cnidocytes are produced from interstitial cells.

●PROBLEM 9-5

The hydra has a unique nervous system. What is this type of system called? Explain how the system operates.

SOLUTION:

The nervous system of the hydra is primitive. The nerve cells, arranged in an irregular fashion, are located beneath the epidermis and are particularly concentrated around the mouth. There is no aggregation or coordination of nerve cells to form a brain or spinal cord as in higher animals. Because of the netlike arrangement of the nerve cells, the system is called a nerve net. For some time it was thought that these nerve cells lacked synapses, but at the present time research indicates that synapses are indeed present. (Synapse is the junction between the axon of one nerve cell, or neuron, and the dendrite of the next.)

It is known that some synapses are symmetrical, that is, both the axon and the dendritic terminals secrete a transmitter substance and an impulse can be initiated in either direction across the synapse; while some are asymmetrical, permitting transmission only in one direction. Impulse in the nerve net can move in either direction along the fibers. The firing of the nerve net results primarily from the summation of impulses from the sensory cells involved, which pick up the external stimuli and the degree to which the response is local or general depends on the strength of the stimulus. When a sensory cell, or receptor, is stimulated, an impulse is relayed to a nerve cell. This in turn relays the impulse to other nerve cells, called effectors, which stimulate muscle fibers and nematocyst discharge.

The rate of transmission of nerve impulses in hydra is usually quite slow. In spite of the fact that the nerve net is very primitive in comparison to the vertebrate type of nervous system, it is apparently adequate for hydra.

Platyhelminthes

What is a hermaphrodite? How and why is self-fertilization in hermaphrodites prevented?

SOLUTION:

Any organism that has both male and female gonads is said to be hermaphroditic. The majority of flowering plants are hermaphroditic in that they bear both the pistil (the female sex organ) and the stamen (the male sex organ). Hermaphroditism is rarer in animals than in plants. It occurs chiefly in sessile forms, notably the sponges and some mollusks. It is also found in the earthworms, the parasitic tapeworms, and flukes. Hermaphroditism due to abnormal embryonic sexual differentiation resulting in individuals born with both a testis and an ovary has also been documented in humans.

Some hermaphroditic animals, the parasitic tapeworms, for example, are capable of self-fertilization. Most hermaphrodites, however, do not reproduce by self-fertilization; instead, two animals, such as two earthworms, copulate and each inseminates the other. Self-fertilization is prevented by a variety of methods. In some animal species, self-fertilization is prevented by the development of the testes and ovaries at different times. In others, such as the oysters, the different gonads produce gametes at different times, so that self-fertilization cannot occur.

The advantage accompanying cross-fertilization is that genetic diversity is enhanced. Self-fertilization preserves the same genetic composition and with mutation occurring at a slow rate genetic variation is limited. Hermaphrodites undergoing cross-fertilization produce offspring showing the same genetic diversity as those resulted from individuals having a distinct sex. Thus, by ensuring gene exchange between individuals, cross-fertilization enhances genetic variation in the population. Only when a population carries a sufficient degree of genetic variation, can physical and environmental forces act to ultimately improve the characteristics of the individuals. And, as we shall see in a later chapter, the survival and propagative ability of a species depends to a large extent on its genetic diversity.

Describe feeding in planarians.

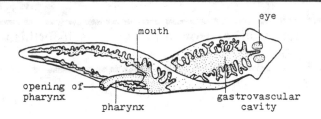

Figure 1. Planaria, showing much-branched gastrovascular cavity and extruded pharynx.

SOLUTION:

Planarians belong to the group of fresh water flatworms and have a digestive system which lacks an anal opening. The mouth of the planarian opens into a cavity that contains the muscular pharynx, or proboscus, which can be protruded through the mouth directly onto the prey (see Figure 1). In feeding, the planarian moves over its food object, which may be a small worm, crustacean, or insect larva, and traps it with its body. The pharynx is then extended and attached to the food material, and by sucking movements produced by muscles in the pharynx, the food is torn into bits and ingested. Digestive enzymes are released in order to assist the planarian in breaking down the food prior to ingestion. The pharynx delivers the food into the three-branched gastrovascular cavity. The branching of the planaria's gastrovascular cavity into one anterior and two posterior branches provides for the distribution of the end products of digestion to all parts of the body. Flatworms with three branched gut cavities are called triclads, in contrast to those with many branches, called polyclads.

Most of the digestion in planaria is intracellular, which means that it occurs in food vacuoles in cells lining the digestive cavity. The end products of digestion diffuse from these cells throughout the tissues of the body. Undigested materials are eliminated by the planaria through its mouth. The mouth, then serves as both the point of ingestion and the point of egestion.

It is interesting to note that planarians can survive without food for months, gradually digesting their own tissues, and growing smaller as time passes.

Discuss the excretory system of planaria.

SOLUTION:

The excretory system of planaria involves a network of tubules running the length of the body on each side. These highly-branching tubules open to the body surface through a number of tiny pores. Side branches of the tubules end in specialized cells called flame cells (see Figure 1), also referred to as protonephridia. Each flame cell consists of a hollow, bulb-shaped cavity containing a tuft of long, beating cilia.

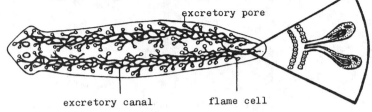

Figure 1. Excretory system of planaria.

It is very probable that flame cells function primarily in the regulation of water balance. The presence of better developed flame cells in freshwater species lends support to the osmoregulatory function of these cells. Primarily, water, and some waste materials, move from the tissues into the flame cells. The constant undulating movement of the cilia creates a current that moves the collected liquid through the excretory tubules to the nephridiopores, through which it leaves the body. The motion of the cilia resembles a flickering flame, hence this type of excretory system is often called a flame-cell system.

Most metabolic wastes move from the body tissues into the gastrovascular cavity, and from there they are eliminated to the outside through the mouth. Nitrogenous wastes are excreted in the form of ammonia via diffusion across the general body surface to the external aquatic environment.

Nemertina (Roundworms)

●PROBLEM 9-9

What are the evolutionary advances shown in the anatomy of the proboscis worms? How do these animals compare with the round worms?

SOLUTION:

The proboscis worms (or nemerteans) are a relatively small group of animals. Almost all are marine forms, excepting a few which inhabit fresh water or damp soil. They have long, narrow bodies, either cylindrical or flattened, and range in length from 5 cm to 20 meters. Their most remarkable organ is the proboscis, a long, hollow, muscular tube which they evert from the anterior end of the body to capture food. A mucus secreted by the proboscis helps the worm in catching and retaining the prey.

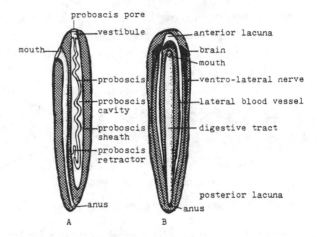

Figure 1. Structure of a typical proboscis worm or nemertean.
A. Lateral view of the digestive tract and proboscis.
B. Dorsal view of the digestive, circulatory, and nervous system.

There are three important evolutionary advances achieved by the proboscis worms. First, these animals have a complete digestive tract, with a mouth at one end for ingesting food, an anus at the other for egesting feces, and an esophagus and intestine in between. This is in contrast to the coelenterates and planarians, in which food enters and wastes leave by the same opening. As in the flatworms, water and metabolic wastes are eliminated from the proboscis' body by flame cells. The second advance exhibited by the proboscis worms is the separation of digestive and circulatory functions. These organisms have a primitive circulatory system consisting of only three muscular blood vessels which extend the length of the body and are connected by transverse vessels. Hemoglobin, the oxygen-carrying protein present in higher animals, is found in the red blood cells of this rudimentary circulatory system. In the absence of a heart, the blood is circulated through the vessels by the movements of the body and the contractions of the muscular blood vessels. Capillaries have not developed in these animals. The third advance in the anatomy of the proboscis worms is seen in the structure of the nervous system. There is a primitive "brain" at the anterior end of the body, consisting of two groups of nerve cells, called ganglia, connected by a ring of nerves. Two nerve cords run posteriorly from the brain.

Compared to the proboscis worms, the round worms (or nematodes) are a far more numerous and ecologically diversified group than the proboscis worms. There are about 8,000 species of round worms, all with a similar basic body plan. They have elongate, cylindrical, threadlike bodies which are pointed at both ends. Their many habitats include the sea, fresh water, the soil, and other animals or plants which they parasitize. This last characteristic is in sharp contrast to the proboscis worms, none of which is parasitic and none is of economic importance. Common parasitic nematodes are the hookworm, trichina worm, ascaris worm, filaria worm, and guinea worm, which all utilize man as the host. Because of their parasitic existence, these worms are covered with a protective cuticle and have only longitudinal muscles for simple bending movements. Contrary to the proboscis worms, which have cilia all over the epithelium and the lining of the digestive tract, none of the nematodes has any cilia at all. However, like the proboscis worms, the round worms have evolved a complete digestive system, a separate circulatory system, and a nervous system composed of a "brain" and nerve cords.

Nematoda

●PROBLEM 9-10

Parasitic organisms often have complex life cycles involving two or more host species. The nematode (round worm) causing elephantiasis has man as its primary host and the mosquito as its intermediate host. Describe the life cycle of this nematode.

SOLUTION:

Adult filaria worms of the genus-species *Wucheria bancrofti*, inhabit the lymph glands of man, particularly in the upper leg or hip. Large numbers of these nematodes block the lymph glands and prevent the return of fluid to the blood stream. This causes enormous swelling of the legs, a condition known as elephantiasis. Blocking of the lymph glands also predisposes the host to microbial infections.

These filara worms mature in the host's lymph glands where they later lay their eggs. The larval nematodes then migrate to the peripheral blood stream. The migration to the peripheral circulation has been found to correlate temporally with the activity of mosquitos. When a mosquito of a certain species bites the infected person, the larval filariae respond by entering the host's peripheral bloodstream. When other mosquitos subsequently bite the host and suck his blood, some larvae move into the bodies of these intermediate hosts. Inside a mosquito, the larvae migrate from the new host's digestive tract to its thoracic muscles, where they undergo further development. After a certain period, the larvae move to the proboscis of the mosquito. The proboscis consists of the upper lip or labium, the mandibles, maxillae, and the hypopharynx, which are long and sharp, modified for piercing man's skin and sucking his blood. The immature filariae are then introduced into another human whom the mosquito bites. Inside this primary host, they are carried by the

293

circulatory system to the lymph glands, where they grow to adults and reach sexual maturity.

Annelida (Segmented Worms)

Explain excretion in the earthworm.

Figure 1. Excretory system of the earthworm (cross-section)

SOLUTION:

The earthworm's body is composed of a series of segments internally partitioned from each other by membranes. In each segment of its body, there are a pair of specialized excretory organs, called nephridia. They open independently from the body cavity to the outside. The various nephridia are not connected to each other. A nephridium consists of an open ciliated funnel or nephrostome (corresponding to the flame cell in planaria) which opens into the next anterior coelomic cavity. A coiled tubule running from the nephrostome empties into a large bladder, which in turn empties to the outside by way of the nephridiopore (see Figure 1). Around the coiled tube is a network of blood capillaries. Materials from the coelomic cavity move into the nephridium through the open nephrostome partly by the beating of the cilia of the nephrostome, and partly by currents created by the contraction of muscles in the body wall. Some materials are also picked up by the coiled tubule directly from the blood capillaries. Substances such as glucose and water are reabsorbed from the tubule into the blood capillaries, while the wastes are concentrated and passed out of the body through the nephridio-pore. The earthworm daily excretes a very dilute, copious urine, which amounts to 60 percent of its total body weight.

The principal advantage of this type of excretory system over the flame cell is the association of blood vessels with the coiled tubule, where absorption and reabsorption of materials can occur.

Explain the locomotory pattern of the earthworm.

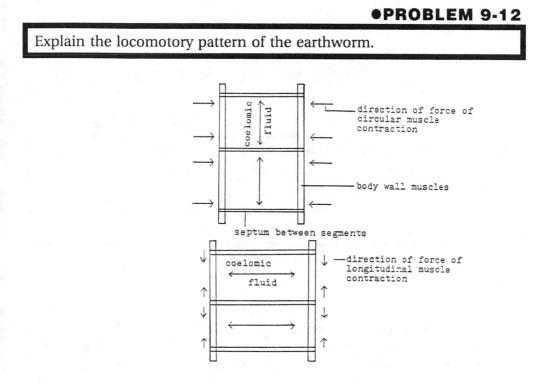

Figure 1. Effects of muscular contraction in the earthworm.

SOLUTION:

In the earthworm, two layers of muscle in the body wall and the four pairs of short bristles or chaetae of each body segment are the structures involved in locomotion. Circular muscle occupies the outer layer of the body wall, and just beneath it is the longitudinal muscle layer. Contractions of these two sets of muscles account for the changes in shape of the worm. Each segment of the body is filled with coelomic fluid that is incompressible. Thus the con-traction of either layer of muscle results in a change of shape. Contractions of the longitudinal muscles make the worm shorter and thicker, while contractions of the circular muscles make it thinner and correspondingly longer (see Figure 1). Circular muscle contraction is most important in crawling, and always generates a pressure pulse in the coelomic fluid. Longitudinal muscle contraction is more important in burrowing. When the worm is crawling, longitudinal contraction may not be strong enough to generate a coelomic pressure pulse, but it does so in burrowing.

Chaetae are extended during longitudinal muscle contraction, functioning to anchor the worm in its burrow and to determine the direction of locomotion. They are retracted during circular muscle contraction. Because of the combined effects of the chaetae and longitudinal muscle contraction, each segment of the body moves in steps of 2 to 3 cm, at the rate of seven to ten steps per minute. The direction of contraction can be reversed, thus enabling the worm to reverse directions. It should be remembered that without the chaetae, no forward movement can take place, but only a change in shape.

●PROBLEM 9-13

The earthworm has a central nerve cord running along the entire length of the body. When an earthworm is cut into several parts, severing its nerve cord in the process, each part will go on crawling around for some time. How can each fragment carry out crawling movement even after the nerve cord is severed?

SOLUTION:

The arrangement of the nervous system in lower invertebrates is quite different from that in higher vertebrates like man. In higher vertebrates, there is an expanded and highly developed anterior end of the spinal cord, forming the brain. The brain coordinates and regulates the activities of the entire body. When the brain is separated from the rest of the body, the animal cannot perform any complicated functions.

However, in the earthworm, a higher invertebrate, coordinated activities such as crawling can still be observed when the body is cut into several transverse sections. This movement is possible because the earthworm has more than one neural center controlling and coordinating its activities. The nervous system of the earthworm consists of a large, two-lobed aggregation of nerve cells, called the brain, located just above the pharynx in the third segment, and a subpharyngeal ganglion just below the pharynx in the fourth segment. A nerve cord connects the brain to the subpharyngeal ganglion and extends from the anterior to the posterior end of the body. In each segment of the body there is a swelling of the nerve cord, called a segmental ganglion.

Sensory and motor nerves arise from each segmental ganglion to supply the muscles and organs of that segment. The segmental ganglia coordinate the contraction of the longitudinal and circular muscles of the body wall, so that the worm is able to crawl. When the earthworm is cut into several pieces, thus severing the connection to the brain (that is, the nerve cord), the resulting fragments still contain segmental ganglia which can fire impulses to the muscles of the body wall, resulting in crawling movement.

Mollusca (The Molluscs)

● **PROBLEM 9-14**

Discuss the basic features of the molluscan body. How do they differ in the several classes of molluscs?

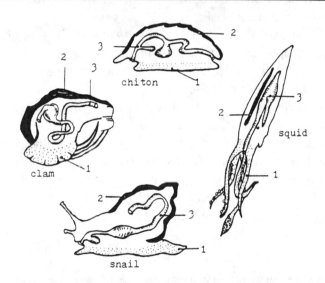

Figure 1. Variations in the basic mulluscan body plan in chitons, snails, clams, and squid. Note how the foot (1), shell (2), and alimentary tract (3) have changed their positions in the evolution.

SOLUTION:

The phylum Mollusca is the second largest in the animal kingdom. Snails, clams, oysters, slugs, squids, and octopuses are among the best known molluscs. The adult body plan is remarkably different from that of any other group of invertebrates. The soft body consists of three principal parts: (1) a large ventral muscular foot which can be extruded from the shell (if a shell is present) and functions in locomotion; (2) a visceral mass above the foot,

297

containing most of the organs of the body; and (3) a mantle, a heavy fold of tissue that covers the visceral mass. In most species, the mantle contains glands that secrete a shell. The mantle often projects over the edges of the foot and overhangs the sides of the visceral mass, thus enclosing a mantle cavity, in which gills frequently lie.

The chitons, members of the class Amphineura, have an ovoid bilaterally symmetrical body with an anterior mouth and posterior anus. They have paired excretory organs, nerves, gonads, and gills. The shell consists of eight dorsal plates.

Class Gastropoda is a large class, containing the snails, slugs, and their relatives. Most gastropods have a coiled shell; however, in some species, coiling is minimal, and in others, the shell has been lost. The body plan of the adult gastropods is not symmetrical. During development, two rotations of the body occur, so that the anus comes to lie dorsal to the head in the anterior part of the body. The organs on one side of the body atrophy, so that the adult has one heart, one kidney, one gonad, and one gill. This embryonic twisting, called torsion, occurs in all gastropods, including those with a flat shell, slugs, and other species without a shell.

Class Pelecypoda or Bivalvia contains the bivalves. These molluscs have two hinged shells. Scallops, clams, mussels, and oysters are well known bivalves. These animals have well-developed muscles for opening and closing the shells. These animals also have a muscular siphon for the intake and output of water.

The nautilus squid, and octopus are members of the class Cephalopoda. Cephalopod means head-foot, and in these molluscs the foot is fused with the head. In squids and octopuses, the foot is divided into ten or eight tentacles, and the shell is greatly reduced or absent. These molluscs have a well-developed nervous system with eyes similar to vertebrate eyes. The mantle is thick and muscular. Giant squids are the largest living invertebrates; they have attained lengths of 55 feet, and weights of two tons.

●PROBLEM 9-15

Discuss feeding mechanisms in different molluscs. Describe the differences in structural organization that have enabled the various classes to adapt to different lifestyles.

SOLUTION:

The chitons lead a sluggish, nearly sessile life. A horny-toothed organ, the radula, is contained within the pharynx, and is capable of being extended from the mouth. Chitons crawl slowly on rocks in shallow water, rasping off fragments of algae for food.

Gastropods occur in a wide variety of habitats. While most are marine forms, there are many fresh water and some land species. Gastropods have a well-developed head with simple eyes. Most feed on bits of plant or animal tissue that they grate or brush loose with a well-developed radula. Gastropods generally move about slowly.

Bivalves lack a radula, and are filter feeders. Sea water is brought to the gills by the siphon. Cilia on the surface of the gills keep the water in motion and food particles are trapped by mucus secreted by the gills. The cilia push the food particles towards the mouth. Most digestion is intracellular. Certain bivalves, such as oysters, are permanently attached to the sea or river floor; others, such as clams, burrow through sand or mud. Scallops are capable of rapid swimming by clapping their two shells together. Enormous amounts of water are filtered by bivalves — an average oyster filters three liters of sea water per hour. Bivalves do not have a well-developed head or nervous system.

The cephalopods are active, predatory molluscs. The tentacles of squids and octopuses enable them to capture and hold prey. Cephalopods have a radula as well as two horny beaks in their mouths. These structures enable the cephalopods to kill the prey and tear it to bits. The nervous system is very well-developed. There is a large and complex brain, and image-forming eyes. The muscular cephalopod mantle is fitted with a funnel. By filling the mantle cavity with water and then ejecting it through the funnel, cephalopods attain rapid speeds in swimming.

●PROBLEM 9-16

Compare the open and the closed type of circulatory systems. Describe molluscan circulation in a bivalve, such as a clam. What is a hemocoel?

SOLUTION:

A closed type of circulatory system is one in which the blood is always contained in well-defined vessels. In an open circulatory system, there are some sections where vessels are absent and the blood flows through large open spaces known as sinuses. All vertebrates have closed circulatory systems, as do the annelids (earthworms and their relatives). All arthropods (insects, spiders, crabs, crayfish, and others) as well as most molluscs have open circulatory systems. Movement of blood through an open system is not as fast, orderly, or efficient as through a closed system.

Aquatic molluscs and most aquatic arthropods respire by means of gills. In bivalves, blood in large open sinuses bathes the tissues directly. The blood drains from the sinuses into vessels that go to the gills, where the blood is oxygenated. The blood then goes to the heart, which pumps it into vessels leading to the sinuses. A typical circuit is heart → sinuses → gills → heart. In arthropods the blood sinuses are termed hemocoels. The hemocoel is not derived from the coelom, but from the embryonic blastocoel.

299

Echinodermata

Discuss the characteristics of the echinoderms and briefly describe several different classes.

SOLUTION:

The echinoderms have pentamerous radial symmetry, that is, the body can be divided into five similar parts along a central axis. Echinoderms have an endoskeleton composed of calcareous ossicles, these may articulate with each other as in sea stars, or may form interlocking plates, as in sand dollars. The skeleton usually bears projecting spines that give the skin a spiny or warty surface. The echinoderm coelom is well developed. The system of coelemic canals and projections, called the water vascular system, is found only in echinoderms.

Class Asteroidea contains the sea stars (starfish). Sea stars have a central disc and usually five arms, although some have more. The mouth is on the lower surface of the disc, and the anus on the upper surface. Locomotion is by means of the tube feet. The surface is studded with many short spines. They have no special respiratory system, but breathe by means of skin gills or dermal branchiae.

Class Ophiuroidea contains the brittle stars. They resemble sea stars, but their arms are longer, more slender, more flexible, and often branched. Locomotion occurs by rapidly lashing the arms, not through the use of tube feet. There is no anus or intestine. Gas exchange occurs through invaginated pouches at the periphery of the disc.

The sea urchins and sand dollars are members of class Echinoidea. The endoskeletal plates are fused to form a rigid case. The body is spherical or oval, and is covered with long spines. Five bands of tube feet are present, and function in respiration in some species. There is a long, coiled intestine, and an anus.

Sea cucumbers, class Holothuroidea, have a much reduced endoskeleton and a leathery body. Many forms have five rows of tube feet. Unlike other echinoderms, they lie on their side. The mouth is surrounded by tentacles attached to the water vascular system. Gas exchange usually occurs through complexly branched respiratory trees attached to the anal opening.

Class Crinoidea contains the sea lilies. They are attached to the sea floor by a long stalk and are sessile. They have long, feathery, branched arms around the mouth, which is on the upper surface.

The same system which enables starfish to cling to rocky substrates is useless on sandy beaches. Explain.

SOLUTION:

Starfish (also called sea star) locomotion occurs by means of tube feet. The tube feet are part of a hydraulic system found only in echinoderms called the water vascular system. The under surface of each arm of a sea star has hundreds of pairs of tube feet, which are hollow, thin-walled, sucker-tipped, muscular cylinders. Internally, the tube foot is connected to a muscular sac, an ampulla, at its base. The tube feet are connected via short lateral canals to a radial canal which extends the length of the arm. The radial canals are joined at the central disc of the sea star by a ring canal. The ring canal leads via a short tube called the stone canal to a sieve-like plate, called a madreporite, on the surface of the animal. The entire system is filled with watery fluid. In order to extend the tube foot, the ampulla contracts, forcing fluid into the tube foot. A valve prevents the fluid from flowing into the radial canals. The tube foot attaches to the sea floor (or substratum) by a sucker at its tip, which acts as a vacuum. Longitudinal muscles cause the tube foot to shorten in length; this pulls the sea star forward, and water is forced back in to the ampulla. The tube foot is released from the substratum, and then again. The rapid repetition of this cycle of events enables sea stars to move slowly.

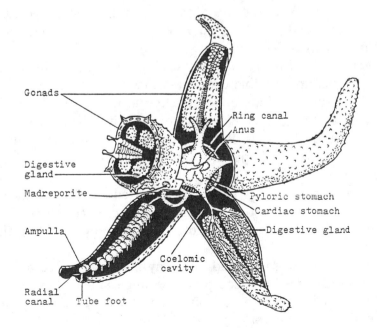

Figure 1. Dissection of a sea star (dorsal view)

One can see that the use of suction in the tube feet would be useless to the sea star in moving on sandy beaches. On a soft surface, the tube feet are employed as legs. Locomotion becomes a stepping process, involving a backward swinging of the middle portion of the podia followed by a contraction, shoving the animal forward. Certain sea stars have tube feet without suckers at their tips; instead the tips are pointed. These sea stars live on soft bottoms, and can feed on buried animals.

Starfish are slow-moving carnivorous animals. Their prey are generally sedentary or slow moving animals, such as clams and oysters.

●PROBLEM 9-19

Describe the function of the sea star's stomach as the animal feeds upon a clam.

SOLUTION:

The sea star places its arms on the clam, and by applying suction with the tube feet, is able to pry the two shells slightly apart. The sea star then everts its cardiac stomach, as it is projected out of its mouth. The stomach then enters the crack between the bivalve shells. Digestive enzymes from the stomach cause the soft body of the clam to be degraded. The clam's adductor muscles are digested and the valves open. The partly digested food is taken into the pyloric stomach and then into the digestive glands, where digestion is completed and the products are absorbed. After the body of the clam is eaten, the sea star retracts the cardiac stomach.

The digestive tract of the sea star consists of a mouth on the lower surface, a short esophagus, an eversible cardiac stomach, a smaller pyloric stomach, a very small intestine, and an anus. Attached to the pyloric stomach are five pairs of large digestive glands. Each pair of digestive glands lies in the coelomic cavity of one of the arms. Both stomachs fill most of the interior of the central disc. The cardiac stomach is capable of entering a gap between the shells of a clam as small as 0.1 mm.

Certain species of sea stars spread the everted cardiac stomach over the ocean bottom, and digest all types of organic matter encountered. The everted stomach of sea stars is also capable of engulfing prey, enabling the prey to be swallowed whole.

Sea stars are carnivous and feed on many marine invertebrates, and even small fish. They also feed on dead matter. Some sea stars have extremely restricted diets, and feed only on certain species. Others have a wide range of prey, but exhibit preferences.

Arthropoda

Arthropods have an exoskeleton. How is movement accomplished?

SOLUTION:

Movement in the arthropods is possible in spite of the hard exoskeleton because the body is segmented and the segments are joined by a thin layer of flexible chitin. Jointed legs are especially characteristic of the arthropods; they consist of a series of cone-like sections with the small end of one fitting into the large end of the next. Only arthropods and vertebrates have jointed appendages; there are more joints, however, in the arthropod legs because each joint does not have as great a degree of movement as the joint of a vertebrate leg.

What characteristics of arthropods have been of primary importance in their evolutionary success?

SOLUTION:

Arthropoda is an extraordinarily large and diverse phylum. There are about a million different arthropod species. Approximately 80 percent of all animal species belong to this phylum. The class Insecta, containing more than 750,000 species, is the largest group of animals; in fact, it is larger than all other animal groups combined.

The development of a chitinous exoskeleton has been an important factor in the evolutionary success of the arthropods. An exoskeletal plate covers each body segment, and movement is possible because the plates of each segment are joined by a flexible, thin articular membrane. In most arthropods, there has been a reduction in the total number of body segments, fusion of many segments, and secondary subdivision of certain segments. This has resulted in body parts specialized for different functions, with movable joints between the parts. Infolding of the embryonic ectoderm has also resulted in an internal skeleton, providing sites for muscle insertions. Arthropod musculature is complex, and quite unlike that of most other invertebrates. The exoskeleton also lines both the anterior and posterior portions of the digestive tract.

The exoskeleton is termed a cuticle and is composed of protein and chitin. The cuticle consists of an epicuticle, an exocuticle, and an endocuticle. The outermost epicuticle often contains wax, as it does in insects, and serves to prevent water loss. The exocuticle is tougher than the innermost endocuticle. The epicuticle and exocuticle are absent at joints to provide for flexibility. The cuticle of the crustaceans is further strengthened by deposition of calcium salts. Where the epicuticle is absent, the cuticle is relatively permeable to gas and water. Fine pore canals in the cuticle permit elimination of secretions from ducts. The support and locomotion provided by the elaborate exoskeleton are major advantages that arthropods have over all other invertebrates, and the ability for modification has enabled the cuticle to serve many functions.

Another evolutionary advantage of the arthropods is the adaptation of well-developed organ systems. The digestive, respiratory, and blood-vascular systems are all complex, and often show improvements over other invertebrates' systems. The reproductive structures are well-developed in many arthropods. Internal fertilization occurs in all terrestrial forms, and in many arthropods, the eggs and the young are brooded and "nursed" by adults. The excretory system is well-developed in terrestrial arthropods.

The complex organization of the nervous tissues in the arthropods is yet another key factor in the evolutionary success. The brain in most arthropods is large, and many complex sense organs are present. Motor innervation to the muscles is precise and allows for many different movements, speeds, and strengths. The compound eyes of insects and crustaceans result in a wide visual field, and a great ability to detect movement. Other sensory receptors are sensitive to touch, chemicals, sound, position, and movement. Arthropods often have complex behavioral patterns, many of which are under hormonal control.

●PROBLEM 9-22

What are the distinguishing features of the different classes of arthropods?

SOLUTION:

The arthropods are generally divided into the subphyla Chelicerates, Mandibulates (or Crustacea), Uniramia, and the extinct Trilobita.

The chelicerate body is divided into two regions, a cephalothorax and an abdomen. Chelicerates have no antennae. The first pair of appendages are mouthparts termed chelicerae. The chelicerae are pincerlike or fanglike. The second pair serves various functions including capturing prey or serving as a sensory device, while the last four pairs of appendages on the cephalothorax function mainly as walking legs. Class Merostomata contains the horseshoe crabs; other members of this class are extinct. The horseshoe crabs have five or six pairs of abdominal appendages that function as gills. The last abdominal segment or telson is long and spinelike. The exoskeleton contains a large amount of calcium salts. The horseshoe crabs are scavengers. Arachnids comprise the other living class of Chelicerates, including spiders, scorpions, mites, and ticks. Arachnids are terrestrial. The first pair of legs is modified to function as feeding devices and are called pedipalps. In most arachnids, the pedipalps seize and tear apart prey. Most arachnids are carnivorous. In spiders, the pedipalps are poisonous fangs. Abdominal appendages are lost, or else function as book lungs, as in spiders. Arachnids usually have eight simple eyes, each eye having a lens, optic rods, and a retina. The eyes are chiefly for the perception of moving objects, and vision is poor.

The mandibulates have antennae and have mandibles as their first pair of mouthparts. Mandibles usually function in biting and chewing, but are never claw-like as are chelicerae. Maxillae are additional mouthparts found in most Mandibulates. The class Crustacea contains an enormous number of diverse aquatic animals. Crabs, shrimp, lobsters, and crayfish are well known crustaceans. There are many small, lesser known crustacean species, such as water fleas, brine shrimp, barnacles, sowbugs, sandhoppers, and fairy shrimps. Crustaceans have two pairs of antennae, a pair of mandibles, and two pairs of maxillae. Compound eyes are often present in adult crustaceans. The larger crustaceans have a calcareous cuticle. Larger crustaceans have gills, but many smaller crustaceans rely on gas exchange across the body surface. There is enormous diversity among crustaceans. A great range of diet and feeding mechanisms are used. Appendages are modified in many different ways, and the body plan varies greatly.

Uniramia encompasses the next three classes. Class Chilopoda contains the centipedes. Their body consists of a head and trunk. There is a pair of mandibles, two pairs of maxillae, and the first pair of trunk appendages are poisonous claws that enable the centipede to capture prey. All other trunk segments bear a pair of walking legs. Centipedes are terrestrial. They have tracheae and Malpighian tubules.

Class Diplopoda contains the millipedes. The body is divided into head and trunk. The trunk segments bear two pairs of legs. There are mandibles and a single fused pair of maxillae, and no poisonous claws. Millipedes are not carnivorous. Respiration and excretion are similar to that of centipedes and insects.

Class Insecta is an enormous group. The insect body has 3 parts: a head, with completely fused segments; a thorax of three segments, each segment bearing a pair of legs; and an abdomen. Two pairs of wings, if present, are attached to the thorax. There is one pair of antennae, and usually a pair of compound eyes. The mouthparts of insects are mandibles, a pair of maxillae, and a lower lip which is formed from fused second maxillae. Respiration is by tracheae and excretion by Malpighian tubules. Insects are the only invertebrates which fly and are mainly terrestrial.

What are the advantages of a segmented body?

SOLUTION:

Segmentation offers the advantage of allowing specialization of different body segments for different functions. More primitive animals have a large number of segments, all very similar to one another. More complex animals have fewer segments, and the specialization of different segments may be so far advanced that the original segmentation of the body plan is obscured. Arthropods are a large group of segmented animals that have evolved in many complex ways. More primitive forms have paired, similar appendages on each segment. More advanced forms have appendages modified for a variety of functions such as sensory antennae, feeding apparatus, walking legs, swimming legs, claws, reproductive apparatus, and respiratory structures, depending upon the species. The more advanced arthropods have a greatly reduced number of segments. These arthropods also have a fusion of body segments into distinct regions, such as a head and trunk, or head, thorax, and abdomen. Internally, there is a great deal of specialization, and septa between segments have been lost. The first six segments always form a head, usually with a well developed brain and sense organs. In primitive forms there are ganglia in every segment, but in masses. Aquatic arthropods may have one pair or several pairs of excretory organs, or coxal glands. In most groups of terrestrial arthropods, the excretory organs are Malpighian tubules. Generally, there is only one pair of reproductive organs; centipedes, however may have 24 testes.

●PROBLEM 9-24

How does the compound eye of crustaceans and insects differ from man's eyes? What advantages do insects' eyes have that man's do not?

SOLUTION:

Compound eyes consist of a varying number of units or ommatidia (see Figure 1). Each ommatidium has its own lens, cornea, and group of neurons. Some arthropods, such as ants, have only a few ommatidia while others, such as dragonflies, have as many as 10,000. Each ommatidium, in gathering light from a narrow sector of the visual field, projects a mean intensity of the light from that sector onto the total retinal field. All the points of light from the various ommatidia form an image, called a mosaic picture. The nature of a mosaic image can be understood by comparing it to the picture of a TV screen or a newspaper photo. The picture is a mosaic of many dots of different intensities. The clarity of the image depends upon the number of dots per unit area. The greater the number, the better the picture. The same is true of the compound eye. Each ommatidial receptor cell with its accompanying nerve-fiber projects a segment of the total picture. The compound eye may contain hundreds of thousands of neurons, clustered in groups of seven or eight per ommatidium.

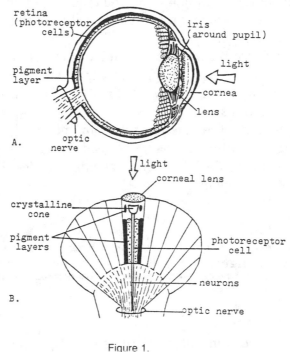

Figure 1.
A. Human eye
B. Compound eye (one ommatidium shown in detail)

The human eye also forms a retinal picture composed of numerous points, each point corresponding to a rod or cone cell with its accompanying neuron. Considering the fact that the human eye contains approximately 125,000,000 rods and 6,500,000 cones, the concentration of corresponding points is much higher than in the compound eye, and the image formed is thus much finer.

In addition, while the compound eye of the arthropod is composed of numerous lenses, the human eye has only one lens for its entire corneal field. Hence, the insect has no structure strictly analogous to the human retina; their critical surface for vision is the outer surface of the compound eye itself, composed of the many closely packed individual lenses.

Many arthropods have very wide visual fields; in some crustaceans, the corneal surface covers an arc of 180°. However, the anthropod cornea and lens are developed from the skeleton, and the eyes are fixed in place. The human eye, has a much smaller visual field, but compensates for this to some extent with movability.

307

Compound eyes are particularly sensitive to motion. This is because the ommatidia recover very rapidly from a light impulse, making them receptive to a new impulse in a very short time. Compound eyes thus can detect flickers at extremely high frequency. Flies detect flickers of a frequency up to 265 per second, as compared to man's limit of about 53 per second. Because flickering light at higher frequency is seen as a continuous light by man, motion pictures are seen as smooth movement, and 60-cycle bulbs give off steady light. The ability of the compound eyes to detect high frequency light changes enables them to rapidly detect motion and facilitates the capture of prey and the avoidance of enemies.

Compound eyes are sensitive to a broader range of light wavelengths than human eyes. Insects can see well into the ultraviolet range. Colors that appear identical to man may reflect ultraviolet light to different degrees, and appear strikingly different to insects.

Compound eyes are also able to analyze the plane of polarization of light. A sky appearing evenly blue to man, reveals different patterns in different areas to insects, because the plane of polarization varies. Honeybees use this ability as an aid to navigation.

●PROBLEM 9-25

What are the distinguishing features of the several orders of insects?

SOLUTION:

Insects are divided into different orders based primarily upon wing structure, type of mouthparts, and the type of metamorphosis they undergo, i.e., complete or incomplete.

There are approximately twenty-five orders of insects. The class Insecta (Hexapoda) is divided into two subclasses. Subclass Apterygota contains the wingless insects, which are believed to be the most primitive living insects. Subclass Pterygota contains most of the insect orders. These are winged insects, or if wingless, the loss of wings is secondary. Some of the better known orders will be further discussed.

Order Thysanura contains primitive wingless insects with chewing mouthparts and long tail-like appendages. Silverfish and bristletails are members of this order. Some species are commonly found in houses and eat books and clothing.

Order Odonata contains dragonflies and damsel flies. The two pairs of long membranous wings are held permanently at right angles to the body. They have chewing mouthparts and large compound eyes. Immature forms of these insects (nymphs) are aquatic (fresh water).

Other winged insects can fold their wings back over the body when they are not flying. Order Orthoptera contains grasshoppers, crickets, and cockroaches. The forewings are usually leather-like. They do not function in flying, but function as covers for the folded hindwings. The chewing mouthparts are strong.

Termites are social insects that belong to the order Isoptera. Both winged and wingless varieties comprise the termite colony.

Order Hemiptera contains the true bugs. They have piercing-sucking mouthparts. The forewing has a distal membranous half and a basal, leathery, thick half.

Order Anoplura contains the sucking lice. These insects are wingless and have piercing-sucking mouthparts. The legs are adapted for attachment to the host. These lice are external parasites on birds and mammals — the headlouse and crablouse are parasites on man. They are often vectors of disease, such as typhus. All of the orders just discussed have incomplete metamorphosis.

Order Lepidoptera contains butterflies and moths. They undergo complete metamorphosis, as do the rest of the orders to be discussed. Lepidoptera have two large pairs of scale covered wings, and sucking mouthparts (in adults).

Order Diptera contains true flies, mosquitoes, gnats, and horseflies. They have one pair of flying wings, with the hind-wings modified as balancing organs. Mouthparts are piercing-sucking, or licking. Adults are often disease vectors.

Order Coleoptera, containing beetles and weevils, is the largest order. They have hard forewings which cover membranous hindwings. They have chewing mouthparts and undergo complete metamorphosis.

Order Siphonaptera contains the fleas. They are small, wingless parasites. They have piercing-sucking mouthparts, and long legs adapted for jumping.

Order Hymenoptera contains ants, wasps, bees, and sawflies. There are winged and wingless species. Wings, when present, are two membranous pairs which interlock in flight. Mouthparts are for chewing, chewing-sucking, or chewing-lapping.

●PROBLEM 9-26

Describe the structure of an insect wing. How are wings used in flight?

SOLUTION:

The wings of an insect are evaginations or folds of the integument, and are composed of two sheets of cuticle. A vein runs through the wing at a point where the two cuticular membranes are thickened and separated, forming an effective supporting skeletal rod for the wing. The wings of the more primitive insects are netlike, but there has been a general tendency in the evolution of wings toward reduction of this netlike appearance.

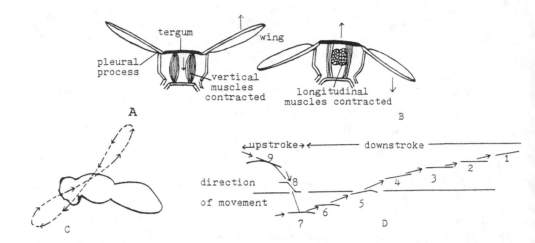

Figure 1. The relationship of wings to tergum and pleura, and the mechanism of the basic wing strokes in an insect. A. Upstroke resulting from the depression of the tergum through the contraction of vertical muscles. B. Downstroke resulting from the arching of the tergum through the contraction of longitudinal muscles. C. An insect in flight, showing the figure 8 described by the wing during an upstroke and a downstroke. D. Changes in the position of the forewing of a grasshopper during the course of a single beat. Short arrows indicate direction of wind flowing over wing and numbers indicate consecutive wing positions.

Each wing articulates with the edge of the dorsal cuticle, called the tergum, but its inner end rests on a dorsal pleural process (the pleura is the cuticle covering the side of the body), which acts as a fulcrum. The wing is thus somewhat analogous to an off-centered seesaw. Upward movement of the wings results indirectly from the contraction of vertical muscles within the thorax, depressing the tergum (see Figure 1A). Downward movement of the wings is produced either directly, by contraction of muscles attached to the wingbase, or indirectly, by the contraction of transverse horizontal muscles raising the tergum. Insects such as dragonflies and roaches exhibit direct contraction, while bees, wasps, and flies show indirect contraction. Downward movement can come about by both direct and indirect muscles in insects such as grasshoppers and beetles. The raising or lowering of the wings involves the alternate contraction of antagonistic muscles.

Up and down movement alone is not sufficient for flight; the wings must also move forward and backward. A complete cycle of a single wing beat describes an ellipse in grasshoppers, and a figure eight in bees and flies; the wings are held at different angles to provide both lift and forward thrust. The wing beat frequency varies from four beats per second in certain gnats. The fastest flying insects are the moths and horse flies, which can fly over 33 miles per hour. Gliding, an important form of flight in birds, occurs in only a few large insects.

Insect flight muscles are very powerful. The fibrils in the muscle cells are relatively large and the mitochondria are huge. Insects are the only poikilothermic (cold-blooded) fliers; their low body temperature and correspondingly low metabolic rate impose limitations on mobility. On a cold day some butterflies are known to literally "warm up" before flight. They remain stationary on a tree trunk or some other location, and move their wings up and down until sufficient internal heat is generated to permit the stroke rate necessary for flight.

●PROBLEM 9-27

The circulatory system of insects does not function in gas exchange. What is its function? Describe the circulatory and respiratory systems in insects.

SOLUTION:

Insects, which have high metabolic rates, need oxygen in large amounts. However, insects do not rely on the blood to supply oxygen to their tissues. This function is fulfilled by the tracheal system. The blood serves only to deliver nutrients and remove wastes.

The insect heart is a muscular dorsal tube, usually located within the first nine abdominal segments. The heart lies within a pericardial sinus. The pericardial sinus is not derived from the coelom, but is instead a part of the hemocoel. It is separated by connective tissue from the perivisceral sinus which is the hemocoel surrounding the other internal structures. Usually, the only vessel besides the heart is an anterior aorta. Blood flow is normally posterior to anterior in the heart and anterior to posterior in the perivisceral sinus. Blood from the perivisceral sinus drains into the pericardial sinus. The heart is pierced by a series of openings or ostia, which are regulated by valves, so that blood only flows in one direction. When the heart contracts, the ostia close and blood is pumped forward. When the heart relaxes, the ostia open and blood from the pericardial sinus is drawn into the heart through the ostia. After leaving the heart and aorta, the blood fills the spaces between the internal organs, bathing them directly. The rate of blood flow is regulated by the motion of the muscles of the body wall or the gut.

A respiratory system delivers oxygen directly to the tissues in the insect. A pair of openings called spiracles is present on the first seven or eight abdominal segments and on the last one or two thoracic segments. Usually, the spiracle is provided with a valve for closing and with a filtering apparatus (composed of bristles) to prevent entrance of dust and parasites.

The organization of the internal tracheal system is quite variable, but usually a pair of longitudinal trunks with cross connections is found. Larger tracheae are supported by thickened rings of cuticle, called taenidia. The tracheae are widened in various places to form internal air sacs. The air sacs have no taenidia and are sensitive to ventilation pressures (see Figure 1). The tracheae

311

branch to form smaller and smaller subdivisions, the smallest being the tracheoles. The smallest tracheoles are in direct contact with the tissues and are filled with fluid at their tips. This is where gas exchange takes place.

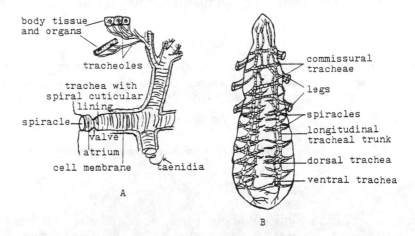

Figure 1. A. Relationship of spiracle, tracheae, taenidia (chitinous bands that strengthen the tracheae), and tracheoles (diagrammatic). B. Generalized arrangement of insect tracheal system (diagrammatic). Air sacs and tracheoles not shown.

Within the tracheae, gas transport is brought about by diffusion, ventilation pressures, or both. Ventilation pressure gradients result from body movements. Body movements causing compression of the air sacs and certain elastic tracheae force air out; those causing expansion of the body wall result in air rushing into the tracheal system. In some insects, the opening and closing of spiracles is coordinated with body movements. Grasshoppers, for example, draw air into the first four pairs of spiracles as the abdomen expands, and expel air through the last six pairs of spiracles as the abdomen contracts.

●PROBLEM 9-28

Discuss the structural and hormonal aspects of insect metamorphosis.

SOLUTION:

Basically, there are two kinds of metamorphosis: incomplete metamorphosis which results in a similar but larger form, and complete metamorphosis, which gives rise to strikingly different forms. Many insects, such as moths, butterflies, and flies undergo complete metamorphosis.

Generally, a wormlike larva — called a caterpillar in moths, maggot in flies, and grub in bees — hatches from the egg. The larva is a relatively active form; it crawls about, eats voraciously, and molts several times, each time becoming larger in size. The last larval molt gives rise to a pupa, an inactive form which typically does not move or eat. Moth and butterfly larvae spin a cocoon around their bodies and molt within the cocoon to form the pupae. During this process all the structures of the larva are broken down and used as raw materials for the development of the adult. Each part of the adult body develops from a group of cells called a disc. The discs are embryonic cells derived directly from the egg and remain quiescent during larval stages. During the pupal stage they grow and differentiate into adult structures such as wings, legs, and eyes. These structures remain collapsed, folded, and thus nonfunctional at first; when the pupa molts into the adult form, blood is pumped in to inflate them, and chitin is deposited to make them hard.

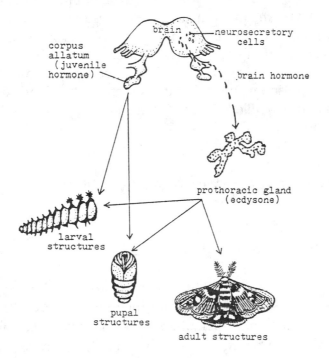

Figure 1. Interactions of juvenile hormone, brain hormone, and molting hormone, (ecdysone) in cecropia silkworm.

Metamorphosis in insects is characterized not only by sharp changes in appearance from the larval to the adult form, but also by striking changes in their modes of life. The butterfly larva eats leaves whereas the adult feeds on nectar from flowers. The mosquito larva lives in ponds and eats algae and protozoa, while the adult sucks the blood of humans and other mammals.

The process of insect metamorphosis involves a brain hormone, a molting hormone called ecdysone, and a regulatory hormone called the juvenile hormone. The brain hormone stimulates glands in the insect's prothorax (the part of the body immediately behind the head, to which the first pair of legs is attached). The prothoracic glands respond by secreting ecdysone which induces molting. Ecdysone is believed to be involved also in many growth and developmental processes in insects. Juvenile hormone is produced by a pair of

313

glands, called corpora allata, which is located just behind the brain and closely associated with it. High concentrations of juvenile hormone at the time of molting result in another immature stage following the molt, while low concentrations lead to a more advanced stage after molting. This is supported by the demonstration that removal of the corpora allata from insects in a highly immature stage resulted in pupation at the next molt, followed by a molt that resulted in a midget adult. Conversely, implantation of an active corpora allata into an advanced pupa resulted in another immature stage after molting rather than an adult. In the larva, juvenile hormone is present in a high concentration, hence the larva molts to form a pupa. In the pupa, juvenile hormone is absent and thus when the pupa molts an adult results.

Notice that insect metamorphosis involves the nervous system as well as endocrine glands. Of the three hormones discussed, one is released directly by the brain (the brain hormone), one is secreted under the influence of the brain hormone (ecdysone), and the third is secreted by glands closely associated with the brain (juvenile hormone). The interactions between these three hormones are shown in Figure 1.

SHORT ANSWER QUESTIONS FOR REVIEW

Choose the correct answer.

1. A planarium has the characteristic of being a *triclad* because: (a) It possesses three different orifices for ingestion of food. (b) It possessed a three-branched muscular pharynx. (c) It possesses three different orifices for egestion of waste-products. (d) It possesses a three-branched gastrovascular cavity.

2. Which of the following best describes the "nervous system" of a hydra? (a) A regularly arranged nerve net concentrated in no one particular area of the hydra. The system lacks synapses and nerve transmission is rapid. (b) An irregularly arranged nerve net, slightly concentrated around the mouth, but not aggregated enough to form a brain or spinal cord. Synapses are present, with some conducting in two directions and others only in one direction. Transmission is slow. (c) Nerve cells are arranged concentrically around the mouth forming a primitive brain. Axons radiate outward forming a "nerve net." The system lacks synapses, so transmission is fast. (d) None of the above.

3. Which of the following is not a type of a nematocyst? (a) Volvent type — used to entangle prey (b) Glutinant type — used for anchoring purposes (c) Buccinant type — used for digestive purposes (d) Penetrant type — used to paralyze prey

4. If an animal is hermaphroditic, does it automatically mean that it reproduces via self-fertilization? (a) Yes, because there is no differentiation of sex, so self-fertilization must take place. (b) No, because if the testes and ovaries develop at different times, self-fertilization cannot take place, but rather copulation can occur between two individuals containing different gonads. (c) No, because if the gonads release gametes at different times, self-fertilization is prevented. (d) Both **b** and **c**

5. Which statement is incorrect? (a) Round worms can be parasitic, while Proboscis worms are usually never parasitic. (b) Both round worms and Proboscis worms are considered to possess a primitive brain. (c) Both round worms and Proboscis worms contain an outer protective cuticle. (d) Round worms do not contain any cilia, while Proboscis worms have a ciliated epithelium.

6. In most species of Mollusca, the shell is secreted by (a) the excretory organ. (b) the visceral mass. (c) the mantle. (d) the ventral foot.

7. Which of the following molluscs are filter feeders? (a) cephalopods (b) gastropods (c) bivalves (d) All of the above

8. The earthworm excretes (a) a very concentrated urine through the nephridiopore. (b) a very concentrated urine through the nephrostome. (c) a dilute, copius urine through the nephridiopore. (d) a dilute, copious urine through the nephrostome.

9. The epicuticle layer of an arthropod's skeleton functions to (a) provide support at the joints. (b) provide tensile strength. (c) provide rigidity. (d) prevent water loss.

10. Segmented worms have the phylum name: (a) Platyhelminthes. (b) Nemathelminthes. (c) Annelida. (d) Echinodermata.

11. Which of the following characteristics does not apply to arthropods as a group? (a) have a notochord (b) includes more species than any other phyla (c) hard exoskeleton composed of chitin (d) jointed legs

12. In the class Insecta, if wings are present they are attached to (a) the head (b) the thorax (c) the abdomen (d) it varies depending on the species

13. The compound eye of an arthropod differs from the human eye in all of the following except: (a) the fact that the image formed is actually a mosaic. (b) the sensitivity to motion. (c) the presence of a retina. (d) the number of lenses.

14. The class of echinoderms which locomote by their long, slender, more flexible arms and do not possess either an anus or an intestine is the: (a) Holothuroidea. (b) Asteroidea. (c) Echinoidea. (d) Ophiuroidea.

Fill in the blanks.

15. Sponges are members of the phylum _____. The surface of a sponge has small openings called _____ that open into a cavity called a _____. This cavity has a direct, larger opening to the top surface called an _____.

16. Regulation of water balance in planaria is a function of the _____, also known as_____. The method by which this occurs is caused by beating _____. Nitrogenous waste is usually eliminated from the planaria via its _____.

17. In an organism such as the hydra, the acellular layer sandwiched between the outer epidermis and the cells lining the gastrovascular cavity is called the _____. In higher invertebrates and all vertebrates, a similarly-placed middle layer of embryonic tissue holds greater importance, as it gives rise to systems such as the _____ and _____ systems. This layer is called the _____.

18. Located in the _____ of the hydra are specialized stinging cells called _____, which contain a bristle-like process at one end called a _____. Inside the _____ is a capsule containing the actual stinging structure, called a _____.

19. Gastropods exhibit an embryonic twisting called _____ in which two rotations of the body occur.

20. The bivalves are molluscs which have two hinged shells and a muscular _____ for the intake and output of water.

21. Most molluscs and all arthropods have an _____ circulatory system which is characterized by some sections where vessels are _____ and the blood flows through _____.

22. The segments in the exoskeleton of an arthropod are joined together by a thin layer of flexible _____.

Determine whether the following statements are true or false.

23. Although sponges are multicellular, there is little communication between the aggregation of cells, hence, there are no organ systems.

24. Planaria can go for long amounts of time without eating, but in the process, will get smaller due to digestion of parts of itself.

25. Although it was once thought that the primitive nervous system of a hydra contained synapses, it is now known that they do not occur.

26. The body wall of a hydra consists of three structural layers: an outer layer called the epidermis, an inner layer called the gastrodermis, and a middle layer called the mesoderm.

27. The nephrostome of the earthworm is analagous in function to the flame cell of the planaria.

28. Locomotion occurs in the earthworm with the contraction of the longitudinal and circular muscles. The contractions compress the coelomic fluid which fills the segments of the body, and thus moves the earthworm along the ground.

29. There are many classes of invertebrates that can fly.

30. Insects are divided into different orders by taking into account their wing structures, mouth parts, and the way in which they undergo metamorphosis.

31. Metamorphosis occurs with the animal maintaining a similar form but its body size becomes progressively larger.

32. In order for flight, an insect only needs up and down movement of its wings.

ANSWER KEY

1. d	2. b	3. c
4. d	5. c	6. c
7. c	8. c	9. d
10. c	11. a	12. b
13. a	14. d	

15. porifera, incurrent pores, spongocoel, osculum

16. flame cells, protone-phridia, cilia, mouth

17. mesoglea, circulatory, excretory, mesoderm

18. epidermis, cnidocytes, cnidocil, cnidocyte, nematocyst

19. torsion	20. siphon	21. open, absent, sinuses
22. chitin	23. True	24. True
25. False	26. False	27. True
28. False	29. False	30. True
31. False	32. False	

CHAPTER 10

ANIMAL KINGDOM —
THE VERTEBRATES

●PROBLEM 10-1

What are the chief characteristics of the subphylum Vertebrata?

SOLUTION:

In addition to the three basic chordate characteristics, the vertebrates have an endoskeleton of cartilage or bone that reinforces or replaces the notochord. The notochord is the only skeletal structure present in lower chordates, but in the vertebrates there are bony or cartilaginous segmental vertebrae that surround the notochord. In the higher vertebrates the notochord is visible only during embryonic development. Later the vertebrae replace the notochord completely. A part of each vertebra consists of an arch, and all of the vertebrae together form a tunnel-like protection for the dorsal nerve cord. A brain case, skull, or cranium, composed either of cartilage or bone, develops as a protective structure around the brain of all vertebrates.

The eyes in vertebrates are unique and differ both in structure and development from those of the invertebrates. The eyes of vertebrates develop as lateral outgrowths of the brain. Invertebrate eyes, such as those of insects, may be highly developed and quite efficient, but they develop from a folding of the skin. The formation of ears for detecting sounds is another vertebrate characteristic. The ears also function as organs of equilibrium, as is the major function of the ears in the lowest vertebrates.

The circulatory system of vertebrates is distinctive in that the blood is confined to blood vessels and is pumped by a ventral, muscular heart. The higher invertebrates such as arthropods and molluscs typically have hearts but they are located on the dorsal side of the body and pump blood into open spaces in the body, called hemocoels. Vertebrates are said to have a closed circulatory system. The invertebrate earthworm is an exception among the lower invertebrates in that it has a closed circulatory system. Arthropods and molluscs have an open circulatory system.

Chordates

What are the three chief characteristics of phylum Chordata?

Figure 1. Cross-section through throat region of a chordate, showing three characteristics of the group: hollow nerve cord, notochord beneath, gill slits connecting gut with exterior.

SOLUTION:

All chordates display the following three characteristics: first, the central nervous system is a hollow tube containing a single continuous cavity, and is situated on the dorsal side of the body. A second characteristic feature is the presence of clefts in the wall of the throat region, usually referred to as gill slits, originally utilized perhaps as a food-catching device. The third characteristic is the presence of a notochord, a rod lying dorsal to the intestine, extending from the anterior to posterior end, and serving as a skeletal support. In the Vertebrata, one of the three subphyla of the chordates, the notochord is partially or wholly replaced by the skull and vertebral column. It should be noted that the dorsal hollow nerve cord, the notochord, and the gill slits need only be present at some time in the life of an organism for it to be considered a chordate. In a tunicate, for example, which belongs to the Chordata subphylum, Urochordata, the dorsal hollow nerve cord and the notochord are confined to the tail in the larval stage, and disappear in the adult stage. In the subphylum, Cephalochordata, all chordate characteristics are retained in the adult.

Fish

The earliest vertebrate fossils date back to the Ordovician period, 500 million years ago. What distinguishes these early vertebrates from later vertebrates?

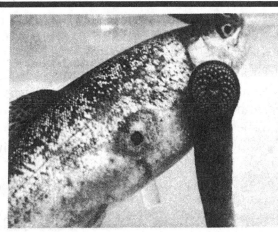

Figure 1. Lamprey detached from rainbow trout to show feeding wound that had penetrated body cavity and perforated guts.

SOLUTION:

These early vertebrates belong to the class Agnatha. The organisms of this class have cylindrical bodies up to a meter long, with smooth scaleless skin. Unlike other vertebrates, these organisms lack jaws ("agnatha" means jawless) and paired fins. In addition, they are also the only parasitic vertebrates, feeding primarily on the fishes. Members of this class include the lampreys and hagfishes, and the extinct ostracoderms (the earliest Agnaths). Lampreys and hagfishes constitute the cyclostomes, and have a circular sucking disc around the mouth, which is located on the ventral side of the anterior end. They attach themselves by this disc to other fish, and using the horny teeth on the disc and tongue, bore through the skin and feed on blood and soft tissues of the host. Some may bore completely through the skin and come to lie within the body of the host. The ostracoderms were the only Agnaths that were not parasitic. Since they were the first vertebrates, there were no fish as yet to exploit as food. It is assumed that the ostracoderms obtained food by filtering mud.

In the cyclostomes, the notochord persists in the adult as a functional supporting structure. The gill slits and dorsal hollow nerve cord are present in the larva called an ammocoetes and adult, and the vertebrae are rudimentary, consisting only of a series of cartilaginous arches that protect the nerve cord.

Describe the function of the lateral-line system in fishes.

SOLUTION:

Just as the sensory hair cells in the semicircular canals of terrestrial verte-brates function in the detection of sound and acceleration, so does the lateral-line system in fishes. The lateral-line system consists of a series of grooves on the sides of a fish. There are sensory hair cells occurring at intervals along the grooves. These sensory cells are pressure sensitive, and enable the fish to de-tect localized as well as distant water disturbances. The lateral-line system bears evolutionary significance in that the sensory hair cells of terrestrial ver-tebrates is believed to have evolved from the sensory cells of the archaic lat-eral-line system in fishes. The lateral-line system of modern fishes functions primarily as an organ of equilibrium. Whether or not a fish can hear in the way that terrestrial vertebrates do is not known.

Contrast the major features of cartilaginous and bony fish.

SOLUTION:

The cartilaginous fish of the class Chondrichthyes are distinguished by, as their name implies, their cartilaginous skeletons. No bone is present in this group. The presence of a cartilaginous skeleton in this class must be regarded as a specialization because there is evidence that the ancestors of the group, the placoderms, had bony skeletons.

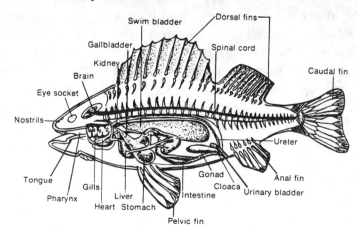

Figure 1. The structure of a perch, a bony fish.

322

Included in the class Chondrichthyes are the sharks, skates, and rays. The sharks are streamlined, fast-swimming, voracious feeders. One kind, the whale shark, is the largest known fish. It may attain a length of 50 feet or more. Rays are sluggish, flattened bottom feeders.

Chondrichthyes have neither swim bladders nor lungs. Osmoregulation in some groups is unusual, involving retention of high concentrations of urea in the body fluids. Fertilization is internal, and the eggs have tough, leathery shells. Most species are predatory but a few are plankton feeders.

Like the cartilaginous fish, the bony fish, belonging to the class Osteichthyes, arose from the placoderms. In most of them, the adult skeleton is composed largely of bone. Unlike cartilaginous fish, fertilization is external in most bony fish. The gills of bony fish are covered by a hinged bony plate, the operculum, on each side of the pharynx. In most bony and cartilaginous fish the body is covered with scales. Unlike the cartilaginous fish, most bony fish have a swim bladder, which arose as a modification of the lungs of the earliest Osteichthyes. There are still some bony fish today that possess lungs instead of swim bladders. By modifying the gaseous content of the swim bladder, the fish can modify its buoyancy. Cartilaginous fish have no swim bladder and are denser than the sea water around them. They would sink to the bottom if it were not for the movements of the pelvic and tail fins which serve to maintain buoyancy in these fish.

The early Osteichthyes gave rise to three main lines of bony fishes: the lobe-finned fish (order Crossopterygii) the lungfish (order Dipnoi), and the telecosts (order Teleostei) which form the dominant group of marine and aquatic animals today). The lungfish and lobe-finned fish have functional lungs as well as gills. Teleosts possess a swim bladder, but no lungs.

Amphibians

●PROBLEM 10-6

Although some adult amphibia are quite successful as land animals and can live in comparatively dry places, they must return to water to reproduce. Describe the process of reproduction and development in the amphibians.

SOLUTION:

The frog (order Anura) will be used as a representative amphibian in this problem. Reproduction in the frog takes place in the water. The male seizes the female from above and both discharge their gametes simultaneously into the water. This process is known as amplexus. Fertilization then takes place externally, forming zygotes. A zygote develops into a larva, or tadpole. The tadpole breathes by means of gills and feeds on aquatic plants. After a time, the larva undergoes metamorphosis and becomes a young adult frog, with lungs and legs. The same type of system is seen in the salamanders (order Urodela).

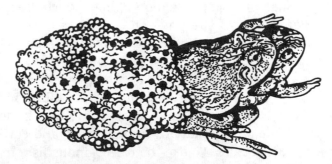

Figure 1. Amplexus in frogs. Male (on top) holds female and both discharge their gametes simultaneously into water. Mass of eggs is visible at left.

Like the metamorphosis of insects and other arthropods, that of the amphibia is under hormonal control. Amphibia undergo a single change from larva to adult in contrast to the four or more molts involved in the development of arthropods to the adult form. Amphibian metamorphosis is regulated by thyroxin, the hormone secreted by the thyroid gland, and can be prevented by removing the thyroid, or the pituitary which secretes a thyroid-stimulating hormone modulating the secretion of thyroxin.

●PROBLEM 10-7

Describe the changes that take place in a larval amphibian which result in adaptation to life on land.

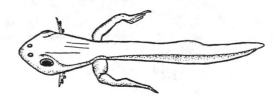

Figure 1. Metamorphosing tadpole.

SOLUTION:

In this problem, the changes that occur in the frog larva which result in the adult frog will be considered. The frog larva is a tadpole which undergoes metamorphosis to become an adult frog. The metamorphosis is a single-step process as opposed to the many molts that an arthropod larva undergoes in reaching the adult form. As in arthropod metamorphosis, amphibian metamorphic processes are hormonally controlled. Thyroxin, secreted by the thyroid gland, is the regulating hormone in amphibian metamorphosis. The tadpole is a completely aquatic organism and breathes via gills. It feeds on microscopic plants in the water. The tadpole also has a tail. During metamorphosis, the gills and gill slits are lost, the lungs develop, forelegs grow out of skin folds, the tail is retracted, the tongue, the eyelids and the tympanic membrane are formed, and the shape of the lens changes. The adult form of the organism, the frog, is a semiaquatic animal which feeds on insects. The frog breathes by means of its lungs as well as through its thin, moist skin. The skin of amphibians functions as a respiratory organ. This is facilitated by the physical nature of the skin, which must remain moist in order to function as a respiratory organ. If terrestrial conditions become very dry, the frog's thin, moist skin will be in danger of desiccation, and hence, the frog will retreat to the aquatic environment.

● PROBLEM 10-8

What hormone is responsible for metamorphosis in amphibians?

SOLUTION:

In amphibians, the thyroid hormones control metamorphosis. This is seen by the fact that very young larvae that have had their thyroids removed did not undergo metamorphosis unless they were immersed in or injected with thyroxine solutions. In addition, normal larvae with thyroids metamorphosize precociously when they have thyroxine added to their water or administered by injection.

The metamorphosis includes regressive changes (ex: resorption of the tadpole tail, gills, and teeth) as well as constructive changes (ex: the development of limbs, tongue, and middle ear). The pituitary gland initiates metamorphosis by releasing thyroid stimulating hormone (TSH), which is carried by the bloodstream to the thyroid. The thyroid is induced to release thyroxine into the circulation.

Metamorphosis involves extensive changes at the biochemical level. A new set of enzymes appears in the liver, a new type of hemoglobin protein is synthesized; and a novel protein is formed in the retina. Structures that are resorbed contain high levels of proteases, nucleases, and other digestive enzymes. These changes are all inducible with a single substance — thyroxine.

Reptiles

Describe the evolution of the reptilian excretory system to account for the transition from an aquatic to a terrestrial habitat.

SOLUTION:

The reptilian excretory system has evolved in a way that enables the animal to conserve most of its water. The conservation of body fluid is a necessary characteristic of a terrestrial animal. Without this feature, the body tissues would become desiccated in the dry environment.

Reptiles conserve water by having a coarse, dry, horny skin. In addition, the glomeruli of the reptilian kidney have diminished in size so that less water is filtered from the blood. Another modification is a greater degree of reabsorption of water from the glomerular filtrate by the kidney tubules. This occurs as the reptiles have evolved kidney tubules with two highly coiled regions and a long loop of Henle extending deep into the medulla of the kidney. These long portions of the tubule function in the reabsorption of water. Their ability to produce a concentrated hypertonic excretory product is an important adaptation to land life.

The conservation of water in the reptile has affected the nature of the excretory product. Nitrogenous wastes are excreted as uric acid in reptiles, as opposed to urea in amphibians (whose ancestors gave rise to primitive reptiles). Uric acid is excreted as a watery paste in reptiles. It is less toxic and less soluble in water than urea. Therefore, it is not necessary for reptiles to use water to dissolve their nitrogenous wastes. In fact, only a comparatively very small amount is required to simply flush the uric acid out of the excretory system. In this way, the reptile conserves most of its body water and prevents dehydration.

Which of the following is not a reptile: snake, lizard, salamander, turtle, or alligator.

SOLUTION:

The class Reptilia is divided into four orders. Turtles are reptiles belonging to the order Chelonia; crocodiles and alligators belong to the order Crocodilia; lizards and snakes are in the order Squamata; and the tuatara belong to the order Rynchocephalia, which has only one surviving species. Of the five animals mentioned in the question, only the salamander is not a reptile. The salamander is an amphibian in the order Urodelia. By anatomical observation, it is easily deduced that the salamander is not of the same class as these other animals. The smooth and moist porous skin of the amphibious salamander contrasts sharply with the coarse dry skin of the reptilian animals. This epidermal variation is based upon the different environmental adaptations that these animals underwent. The skin of the amphibian is adapted for a semi-aquatic environment whereas that of the reptile is adapted for a strictly terrestrial environment.

Birds

●PROBLEM 10-11

How does the wing shape of a bird correlate with its distinctive flight?

SOLUTION:

The shape of a wing is correlated with both the power and type of flight for which it is used. Long, slender, pointed wings, sometimes reaching beyond the tail, are seen in birds having great flying powers and soaring habits, such as gulls, eagles, hawks, and vultures. Birds which do not soar, but which fly by continuous wing strokes, have shorter, more rounded wings. Very short, broad wings occur in the fowls, pheasants, grouses, and quails. These are habitual ground dwellers with feet adapted for running. They occasionally make short powerful flights by rapid wing strokes.

Degeneration of the wings to a flightless condition has occurred in a number of birds, such as the penguins and the ostriches. In the ostrich group, many other changes accompany the loss of flight, such as the disappearance of the keel of the breast bone, which supports the flight muscles, and the development of strong running legs and feet.

Which of the following would maintain a constant body temperature in spite of changes in the environmental temperature: frog, robin, fish, dog, or lizard?

SOLUTION:

Animals that can regulate their internal body temperature so that it remains constant in varying environmental temperatures are known as homeotherms. Of the phylum Chordata, only mammals and birds can therm-regulate — i.e., they possess temperature-regulating systems. They are considered to be warm-blooded animals. From the list of animals given, two of them are homeotherms. The robin, since it is a bird, belongs to the class Aves, and the dog is a member of the class Mammalia. Hence these two animals are homeothermic and will maintain a constant body temperature. The remaining animals are poikilotherms. They possess no temperature-regulating system and as a result, their internal body temperature varies directly with the environmental temperature. This poikilothermic characteristic places strict limitations on the environment exploited by the animal, which in turn affects its behavioral patterns. The frog is an amphibian whereas the lizard is a reptile. A fish belongs to the superclass pisces. These three animals are poikilotherms and hence do not maintain a constant body temperature independent of changes in environmental temperature.

Mammals

Describe the characteristic differences between the monotreme, marsupial, and placental mammals.

Figure 1. Duck billed platypus, an egg-laying mammal.

Figure 1. Euro kangaroo, a marsupial mammal, with young in pouch.

Figure 2. Ring-tailed lemur, a placental mammal.

SOLUTION:

The class Mammalia is divided into three subclasses: Prototheria (monotremes), Metatheria (marsupials), and Eutheria (placental mammals). Of these three, the monotremes can be considered the most primitive. They are an early offshoot of the main mammalian groups. The marsupials and placentals appeared at about the same time. Major characteristics of mammals include the possession of mammary glands and hair. Most mammals have sweat glands. All mammals are homeotherms.

Monotremes are peculiar in that they possess mammalian as well as reptilian traits. They are classified as mammals, however, because the number of mammalian traits far exceed the number of reptilian traits. Some of the more outstanding mammalian traits include: a layer of hair covering the body and the secretion of milk by mammary glands. There are only two surviving species of monotremes: the duck-billed platypus and the spiny anteater, both of which are found in Australia. The trait that most clearly distinguishes monotremes from other groups of mammals is their ability to lay eggs. In marsupials and placentals, embryonic development occurs in the uterus of the female.

The characteristic difference between the marsupials and the placentals is the time of embryonic development within the uterus. Marsupial embryos undergo a short developmental period before they leave the uterus. Embryonic development is completed in an abdominal pouch of the mother where the embryo is attached to a nipple. In contrast to this is the placentals. In this group, the embryo develops completely in the uterus of the mother. In both marsupial and placental mammals, the young are born alive.

● PROBLEM 10-14

How are whales adapted for their life in cold waters?

SOLUTION:

Whales are animals that belong to the order Cetacea of the class Mammalia. Only animals belonging to the classes Mammalia and Aves possess a temperature regulating system within their body. They are homeothermic. These animals maintain a nearly constant internal body temperature that is independent of the environmental temperature. Whales, sea cows, and pigeons are animals that have this temperature maintenance ability. All animals not belonging to the class Mammalia or Aves are poikilothermic — their internal body temperature varies directly with the environmental temperature. Another feature of the whale that helps it survive in cold waters is the tremendous amount of subcutaneous fat serving an insulating function. All mammals have a layer of fat underlying the skin. An extreme case of this is seen in the whale.

SHORT ANSWER QUESTIONS FOR REVIEW

Choose the correct answer.

1. Tunicates are best described as (a) terrestrial animals very similar to chordates. (b) urochordates, with a chordate larval stage, and lacking a notochord as an adult. (c) always maintaining a notochord. (d) never having a notochord.

2. Vertebrate characteristics include (a) an open circulatory system, internal skeleton of cartilage or bone, ears, and eyes developed from outgrowths of brain. (b) a closed circulatory system, external skeleton of cartilage or bone, ears, and eyes developed from a folding of skin. (c) a closed circulatory system, internal skeleton of cartilage or bone, ears, and eyes developed from outgrowths of brain. (d) none of the above

3. The chondrichthyes are characterized as (a) having a skeleton of cartilage which is always calcified. (b) having paired jaws and two pairs of fins. (c) the only fish that do not have highly vascular gills. (d) having swim bladders enabling them to float.

4. The bony fish or osteichthes (a) evolved independently of and at about the same time as, the cartilaginous fishes. (b) evolved from the cartilaginous fishes. (c) do not contain swim bladders. (d) do not have their gills covered by a protective structure called the operculum.

5. The correct characteristics of all birds include: (a) cold-blooded, all fly, internal fertilization. (b) warm-blooded, some fly, internal fertilization. (c) warm-blooded, all fly, internal fertilization. (d) warm-blooded, some fly, external fertilization.

6. The distinguishing characteristics of mammals are: (a) hair and mammary glands. (b) carnivorous. (c) sweat glands and differentiation of teeth into incisors, canines, and molars. (d) Both **a** and **c**.

Fill in the blanks.

7. _____ are present in all chordate embryos but are not found in higher adult vertebrates.

8. Vertebrates have a _____ circulatory system.

9. Unlike the bony fishes, cartilaginous fishes have no _____.

10. All chordates contain a hollow, tubular, dorsal _____.

11. The agnatha are eel-shaped animals which are characterized by the complete lack of _____.

12. _____ control metamorphosis in amphibians.

Determine whether the following statements are true or false.

13. The most advanced vertebrates contain a notochord and simpler vertebrates do not.

14. Higher forms of vertebrates lack the notochord as adults, and the vertebrae take over its functions.

15. The placenta of mammals allows an embryo to obtain nourishment from the mother before birth.

16. Reptiles are true land dwellers and do not have to return to water to reproduce as amphibians do.

17. The skeleton of the ostheichthyes consists mostly of cartilage.

18. Birds which fly by continuous strokes have longer and pointier wings.

ANSWER KEY

1. b	2. c	3. b
4. a	5. b	6. d
7. Gill slits	8. closed	9. swim bladders
10. nerve cord	11. jaws	12. Thyroid hormones
13. False	14. True	15. True
16. False	17. False	18. False

CHAPTER 11

HUMAN ANATOMY

Digestive System

● PROBLEM 11-1

Name the major organs of the human digestive tract and explain their functions.

SOLUTION:

The human digestive system begins at the oral cavity. The teeth break up food by mechanical means, increasing the substrates' surface area available to the action of digestive enzymes. There are four types of teeth. The chisel-shaped incisors are used for biting, while the pointed canines function in tearing, and the flattened, ridged premolars and molars are used for grinding and crushing food. In addition to tasting, the tongue manipulates food and forms it into a semi-spherical ball (bolus) with the aid of saliva.

The salivary glands consist of three pairs of glands. The parotid glands, located in the cheek in front of the ear, produce only watery saliva which dissolves dry foods. The submaxillary and sublingual glands, located at the base of the jaw and under the tongue, produce watery and mucous saliva which coagulates food particles and also lubricates the throat for the passage of the bolus. Saliva also contains amylases which break down starches.

The tongue pushes the bolus into the pharynx which is the cavity where the esophagus and trachea (windpipe) meet (see Figure 2). The larynx is raised against the epiglottis and the glottis is closed, preventing food from passing into the trachea. The act of swallowing initiates the movement of food down through a tube connecting the mouth to the stomach called the esophagus. Once inside the esophagus, the food is moved by involuntary peristaltic waves towards the stomach. At the junction of the stomach and the esophagus, is a special ring of muscles called the lower esophageal sphincter. These muscles are normally contracted, but when food from the esophagus reaches the sphincter, it opens reflexively and allows food to enter the stomach.

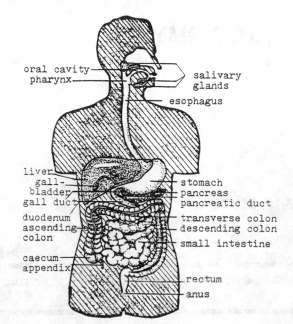

Figure 1. Human digestive system.
(The organs are slightly displaced, and the small intestine is greatly shortened.)

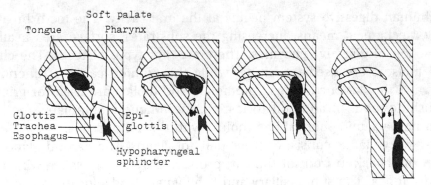

Figure 2. Movement of a bolus of food through the pharynx and upper esophagus during swallowing.

The stomach is a thick muscular sac positioned on the left side of the body just beneath the ribs. The upper region of the stomach, closest to the heart, is called the cardiac region. Below that is the crescent part of the sac called the fundus. The pyloric region is tubular and connects the stomach to the small intestines. The wall of the stomach is made up of three thick layers of muscle. One layer is composed of longitudinal, one of circular, and the other

334

of oblique (diagonal) fibers. The powerful contractions of these muscles break up the food, mix it with gastric juice, and move it down the tract. Gastric juice is a mixture of hydrochloric acid and enzymes that further digest the food. Gastric juice and mucus are secreted by the small gastric glands in the lining of the stomach. The mucus helps protect the stomach from its own digestive enzymes and acid. The partially digested food, called chyme, is pushed through the pyloric sphincter into the small intestine. The pyloric sphincter is similar in structure and function to the lower esophageal sphincter.

The first part of the small intestine, called the duodenum, is held in a fixed position. The rest of the intestine is held loosely in place by a thin membrane called mesentery which is attached to the back of the body wall. In the duodenum, bile from the liver that has been stored in the gallbladder is mixed with pancreatic juice from the pancreas. The secretions of the pancreas and glandular cells of the intestinal tract contain enzymes that finish digesting the food. As digestion continues in the lower small intestine, muscular contractions mix the food and move it along. Small finger-like protrusions, called villi, line the small intestine facing the lumen. They greatly increase the intestinal surface area and it is through the villi that most of the nutrient absorption takes place.

The small intestine joins the large intestine (colon) at the cecum. The cecum is a blind sac that has the appendix protruding from one side. Neither the appendix nor the cecum are functional. At the junction of the cecum and the lower small intestine (ileum) is a sphincter called the ileocecal valve. Undigested food passes through this valve into the large intestine.

The large intestine has the function of removing water from the unabsorbed material. At times there is an excretion of certain calcium and iron salts when their concentrations in the blood are too high. Large numbers of bacteria exist in the colon. Their function is not fully understood, but some can synthesize vitamin K which is of great importance to blood clotting. The last section of the colon stores feces until it is excreted through the anal sphincter.

●PROBLEM 11-2

What is the basic mechanism of digestion and what digestive processes take place in the mouth and stomach?

SOLUTION:

The process of digestion is the breakdown of large, ingested molecules into smaller, simple ones that can be absorbed and used by the body. The breakdown of these large molecules is called degradation. During degradation, some of the chemical bonds that hold the large molecules together are split. The digestive enzymes cleave molecular bonds by a process called hydrolysis. In hydrolysis a water molecule is added across the bond to cleave it.

$$H - \underset{\underset{H}{|}}{\overset{\overset{R}{|}}{N}} - \underset{\underset{H}{|}}{\overset{R}{C}} - \overset{\overset{O}{\|}}{C} - \underset{\underset{H}{|}}{\overset{\overset{R'}{|}}{N}} - \underset{\underset{H}{|}}{\overset{R'}{C}} - \overset{\overset{O}{\|}}{C} - OH + H_2O \xrightarrow{\quad Enzyme \quad}$$

Dipeptide

$$H_2N - \underset{\underset{H}{|}}{\overset{\overset{R}{|}}{C}} - \overset{\overset{O}{\|}}{C} - OH \quad + \quad H - \underset{\underset{H}{|}}{\overset{\overset{R'}{|}}{N}} - \underset{\underset{H}{|}}{\overset{R'}{C}} - \overset{\overset{O}{\|}}{C} - OH$$

Figure 1. Hydrolysis of a dipeptide, R and R' represent different side chains.

Within living systems, chemical reactions require specific enzymes to act as catalysts. Enzymes are very specific, acting only on certain substrates. In addition, different enzymes work best under unlike conditions. Digestive enzymes work best outside of the cell, for their optimum pHs lie either on the acidic (e.g., gastric enzymes) or basic side (e.g., intestinal and pancreatic enzymes). The cell interior, however, requires an almost neutral (about 7.4) pH constantly. Digestive enzymes are secreted into the digestive tract by the cells that line or serve it.

Digestion begins in the mouth. Most foods contain polysaccharides, such as starch, which are long chains of glucose molecules. Saliva (and the intestinal secretions) contain enzymes that degrade such molecules. Salivary amylase, an enzyme that is also called ptyalin, hydrolyzes starch into maltose. (Compounds whose names end with "-ase" are enzymes, and those with the suffix "-ose" are sugars.) Glucose is eventually absorbed by the epithelial cells lining the small intestine.

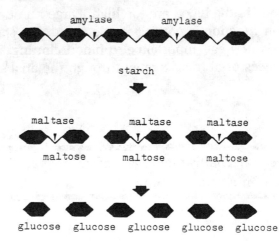

Figure 2. Digestion of starch. Amylase in the saliva and in the pancreatic juice hydrolyzes the bonds between every other pair of glucose units, producing the disaccharide maltose. Maltose is digested to glucose by maltase, secreted by intestinal glands.

The saliva has a pH of 6.5–6.8. This is the optimal range for salivary enzyme activity. Food spends a relatively short amount of time in the mouth, and eventually enters the stomach. The stomach is very acidic, with a pH of 1.5–2.5. The acid is secreted by special cells in the lining of the stomach called parietal cells. The low pH is required for the activity of the stomach enzyme pepsin. Rennin coagulates milk proteins in the infant's stomach, making them more susceptible to enzyme attack. Pepsin is a proteolytic enzyme (protease): it degrades proteins. Pepsin starts the protein digestion in the stomach by splitting the long proteins into shorter fragments, or peptides, that are further digested in the intestine. Pepsin will split any peptide bond involving the amino acids tyrosine or phenylalanine. There are 20 different kinds of amino acids that can make up a protein and some proteins are thousands of amino acids long. The body needs the amino acids it obtains from digestion to synthesize its own proteins.

●PROBLEM 11-3

Explain how peristalsis moves food through the digestive tract.

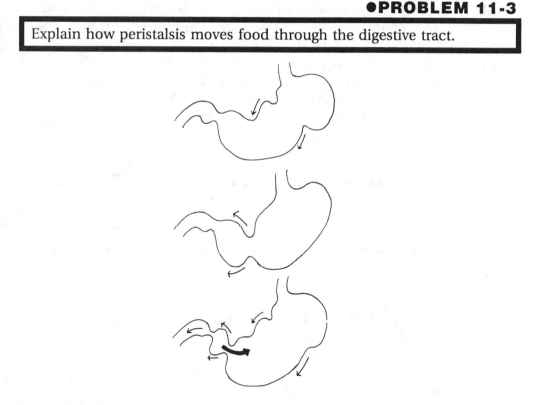

Figure 1. Peristaltic waves passing over the stomach empty a small amount of material into the duodenum. Most of the material is forced back into the antrum.

SOLUTION:

In each region of the digestive tract, rhythmic waves of constriction move food down the tract. This form of contractile activity is called peristalsis, and involves involuntary smooth muscles. There are two layers of smooth muscle throughout most of the digestive tract. Circular muscles run around the circumference of the tract while longitudinal muscles traverse its length.

Once a food bolus is moved into the lower esophagus, circular muscles in the esophageal wall just behind the bolus contract, squeezing and pushing the food downward. At the same time, longitudinal muscles in the esophageal wall in front of the bolus relax to facilitate movement of the food. As the bolus moves, the muscles it passes also contract, so that a wave of contraction follows the bolus and constantly pushes it forward. This wave of constriction alternates with a wave of relaxation.

Swallowing initiates peristalsis and once started, the waves of contraction cannot be stopped voluntarily. Like other involuntary responses, peristaltic waves are controlled by the autonomic nervous system. When a peristaltic wave reaches a sphincter, the sphincter opens slightly and a small amount of food is forced through. Immediately afterwards, the sphincter closes to prevent the food from moving back. In the stomach, the waves of peristalsis increase in speed and intensity as they approach the pyloric end. As this happens, the pyloric sphincter of the stomach opens slightly. Some chyme escapes into the duodenum but most of it is forced back into the stomach (see Figure 1). This allows the food to be more efficiently digested. There is little peristalsis in the intestine, and more of a slower oscillating contraction. This is why most of the 12-24 hours that food requires for complete digestion is spent in the intestine.

●PROBLEM 11-4

The intestine, especially the small intestine, is a vital organ for absorption of nutrients required by the body. In what ways is it suitable for such a function?

SOLUTION:

The small intestine is that region of the digestive tract between the stomach and the cecum. Its long, convoluted structure is an adaptation for absorption of nutrients. Structural modifications of the internal surfaces of the small intestine act to increase its surface area for absorption. First, the mucosa lining the intestine is thrown into numerous folds and ridges. Second, small fingerlike projections called villi cover the entire surface of the mucosa (see Figure 1). These villi are richly supplied with blood capillaries and lacteals (for absorption of fats) in order to facilitate absorption of nutrients. Third, individual epithelial cells lining the folds and villi have a "brush-border" on the surface facing the lumen, consisting of countless, closely-packed, cylindrical processes known as microvilli. These microvilli add an enormous amount of surface area to that already present. The total internal surface area of the small intestine is thus incredibly large; this is advantageous for the purpose of absorption.

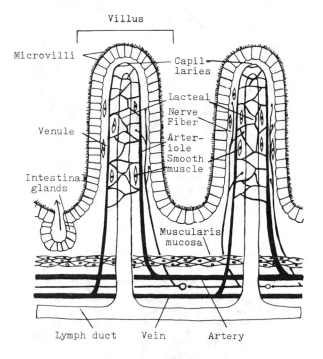

Figure 1. Structure of intestinal villi.

The large intestine also has villi to increase its surface area. However, the number of villi present in the small intenstine far exceeds that found in the large intestine. The main function of the large intestine is to absorb water from the undigested food substances and reduce the remains to a semi-solid state before it is expelled through the anus.

Circulatory System

●PROBLEM 11-5

Trace the path of blood through the human heart.

SOLUTION:

The heart is the muscular organ that causes the blood to circulate in the body. The heart of birds and mammals is a pulsatile four-chambered pump composed of an upper left and right atrium (pl., atria) and a lower left and right ventricle. The atria function mainly as entryways to the ventricles, whereas the ventricles supply the main force that propels blood to the lungs and throughout the body.

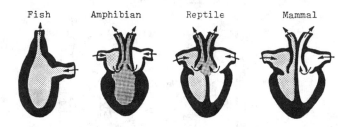

Figure 1. The hearts of four classes of vertebrates. From fish to mammal, there is increasing separation between the two sides of the heart, with consequent decrease in the amount of mixing between oxygenated and deoxygenated blood.

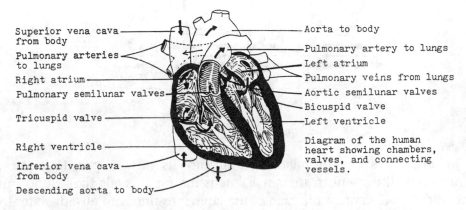

Figure 2. The human heart showing chambers, valves, and connecting vessels.

Depending on where the blood is flowing from, it would enter the heart via one of the two veins: the superior vena cava carries blood from the head, neck and arms; the interior vena cava carries blood from the rest of the body. The blood from these two veins enters the right atrium. When this chamber is filled with blood, the chamber contracts and forces the blood through a valve called the tricuspid valve and into the right ventricle. Since this blood has returned from its circulation in the body's tissues, it is deoxygenated and contains much carbon dioxide. It therefore must be transported to the lungs where gas exchange can take place. The right ventricle contracts, forces the blood through the pulmonary semilunar valve into the pulmonary artery. This artery is unlike most arteries in that it carries deoxygenated blood. The artery splits into two, with one branch leading to each lung. The pulmonary arteries further divide into many arterioles, which divide even further and connect with dense capillary networks surrounding the alveoli in the lungs. The alveoli are small sac-like cavities where gas exchange occurs. Carbon dioxide diffuses into the alveoli, where it is expelled, while oxygen is picked up by the hemoglobin of the erythrocytes. The capillaries join to form small venules which further combine to form the four pulmonary veins leading back to the heart. The pulmonary veins are unlike most veins in that they carry oxygenated blood.

340

These veins empty into the left atrium, which contracts to force the blood through the bicuspid (or mitral) valve into the left ventricle. When the left ventricle, filled with blood, contracts, the blood is forced through the aortic semilunar valve into the aorta, the largest artery in the body (about 25 millimeters in diameter).

The aorta forms an arch and runs posteriorly and inferiorly along the body. Before it completes the arch, the aorta branches into the coronary artery, which carries blood to the muscular walls of the heart itself, the carotid arteries, which carry blood to the head and brain, and the subclavian arteries, which carries blood to the arms. As the aorta runs posteriorly, it branches into arteries which lead various organs such as the liver, kidney, intestines and spleen, and also the legs.

The arteries divide into arterioles which further divide and become capillaries. It is here that the oxygen and nutrients diffuse into the tissues and carbon dioxide and nitrogenous wastes are picked up. The capillaries fuse to form venules which further fuse to become either the superior or inferior vena cava. The entire cycle starts once again.

The part of the circulatory system in which deoxygenated blood is pumped to the lungs and oxygenated blood returned to the heart is called the pulmonary circulation. The part in which oxygenated blood is pumped to all parts of the body by the arteries and deoxygenated blood is returned to the heart by the veins is called the systemic circulation.

● PROBLEM 11-6

Explain why blood is such an important tissue in many animals. Discuss the major functions of blood.

SOLUTION:

All cells, in order to survive, must obtain the necessary raw materials for metabolism, and have a means for the removal of waste products. In small plants and animals living in an aquatic environment, these needs are provided for by simple diffusion. The cells of such organisms are very near the external watery medium, and so nutrients and wastes do not have a large distance to travel. However, as the size of the organism increases, more and more cells become further removed from the media bathing the peripheral cells. Diffusion cannot provide sufficient means for transport. In the absence of a specialized transport system, the limit on the size of an aerobic organism would be about a millimeter, since the diffusion of oxygen and nutrients over great distances would be too slow to meet the metabolic needs of all the cells of the organism. In addition, without internal transport, organisms are restricted to watery environments, since the movement to land requires an efficient

341

system for material exchange in non-aqueous surroundings. Therefore, larger animals have developed a system of internal transport, the circulatory system. This system, consisting of an extensive network of various vessels, provides each cell with an opportunity to exchange materials by diffusion.

Blood is the vital tissue in the circulatory system, transporting nutrients and oxygen to all the cells and removing carbon dioxide and other wastes from them. Blood also serves other important functions. It transports hormones, the secretions of the endocrine glands, which affect organs sensitive to them. Blood also acts to regulate the acidity and alkalinity of the cells via control of their salt and water content. In addition, the blood acts to regulate the body temperature by cooling certain organs and tissues when an excess of heat is produced (such as in exercising muscle) and warming tissues where heat loss is great (such as in the skin).

Some components of the blood act as a defense against bacteria, viruses, and other pathogenic (disease-causing) organisms. The blood also has a self-preservation system called a clotting mechanism so that loss of blood due to vessel rupture is reduced.

● PROBLEM 11-7

Both myoglobin and hemoglobin are oxygen-carrying molecules. Why is hemoglobin the molecule of choice to carry oxygen in the blood?

SOLUTION:

In vertebrates, both myoglobin and hemoglobin act as oxygen carriers. Hemoglobin, however, is the only one that acts in the blood, carrying oxygen from the lungs to the tissues where it is needed for metabolic processes. Myoglobin is located in muscle, and serves as a reserve supply of oxygen. What accounts for the functional differences between these two proteins?

Myoglobin is a single-chain protein containing only one heme group, which serves to bind an oxygen molecule. Hemoglobin is composed of four polypeptide chains (each chain similar to the one of myoglobin) and thus has four binding sites for oxygen. It is the interaction of these four polypeptide chains that confers special properties to the hemoglobin molecule, making it a better oxygen-carrier in the blood.

One of these important properties is the ability to transport CO_2 and H^+ in addition to O_2. Myoglobin does not have this ability. The binding of oxygen by hemoglobin is regulated by specific substances in its environment such as H^+, CO_2, and organic phosphate compounds. These regulatory substances bind to sites on hemoglobin that are far from the heme groups. The binding of these substances affects the binding of oxygen by producing conformational changes in the protein, that lower hemoglobin's affinity for oxygen. A change at the regulatory site (where these regulatory substances bind) is translated to the heme site by changes in the way the four polypeptide chains are spatially arranged. This results in a structural change in the protein. Such interactions between spatially distinct sites are termed allosteric interactions. Hemoglobin is an allosteric protein (whereas myoglobin is not) and therefore exhibits certain allosteric effects which account for the functional differences between the molecules.

This essential difference between myoglobin and hemoglobin is reflected in their respective oxygen dissociation curves. The curve is a plot of the amount of saturation of the oxygen-binding sites as a function of the partial pressure of oxygen:

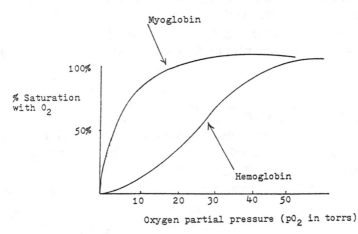

The shape of the oxygen dissociation curve reflects the crucial difference: the shape of the hemoglobin curve is sigmoidal (S-shaped) whereas that of myoglobin is hyperbolic. The sigmoidal shape is ideally suited to hemoglobin's role as an oxygen carrier in the blood. When the partial pressure of the oxygen is high, hemoglobin tends to bind oxygen; that is, many of the binding sites are filled with oxygen. There is a high partial pressure of oxygen (~ 100 torrs) in the alveoli of the lungs, so that hemoglobin tends to pick up oxygen there. When the partial pressure of oxygen is low, hemoglobin tends to release oxygen. There is a low partial pressure of oxygen (~ 20 torrs) in the capillaries in active muscle, where oxygen is being rapidly consumed by cellular respiration. CO_2 is being rapidly produced, and its concentration is correspondingly high. Hemoglobin tends to release oxygen.

Hemoglobin thus acts to pick up oxygen where it is available and release it where it is needed. Myoglobin, on the other hand, has a higher affinity for oxygen than does hemoglobin. Thus, even at relatively low partial pressures, myoglobin still tends to bind oxygen. Only when the pressure is very low does myoglobin release oxygen. This behavior makes it unsuitable to carry oxygen in the blood. An oxygen carrier in the blood must be able to readily release oxygen at places where oxygen is needed.

On a molecular level, the sigmoidal shape means that the binding of oxygen to hemoglobin is cooperative — that is, the binding of oxygen at one heme facilitates the binding of oxygen at another heme on the same hemoglobin molecule. The binding of the first oxygen molecule is thought to be most thermodynamically unfavorable. Subsequent oxygen molecules can bind more easily because the first molecule alters the structure (disrupt certain electostatic interactions) upon binding. The increasing affinity of the hemoglobin molecule for oxygen thus accounts for its sigmoidal dissociation curve.

●PROBLEM 11-8

If blood is carefully removed from a vessel and placed on a smooth plastic surface, will it clot? Explain why or why not.

SOLUTION:

Vertebrates have developed a mechanism for preventing the accidental loss of blood. Whenever a blood vessel is ruptured, one of the soluble plasma proteins, fibrinogen, is enzymatically converted into an insoluble protein, fibrin, which forms a semisolid clot.

Many people think that blood clots when it becomes exposed to the air or when it stops flowing. However, if one were to carefully remove blood from a vessel without allowing it to contact the damaged part of the vessel, and then place this blood on a smooth plastic dish or one lined with paraffin, it would not clot. However, if this blood were allowed to touch any damaged tissues or were placed on glass or some other relatively rough surface, the blood would clot. Either the damaged tissues or the blood itself must release some chemical which initiates the clotting mechanism. Actually, it is both damaged tissues and disintegrated platelets in the plasma that release substances responsible for the clotting reaction. Platelets are very small disc-shaped bodies found in mammalian blood and formed in the bone marrow from large cells called megakaryocytes. Platelets seem to disintegrate more readily upon contacting glass surfaces than on plastic surfaces. Platelets are also called thrombocytes.

When a blood vessel is cut, the damaged tissues release a lipoprotein, called thromboplastin, which initiates the clotting mechanism. Calcium ions and certain protein factors in the plasma must be present in order for thromboplastin to be effective. Thromboplastin interacts with Ca^{2+} and these proteins to produce prothrombinase, the enzyme that catalyzes the second step in the clotting mechanism. Prothrombinase can also be made by the interaction of a substance released from the disintegrated platelets (platelet factor #3) and other factors in the plasma, including Ca^{2+} and proteins. The prothrombinase made from either the tissues or the platelets catalyses the conversion of prothrombin, a plasma globulin, into thrombin. Finally, thrombin enzymatically converts fibrinogen into fibrin, an insoluble protein. Fibrin forms long fibers which mesh and trap red cells, white cells, and platelets, forming the clot. Usually the clot forms within five minutes of the rupturing of the vessel. The clot then begins to contract and squeeze out most of the plasma from itself within an hour. This process, called clot retraction, serves to increase the strength of the clot, and also pulls the vessel walls adhering to the clot closer together. The extruded plasma is now called serum, since all the fibrinogen and most other clotting factors have been removed. Because it lacks these constituents, serum cannot clot.

The entire process is summarized in the following diagram:

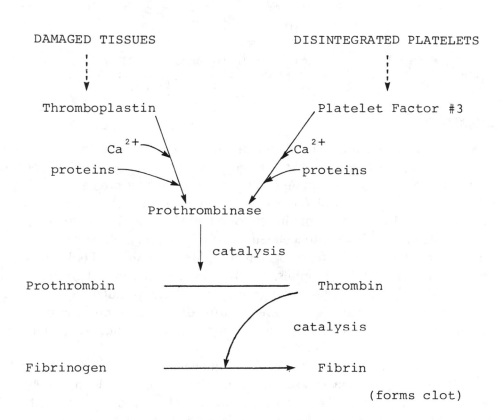

Immune System

What are the basic structural and functional differences between white blood cells and red blood cells? Describe two different ways that white blood cells act to protect the body from foreign agents such as micro-organisms.

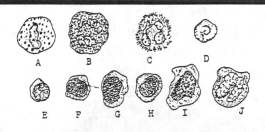

Figure 1. Types of white blood cells. (A) basophil; (B) eosinophil; (C) neutrophil; (E-H) a variety of lymphocytes; (I and J) monocytes. (D) is a red blood cell drawn to the same scale.

SOLUTION:

In addition to red blood cells, human blood contains five types of white blood cells, or leukocytes. Unlike the red blood cells, all types of leukocytes contain nuclei and do not contain hemoglobin. Leukocytes are generally larger than erythrocytes and are far less numerous. There are approximately 5,400,000 red cells per cubic millimeter of blood in an adult male (4.6 million in females), while only about 7,000 leukocytes per cubic millimeter.

There are five different types of leukocytes (see Figure 1). Leukocytes are classified as granular (eosinophils, neutrophils, and basophils) or agranular (monocytes and lymphocytes). The granulocytes have granules in their cytoplasm, have lobed nuclei, and are produced in red bone marrow. The agranulocytes are produced in organs such as the lymph nodes, spleen, and thymus.

Neutrophils make up over 60 percent of the leukocytes present in the body. Like other leukocytes, they can squeeze through the pores of blood vessels and enter the tissue spaces. They then move by amoeboid movement to sites of infected tissue. For example, when bacteria enter a certain tissue of the body, they can either attack cells or produce damaging toxins. The blood vessels in the infected region dilate and allow more blood flow to the site, causing the heat and redness characteristic of inflammation. Blood vessel permeability also increases, causing fluid to enter the tissue and swelling to result. Neutrophils and monocytes pass through the blood vessels and engulf, ingest, and destroy

346

the bacteria. Foreign particles and dead tissue can also be engulfed by this process of phagocytosis. These leukocytes are chemically attracted to the inflamed site by products released from the damaged tissues.

The monocytes (5.3 percent) usually appear after the neutrophils and are more important in fighting chronic infections. Monocytes can phagocytize bacteria but more often, they enlarge and become wandering macrophages, which can move more quickly and engulf more bacteria. Eosinophils (2.3 percent) are weakly phagocytic, and are involved in allergic reactions (by releasing antihistamines) and in fighting trichinosis (an infection caused by the parasitic worm, trichinella). Basophils (.5 percent) liberate the anticoagulant heparin which combats the coagulative processes that sometimes occurs in prolonged inflammation.

The second means by which leukocytes protect the body from invasion is carried out by the lymphocytes. Lymphocytes (30 percent) function in the process of immunity. Lymphocytes are involved in the production of antibodies, proteins made by the body in response to specific foreign substances. These foreign substances are subsequently attacked and destroyed by the antibodies. Immunity and its agents will be discussed in further questions.

The main functions of the leukocytes are thus protective: phagocytosis and immunity. The major function of the erythrocytes is to carry hemoglobin for gaseous transport and exchange, which is essential to the continuation of cellular metabolic processes.

●PROBLEM 11-10

Distinguish between active and passive immunity. How are they produced? Are vaccines and toxoids used to induce active immunity or passive immunity?

SOLUTION:

Immunity is a natural or acquired resistance to a specific disease. A host is immune to a certain pathogen as long as the antibodies specific for the pathogen are present in his circulatory system. The crucial difference between active and passive immunity lies in the answer to the host's question, "Are these antibodies made by me or were they formed in some other organism?"

Active immunity results when antibodies are produced by the cells (lymphocytes) of the host as a result of contact with an antigen. The antigen may be a microorganism or its product. Active immunity usually develops slowly within a couple of weeks (as antibody production reaches a maximum level), yet it may last up to many years for some antigens. Active immunity may be induced naturally, while recovering from an infectious disease such as mumps, measles, or chicken pox; or artificially, by vaccines. Vaccines are inactivated or attenuated microorganisms which can still stimulate antibody production. Attenuated microorganisms are living, yet too weak to be virulent. Vaccines are available for typhoid fever, poliomyelitis, rabies, smallpox, and various other diseases. Also used to induce active immunity are toxoids, made by destroying the poisonous parts of the toxins produced by some pathogens. The antigenic part of the toxin is not affected and can still induce antibody production for protection against diphtheria, tetanus, and other diseases.

Passive immunity is conferred when antibodies produced by active immunity in one organism are transferred to another. Since no antigen is introduced, there is no stimulation of antibody production; hence, passive immunity is of short duration. It does provide immediate protection, unlike active immunity which requires time for development. Passive immunity is also conferred by both natural or artificial means: naturally, by antibody transfer to the fetus from an immune mother (that is, by placental transfer), or artificially, by injection of serum containing antibodies from an immune individual to a susceptible one. In the latter case, it is not necessary that the donor and the recipient be of the same species. It is, however, dangerous for people who are allergic to animal serum, and so must be used with caution.

If the answer to the host's question is "These are my own antibodies," then active immunity is involved; if the answer is "These are not my antibodies," then passive immunity is involved.

●PROBLEM 11-11

Distinguish between cell-mediated immunity and humoral immunity. What structures are responsible for each type of immunity?

SOLUTION:

It was originally thought that all antibodies were secreted into the blood or other body fluids, such as saliva, mucous, and tears. Such antibodies, which function only after they are secreted into body fluids, are called humoral antibodies, and the immunity mediated by them is called humoral immunity. It eventually became clear that other types of immunological responses were due to antibodies which remain bound to their parent lymphocyte. The immunity mediated by these special lymphocytes is called cell-mediated immunity. A variety of antigens evoke the cell-mediated immune response for example, the bacterium *Mycobacterium tuberculosis* (the causative agent of tuberculosis).

We can now distinguish two different types of lymphocytes involved in the immunological response. The T, or thymus lymphocytes are responsible for cell-mediated immunity, whereas the B, or bursal lymphocytes are responsible for humoral immunity. Both types of lymphocytes originate from bone marrow stem cells. Those stem cells which migrate to the thymus differentiate into T cells while those which migrate into the bursa differentiate into B cells. (The bursa is a gland in birds, although we do not yet know its mammalian counterpart.) Both B and T lymphocytes enter the circulation and colonize in lymphoid tissue such as the spleen and lymph nodes.

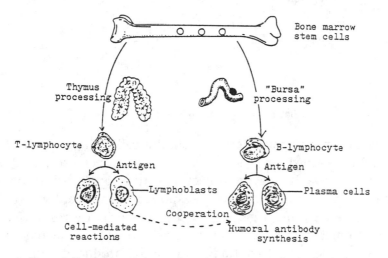

Figure 1. Bone marrow stem cells undergoing maturation in the thymus or the bursal tissue to become T- or B-lymphocytes.

In the presence of antigens, T lymphocytes transform into lymphoblasts, cells which do not secrete their antibodies, but which are involved in cell-mediated immunity. When B lymphocytes are antigenically stimulated, they transform into plasma cells which produce and secrete the immunoglobulins involved in humoral immunity.

A given antigen predominately leads to either a cell-mediated or humoral immunological response. As a general rule, the humoral response is seen as a defense against bacteria and viruses in the body's fluids, while the cellular response is effective against bacteria and viruses in infected host cells as well as against fungal and protozoan infections.

●PROBLEM 11-12

How would you explain the secondary response to antigens on the basis of the clonal selection theory?

SOLUTION:

When an antigen is first injected into an animal, only a small number of

349

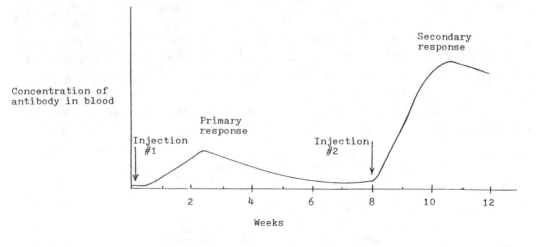

Figure 1. Concentration of antibody in blood

lymphocytes become transformed into plasma cells. The amount of antibodies produced rises slowly to a low peak and then decreases. This is termed the primary response. If a second injection of the same antigen occurs some weeks later, a much more vigorous response is induced. Not only is the amount of antibodies much greater than in the primary response, but their production is much more rapid (see Figure 1). Further injections will result in the maximum amount of antibody that can be produced. Primary and secondary responses of antibody formation can be explained on the basis of the clonal selection theory. When an antigen first comes in contact with its corresponding lymphocyte, it stimulates the lymphocyte to divide and differentiate into plasma cells (or lymphoblasts). The antibodies of these cells interact with the antigen to form complexes which are engulfed and destroyed by macrophages. Some days after the primary response, these plasma cells (or lymphoblasts) eventually die. However, the antigen caused production of many more copies of the originally stimulated small lymphocytes. It is thought that these lymphocytes, called memory cells, arise from division of the originally stimulated cells without concomitant differentiation into plasma cells (lymphoblasts). This immunological memory explains the process in which an animal "remembers" previous exposure to an antigen. When the animal is exposed to the antigen the second time, many more lymphocytes (specific for the antigen) are stimulated, resulting in a greater and more rapid production of antibodies. This explains the characteristics of the secondary response.

Respiratory System

●PROBLEM 11-13

Differentiate clearly between "breathing" and "respiration."

SOLUTION:

Respiration has two distinct meanings. It refers to the oxidative degradation of nutrients such as glucose through metabolic reactions within the cell, resulting in the production of carbon dioxide, water, and energy. Respiration also refers to the exchange of gases between the cells of an organism and the external environment. Many different methods for exchange are utilized by different organisms. In man, respiration can be categorized by three phases: ventilation (breathing), external respiration, and internal respiration.

Breathing may be defined as the mechanical process of taking air into the lungs (inspiration) and expelling it (expiration). It does not include the exchange of gases between the bloodstream and the alveoli. Breathing must occur in order for respiration to occur; that is, air must be brought to the alveolar cells before exchange can be effective. One distinction that can be made between respiration and breathing is that the former ultimately results in energy production in the cells. Breathing, on the other hand, is solely an energy consuming process because of the muscular activity required to move the diaphragm.

●PROBLEM 11-14

Differentiate between direct and indirect respiration, and between external and internal respiration.

SOLUTION:

The phenomenon in which the cells of an organism exchange oxygen and carbon dioxide directly with the surrounding environment is termed direct respiration. This form of respiration is a fairly simple process and occurs in small, aquatic animals such as paramecia or hydras. In these animals, dissolved oxygen from the surrounding water diffuses into the cells, while carbon dioxide within the cell diffuses out; no special respiratory system is needed.

With the evolution of animals into larger and more complex forms, it became impossible for each cell to exchange gases directly with the external environment. Consequently, it became necessary for these organisms to have a specialized organ system that would function in gas exchange with the environment. This structure must be thin-walled, and its membrane must be differentially permeable. In addition, the membrane must be kept moist so that oxygen and carbon dioxide could dissolve in it, and it must have a good blood supply. The process of respiration employing this organ system is called indirect respiration. For indirect respiration, the lower vertebrates developed gills and the higher vertebrates developed lungs.

During indirect respiration, gas exchange between the body cells and the environment may be categorized into two phases: an external and an internal phase. External respiration is the exchange of gases by diffusion that occurs between the lungs and the bloodstream. Oxygen passes from the lungs to the blood and carbon dioxide passes from the blood to the lungs. Internal respiration takes place throughout the body. In the latter, there is an exchange of gases between the blood and other tissues of the body, with oxygen passing from the blood to the tissue cells and carbon dioxide passing from the cells to the blood. This phase, along with the external phase, relies on the movement of gases from a region of higher concentration to one of lower concentration.

●PROBLEM 11-15

List the parts of the human respiratory system. How is each adapted for its particular function?

SOLUTION:

The respiratory system in man and other air-breathing vertebrates includes the lungs and the tubes by which air reaches them. Normally air enters the human respiratory system by way of the external nares or nostrils, but it may also enter by way of the mouth. The nostrils, which contain small hairs to filter incoming air, lead into the nasal cavities, which are separated from the mouth below by the palate. The nasal cavities contain the sense organs of smell, and are lined with mucus-secreting epithelium which moistens the incoming air. Air passes from the nasal cavities via the internal nares into the pharynx, then through the glottis and into the larynx. The larynx is often called the "Adam's apple," and is more prominent in men than women. Stretched across the larynx are the vocal cords.

The opening to the larynx, called the glottis, is always open except when swallowing, when a flap-like structure (the epiglottis) covers it. Leading from the larynx to the chest region is a long cylindrical tube called the trachea, or windpipe. In a dissection, the trachea can be distinguished from the esophagus by its cartilaginous C-shaped rings which serve to hold the tracheal tube open. In the middle of the chest, the trachea bifurcates into bronchi which lead to the lungs. In the lungs, each bronchus branches, forming smaller and smaller tubes called bronchioles. The smaller bronchioles terminate in clusters of cup-shaped cavities, the air sacs. In the walls of the smaller bronchioles and the air sacs are the alveoli, which are moist structures supplied with a rich network of capillaries. Molecules of oxygen and carbon dioxide diffuse readily through the thin, moist walls of the alveoli. The total alveolar surface area across which gases may diffuse has been estimated to be greater than 100 square meters.

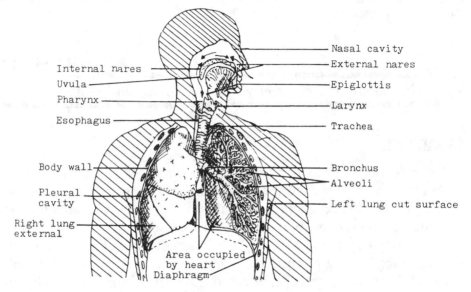

Figure 1. Diagram of the human respiratory system.

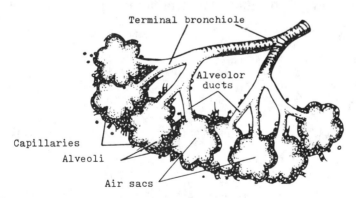

Figure 2. Diagram of a small portion of the lung, highly magnified showing the air sacs at the end of the alveolar ducts, the alveoli in the walls of the air sacs, and the proximity of the alveoli and the pulmonary capillaries containing red blood cells.

Each lung, as well as the cavity of the chest in which the lung rests, is covered by a thin sheet of smooth epithelium, the pleura. The pleura is kept moist, enabling the lungs to move without much friction during breathing. The pleura actually consists of two layers of membranes which are continuous with each other at the point at which the bronchus enters the lung, called the hilus (roof). Thus, the pleura is more correctly a sac than a single sheet covering the lungs.

The chest cavity is closed and has no communication with the outside. It is bounded by the chest wall, which contains the ribs on its top, sides, and back, and the sternum anteriorly. The bottom of the chest wall is covered by a strong, dome-shaped sheet of skeletal muscle, the diaphragm. The diaphragm separates the chest region (thorax) from the abdominal region, and plays a crucial role in breathing by contracting and relaxing, changing the intrathoracic pressure.

●PROBLEM 11-16

Explain the physical changes which take place during inspiration.

SOLUTION:

Just prior to inspiration, at the conclusion of the previous expiration, the respiratory muscles are relaxed and no air is flowing into or out of the lungs. Inspiration is initiated by the contraction of the dome-shaped diaphragm and the intercostal muscles. When the diaphragm contracts, it moves downward into the abdomen. Simultaneously, the intercostal muscles which insert on the ribs contract, leading to an upward and outward movement of the ribs. As a result of these two physical changes, the volume of the chest cavity increases and hence the pressure within the chest decreases. Then, the atmospheric pressure, which is now greater than the intrathoracic pressure, forces air to

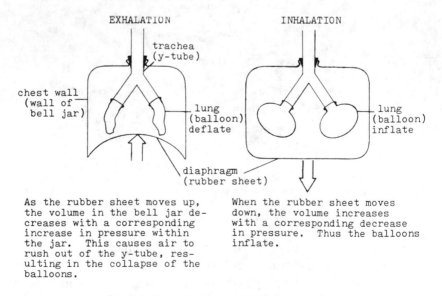

As the rubber sheet moves up, the volume in the bell jar decreases with a corresponding increase in pressure within the jar. This causes air to rush out of the y-tube, resulting in the collapse of the balloons.

When the rubber sheet moves down, the volume increases with a corresponding decrease in pressure. Thus the balloons inflate.

Figure 1. Model of how the diaphragm works.

enter the lungs, and causes them to inflate or expand. During exhalation, the intercostal muscles relax and the ribs move downward and inward. At the same time, the diaphragm relaxes and resumes its original dome shape. Consequently, the thoracic volume returns to its pre-inhalation state, and the pressure within the chest increases. This increase in pressure, together with the elastic recoil of the lungs, forces air out of the lungs causing them to deflate. The role of the diaphragm in breathing can be demonstrated by Figure 1.

Nervous System

●PROBLEM 11-17

Describe the primary functions of the nervous system. What other systems serve similar functions?

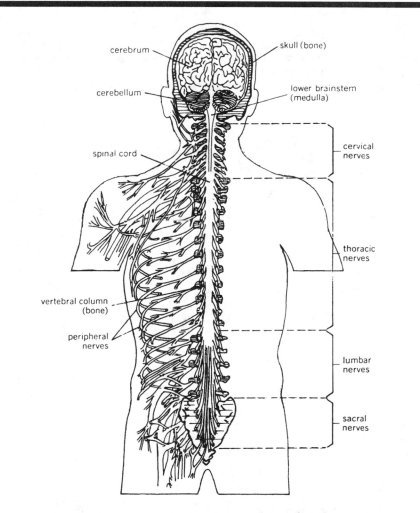

Figure 1. Nervous system viewed from behind.

The human nervous system, composed of the brain, spinal cord, and peripheral nerves, connects the eyes, ears, skin, and other sense organs (the receptors) with the muscles, organs, and glands (the effectors). The nervous system functions in such a way that when a given receptor is stimulated, the proper effector responds appropriately.

The chief functions of the nervous system are the conduction of impulses and the integration of the activities of various parts of the body. Integration means a putting together of generally dissimilar things to achieve unity.

Other systems involved in similar functions are the endocrine system and the regulatory controls intrinsic in the enzyme systems within each cell. Examples of the latter are inhibition and stimulation of enzymatic activities. The endocrine system utilizes substances, known as hormones, to regulate metabolic activities within the body.

●PROBLEM 11-18

What is the structure of a typical neuron?

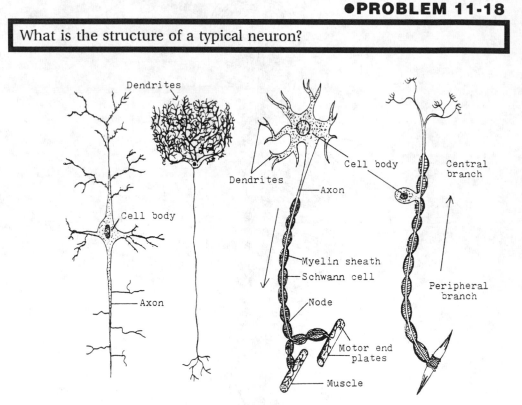

Figure 1. A variety of neuron types in human beings.

SOLUTION:

Before we get to the answer, it is important to recognize the fact that the term "typical neuron" is rather vague. Neurons, which are the basic structural and functional units of the nervous systems of multicellular animals, show a great diversity in types. In humans, many types of neurons are present (Figure 1). Nevertheless, often three parts of a neuron can be distinguished: a cell body, an axon, and a group of processes called dendrites.

Dendrites are usually rather short and numerous extensions from the cell body. They frequently branch profusely, and their many short terminals may give them a spiny appearance. When stained, they ordinarily show many dark granules. There is usually only one axon per neuron (very rarely two), and it is frequently longer than the dendrites. It may branch extensively, but unlike dendrites it does not have a spiny appearance and does not show dark granules when stained. The most fundamental distinction between dendrites and axons is that dendrites receive excitation from other cells whereas axons generally do not, and that axons can stimulate other cells whereas dendrites cannot. Thus, dendrites carry information to the cell body while axons carry information away from the cell body.

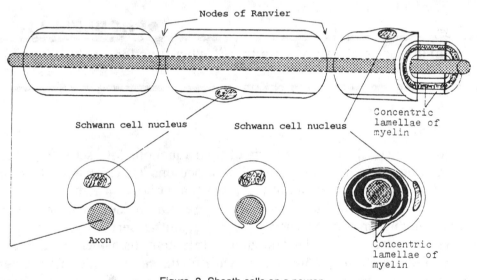

Figure 2. Sheath cells on a neuron.
(upper) Dissection of a myelinated nerve fiber.
(lower) Envelopment of axis cylinder by a sheath cell.

Axons may be several feet long in some neurons. A bundle of many axons wrapped together by a sheath of connective tissue is what we commonly call a nerve. Each vertebrate axon is usually enveloped in a myelin sheath formed by special cells, the Schwann cells, that almost completely encircle the axon. Schwann cells play a role in the nutrition of the axons, and provide a conduit within which damaged axons can grow from the cell body back to their original position. The myelin sheath is interrupted at regular intervals; the interruptions are called nodes of Ranvier. At these nodes, the myelin sheath disappears. The myelin functions in speeding up the transmission of impulses in the axon it envelopes. This is because transmission of impulses do not oc-

357

cur at myelinated regions. Therefore, transmission is faster as impulses jump across the myelination into the nodes of Ranvier (a process known as saltatory conductance). It is crucial to note that the myelin sheath is not a separate layer by itself. Through electron microscopy, it has been proved that the sheath is not a secretion product of the axon or Schwann cells, as was once believed, but a tightly packed spiral of the cell membrane of the Schwann cells. Thus the sheath is composed of the lipid from the membrane's bilayer. The nucleus and cytoplasm of the Schwann cell are pushed aside to form the neurolemma. The nodes in the myelin sheath are simply the points at which one Schwann cell ends and another begins (see Figure 2).

The neuronal cell body, or perikaryon, contains the nucleus and cytoplasmic organelles distributed around the nucleus. The perikaryon has well-developed endoplasmic reticulum and Golgi apparatus for manufacturing all the substances needed for the maintenance and functioning of the axon and dendrites.

●PROBLEM 11-19

How many kinds of neurons are there? What functions are performed by each type?

SOLUTION:

Neurons are classified on the basis of their functions into sensory, motor, or interneurons. Sensory neurons, or afferent neurons, are either receptors that receive impulses or connectors of receptors that conduct information to the central nervous system (brain and spinal cord). Motor neurons, or efferent neurons, conduct information away from the central nervous system to the effectors, for example, muscles and glands. Interneurons, which connect two or more neurons, usually lie wholly within the central nervous system. Therefore, they have both axonal and dendritic ends in the central nervous system. In contrast, the sensory and motor neurons generally have one of their endings in the central nervous system and the other close to the periphery of the body.

●PROBLEM 11-20

Discuss the events which constitute the reflex arc.

SOLUTION:

Motor neurons and sensory (or afferent) neurons usually occur in the same "mixed" nerve. The simplest manner in which sensory and motor neurons are integrated to evoke behavior is in a reflex arc. For example, the knee jerk response when striking the patella stimulates a stretch receptor neuron which sends an impulse to the spinal cord. Within the gray matter of the spinal cord the axon of the sensory neuron forms a synapse with a dendrite of an anterior motor neuron. The impulse travels via the anterior motor neuron to the quadriceps femoris muscle which responds by contracting and causing an extension of the leg.

Most of the sensory neurons that enter the spinal cord do not terminate on anterior neurons but rather on interneurons and they have numerous connections to each other and also to anterior motor neurons. These interconnections provide the basis for complex reflex responses such as the withdrawal reflex.

Excretory System

●PROBLEM 11-21

In humans, the liver is one of the largest and most active organs in the body. Describe its functions.

SOLUTION:

One of the most important functions of the liver is to regulate the level of glucose in the blood stream. The maintenance of a constant level of blood glucose is essential because specialized cells, such as the brain cells, are easily damaged by slight fluctuations in glucose levels. Excess glucose is stored in the liver as glycogen while declining blood glucose can be restored by conversion of liver glycogen into glucose. In addition to the formation of glycogen, the liver can convert glucose into fat, which is then either stored in the liver itself or in special fat-deposit tissues known as adipose tissues.

The production of bile occurs in the liver. Bile is of major importance in aiding the digestion of fats. It is secreted by the liver cells into a number of small ducts which drain into a common bile duct. Bile is stored in the gallbladder, which releases its contents upon stimulation by the presence of fats in the duodenum.

When proteins are metabolized, ammonia, a toxic substance, is formed. The cells of the liver are able to detoxify ammonia rapidly by transforming it into the relatively inert substance urea. Urea can then be excreted from the body in the urine.

The liver also produces a lipid which has been frequently associated with heart diseases — cholesterol. In fact, a diet with reduced cholesterol content may not be effective in lowering cholesterol level in the body because the liver

359

responds by producing more.

The liver plays some important roles in blood clotting. It is the site of production of prothrombin and fibrinogen, substances essential to the formation of a blood clot. In addition, bile secreted by the liver aids in the absorption of vitamin K by the intestine. Vitamin K is an essential cofactor in the synthesis of prothrombin and the plasma clotting cofactors.

Vitamin D, produced by the skin, is relatively inactive and requires biochemical transformation, first by the liver and then by the kidneys, before it is fully able to stimulate absorption of calcium by the gut. The mechanism of activating vitamin D is not yet fully understood. However, the presence of liver and kidney enzymes is essential to the process.

●PROBLEM 11-22

What is bile and what is its role in digestion? Where is bile manufactured and how does it reach the food undergoing digestion?

SOLUTION:

Bile is very important for proper digestion, although it contains no enzymes. It is highly alkaline and helps neutralize the acid in the chyme as it leaves the stomach and enters the small intestine. This is necessary in order for the intestinal enzymes to function properly. Bile is composed of bile salts, lecithin, cholesterol, and bile pigments. The first three are involved in the emulsification of fat in the small intestine. The bile pigments give bile its color.

The major bile pigment is bilirubin. Bilirubin is actually a breakdown product of hemoglobin, the oxygen-carrying protein in red blood cells. In the large intestine, bilirubin and other bile pigments are further converted by bacteria into brown pigments, which give rise to the color of feces. If the bile duct is blocked so that the pigments cannot be excreted in the bile, they will be reabsorbed by the liver. Eventually, the pigments will accumulate in the blood and tissues, giving the skin a yellow color; this condition is called jaundice.

Cholesterol is a large fat-like molecule that has a very low solubility in body fluids. This may lead to deposits of cholesterol in the heart and arteries, which could result in heart disease or arteriosclerosis. The liver excretes excess cholesterol in the bile. Gallstones result from the accumulation of excess insoluble cholesterol in the gallbladder.

Bile salts are the most active part of bile. They are salts of glycocholic acid, which is made from cholesterol. Unlike cholesterol, bile salts are very soluble. These salts are essential for digestion of fats. Butter and oil are fats which constitute part of a group of molecules called lipids. Lipid molecules are insoluble in water and tend to coalesce to form globules. The enzymes that digest lipids, called lipases, can only work on the surface of these globules. Alone, it would take weeks for lipases to complete fat digestion in this manner. Bile salts solve this problem by having detergent-like properties — they coat the globules and break them up into millions of tiny droplets called micelles. This process, called emulsification, greatly increases the surface area exposed to attack by lipases, speeding up lipid digestion. Bile salts are conserved by the body, and are reabsorbed in the lower part of the intestine, carried back to the liver through the bloodstream, and secreted again.

The liver, one of the body's largest organs, constantly secretes bile (600–800 ml. a day). A network of ducts collects the bile and passes it into the gallbladder, where it is stored until needed. The gallbladder is a small muscular sac that lies on the surface of the liver. When food enters the duodenum, certain receptor cells in the wall of the intestine sense the presence of fats in the chyme. Stimulated by the fats, the receptor cells in the duodenum secrete a hormone, called cholecystokinin (CCK) into the bloodstream. This hormone causes inhibition of gastric motility and contraction of the gallbladder, forcing bile out through the bile duct and into the small intestine.

●PROBLEM 11-23

The kidney performs the bulk of the excretion of wastes from the human body. Outline the structure of the human kidney and urinary system.

SOLUTION:

Located on each posterior side of the human body just below the level of the stomach are the bean-shaped kidneys. Each kidney is about 10 cm long, and consists of three parts: an outer layer called the cortex, an inner layer called the medulla, and a sac-like chamber called the pelvis (see Figure 1). The functional unit of a kidney is the nephron; there are about a million nephrons per kidney. A nephron consists of two components: a tubule for conducting cell-free fluid and a capillary network for carrying blood cells and plasma. The mechanisms by which the kidneys perform their functions depend on both the physical and physiological relationships between these two components of the nephron.

Throughout its course, the kidney tubule is composed of a single layer of epithelial cells which differs in structure and function from one portion of the tubule to another. The blind end of the tubule is Bowman's capsule, a sac embedded in the cortex and lined with thin epithelial cells. The curved side of Bowman's capsule is in intimate contact with the glomerulus, a compact tuft of branching blood capillaries, while the other opens into the first portion of the tubular system called the proximal convoluted tubule. The proximal convoluted tubule leads to a portion of the tubule known as the loop of Henle.

361

This hairpin loop consists of a descending and an ascending limb, both of which extend into the medulla. Following the loop, the tubule once more becomes coiled as the distal convoluted tubule. Finally, the tubule runs a straight course as the collecting duct. From the glomerulus to the beginning of the collecting duct, each of the million or so nephrons is completely separate from its neighbors. However, the collecting ducts from separate nephrons join to form common ducts, which in turn join to form even longer ducts, which finally empty into a large central cavity, the renal pelvis, at the base of each kidney. The renal pelvis is continuous with the ureter, which empties into the urinary bladder where urine is temporarily stored. The urine remains unchanged in the bladder, and when eventually excreted, has the same composition as when it left the collecting ducts.

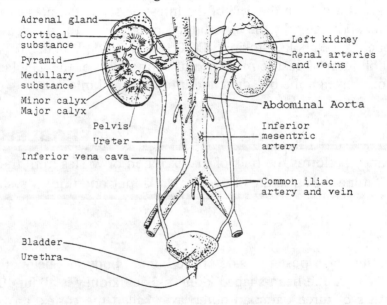

Figure 1. The human urinary system seen from the ventral right side.
The right kidney is shown cut open to reveal the internal structures.

Blood enters the kidney through the renal artery, which upon reaching the kidney divides into smaller and smaller branches. Each small artery gives off a series of arterioles, each of which leads to a glomerulus. The arterioles leading to the glomerulus are called afferent arterioles. The glomerulus protrudes into the cup of Bowman's capsule and is completely surrounded by the epithelial lining of the capsule. The functional significance of this anatomical arrangement is that blood in the capillaries of the glomerulus is separated from the space within Bowman's capsule only by two extremely thin layers: (1) the single-celled capillary wall, and (2) the one-celled lining of Bowman's capsule. This thin barrier permits the filtration of plasma (the non-cellular blood fraction) from the capillaries into Bowman's capsule.

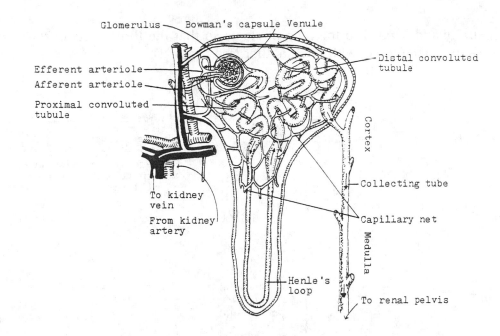

Figure 2. Diagram of a single nephron and its blood vessels.

Ordinarily, capillaries recombine to form the beginnings of the venous system. However, glomerular capillaries instead recombine to form another set of arterioles, called the efferent arterioles. Soon after leaving the region of the capsule, these arterioles branch again forming a capillary network surrounding the tubule. Each excretory tubule is thus well supplied with circulatory vessels. The capillaries eventually rejoin to form venous channels, through which the blood ultimately leaves the kidney.

●PROBLEM 11-24

When the higher vertebrates left the water to take on a terrestrial existence, they had to adopt mechanisms to conserve body water. One of these was the evolution of a concentrated urine. How is this achieved physiologically?

SOLUTION:

The higher vertebrates have evolved a final urine having a greater osmolarity than blood plasma. This is advantageous in that water can be retained within the body making the organism less likely to suffer dehydration. In the absence of a special renal mechanism, the urine would be highly dilute and severe water loss from the organism could become fatal.

The loop of Henle is a hairpin segment of the renal tubule having an ascending limb and a descending limb. The connecting tubule lies in close

363

proximity and parallel to the loop of Henle so that the three parts of the renal tubule can interact with one another (see Figure 1).

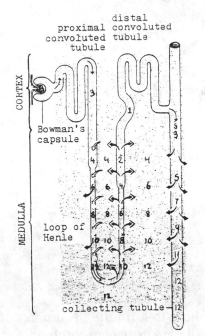

Figure 1. Countercurrent flow mechanism of the mammalian kidney.

The walls of these three portions differ in their permeabilities to substances such as sodium and water. Both the anatomical and physiological aspects of the renal tubule determine the concentration of the urine excreted.

The ascending limb of the loop of Henle actively pumps sodium ions out of its tubular space into the interstitial fluid, with chloride following passively due to electrostatic attraction. The ascending limb is impermeable to water and thus the osmolarity of fluid inside the ascending limb decreases as the loop ascends and a concentration gradient is established between the loop and the interstitial fluid. The descending limb is permeable both to water and sodium, so that some of the sodium and chloride ions diffuse passively into its tubular space. The cycling of sodium from ascending limb to interstitial fluid to descending limb results in the establishment of a concentration gradient of sodium and chloride in the tissue fluid surrounding the loop, with the lowest concentration near the cortex and the highest concentration deep in the medulla. (See accompanying figure). This mechanism of flow in the mammalian kidney, called the countercurrent flow, permits the concentration gradient in the interstitial fluid to be maintained — this gradient is essential in establishing the final concentration of the urine.

With this in mind, we can understand how the final urine becomes highly concentrated relative to the blood. The urine that leaves the ascending limb is not more concentrated than the glomerular filtrate since it has been diluted in the ascending loop. But as the urine flows through the collecting tubule, it is essentially flowing through a concentration gradient in the interstitial fluid from the cortex to the medulla. Moreover, the collecting tubule is permeable only to water. Since the osmolarity of the interstitial fluid is lowest near the cortex and increases toward the medulla, the urine flowing down the collecting tubule will lose water during its course to the medulla. The final urine that emerges from the collecting tubule is substantially hypertonic to blood and remains in this same concentration until it is excreted to the outside.

●PROBLEM 11-25

In the human, many organs in addition to the kidneys perform excretory functions. What are these organs and what do they excrete?

SOLUTION:

The organs of excretion include the lungs, liver, skin, and the digestive tract, in addition to the kidneys. Water and carbon dioxide, important metabolic wastes, are excreted by the lungs. Bile pigments, hemoglobin, red blood cells, some proteins, and some drugs are broken down by the liver for excretion. Certain metal ions, such as iron and calcium, are excreted by the colon. The sweat glands of the skin are primarily concerned with the regulation of body temperature, but they also serve in the excretion of 5 to 10 percent of the metabolic wastes formed in the body. Sweat and urine have similar composition (water, salts, urea, and other organic compounds) but the former is much more dilute than the latter, having only about one eighth as much solute matter. The volume of perspiration varies from about 500 ml. on a cool day to as much as 2 to 3 liters on a hot day. While doing hard work at high temperatures, a man may excrete from 3 to 4 liters of sweat in an hour.

Endocrine System

●PROBLEM 11-26

Define a hormone.

SOLUTION:

The endocrine system constitutes the second great communicating system of the body, with the first being the nervous system. The endocrine system consists of ductless glands which secrete hormones. A hormone is a chemical substance synthesized by a specific organ or tissue and secreted directly into the blood. The hormone is carried via the circulation to other sites of the body where its actions are exerted. Hormones are typically carried in the blood from the site of production to the site(s) of action, but certain hormones produced by neurosecretory cells in the hypothalamus act directly on their target areas without passing through the blood. The distance traveled by hormones before reaching their target area varies considerably. In terms of chemical structure, hormones generally fall into three categories: The steroid hormones include the sex hormones and the hormones of the adrenal cortex; the amino acid derivatives (of tyrosine) include the thyroid hormones and hormones of the adrenal medulla; proteins and polypeptides make up the majority of the hormones. The chemical structure determines the mechanism of action of the hormone. Hormones serve to control and integrate many body functions such as reproduction, organic metabolism and energy balance, and mineral metabolism. Hormones regulate a variety of behaviors, including sexual behaviors.

● PROBLEM 11-27

The thyroid gland is located in the neck and secretes several hormones, the principal one being thyroxine. Trace the formation of thyroxine. What functions does it serve in the body? What happens when there is a decreased or increased amount of thyroxine in the body?

SOLUTION:

The thyroid gland is a two-lobed gland which manifests a remarkably powerful active transport mechanism for uptaking iodide ions from the blood. As blood flows through the gland, iodide is actively transported into the cells. Once within the cell, the iodide is converted to an active form of iodine. This iodine combines with an amino acid called tyrosine. Two molecules of iodinated tyrosine then combine to form thyroxine. Following its formation, the thyroxine becomes bound to a polysaccharide-protein material called thryroglobulin. The normal thyroid gland may store several weeks supply of thyroxine in this "bound" form. An enzymatic splitting of the thyroxine from the thyroglobulin occurs when a specific hormone is released into the blood. This hormone, produced by the pituitary gland, is known as thyroid-stimulating hormone (TSH). TSH stimulates certain major rate-limiting steps in thyroxine secretion, and thereby alters its rate of release. A variety of bodily defects, either dietary, hereditary, or disease-induced, may decrease the amount of thyroxine released into the blood. The most popular of these defects is one which results from dietary iodine deficiency. The thyroid gland enlarges, in the continued presence of TSH from the pituitary, to form a goiter. This is a futile attempt to synthesize thyroid hormones, for iodine levels are low. Normally, thyroid hormones act via a negative feedback loop on the pituitary to decrease stimulation of the thyroid. In goiter, the feedback loop cannot be in operation — hence continual stimulation of the thyroid and the inevitable protuberance on the neck. Formerly, the principal source of iodine came from seafood. As a result, goiter was prevalent amongst inland areas far removed from the sea. Today, the incidence of goiter has been drastically reduced by adding iodine to table salt.

Thyroxine serves to stimulate oxidative metabolism in cells; it increases the oxygen consumption and heat production of most body tissues, a notable exception being the brain. Thyroxine is also necessary for normal growth, the most likely explanation being that thyroxine promotes the effects of growth hormone on protein synthesis. The absence of thyroxine significantly reduces the ability of growth hormone to stimulate amino acid uptake and RNA synthesis. Thyroxine also plays a crucial role in the closely related area of organ development, particularly that of the central nervous system.

If there is an insufficient amount of thyroxine, a condition referred to as hypothyroidism results. Symptoms of hypothyroidism stem from the fact that there is a reduction in the rate of oxidative energy-releasing reactions within the body cells. Usually the patient shows puffy skin, sluggishness, and lowered vitality. Hypothyroidism in children, a condition known as cretinism, can result in mental retardation, dwarfism, and permanent sexual immaturity. Sometimes the thyroid gland produces too much thyroxine, a condition known as hyperthyroidism. This condition produces symptoms such as an abnormally high body temperature, profuse sweating, high blood pressure, loss of weight, irritability, and muscular weakness. It also produces one very characteristic symptom that may not be predicted because it lacks an obvious connection to a high metabolic rate. This symptom is exophthalmia, a condition where the eyeballs protrude in a startling manner. Hyperthyroidism has been treated by partial removal or by partial radiation destruction of the gland. More recently, several drugs that inhibit thyroid activity have been discovered, and their use is supplanting the former surgical procedures.

●PROBLEM 11-28

The pituitary gland has been called the master gland. Is this term justified? Where is the gland located and what does it secrete?

SOLUTION:

The pituitary gland, also known as the hypophysis, lies in a pocket of bone just below the hypothalamus. The pituitary gland is composed of three lobes, each of which is a functionally distinct gland. They are the anterior, intermediate, and posterior lobes. The anterior and posterior lobes are also known as the adenohypophysis and neurohypophysis, respectively.

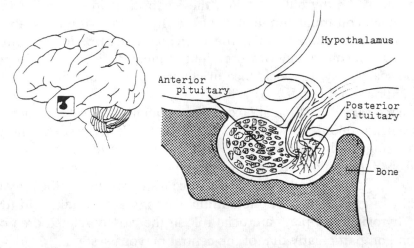

Figure 1. Relationship of the pituitary to the brain and hypothalamus.

In humans, the intermediate lobe is only rudimentary and its function remains unclear. It secretes melanocyte stimulating hormones (MSH) which is known to cause skin darkening in the lower vertebrates.

The anterior lobe is made up of glandular tissue which produces at least six different protein hormones. Evidence suggests that each hormone is secreted by a different cell type. Secretion of each of the six hormones occurs independently of the others.

One of the hormones secreted by the anterior pituitary is known as TSH (thyroid stimulating hormone), which induces secretion of the thyroid hormones from the thyroid gland. Thyroid hormones refers to two closely related hormones, thyroxine (T_4) and triiodothyronine (T_3). Another hormone secreted by the anterior pituitary is ACTH (adrenocorticotrophic hormone), which stimulates the adrenal cortex to secrete cortisol. The anterior pituitary is also responsible for the release of the gonadotropic hormones, FSH (follicle stimulating hormone), and LH (luteinizing hormone). These hormones primarily control the secretion of the sex hormones estrogen, progesterone, and testosterone by the gonads. FSH and LH also regulate the growth and development of the reproductive cells (sperm and ovum). TSH, ACTH, FSH, and LH are all trophic hormones in that they stimulate other endocrine glands to secrete hormones. There are two hormones secreted by the anterior pituitary that do not affect other hormonal secretions, but rather act directly on target tissues. One of these is called prolactin, which stimulates milk production by the mammary glands of the female shortly after giving birth. The other hormone is called growth hormone, which plays a critical role in the normal processes of growth.

The posterior lobe of the pituitary gland is actually an outgrowth of the hypothalamus and is true neural tissue. The posterior pituitary differs from

368

the anterior pituitary with respect to embryological origin as well as types of hormones secreted. It releases two hormones called oxytocin and vasopressin. Oxytocin principally acts to stimulate contraction of the uterine muscles as an aid to parturition. Emotional stress may also cause the release of this hormone, and is frequently the cause of a miscarriage. Oxytocin is also responsible for the milk let-down reflex. It stimulates smooth muscle cells of the mammary glands which causes milk ejection.

Antidiuretic hormone (ADH) stimulates the kidney tubules to reabsorb water and thus plays an important role in the control of plasma volume. In addition, ADH can increase blood pressure by causing arteriolar constriction. Thus ADH is also called vasopressin.

It should now be clear why the pituitary is sometimes referred to as the master gland; it secretes at least nine hormones, some of which directly regulate life processes while others control the secretion of other glands important in development, behavior, and reproduction.

●PROBLEM 11-29

The pancreas is a mixed gland having both endocrine and exocrine functions. The exocrine portion secretes digestive enzymes into the duodenum via the pancreatic duct. The endocrine portion secretes two hormones (insulin and glucagon) into the blood. What are the effects of these two hormones?

SOLUTION:

Insulin is a hormone which acts directly or indirectly on most tissues of the body, with the exception of the brain. The most important action of insulin is the stimulation of the uptake of glucose by many tissues, particularly liver muscle and fat. The uptake of glucose by the cells decreases blood glucose and increases the availability of glucose for those cellular reactions in which glucose participates. Thus, glucose oxidation, fat synthesis, and glycogen synthesis are all accentuated by an uptake of glucose. It is important to note that insulin does not alter glucose uptake by the brain, nor does it influence the active transport of glucose across the renal tubules and gastrointestinal epithelium.

As stated, insulin stimulates glycogen synthesis. In addition, it also increases the activity of the enzyme which catalyzes the rate-limiting step in glycogen synthesis. Insulin also increases triglyceride levels by inhibiting triglyceride breakdown, and by stimulating production of triglyceride through fatty acid and glycerophosphate synthesis. The net protein synthesis is also increased by insulin, which stimulates the active membrane transport of amino acids, particularly into muscle cells. Insulin also has effects on other liver enzymes, but the precise mechanisms by which insulin induces these changes are poorly understood.

Insulin secretion is directly controlled by the glucose concentration of the blood flowing through the pancreas. This is a simple system which requires no participation of nerves or other hormones.

Insulin is secreted by beta cells, which are located in the part of the pancreas known as the Islets of Langerhans. These groups of cells, which are located randomly throughout the pancreas, also consist of other secretory cells called alpha cells. It is these alpha cells which secrete glucagon. Glucagon is a hormone which has the following major effects: it increases glycogen breakdown thereby raising the plasma glucose level; it increases hepatic synthesis of glucose from pyruvate, lactate, glycerol, and amino acids (a process called gluconeogenesis, which also raises the plasma glucose level), it increases the breakdown of adipose-tissue triglyceride, thereby raising the plasma levels of fatty acids and glycerol. The glucagon-secreting alpha cells in the pancreas, like the beta cells, respond to changes in the concentration of glucose in the blood flowing through the pancreas; no other nerves or hormones are involved.

It should be noted that glucagon has the opposite effects as insulin. Glucagon elevates the plasma glucose whereas insulin stimulates its uptake and thereby reduces plasma glucose levels; glucagon elevates fatty acid concentrations whereas insulin converts fatty acids (and glycerol) into triglycerides, thereby inhibiting triglyceride breakdown.

Thus the alpha and beta cells of the pancreas constitute a "push-pull" system for regulating the plasma glucose level.

●PROBLEM 11-30

The two adrenal glands lie very close to the kidneys. Each adrenal gland in mammals is actually a double gland, composed of an inner corelike medulla and an outer cortex. Each of these is functionally unrelated. Outline the function of the adrenal medulla.

SOLUTION:

The adrenal medulla secretes two hormones, adrenalin (epinephrine) and noradrenalin (norepinephrine, NE), whose functions are very similar but not identical. The adrenal medulla is derived embryologically from neural tissue. It has been likened to an overgrown sympathetic ganglion whose cell bodies do not send out nerve fibers, but release their active substances directly into the blood, thereby fulfilling the criteria for an endocrine gland. In controlling epinephrine secretion, the adrenal medulla behaves just like any sympathetic ganglion, and is dependent upon stimulation by sympathetic preganglionic fibers, as shown below:

Preganglionic fiber ——————— Adrenal medulla Synapse · NE & epinephrine released into blood. →

Epinephrine promotes several responses, all of which are helpful in coping with emergencies: the blood pressure rises, the heart rate increases, the glucose content of the blood rises because of glycogen breakdown, the spleen contracts and squeezes out a reserve supply of blood, the clotting time of blood is decreased, the pupils dilate, the blood flow to skeletal muscle increases, the blood supply to intestinal smooth muscle decreases, and hairs become erect. These adrenal functions, which mobilize the resources of the body in emergencies, have been called the fight-or-flight response. Norepinephrine stimulates reactions similar to those produced by epinephrine, but is less effective in the conversion of glycogen into glucose.

The significance of the adrenal medulla may seem questionable since the complete removal of the gland causes few noticeable changes in the animal; the animal can still exhibit the fight-or-flight response. This occurs because the sympathetic nervous system compliments the adrenal medulla in stimulating the fight-or-flight response, and the absence of the hormonal control will be compensated for by the nervous system.

●PROBLEM 11-31

The thymus gland is a two-lobed, glandular-appearing structure located in the upper region of the chest just behind the sternum. What are the two principal functions that have been attributed to this gland?

SOLUTION:

It is thought that one of the functions of the thymus is to provide the initial supply of lymphocytes for other lymphoid areas, such as the lymph nodes and spleen. These primary cells then give rise to descendent lines of lymphocytes, making further release from the thymus unnecessary. This first function of the thymus is non-endocrine in nature.

The second function attributed to the thymus is the release of the hormone thymosin which stimulates the differentiation of incipient plasma cells in the lymphoid tissues. The cells then develop into functional plasma cells, capable of producing antibodies when stimulated by the appropriate antigens. To summarize, full development of plasma cells requires two types of inducible stimuli. They are: (1) stimulation by thymosin which initiates differentiation of all types of incipient plasma cells, and (2) stimulation by a specific antigen, which affects the functional maturation of *only* those cells with a potential for making antibodies against that particular antigen.

Skeletal and Muscular Systems

> Bone, like other connective tissues, consists of cells and fibers, but unlike the others its extracellular components are calcified, making it a hard, unyielding substance ideally suited for its supportive and protective function in the skeleton. Describe the macroscopic and microscopic structure of bone.

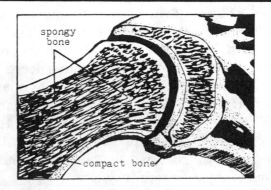

Figure 1. Longitudinal section of the end of a long bone.

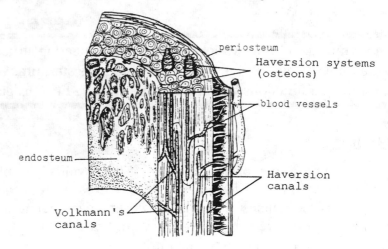

Figure 2. Cross-section of a long bone showing internal structures.

SOLUTION:

Upon inspection of a long bone with the naked eye, two forms of bone are distinguishable: cancellous (spongy) and compact. Spongy bone consists of a network of hardened bars having spaces between them filled with marrow. Compact bone appears as a solid, continuous mass, in which spaces can be seen only with the aid of a microscope. The two forms of bone grade into one

372

another without a sharp boundary. (See Figure 1.)

In typical long bones, such as the femur or humerus, the shaft (diaphysis) consists of compact bone surrounding a large central marrow cavity composed of spongy bone. In adults, the marrow in the long bones is primarily of the yellow, fatty variety, while the marrow in the flat bones of the ribs and at the ends of long bones is primarily of the red variety and is active in the production of red blood cells. Even this red marrow contains about 70 percent fat.

The ends (epiphyses) of long bones consist mainly of spongy bone covered by a thin layer of compact bone. This region of the long bones contains a cartilaginous region known as an epiphyseal plate. The epiphyseal cartilage and the adjacent spongy bone constitute a growth zone, in which all growth in length of the bone occurs. The surfaces at the ends of long bones, where one bone articulates with another are covered by a layer of cartilage, called the articular cartilage. It is this cartilage which allows for easy movement of the bones over each other at a joint.

Compact bone is composed of structural units called Haversian systems. Each system is irregularly cylindrical and is composed of concentrically arranged layers of hard, inorganic matrix surrounding a microscopic central Haversian canal. Blood vessels and nerves pass through this canal, supplying and controlling the metabolism of the bone cells. The bone matrix itself is laid down by bone cells called osteoblasts. Osteoblasts produce a substance, osteoid, which is hardened by calcium, causing calcification. Some osteoblasts are trapped in the hardening osteoid and are converted into osteocytes which continue to live within the bone. These osteocytes lie in small cavities called lacunae, located along the interfaces between adjoining concentric layers of the hard matrix. Exchange of materials between the bone cells and the blood vessels in the Haversian canals is by way of radiating canals. Other canals, known as Volkmann's canals, penetrate and cross the layers of hard matrix, connecting the different Haversian canals to one another. (See Figure 2.)

With few exceptions, bones are invested by the periosteum, a layer of specialized connective tissue. The periosteum has the ability to form bone, and contributes to the healing of fractures. Periosteum is lacking on those ends of long bones surrounded by articular cartilage. The marrow cavity of the diaphysis and the cavities of spongy bone are lined by the endosteum, a thin cellular layer which also has the ability to form bone (osteogenic potencies).

Haversian type systems are present in most compact bone. However, certain compact flat bones of the skull (the frontal, parietal, occipital, and temporal bones, and part of the mandible) do not have Haversian systems. These bones, termed membrane bones, have a different architecture and are formed differently than bones with Haversian systems.

Besides their function in locomotion and support, bones also serve several other important functions. What are they?

SOLUTION:

Bones are an important reservoir for certain minerals. The mineral content of bones is constantly being renewed. Roughly all the mineral content of bone is removed and replaced every nine months. Calcium and phosphorus are especially abundant in the bones and these are minerals which must be maintained in the blood at a constant level. When the diet is low in these minerals, they can be withdrawn from the bones to maintain the proper concentration in the blood. Stress seems to be necessary for the maintenance of calcium and phosphate in the bones, for in the absence of stress these minerals pass from the bones into the blood faster than they are taken in. This elevates the blood concentration of these minerals to a very high level, which may ultimately lead to the development of kidney stones. Before special stress exercise programs were developed, astronauts in space often became victims of this type of kidney trouble.

During pregnancy, when the demand for minerals to form bones of a growing fetus is great, a woman's own bones may become depleted unless her diet contains more of these minerals than is normally needed. During starvation, the blood can draw on the storehouse of minerals in the bones and maintain life much longer than would be possible without this means of storage.

Bones are also important in that they give rise to the fundamental elements of the circulatory system.

Bone marrow is the site of production of lymphocyte precursor cells, which play an integral role in the body's immune response system. Red blood cells, or erythrocytes, also originate in the bone marrow. As the erythrocytes mature, they accumulate hemoglobin, the oxygen carrier of blood. Mature erythrocytes, however, are incomplete cells lacking nuclei and the metabolic machinery to synthesize new protein. They are released into the bloodstream, where they circulate for approximately 120 days before being destroyed by the phagocytes. Thus, the bone marrow must perform the constant task of maintaining the level of erythrocytes for the packaging of hemoglobin.

The vertebrate skeleton may be divided into two general parts, the axial skeleton and the appendicular skeleton. What bones constitute these in man?

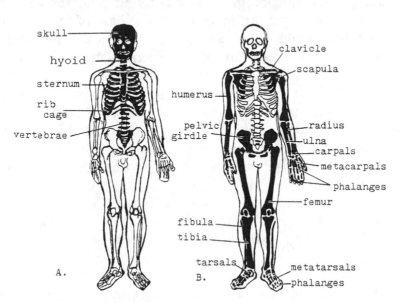

Figure 1. The human body showing, A, the bones of the axial skeleton and B, the bones of the appendicular skeleton.

SOLUTION:

The axial skeleton consists of the skull, vertebral column, ribs, sternum, and hyoid bone. The primary function of the vertebrate skull is the protection of the brain. The part of the skull that serves this function is the cranium. The rest of the skull is made up of the bones of the face. In all, the human skull is composed of 28 bones, 6 of which are very small and located in the middle ear. At the time of birth, several of the bones of the cranium are not completely formed, leaving 5 membraneous regions called fontanelles. These regions are somewhat flexible and can undergo changes in shape as necessary for safe passage of the infant through the birth canal.

The human vertebral column, or spine, is made up of 33 separate bones known as vertebrae, which differ in size and shape in different regions of the spine. In the neck region there are 7 cervical vertebrae; in the thorax there are 12 thoracic vertebrae; in the lower back region there are 5 lumbar vertebrae, in the sacral or hip region, 5 fused vertebrae form the sacrum to which the pelvic girdle is attached; and at the end of the vertebral column is the coccyx or tailbone, which consists of four, or possibly five, small fused vertebrae. The vertebrae forming the sacrum and coccyx are separate in childhood, with fusion occurring by adulthood. The coccyx is the vestige of a tail.

A typical vertebra consists of a basal portion, the centrum, and a dorsal ring of bone, the neural arch, which surrounds and protects the delicate spinal cord which runs through it. Each vertebra has projections for the attachment of ribs or muscles or both, and for articulating (joining) with neighboring vertebrae. The first vertebra, the atlas, has rounded depressions on its upper surface into which fit two projections from the base of the skull. This articulation allows for up and down movements of the head. The second vertebra, called the axis, has a pointed projection which fits into the atlas. This type of articulation allows for the rotation of the head.

In humans there are 12 pairs of ribs, one pair articulating with each of the thoracic vertebrae. These ribs support the chest wall and keep it from collapsing as the diaphragm contracts. Of the twelve pairs of ribs, the first seven are attached ventrally to the breastbone, the next three are attached indirectly by cartilage, and the last two, called "floating ribs," have no attachments to the breastbone.

The sternum or breastbone consists of three bones — the manubrium, body, and xiphoid process — which usually fuse by middle-age. The sternum is the site for the anterior attachment of most of the ribs. The ribs and sternum together make up the thoracic cage which functions to protect the heart and lungs.

The hyoid bone supports the tongue and its muscles. It has no articulation with other bones, but is held in place by muscles and ligaments.

The bones of the girdles and their appendages make up the appendicular skeleton. In the shoulder region the pectoral girdle, which is generally larger in males than in females, serves for the attachment of the forelimbs. The pectoral girdle consists of two collarbones, or clavicles, and two shoulder blades, or scapulas. In the hip region, the pelvic girdle serves for the attachment of the hindlimbs. The pelvic girdle, which is wider in females so as to allow room for fetal development, consists of three fused hipbones, called the ilium, ischum, and pubis, which are attached to the sacrum. Collectively, the "hip bone" is called the oscoxae or innominate bone.

Articulating with the scapula is the single bone of the upper arm, called the humerus. Articulating with the other end of the humerus are the two bones of the forearm called the radius and the ulna. The radius and ulna permit rotation of the forearm. The ulna has on its end next to the humerus a process often referred to as the "funny bone." The wrist is composed of eight small bones called the carpals. The arrangement of these bones permits the rotating movements of the wrist. The palm of the hand consists of 5 bones, known as the metacarpals, each of which articulates with a bone of the finger, called a phalanx. Each finger has three phalanges, with the exception of the thumb, which has two.

The pattern of bones in the leg and foot is similar to that in the arm and hand. The upper leg bone, called the femur, articulates with the pelvic girdle.

The two lower leg bones are the tibia (shinbone) and fibula, corresponding to the radius and ulna of the arm, respectively. These two bones are responsible for rotation of the lower leg. Ventral to the joint between the upper and lower leg bones is another bone, the patella or knee cap, which serves as a point of muscle attachment for upper and lower leg muscles. This bone has no counter part in the arm. The ankle contains seven irregularly shaped bones, the tarsals, corresponding to the carpals of the wrist. The foot proper contains five metatarsals, corresponding to the metacarpals of the hand, and the bones in the toes are the phalanges, two in the big toe and three in each of the others.

●PROBLEM 11-35

List and describe the several types of joints.

SOLUTION:

The point of junction between two bones is called a joint. Some joints, such as those between the bones of the skull, are immovable and extremely strong, owing to an intricate intermeshing of the edges of the bones. The truly movable joints of the skeleton are those that give the skeleton its importance in the total effector mechanism of locomotion. Some are ball and socket joints, such as the joint where the femur joins the pelvis, or where the humerus joins the pectoral girdle. These joints allow free movement in several directions. Both the pelvis and the pectoral girdle contain rounded, concave depressions to accommodate the rounded convex heads of the femur and humerus, respectively. Hinge joints, such as that of the human knee, permit movement in one place only. The pivot joints at the wrists and ankles allow freedom of movement intermediate between that of the hinge and the ball and socket types.

●PROBLEM 11-36

The most widely accepted theory of muscle contraction is the sliding filament theory. What is the major point of this theory?

SOLUTION:

The major premise of the sliding filament theory is that muscle contraction occurs as the result of the sliding of the thick and thin filaments past one another; the lengths of the individual filaments remain unchanged. Thus the width of the A band remains constant, corresponding to the constant length of the thick filaments. The I band narrows as the thin filaments approach the center of the sarcomere. As the thin filaments move past the thick filaments, the width of the H zone between the ends of the thin filaments becomes smaller, and may disappear altogether when the thin filaments meet at the center of the sarcomere. With further shortening, new banding patterns appear as thin filaments from opposite ends of the sarcomere begin to overlap. The shortening of the sarcomeres in a myofibril is the direct cause of the shortening of the whole muscle.

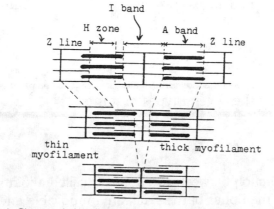

Figure 1. Changes in banding pattern resulting from the movements of thick and thin filaments past each other during contraction.

The question arises as to which structures actually produce the sliding of the filaments. The answer is the myosin cross bridges. These cross bridges are actually part of the myosin molecules which compose the thick filaments. The bridges swivel in an arc around their fixed positions on the surface of the thick filaments much like the oars of a boat. When bound to the actin filaments, the movement of the cross bridges causes the sliding of the thick and thin filaments past each other. Since one movement of a cross bridge will produce only a small displacement of the filaments relative to each other, the cross bridges must undergo many repeated cycles of movement during contraction.

●PROBLEM 11-37

What are the properties of actin and myosin which produce the cyclic activity of the cross bridges responsible for contraction? What causes rigor mortis?

SOLUTION:

Myosin, the larger of the two molecules, is shaped like a lollypop (see Figure 1). The myosin molecules are arranged within the thick filaments so that they are oriented tail-to-tail in the two halves of the filament; the globular

378

ends extend to the sides, forming the cross bridges which bind to the reactive site on the actin molecule. Actin is a globular-shaped molecule having a reactive site on its surface that is able to combine with myosin. These globular proteins are arranged in two chains which are helically intertwined to form the thin myofilaments (See Figure 2).

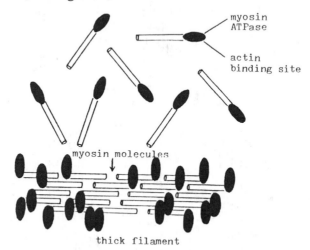

Figure 1. Aggregation of myosin molecules to form thick filaments, with the globular heads of the myosin molecules forming the cross bridges.

Figure 2. Structure of thin myofilament composed of two helical chains of globular actin monomers.

The globular end of the myosin molecule, in addition to being a binding site for the actin molecule, contains a separate binding site for ATP. This active site has ATPase activity, and the reaction that is catalyzed is the hydrolysis of ATP:

$$H_2O + ATP \rightarrow ADP + P_i$$

However, myosin alone has a very low ATPase activity. It appears that an allosteric change occurs in the active site of myosin ATPase when the myosin cross bridge combines with actin in the thin filaments, considerably increasing the ATPase activity. The energy that is released from the splitting of ATP produces cross bridge movement by an as yet unknown mechanism. It is believed that the oscillatory movements of myosin cross bridges produce the relative movement of thick and thin filaments, resulting ultimately in the shortening of a muscle fiber (see Figure 3).

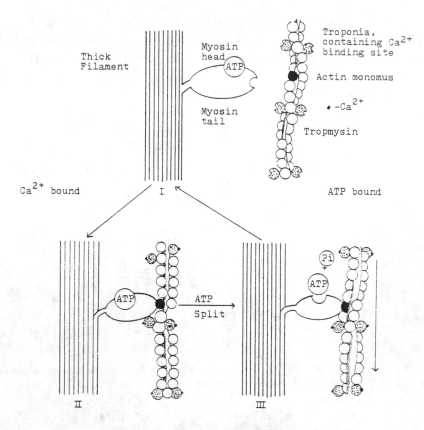

Figure 3. Schematic representation of the interactions involved in muscle contractions.

Since many cycles of activity are needed to produce the degree of shortening observed during muscle contraction, the myosin bridge must be able to detach from the actin and then rebind again. This is accomplished by the binding of ATP to the myosin in the cross bridge, forming what is known as a low-energy complex. The low-energy complex has only a weak affinity for actin; the actin-myosin bond is broken, allowing the cross bridges to dissociate from actin. Shortly after this event, a conformational change occurs in the myosin — ATP complex and a high energy complex is formed. The high energy complex has a very high affinity for actin, and the cross bridges are able to rebind to the actin. In this manner, the cross bridges are able to bind and dissociate from actin in a cycle of coordinated actions. This cycle may be summarized in the following sequence of events:

A = actin   M = myosin

M – ATP   →   M* – ATP
(low-energy complex)   (high-energy complex capable
                                    of binding actin)

A + M* – ATP   →   A – M* – ATP (with actin bound,
                                    myosin is able to split ATP)

380

$$A - M^* - ATP \qquad \rightarrow \qquad A - M + ADP + P_i \text{ (as ATP is split,}$$

cross bridge movement occurs)

$$A - M + ATP \qquad \rightarrow \qquad A + M - ATP \text{ (low-energy complex}$$

dissociates from actin)

Rigor mortis is a phenomenon in which the muscles of the body become very stiff and rigid after death. It results directly from the loss of ATP in the dead muscle cells; the myosin cross bridges are unable to combine with actin and those bonds already formed cannot be broken — thus the rigid condition.

At the molecular level, we can identify two specific roles for ATP: 1) to provide energy for movement of cross bridge, and 2) to dissociate actin from the myosin cross bridges during the contraction cycle of the bridges. ATP is also needed to restore Ca^{2+} in the sarcoplasmic reticulum following contraction.

Two regulatory proteins, troponin and tropomyosin, are associated with actin. During nervous stimulation of a muscle, there is an increase in free intracellular calcium ions: calcium diffuses in from the terminal cisternae and from the extracellular fluid in the T tubules. Calcium binds to troponin which causes tropomyosin to shift its position along the actin helix. This exposes the binding site on actin for myosin.

●PROBLEM 11-38

What are the distinguishing characteristics of cardiac and smooth muscle.

SOLUTION:

Smooth muscle fibers are considerably smaller than skeletal muscle fibers. Each smooth muscle fiber has a single nucleus located in the central portion of the cell. By contrast, each skeletal muscle fiber is multinucleated with the nuclei located peripherally. The most noticeable morphological factor distinguishing smooth from either skeletal or cardiac muscle is the absence of striated banding patterns in the cytoplasm of smooth muscle. Smooth muscle does not contain myofibrils. However, myosin thick filaments and actin thin filaments can be seen distributed throughout the cytoplasm, oriented parallel to the muscle fiber, but not organized into regular units of filaments as in skeletal and cardiac muscle.

It is believed that the molecular events of force generation in smooth muscle cells are similar to those in skeletal muscle. Smooth muscle exhibits wide variations in tonus; it may remain almost entirely relaxed or tightly contracted. Also, it apparently can maintain the contracted condition of tonus without the expenditure of energy, perhaps owing to a reorganization of the protein chains making up the fibers. Smooth muscle cells are not under voluntary control. Their activity is under the regulation of the autonomic nervous system and they have an ability to perform work for long periods of time, since their contraction is slow and sustained. Smooth muscle is often referred to as a visceral muscle since it regulates the internal environment of a great many systems and organs. It is found in the walls of hollow organs such as the intestinal tract, the bronchioles, the urinary bladder, and the uterus. Vascular smooth muscle lines the walls of blood vessels. It may also be found as single cells distributed throughout an organ such as the spleen or in small groups of cells attached to the hairs in the skin.

Cardiac muscle has properties similar to those of skeletal muscle. It is multinucleated and striated, with its thick and thin myofilaments organized into myofibrils. The sliding-filament type of contraction is also found in cardiac muscle. Unlike skeletal muscle but like smooth muscle, cardiac muscle is involuntary. Each beat of the heart represents a single twitch. Cardiac muscle has a long refractory period. Consequently, it is unable to contract tetanically, since one twitch cannot follow another quickly enough to maintain a contracted state. A unique feature of cardiac muscle is its inherent rhythmicity; it contracts at a rate of about 72 beats per minute. The muscle is innervated by nerves, but these nerves only serve to speed up or slow down the inherent cardiac rhythm. In addition, cardiac muscle is unique in having intercalated discs, or tight junctions, between cells; these aid in the transmission of electrical impulses throughout the heart.

Reproduction

●PROBLEM 11-39

Give a brief summary of the events occurring in spermatogenesis and oogenesis. Compare the two processes.

SOLUTION:

Spermatogenesis is the production of sperm (male sex cells). It begins with spermatogonia, which are primitive, unspecialized germ cells lining the walls of the tubules in the testes. Throughout embryonic development and during childhood, the diploid spermatogonia divide mitotically, giving rise to additional spermatogonia to provide for growth of the testes. After sexual maturity is reached, some of the spermatogonia grow and enlarge into cells known as primary spermatocytes (see Figure 1), which are still diploid. The primary spermatocytes then undergo the first meiotic division, each producing two equal-sized secondary spermatocytes. Each of these in turn undergoes the second meiotic division, forming two spermatids of equal size. The haploid spermatids then undergo a complicated process of maturation, including development of a tail, to become functional sperm.

Oogenesis is the process of ovum (female gamete) formation. The immature germ cells of the female are called oogonia and are located in the ovary. Early in development, they undergo numerous mitotic divisions. Then some oogonia develop and enlarge into primary oocytes. At maturation, the primary oocyte undergoes the first meiotic division. The nuclear events are the same as in spermatogenesis, but the cytoplasm divides unequally to produce two cells of different sizes. The small cell is the first polar body and the large cell is the secondary oocyte. This haploid secondary oocyte undergoes the second meiotic division, which also involves unequal, cytoplasmic distribution, and forms a second polar body and a large ootid. The first polar body divides to form two additional second polar bodies. The ootid matures into the egg, or ovum. The polar bodies disintegrate and do not become functional gametes.

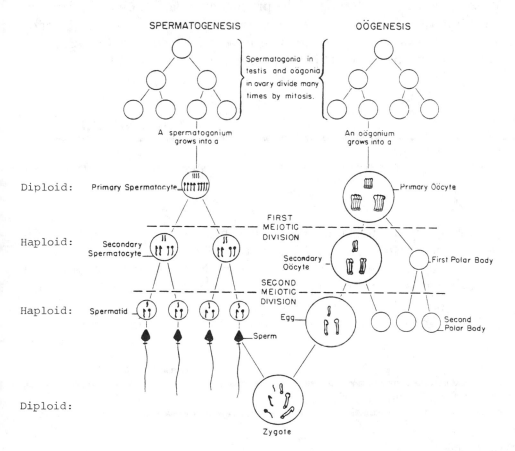

Figure 1. Comparison of the formation of sperm and eggs.

Both spermatogenesis and oogenesis involve the production and maturation of the gametes. However, there are a few notable differences intrinsic in each process with the most important being the differences in the amount of cytoplasm and the number of viable gametes produced.

The egg cell accumulates much more nutrient material during its development than does the sperm. The sperm actually loses cytoplasm during maturation. In addition, the unequal meiotic division of the oocyte results in a much larger gamete than would normal division. As a result, one viable gamete with a considerable amount of cytoplasm is produced in oogenesis. In spermatogenesis, four viable gametes with very little cytoplasm are produced. These differences are a reflection of the different roles of the egg and sperm in reproduction. It is the fertilized egg which will ultimately develop into the new individual. Large amounts of cytoplasm are necessary to provide adequate nutrition for the developing embryo. The unequal cytoplasmic division solves the problem of reducing chromosome number without losing cytoplasm.

Sperm, on the other hand, are specialized for their role in fertilization. Their small size is necessary for motility. The production of large numbers of sperm, in contrast to eggs, is to ensure the occurrence of fertilization against the odds resulting from physical barriers and environmental factors. Fertilization of the haploid ovum by the haploid sperm restores the diploid number in the resultant zygote.

● **PROBLEM 11-40**

List the male reproductive organs.

SOLUTION:

In males the reproductive organs include two testes as well as accessory internal organs (i.e., the epididymides, the vas deferentia, the seminal vesicles, ejaculatory ducts, the prostate gland, the urethra, and the bulbourethral glands) and accessory external organs (i.e., the scrotum, penis). These accessory organs primarily serve to store and deliver the sperm (or spermatozoa) to the female genitalia. Various glands secrete fluids to aid this process.

● **PROBLEM 11-41**

List the female reproductive organs.

SOLUTION:

The female reproductive system produces, transports, and temporarily stores ovum. Ovum are produced in the ovaries which are the primary reproductive organ. The female reproductive system is specialized to accept sperm, to aid in the process of fertilization, to provide a highly controlled environment for long term fetal development, and to deliver the new born from an intrauterine to an extrauterine environment. The ovaries also secrete hormones. The accessory internal organs include the fallopian tubes and the vagina. The external accessory organs include the labia majora, the labia minora, the clitoris, and the vestibule.

FERTILIZATION, IMPLANTATION, AND DEVELOPMENT

● PROBLEM 11-42

What do each of the embryonic germ layers give rise to?

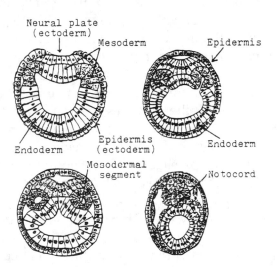

Figure 1. Early germ layer development.

SOLUTION:

Ectoderm gives rise to the epidermis of the skin, including the skin glands, hair, nails, and enamel of teeth. In addition, the epithelial lining of the mouth, nasal cavity, sinuses, sense organs, and the anal canal are ectodermal in origin. Nervous tissue, including the brain, spinal cord, and nerves, are all derived from embryonic ectoderm.

Mesoderm gives rise to muscle tissue, cartilage, bone, and the notochord which is replaced in the human embryo by vertebrae. It also provides the foundation for the organs of circulation (bone marrow, blood, lymphoid tissue, blood vessels), excretion (kidneys, ureters), and reproduction (gonads, genital ducts). The mesoderm produces by far the greatest amount of tissue in the vertebrate body.

Endoderm gives rise to the epithelium of the digestive tract, the tonsils, the parathyroid and thymus glands, the larynx, trachea, lungs, the bladder, and the urethra with its associated glands.

●PROBLEM 11-43

Which are the first two organs to appear in the human embryo, and how are they formed?

SOLUTION:

The first two organs to appear in the embryo are the brain and spinal cord, which form by a process termed neurulation. During the third week of development, the ectoderm in front of the primitive streak develops a thickened plate of cells called the neural plate. At the center of this plate there appears a depression, known as the neural groove. At the same time, the outer edges of the plate rise in two longitudinal neural folds that meet at the anterior end. These appear, when viewed from above, like a horseshoe. These folds gradually come together at the top, forming a hollow neural tube. The cavity of the anterior part of this neural tube becomes the ventricles of the brain. At the same time, the cavity of the posterior part becomes the neural canal, extending the length of the spinal cord. The brain region is the first to form, and the long spinal cord develops slightly later. The anterior part of the neural tube, which gives rise to the brain, is much larger than the posterior part and continues to grow so rapidly that the head region comes to bend down at the anterior end of the embryo. By the fifth week of development, all the regions of the brain, i.e., the forebrain, midbrain, and hindbrain are established. A short time later, the outgrowths that will form the large cerebral hemispheres begin to grow. While the various motor nerves grow out of the brain and spinal cord, the sensory nerves do not, having a separate origin. During the formation of the neural tube, bits of nervous tissue, known as neural crest cells, are left over on each side of the tube. These cells migrate downward from their original position and form the dorsal root ganglia of the spinal nerves and the postganglionic sympathetic neurons. From sensory cells in the dorsal root ganglia, dendrites grow out to the sense organs and axons grow in to the spinal cord. Other neural crest cells migrate and form the medullary cells of the adrenal glands, the neurilemma sheath cells of the peripheral neurons, and certain other structures.

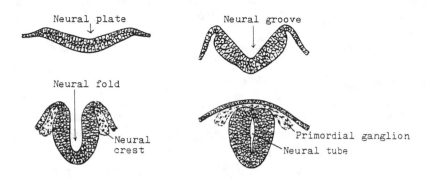

Figure 1. Cross section of the ectoderm of human embryos at successively later stages illustrating the origin of the neural tube and neural crest, which forms the dorsal root ganglia and the sympathetic nerve ganglia.

Fertilization

What are the results of fertilization?

SOLUTION:

There are four results of fertilization. First, fusion of the two haploid sex cells produces a zygote with a diploid number of chromosomes. For higher organisms in which the prominent generation is the diploid one, fertilization allows the diploid state to be restored. Second, fertilization results in the initiation of cleavage of the zygote. It sets off cleavage by stimulating the zygote to undergo a series of rapid cell divisions, leading to the formation of the embryo. Third, fertilization results in sex determination. It is at fertilization that the genetic sex of a zygote is determined. Hormonal factors, which are dependent upon the genotypic sex, regulate the development of the reproductive system during the embryonic period and of the secondary sex characteristics after birth, completing the sex differentiation of an individual. In humans, the male genetic sex is determined by the presence of the XY chromosomal pair, whereas the female is determined by the XX chromosomal pair. The fourth result of fertilization is the rendering of species variation. Because half of its chromosomes have a maternal source and the other half a paternal source, the zygote contains a new, unique combination of chromosomes, and thus a new set of genetic information. Hence fertilization provides for the genetic diversity of a species.

387

Trace the path of the sperm from the testes to its union with the egg in the human.

SOLUTION:

In order to trace this path, we must first outline some aspects of the human male and female reproductive systems, illustrated in Figures 1 and 2, respectively. In normal males, the testes lie in the scrotum, a sac attached to the lower anterior wall of the abdomen. The testes reside in the body cavity during early embryonic development, but before birth they descend into the cavities of the scrotum. The inguinal canals are connections between the scrotum and body cavity; these canals are blocked off by connective tissue after the testes descend. The testes are located in the scrotal sacs because the sperm within them require cooler temperatures than the internal body temperature in order to survive and mature.

Each testis consists of roughly 1,000 coiled tubules called seminiferous tubules. It is in these tubules that the germ cells produce the sperm. Sertoli cells are also present and nourish the developing sperm. Connected to the seminiferous tubules via fine tubes called vasa efferentia is the epididymis, which is a single, complexly coiled tube in which sperm are stored and mature. The epididymis, which is derived from the embryonic kidney, empties into the vas deferens. This duct passes from the scrotum through the inguinal canal into the abdominal cavity, over the urinary bladder to a point where it opens into the ejaculatory duct, which empties into the urethra, the duct that leads from the urinary bladder to the exterior. Thus in the male, the urethra serves as a common passageway for both reproductive and excretory functions. The urethra passes through the penis and is flanked by three columns of erectile tissue. This tissue becomes enlarged with blood during periods of sexual excitement, causing the penis to become erect. The engorgement of the penis is caused by arterial dilation and increased blood flow at unchanged arterial pressure. Prior to ejaculation, sperm from the testes pass through the vasa efferentia into the epididymis. During ejaculation, sperm from the epididymis are moved through the vas deferens by peristaltic contractions of its walls. Fluids are added to the sperm at the time of ejaculation. These fluids come from three pairs of glands; the seminal vesicles, the prostate glands (which in the human are fused into a single gland), and Cowper's bulbourethral glands. The mixture of secretions from these three sets of glands is termed seminal fluid. The semen consists of the sperm and seminal fluid. The seminal fluid consists of mucus (from seminal and bulbourethral secretions) and nutrients (seminal secretions), in a milky alkaline fluid (prostatic secretions).

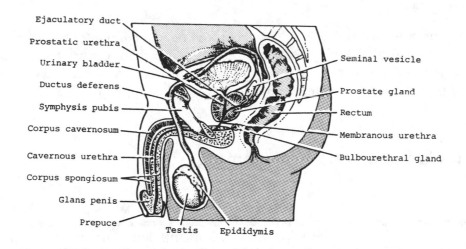

Figure 1. Reproductive system of the human male, lateral view.

During copulation, the male's penis is inserted into the female vagina and the semen is released there. Surrounding the vagina are the labia majora, two folds of fatty tissue covered by skin richly endowed with hair and sebaceous glands. These folds extend dorsally and down, enclosing the openings of the urethra and the vagina and merging behind them. The labia minora — thin folds of tissue devoid of hair — lie within the folds of the labia majora and are usually concealed by them. At the ventral junction of these two is the clitoris, a sensitive, erectile organ, which is the major site of female sexual excitement. The external female sex organs are collectively known as the vulva.

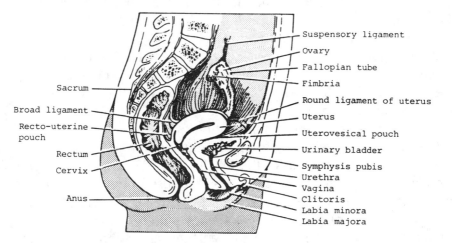

Figure 2. Reproductive system of the human female, lateral view.

The vagina is a single, muscular tube which extends from the exterior to the uterus. From the vagina, the sperm swim, by motion of their flagella, through the cervix, the muscular ring of the uterus which projects into the vagina and pass into the uterus. From there, they enter the Fallopian tubes (also known as the oviducts) where one may fertilize the secondary oocyte, if

389

it is present. If fertilization does occur, the oocyte completes the second meiotic division and the zygote (fertilized egg) is formed. Cleavage of the zygote begins in the Fallopian tube and will have proceeded to a multicellular state by the time the egg enters into the uterus and is implanted.

Implantation and Nourishment

Describe the early development and implantation of the human embryo.

SOLUTION:

The ovum must be fertilized while in the upper regions of the Fallopian tube or oviduct to develop successfully. Upon fertilization, it begins the series of cell divisions and differentiation which will eventually lead to development of the embryo (see Figure 1). The fertilized ovum continues its passage through the oviduct to the uterus, which requires three to four days. Once in the uterus, the egg floats free in the intrauterine fluid, from which it receives nutrients for several more days. During this time, it continues dividing and begins to differentiate into the blastocyst. The blastocyst stage (a fluid-filled sphere of cells) is attained by the time or shortly after the egg reaches the uterus. The egg would have slowly disintegrated during its passage to the uterus if fertilization had not occurred.

While the egg had been traveling to the uterus, the uterus was being prepared under the combined stimulation of estrogen and progesterone to receive the egg. If the fertilized egg were to pass too quickly through the oviduct, it would reach the uterus prematurely, when both it and the uterus had not yet reached a suitable state for implantation.

For the egg, the necessary event for implantation is the disintegration of the zona pellucida, a remnant of the follicle. This disintegration is completed at the blastocyst stage. The blastocyst is composed of an outer layer of specialized cells called trophoblasts, which are responsible for implantation, and an inner cell mass destined to become the fetus itself. The trophoblast layer, upon disintegration of the zona pellucida, enlarges and adheres to the uterine wall. These trophoblasts secrete lytic enzymes which will digest the uterine endometrium, allowing the blastocyst to completely embed itself in the uterine lining. This digestion of tissue continues for a period, with the breakdown products of the endometrium serving as a nutrient source for the developing embryo until both the fetal circulation and the placenta have developed. The placenta will form from an intermeshing of the trophoblast layer with the endometrium, and provides for contact and nutrient exchange between the mother and the fetus.

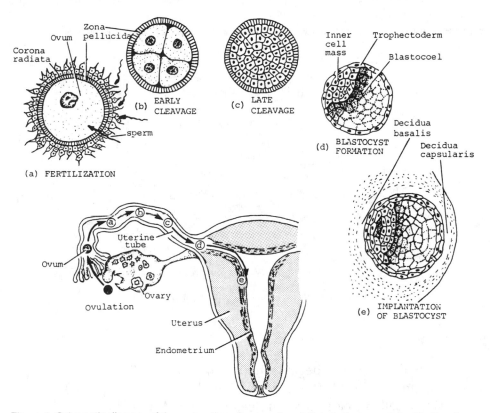

Figure 1. Schematic diagram of the maturation of an egg in a follicle in the ovary following its release (ovulation). a) fertilization in the upper part of the oviduct b) early cleavage as it descends c) late cleavage continuing descent d) blastocyst development in the uterus before implantation e) implantation of blastocyst in the wall of the uterus.

In addition to enzymes, the trophoblast secretes hormones, including chorionic gonadotropin. This important hormone is necessary for retention of the corpus luteum, which would have involuted if its ovum had not been fertilized. The hormonal secretions of the corpus luteum and later the placenta, maintain the uterus in the proper condition for pregnancy and prevent menstruation. Detection of the presence of chorionic gonadotropin in the urine is the basis for most pregnancy tests.

Because of the time required for the ovum to traverse the oviduct and for the uterus to be prepared, the total time that elapses from ovulation to implantation is from seven to eleven days.

What is meant by embryonic development? Describe the various stages of embryonic development.

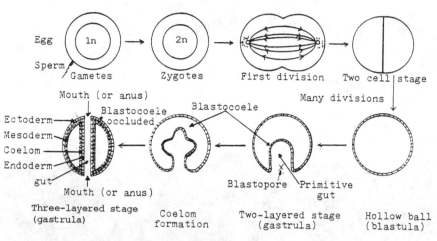

Figure 1. Early embryonic development in animals.

SOLUTION:

Embryonic development begins when an ovum is fertilized by a sperm and ends at parturition (birth). It is a process of change and growth which transforms a single cell zygote into a multicellular organism.

The earliest stage of embryonic development is the one-celled, diploid zygote which results from the fertilization of an ovum by a sperm. Next is a period called cleavage, in which mitotic division of the zygote results in the formation of daughter cells called blastomeres. At each succeeding division, the blastomeres become smaller and smaller. When 16 or so blastomeres have formed, the solid ball of cells is called a morula. As the morula divides further, a fluid-filled cavity is formed in the center of the sphere, converting the morula into a hollow ball of cells called a blastula. The fluid filled cavity is called the blastocoel. When cells of the blastula differentiate into two, and later three, embryonic germ layers, the blastula is called a gastrula. The gastrula period generally extends until the early forms of all major structures (for example, the heart) are laid down. After this period, the developing organism is called a fetus. During the fetal period (the duration of which varies with different species), the various systems develop further. Though developmental changes in the fetal period are not as dramatic as those occurring during the earlier embryonic periods, they are extremely important.

Congenital defects may result from abnormal development during this period.

Describe the development of a mammalian egg from cleavage up to the development of the fetal membranes.

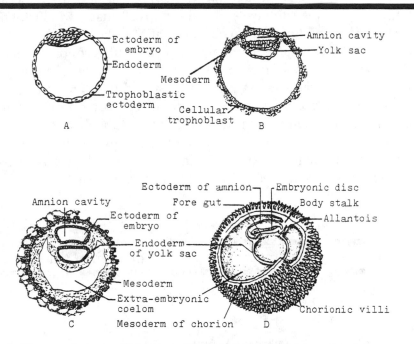

Figure 1. Human embryos ten (A) to twenty (D) days old showing the formation of the amniotic and yolk sac cavities and the origin of the embryonic disc.

SOLUTION:

Cleavage in a mammalian egg takes place as the egg moves slowly down the oviduct, driven along by cilia and muscular contraction of the wall of the duct. The journey takes about four days in the case of cells, the morula, which divides and rearranges into a hollow ball of cells, the blastocyst. The blastocyst subdivides into an inner cell mass from which the embryo develops, and an enveloping layer of cells, the trophoblast. The cavity of the blastocyst may be compared to the blastocoel, but the embryo is not a blastula, for its cells are differentiated into two types. The cells of the inner cell mass differentiate further into a thin layer of flat cells, the hypoblast, which is located on the interior surface of the mass adjacent to the blastocoel, and which represents the endoderm. The remaining cells of the inner cell mass become the epiblast. The cells of the hypoblast, spreading along the inner surface of the trophoblast, eventually surround the cavity of the blastocyst, forming a "yolk sac," which is filled with fluid, not yolk.

As the hypoblast spreads out, the inner cell mass also spreads and becomes a disc shaped plate of cells similar to the blastodisc of bird and reptilian eggs. The blastodisc becomes delimitated from the rest of the embryo. Gastrulation

393

begins with the formation of a primitive streak and Hensen's node in which cells migrate downward, laterally and anteriorly between the epiblast and hypoblast. Those cells which remain between these two layers comprise the mesoderm. Those cells which join the hypoblast become endoderm. A crevice appears between the cells of the inner cell mass, which then enlarges to become the amniotic cavity. The cavity of the blastocyst becomes filled with mesodermal cells, and is comparable to the subgerminal cavity in the bird. The embryonic disc comes to lie as a plate between the two cavities, connected to the trophoblast at the posterior end by a group of extraembryonic mesoderm cells, the body stalk or allantoic stalk. The nonfunctional endodermal part of the allantois, which develops as a tube from the yolk sac, is rudimentary and never reaches the trophoblast. Thus, after two weeks of development the human embryo is a flat, two-layered disc of cells about 250 microns across, connected by a stalk to the trophoblast.

●PROBLEM 11-49

Describe the structure and function of the human placenta.

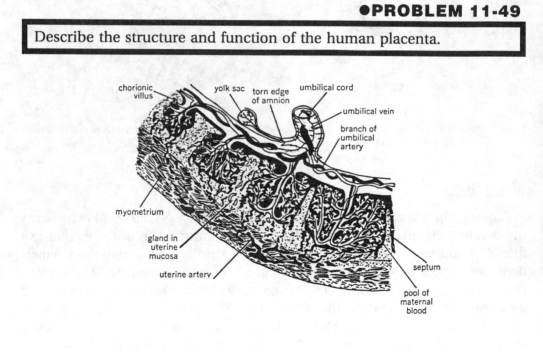

Figure 1. Interrelations of fetal and maternal tissues in formation of placenta.
The placenta becomes progressively more developed from left to right.

SOLUTION:

The placenta is an organ composed of both maternal and fetal tissues that supplies the developing embryo with nutrients and oxygen and enables the embryo to excrete carbon dioxide and other metabolic wastes. It also functions as an endrocrine gland, secreting estrogens, progesterone, human chorionic gonadotropin (HCG), and human placental lactogen (HPL). The former two are steroids, while the latter two are protein hormones. HCG functions to prevent regression of the corpus luteum, while HPL stimulates secretion of the steroid hormones from the corpus luteum.

The placenta forms following the implantation of the embryo within the uterine wall. Lytic enzymes secreted by the trophoblasts break down the capillaries of the uterine endometrium causing the maternal blood to pool in that area. Subsequently, the trophoblast layer surrounds and sends out villi into this region (see Figure 1). These villi become integrated by the umbilical arteries and veins which are extensions of the fetal circulatory system. The fetal blood in the capillaries of the villi come in close contact with the maternal blood in the tissue sinuses between the villi. Nutrients diffuse from the maternal blood through the trophoblast layer into the fetal capillaries, and waste products from the fetus is eliminated into the maternal blood. Note, however, that at no time or place does the blood of the fetus mix with that of the mother. Blood from the mother enters the placenta via the uterine artery and leaves the region via the uterine veins. Similarly, the fetal blood never leaves the fetal vessels, which consist of umbilical arteries, the capillary network in the placental villi, and the umbilical vein.

●PROBLEM 11-50

Differentiate between a placenta and an umbilical cord.

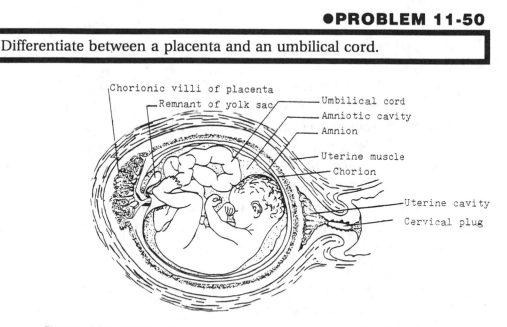

Figure 1. Advanced fetus shows its membranes and their relationship to the uterus.

SOLUTION:

As the human embryo grows, the region on the ventral side from which the folds of the amnion, the yolk sac, and the allantois grow, becomes relatively smaller, and the edges of the amniotic folds come together to form a tube which encloses the other membranes. This tube is called the umbilical cord and contains, in addition to the yolk sac and allantois, the large umbilical blood vessels through which the fetus obtains nourishment from the wall of the uterus. The umbilical cord, about 1 cm in diameter and about 70 cm long at birth, is composed chiefly of a peculiar jellylike material found nowhere else.

The placenta is the area where a portion of the chorion and a portion of the uterine wall join. The placenta is thus a structure of double origin, partly embryonic (chorion) and partly maternal (uterus). It functions to exchange nutrients, wastes, and gases between the mother and the fetus. In mammals such as the human, the placenta is a disk about 7 inches in diameter and about 1 to 1-1/2 inches thick. Not all mammals have such disklike placentas. For example, cows have numerous isolated clusters of fetal-maternal associations, other animals have fingerlike projections of the chorion that provide a very diffuse type of association. In cats and dogs the placenta forms a ring around the fetus.

SHORT ANSWER QUESTIONS FOR REVIEW

Choose the correct answer.

1. Which of the following best describes how a peristaltic wave is formed? (a) Circular smooth muscle immediately in front of a bolus of food contracts, while smooth muscle behind the bolus of food relaxes. (b) Skeletal muscle surrounding the entire alimentary tract relaxes and contracts intermittently, causing food to move in a forward direction. (c) Circular smooth muscle immediately behind the bolus of food contracts, while the smooth muscle in front of the bolus relaxes. (d) Smooth muscle both in front of and behind a bolus of food contract together, causing the bolus to move toward the anus.

2. Which of the following is not a proteolytic enzyme? (a) trypsin (b) lipase (c) carboxypeptidase (d) pepsin

3. Which is not a function of the blood? (a) transport of nutrients and oxygen to the cells (b) removal of carbon dioxide and other wastes (c) transport of hormones to target organs (d) regulation of acidity and alkalinity of the cells (e) all of the above are functions of the blood.

4. Hematocrit refers to (a) the cellular component of blood. (b) small blood sucking organisms. (c) the leukocytes and erythrocytes found in the blood. (d) a dye used to stain the blood plasma. (e) none of the above.

5. During the clotting process fibrinogen is converted into (a) thrombo-plastin. (b) fibrin. (c) platelets. (d) prothrombin. (e) thrombin.

6. The process by which gases are exchanged in the alveoli of our lungs is called: (a) external respiration. (b) indirect respiration. (c) internal respiration. (d) direct respiration.

7. Which of the following mechanisms cause air to rush into our lungs during inspiration? (a) The diaphragm moves up, while the external intercostal muscles contract, causing the chest cavity to decrease in size. That raises the intrathoracic pressure, and air rushes in. (b) The diaphragm moves down, while the internal intercostal muscles relax, causing the chest cavity to increase in size. That raises the in-trathoracic pressure above atmospheric pressure, and air rushes in. (c) The diaphragm contracts and moves downward, while the inter-nal intercostal muscles contract, causing the ribs to move upward. The result is a larger chest cavity, causing intrathoracic pressure to fall below that of atmospheric pressure. (d) None of the above

8. Which of the following is incorrect concerning bile? (a) It consists of bile acids, pigments, cholesterol, and lecithin. It is synthesized in the liver and stored in the gall bladder. (b) It is released when the gall bladder contracts. This is caused by stimulation from the hormone cholecystokinin. (c) Its main function is the emulcification of fats. It does this by breaking up fat into smaller units called micelles. This increases the surface area available for lipase activity. (d) All con-stituents of bile are excreted out of the body as part of the feces. Es-sentially, there is no recirculation of components.

9. Which of the following is not a function of the liver? (a) hydroxyla-tion of vitamin D (b) regulation of blood sugar levels via synthesis and secretion of insulin and glucagon (c) detoxification of ammonia via its conversion to urea (d) conversion of glucose into fat, which can then be stored in adipose tissue.

10. The functional unit of the kidney is called a (a) tubule. (b) urethra. (c) neuron. (d) nephron.

11. If someone suffers from kidney failure, it might be traced to a breakdown in (a) secretion. (b) filtration. (c) reabsorption. (d) any of the above.

12. Choose the correct statement: (a) The ascending limb of the loop of Henle pumps sodium ions out. (b) Chloride ions pass into the ascending limb. (c) The ascending limb is permeable to water. (d) The descending limb is impermeable to water and sodium.

13. The thin barrier at Bowman's capsule allows for the filtration of (a) whole blood. (b) plasma. (c) oxygen. (d) electrolytes only.

14. The hormone glucagon: (a) has the opposite effect on the liver than insulin does. (b) converts glycogen into glucose. (c) is produced in the beta cells of the pancreas. (d) **a** and **b** (e) **b** and **c**

15. The "Fight-or-Flight" reaction is characterized by the increase of glucose levels and oxygen content to the skeleton and muscles, with a decrease in glucose level and oxygen content to the digestive system. What hormone(s) are responsible for this reaction? (a) adrenalin (b) noradrenalin (c) cortisone (d) **a** and **b** (e) **b** and **c**

16. Myosin bridges can be prevented from combining with actin by (a) troponin. (b) tropomyosin. (c) calcium. (d) both **a** and **b**

17. Choose the correct statement. (a) Skeletal muscle fibers are multi-nucleated. (b) Smooth muscle shows a striated banding pattern. (c) Cardiac muscle is striated and has a single nucleus. (d) All of the above are correct.

18. According to the sliding filament theory of muscle contraction (a) the thick and thin filaments change their length as they slide past each other. (b) the lengths of the individual thick and thin filaments remain the same during muscle contraction. (c) groups of muscles slide over each other during stress. (d) none of the above.

19. The phenomenon of rigor mortis is a direct result of (a) the breaking of ATP to myosin bonds. (b) the loss of ATP in the dead muscle cells. (c) the myosin crossbridges being unable to combine with actin. (d) none of the above.

20. Bone matrix is laid down by cells called (a) osteocytes. (b) chondrocytes. (c) osteoblasts. (d) chondroblasts.

21. Which of the following is not a function of bone? (a) replacement of certain minerals (b) production of lymphocyte precursor cells (c) production of erythrocytes (d) All of the above

22. Which of the following is not a part of the axial skeleton? (a) skull (b) humerus (c) ribs (d) sternum

23. At which stage of development is the egg ovulated? (a) oogonium (b) primary oocyte (c) secondary oocyte (d) ootid (e) None of the above

24. Which is not a result of fertilization? (a) restoration of the diploid state in the zygote (b) stimulation of zygotic cleavage (c) genetic determination of sex (d) increase in species variability (e) None of the above

25. The coiled tube in which mature sperm are stored is known as the (a) vasa efferentia. (b) epididymis. (c) vas deferens. (d) scrotal sac. (e) Sertoli cells.

26. Following fertilization, the zygote undergoes a series of rapid mitotic divisions. The stage at which a solid ball of cells is formed is called: (a) morula. (b) blastula. (c) gastrula. (d) fetus. (e) None of the above

27. The first stage of embryonic development in which three distinct germ layers are seen is: (a) morula. (b) blastula. (c) gastrula. (d) fetus. (e) None of the above

28. The primitive gut formed during gastrulation is called the (a) blastopore. (b) gastrocoel. (c) blastocoel. (d) archenteron. (e) ventral pore.

Fill in the blanks.

29. The sudden relaxing of the _____ sphincter allows food to pass from the pharynx into the esophagus. It then contracts and closes immediately thereafter. At the same time, the closure of the _____ prevents food from entering the trachea.

30. Some of the macrophages wander around in the tissue spaces, others are fixed in one place. Together the two constitute the _____ system of phagocytes.

31. The most severe reaction to an allergy, commonly associated with insect bites, is _____.

32. Air entering the nose passes through the internal nares, and from there, enters the _____. The larynx is the next landmark passed, air entering it via an opening called the _____, which is where the _____ are located. Air then passes through the trachea, which divides eventually into two _____.

33. During exhalation, the intercostal muscles _____ (contract, relax) and the ribs move _____ (up, down) and _____ (in, out).

34. The human nervous system is composed of _____, _____, and _____.

35. When bile pigments such as bilirubin are not able to be incorporated into bile, they can accumulate in the blood and tissues. This gives rise to a condition called _____.

36. The hormone secreted by the posterior pituitary and responsible for contraction of uterine muscles is _____.

37. Vasopressin reabsorbs water at the kidney. An alternate name for this hormone is _____.

38. The two hormones secreted by the endocrine portion of the pancreas are _____ and _____.

39. TSH produced by the pituitary gland stimulates the secretion of the hormone _____.

40. During muscle contraction, the length of the individual thick and thin filaments are _____ (changed, unchanged).

41. The globular-shaped molecule called _____ has a surface reactive site able to combine with _____.

42. Haversian systems are characteristic of _____ bone.

43. Hormones are placed into three categories because of a difference in chemical structure. The three categories are: _____, _____, and _____.

44. The point of junction between two bones is called a _____.

45. Following the formation of the primary oocyte from mitotic enlargement of the oogonia, meiosis takes place. Unequal meiotic division of the primary oocyte results in the formation of the _____ and a(n) _____.

46. Cleavage of the egg is stimulated by the process of _____.

47. Production of sperm from germ cells occurs in the _____.

48. Semen is a mixture of the sperm and seminal fluid. The seminal fluid is composed of the secretions from the _____ gland, _____ glands, and the _____ vesicles.

49. The _____ is an organ composed of both maternal and fetal tissue that supplies the developing embryo with nutrients and oxygen, and enables the embryo to excrete carbon dioxide and other metabolic wastes.

50. As the lateral cells continue to invaginate, they move into the space between the _____ and the _____.

51. The region where the chorion and uterine wall join is called the _____.

52. The structure through which the embryo receives nourishment from the uterine wall is the _____.

Determine whether the following statements are true or false.

53. If an individual so desires, swallowing can be voluntarily halted before completion.

54. The large intestine has fewer villi than the small intestine, but plays an important role in concentrating feces.

55. Monocytes and lymphocytes are capable of fighting against bacterial infection by phagocytosis.

56. Respiration is an energy consuming process and breathing is an energy producing process.

57. Bile is produced in the liver and stored in the gall bladder. Its function is to aid in the digestion of the nucleic acid, DNA, and RNA.

58. By reducing one's intake of cholesterol, one can effectively, with no exception, lower the amount of circulating cholesterol in the body.

59. Possible explanations for depletion of minerals in bones are pregnancy and starvation.

60. Smooth muscle does not contain sarcomeres.

61. The simplest manner in which sensory and motor neurons are integrated to evoke behavior is in a reflex arc.

62. Hormones always travel to the target area via the blood.

63. After numerous divisions, the embryo develops into a hollow ball called a morula.

64. The blastula indents on one side to form a two-layered gastrula.

65. After continued development, the embryo contains three layers: epiderm, mesoderm, endoderm.

66. The inner layer of endoderm forms the digestive tract.

ANSWER KEY

1. c	2. b	3. e
4. a	5. e	6. b
7. c	8. d	9. b
10. d	11. d	12. a
13. b	14. d	15. d
16. d	17. a	18. b
19. b	20. c	21. d
22. b	23. c	24. e
25. b	26. a	27. c

28. d   29. hypopharyngeal, glottis

30. reticulo-endothelial   31. anaphylaxis

32. pharynx, glottis, vocal cords, main bronchi   33. relax, down, in

34. brain, spinal cord, peripheral nerves   35. jaundice

36. oxytocin   37. antidiuretic hormone

38. insulin, glucagon   39. thyroxin   40. unchanged

41. actin, myosin   42. compact

43. steroid hormones, amino acid derivatives, proteins and polypeptides

44. joint

45. secondary oocyte, polar body

46. fertilization

47. seminiferous tubules

48. prostate, Cowper's, seminal

49. placenta

50. hypoblast, epiblast

51. placenta

52. umbilical cord

53. False

54. True

55. True

56. False

57. False

58. False

59. True

60. True

61. True

62. False

63. False

64. True

65. False

66. True

INDEX

Numbers on this page refer to PROBLEM NUMBERS, not page numbers.

Numbers on this page refer to PROBLEM NUMBERS, not page numbers.